THE QUIET AVANT-GARDE

Crepuscular Poetry and the Twilight of Modern Humanism

The Quiet Avant-Garde

Crepuscular Poetry and the Twilight of Modern Humanism

DANILA CANNAMELA

UNIVERSITY OF TORONTO PRESS
Toronto Buffalo London

Toronto Buffalo London
utorontopress.com

ISBN 978-1-4875-0506-6

Toronto Italian Studies

Library and Archives Canada Cataloguing in Publication

Cannamela, Danila, 1983–, author
The quiet avant-garde : crepuscular poetry and the twilight of modern humanism / Danila Cannamela.

(Toronto Italian studies)
Includes bibliographical references and index.
ISBN 978-1-4875-0506-6 (hardcover)

1. Italian poetry – 20th century – History and criticism.
2. Avant-garde (Aesthetics) – Italy – History – 20th century.
3. Modernism (Literature) – Italy. I. Title. II. Series: Toronto Italian studies

PQ4113.C36 2019 851'.9109 C2018-906429-3

This book has been published with the assistance of the University of St Thomas.

University of Toronto Press acknowledges the financial assistance to its publishing program of the Canada Council for the Arts and the Ontario Arts Council, an agency of the Government of Ontario.

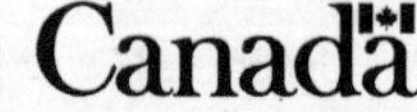

Contents

Acknowledgments

Writing this book led me into a research journey that was enriched by many encounters – either in person or mediated by other texts. Although it would take too long to retrace this path entirely, I would like to mention a few people who have been particularly helpful.

For sparking my interest in the crepusculars and advising my undergraduate research into these poets, I thank Mauro Novelli and Roberto Carnero. My investigation of the crepuscular poets has enormously benefited from the work of Angela Ida Villa and Giuseppe Farinelli, and from the conversations I had with them. In a similar way, I am thankful to Federico Luisetti for suggesting critical perspectives that reframed my understanding of the futurist avant-garde. Overall, my theoretical approach was inspired by the work of many colleagues. A special thanks goes to Serenella Iovino for suggesting readings about feminist environmentalism that, in a later phase of my writing process, contributed in shaping this book and my current research. I would also like to thank Levi Bryant for talking with me about his view of object-oriented ontology, Elena Past for her valuable insights on nonhuman sounds, and Matteo Gilebbi for sharing with me his knowledge of animal studies. Also, thank you to Mimmo Cangiano for offering advice on Italian modernism, Achille Castaldo for providing feedback on passages of the book, and Paola Ehrmantraut for discussing with me her research on masculinity studies and affect theory. Finally, Valeria Finucci was the first to encourage me to revise my doctoral dissertation. "I see a book here," she said.

However, this book would not have been possible without the work of Mark Thompson, acquisition editor at University of Toronto Press, who believed in this project and assisted me during the revision process with great professionalism. In this process, the constructive criticism of the anonymous external reviewers was crucial in helping me to improve my manuscript.

Also, as a non-native speaker of English, I found that writing a book in the English language requires extra time and effort. Thank you, Mary Reichardt and Betsy Tremmel, for reading drafts of my chapters and offering suggestions on language and style.

Last but not least, I would like to thank Mike, my husband, for becoming the most knowledgeable non-academic expert in crepuscularism and supporting – with a good dose of crepuscular irony – the ups and downs of my writing process. Thank you, Felicita, for being the best more-than-human companion of long writing sessions and making me laugh when I found you asleep on my poetry books several times. I am concluding this page with a personal note: I signed the contract for this book a few weeks before my daughter, Maria-Sofia, was born, and I submitted the final revisions a few weeks after she was born. In an academic world in which many women in tenure-track careers still think that they must choose between being a scholar and being a mother, this book is an invite to challenge the system that fuels this idea.

Abbreviations

The titles listed below refer to the works of crepuscular and futurist authors most frequently referenced in this book. Other primary sources and all secondary sources appear in notes. When not otherwise indicated, translations from the original Italian are mine.

F	Rainey, Lawrence, Christine Poggi, and Laura Wittman, eds. *Futurism: An Anthology*. New Haven, London: Yale University Press, 2009.
M	Marinetti, Filippo Tommaso. *Mafarka il futurista*. Edited by Luigi Ballerini. Milan: Mondadori, 2003.
MDF	Birolli, Viviana, ed. *Manifesti del futurismo*. Milan: Abscondita, 2008.
MF	Marinetti, Filippo Tommaso. *Mafarka the Futurist: An African Novel*. Translated by Carol Diethe and Steve Cox. London: Middlesex University Press, 1998.
MT	Ginanni, Maria. *Montagne trasparenti*. Florence: Edizioni dell'Italia Futurista, 1917.
O	Corazzini, Sergio. *Opere. Poesie e prose*. Edited by Angela Ida Villa. Pisa, Rome: Istituti editoriali e poligrafici internazionali, 1999.
P	Govoni, Corrado, *Poesie (1903–1958)*. Edited by Gino Tellini. Milan: Mondadori, 2000.
PF	Altomare, Libero, et al. *I poeti futuristi*. Milan: Edizioni di Poesia, 1912.
PO	Oxilia, Nino. *Poesie*. Edited by Roberto Tessari. Naples: Guida, 1973.
SE	Corazzini, Sergio. *Sunday Evening: Selected Poems of Sergio Corazzini*. Edited and translated by Michael Palma. Stony Brook, New York: Gradiva Publications, 1997.
SF	Bello Minciacchi, Cecilia, ed. *Spirale di dolcezza + serpe di fascino. Scrittrici futuriste. Antologia*. Naples: Bibliopolis, 2007.

TIF Marinetti, Filippo Tommaso. *Teoria e invenzione futurista*. Edited by Luciano De Maria. Milan: Mondadori, 2010.

TLP Moretti, Marino. *Tutte le poesie*. Milan: Mondadori, 1966.

TM Gozzano, Guido. *The Man I Pretend to Be: The Colloquies and Selected Poems of Guido Gozzano*. Translated by Michael Palma. Princeton: Princeton University Press, 1981.

TP Gozzano, Guido. *Tutte le poesie*. Edited by Andrea Rocca. Milan: Mondadori, 1980.

TTP Palazzeschi, Aldo. *Tutte le poesie*. Edited by Adele Dei. Milan: Mondadori, 2002.

UG Vallini, Carlo. *Un giorno e La rinunzia*. Genoa: San Marco dei Giustiniani, 2010.

THE QUIET AVANT-GARDE

Crepuscular Poetry and the Twilight of Modern Humanism

Introduction

Poetry at the Twilight

So many sunsets
Facebook and Instagram couldn't contain them.

Robert Sullivan, "Hello Great North Road"

The Avant-Garde Has Never Been Modern

In the last few decades, the complex relationship that links the human and the nonhuman has deeply shaped the imagery of science fiction. In looking back over even just the past five years, examples are not hard to find. One might think of the successful recent television series *Westworld*, in which a Western theme park is inhabited by artificial-intelligence androids who are gaining sentience and impacting the lives of their human guests in unexpected ways. Similarly, *Black Mirror*, a British science fiction television series, has portrayed dystopic near futures in which the divide between technology and humankind is progressively thinning. The first episode of the second season, "Be Right Back," is particularly evocative of the hybridity that shapes the human and nonhuman, as well as virtual and material realities: after the loss of her partner, Martha orders an intelligence that can access his social media life. The android gradually comes to substitute for Ash, the woman's late boyfriend, and augment her life with new experiences and memories.[1] This *Black Mirror* episode recalls the plot of the 2013 film *Her*, which features the romance of a businessman with Samantha, an operating system with a female persona.[2] Both the movie and the aforementioned TV series share a fundamental question: Who is in control – humans or machines – in the development of affective relationships that muddle the division between a living person and an inert object?

Science fiction envisions a near future in which technology not only simulates humanity but also, in many cases, goes beyond simulation to having its own agency. In this future, neither is life solely biological, nor does intelligence belong only to humans: "In addition to *Homo sapiens*, there will be *Homo nexus*," Italian science fiction author Francesco Verso writes in his 2013 novel *Livido* [translated as *Nexhuman*], imagining a world in which it is possible to upload people's minds to electronic platforms.[3] Yet this effort to redefine the traditional human-nonhuman divide is not unique to the techno-universe of science fiction but has emerged, from various perspectives, in the art world. Here, artists ask the profound question: can we draw a clear line of demarcation between human and nonhuman animals, or between individual bodies and surrounding "matter"? In exploring their answers to this question, artists across the world created "bio-art," featuring cheese made from human milk, monstrous synthetic organisms, and test animals like Xenopus frogs. These works were exhibited at "The Multispecies Salon" (2010), an itinerant salon that combined art, ecology, anthropology, and biology to show how diverse organisms, including insects, infectious spores, and plants, are actively involved in political, economic, and cultural systems.[4]

Artists have also engaged in a meta-reflection on art, exploring how materiality intertwines with human thought and emotion. The collection *Photographs Not Taken* (2012) offers a peculiar example of how even pictures not taken – quintessential "non-objects" – can illustrate the intermingling of physicality and virtuality that informs both life and artistic representation. This book features essays from sixty photographers who used words rather than images to describe "the moments that slipped from their photographic grip, either because they couldn't take the picture, or wouldn't."[5] On the written page, the "objects" that the camera did not capture form slippery clusters of material and immaterial "things." Unrecorded images, bodies, human emotions, nonhuman landscapes, and symbolic contents interweave the fabric of these stories. In this case, too, it is hard to mark a clear boundary between the tangible objects that escaped being photographed and the "mental negatives" that these missed objects impressed on the narrators' minds and, through their descriptions, on the minds of their readers.[6]

As Paolo Bartoloni highlights in *Objects in Italian Life and Culture* (2016), tangible objects retain "the life that has attached to them, but ignore that life lingers around them ready to be recomposed and rearranged by the others that will come."[7] Art often attains this recomposition by estranging everyday objects from their original settings. A paradigmatic case of aesthetic rearrangement emerges in the work of carpenter Franco Tuccio. A native of Lampedusa, Tuccio has made crosses out of the wood of shipwrecked boats that carried immigrants from the African shores to his island, an Italian territory.[8] The Lampedusa cross is wood wherein human flesh, ethics, politics, religious symbolism, and natural agents intermingle in an uncomfortable and hybrid materiality.

Contemporary science fiction and art have effectively portrayed how the line that divides the dominion of the *animal rationale* from the supposedly chaotic realm of matter and "things" is an artificial vanishing line. Yet, as anthropologist Bruno Latour has pinpointed, this dividing line has shaped modernity for centuries. The modern mindset has fostered a system of dichotomies – human-nonhuman, culture-nature, mind-body. Nevertheless, these dualistic frameworks have also created a variety of (concealed) hybrids like the "Lampedusa cross," from environmental disasters to bio-technological and bio-ethical issues. Dismantling this binary mindset involves facing the threatening realization that human nature is a site of intermeshing, rather than a purified, rational, and privileged animality.

Scientific research has substantiated the fact that the human animal is not as unique as previously thought. Research conducted on primates has proved, among other things, the ability of chimpanzees to understand the idea of art, engage with human vocabulary, and adopt cultural rituals. Commenting on these results, historian Felipe Fernández-Armesto has effectively summarized:

> Even if it were true that there are elements of culture that are capable of being used to define humankind, it would not necessarily justify us in hiving our species off from the rest of creation in a special category of our own. Most of the uniquely or typically human features of what we call culture could be evolutionary in origin, and although handling tools and fire, recognizing art or music, and so on are behaviours we learn, our general propensity to adopt those behaviours may be inherited or – for those who like the word – instinctive.[9]

Humanitas might then be broadly reconceived of as "something" that connects us with other beings, the embodied site of our "interspecies relation(s)."[10] From this non-exclusive point of view, the notion of Western subjectivity loses its ontological singularity, and enters into dialogue with the notion of agency, namely, a rethinking of the nonhuman, be it nature, animal life, or *techne*, as inherently agentic. The category of agency leads us to overcome the reductive "dualism[s] of persons and things" and explore new possible "alliance(s) between animism and materialism."[11]

If anthropocentrism, understood as a divide, has proved to offer a limited platform, the current "nonhuman turn" in the humanities and social sciences aims to reconceive the meaning of humanism from a revised ontological view that undermines centuries of a "colonial" attitude towards the nonhuman. The need to redefine humanism as a more inclusive ethical and political platform has developed across scholarly frameworks, including actor-network theory (ANT), new materialism, object-oriented ontology, affect theory, and ecocriticism. As Richard Grusin has remarked, the nonhuman turn "should be a politically liberatory project in very much the same way that earlier, similar turns toward a concern for gender, race, ethnicity, or class were politically liberatory for groups of humans."[12]

However, if the theories gathered under the umbrella term "nonhuman turn" share a methodological decentring of the human and an overall liberatory project, their objectives are quite different and, at times, even divergent. For instance, since the 1990s, Latour has engaged in a redefinition of "the social not as a special domain ... but only as a very peculiar movement of re-association and reassembling"[13] in which human as well as nonhuman actors come into play. This revised sociological approach implies rethinking the social as an arena of complex interactions and transformations; for example, in the last few decades, natural catastrophes and, on a larger scale, climate change have been central actors in shaping socio-political policies, media communication, and public opinion. At a broader theoretical level, the relational and dynamic perspective that informs ANT resonates with the core argument of vital materialism, as elaborated by political scientist Jane Bennett. She posits that material life is "as much force as entity, as much energy as matter, as much intensity as extension," and, moving away from an atomistic view, she endorses a "congregational understanding of [material] agency."[14] Bennett proceeds to explain that "while the smallest or simplest body or bit may indeed express a vital impetus, conatus or *clinamen*, an actant never really acts alone. Its efficacy or agency always depends on the collaboration, cooperation, or interactive interference of many bodies and forces."[15] The perspective of relational interconnectedness embraced by vital materialism can be immediately pictured if we refer to an example that Bennett discusses in her seminal book, *Vibrant Matter* (2010). She examines the active role that electricity, as living matter gifted with agency, played in the 2003 power outage in New York City. The blackout triggered a chain of human-nonhuman interactions that affected the life of the city for several hours.

Human-nonhuman relations are also a fundamental topic of inquiry for environmental theories. In exploring this system of material and embodied relations, this interdisciplinary platform extends its research far beyond what we generally picture as the natural environment – say, a separate "green space" inhabited by vegetal life and nonhuman animals. Ecocritical perspectives, in particular material ecocriticism, rethink nature as "storied matter" – to recall an expression of theorist Serenella Iovino. According to this view, nature is a collective narrative agent that can be ultimately approached as a material text.

Furthermore, exploring topics such as toxicity and waste management, environmental humanities has proved that toxic narratives are not only an issue of social constructs but can, rather, be matter that physically challenges the vulnerability of human bodies. Touching on the body and its vulnerable exposure to the nonhuman, it is essential to mention that, beginning with 1970s ecofeminism and more recently with feminist environmentalism and queer ecology, body and gender have been important topics of debate. We may think of the many attempts to redefine the traditional patriarchal association between woman and nature, and of the more recent acknowledgment of the queer *nature* of the natural environment, observed in its inexhaustible reservoir of diverse and transformative behaviours.

Finally, environmental humanities are a growing field within Italian Studies. As Monica Seger highlights in *Landscapes in Between* (2015), one of the first English-language monographs analysing Italian culture through the lens of ecocriticism, the latter "has historically been rooted in North American traditions of nature writing, [yet] scholars have widened their reach beyond national borders in the past decade, and the field has benefited immeasurably."[16] Seger's reckoning is especially true if we consider that in the last few years, a variety of research has explored new ecocritical approaches to Italian written and visual culture, investigated the crossroads of ecology and creative imagination in what has been dubbed "Bel paese," and suggested new ways to think about nonhuman animals and landscapes in Italy.[17]

Broadly speaking, theories like environmental humanities, ANT, and vital materialism tightly connect the notion of agency with dynamic processes of interaction and transformation in which humans and nonhumans intermesh. Consequently, it might be difficult to draw a neat divide between a single agent and its intrinsic relational ability to affect and be affected. This is why feminist physicist Karen Barad has revised the notion of interaction into the neologism *intra-action*. The term highlights that agency always implies the creation of an entangled matter, in which nature and culture merge: it is only *within* material and discursive entanglements that the ability to act emerges and is collectively performed. Barad's perspective challenges not only the distinctions between subject and object, or culture and nature, but also the one between being, doing, and becoming.

However, relationality becomes a much more problematic aspect when analysed from the perspective of object-oriented ontology (OOO). OOO officially took its name and developed as a movement in 2010, during a conference hosted at Georgia Tech, although many of its proponents had been active for a decade. Its philosophical speculation is a sub-branch of speculative realism – a broader theory that rejects correlationism, or the idea that perception and knowledge of the world ultimately depend on human categories. OOO asserts a type of flat ontology by stating that everything exists equally – "plumbers, cotton, bonobos, DVD players, and sandstone, for example."[18] Yet, *how* do things exist or manifest themselves in the world? As Graham Harman, one of the main OOO theorists, states in his blog, "1. Individual entities of various different scales (not just tiny quarks and electrons) are the ultimate stuff of the cosmos. 2. These entities are never exhausted by any of their relations or even by their sum of all possible relations. Objects withdraw from relation."[19] OOO criticizes both scientific naturalism, for reducing objects to atomic particles, and social relativism, for turning objects into human mental constructs. Yet, as Levi Bryant highlights in a 2010 blog post (OOO philosophers have been very active on social media), a widespread misconception exclusively identifies OOO with a radical denial of relationality. As Bryant clarifies, "OOO has never argued that relations are unimportant. [Rather, it] has argued that objects cannot be *reduced to* their relations, that they always exceed their relations."[20] This is in fact the main critique that object-oriented ontologists pose, for instance, to Latour, for having reduced actants to their relations.

Through its flat ontology, OOO proposes an intriguing decentring of the human that Timothy Morton has successfully adopted in his ecological theories. We may recall, in particular, Morton's definition of large-scale environmental phenomena, like global warming, as hyperobjects. While pervading human life with their overwhelming presence, hyperobjects can hardly be localized or exactly defined. OOO has also influenced Morton's critique of taken-for-granted images, such as the natural environment and ecological behaviours. To defamiliarize these commonly accepted notions, he has proposed to "measure" our own coexistence and interconnection with other nonhuman beings on uncanny scales. If we try to think, for instance, about our close intimacy with nature, nature loses its obvious semblance to become a puzzling "strange stranger"; similarly, if we imagine our life from inhuman distances – what Morton defines as "Earth Magnitude" – our relevance and perspective are uncomfortably altered.[21]

The notion of inhuman scale has been a prominent one in the current debate on the Anthropocene, a geological epoch in which the *anthropos* is simultaneously a major agent of change and the accomplice/victim of an irreversible and multi-agentic process of transformation that greatly exceeds human perception but has a detrimental impact on human and nonhuman lives.

Having briefly explored the richness and complexity of the "nonhuman turn," we shall now move to a central point of investigation and consider whether this liberatory project is a true novelty of twenty-first-century theory or if its various efforts to redefine human-nonhuman relations echo from an earlier time. In this work, I argue that, in the early twentieth century, the Italian avant-garde challenged modern anthropocentrism, portraying a world swarming with "living" machines and objects, a fictional universe in which the identification of humans as subjects and nonhumans as inert "still life" loses its clear meaning. As Walter Benjamin noticed, the avant-garde worked to make known that the world is full of "quasi-objects" and "quasi-subjects."[22] *The Quiet Avant-Garde* advances the hypothesis that at the heart of the groundbreaking avant-garde action – its quiet rebellion – lies a peculiar decolonization of the world of things from the human. Exploring pioneering proposals of flat ontology, this book introduces *crepuscolarismo* [crepuscularism], a "quiet" (proto-)avant-gardist movement that developed roughly between 1903 and 1918, and analyses it as a precursor to the material vitalism of the futurist avant-garde. Since a literary or visual text is also materially in relation with other texts and readers across epochs, the purpose of this analysis is to contextualize the crepuscular and futurist poetics of the object in their original historical context, while drawing new connections between their experimental proposals and the twenty-first-century discussion on the nonhuman. My work furthers the dialogue in the area of environmental humanities in two ways: it offers a new ecocritical interpretation of early twentieth-century Italian movements and links ecocriticism to other theoretical frameworks, including object-oriented ontology, vital materialism, affect theory, and gender studies.

Unlike futurism, which initiated the avant-garde wave in Europe, crepuscularism is an anticipatory linchpin movement, at the intersection of nineteenth-century tradition, early modernism, and the historical avant-gardes. Although crepuscularism and futurism produced very different literary and cultural outcomes, they share some common polemical targets, including the fading poetics of stylistic refinement and civic engagement, and the conformism of bourgeois society. In addition, the two movements present a similar fascination with the nonhuman that inspired complementary representations of material "life." In representing objects as free and agentic, crepuscular poetry portrays a world of discarded "little things" that silently undermines human certitudes. Futurism later experiments with breathing machines and ferocious cyborgs, which become main actors in its all-encompassing reinvention of the universe and implicitly cast doubts on the role of humans in a fast-industrialized society. As we will see, the crepuscular poetics of the object is the "missing link" to retrace an important, yet often overlooked, transition from a humanistic tradition that glorified human enterprise through objects to the futurist glorification of living machines and human-nonhuman hybrids. Ultimately, this non-anthropocentric transition can lead to a contemporary interpretation of crepuscularism and futurism as two parallel discourses on materiality that can give rise to thought-provoking insights on the current debate on the nonhuman.

Through their complementary perspectives, these movements envision the twilight of modern humanism, as human characters discover that they have developed their hybrid personae through transcorporeal relations of "co-belonging" with the nonhuman.[23] In the early twentieth century, the crepusculars' and futurists' reflections on materiality foreshadow the sunset of an anthropocentric approach to life, which, as we now fully realize, is ultimately incompatible with the challenges that progress poses to humankind and "nonhuman-kind." Not without incoherencies and paradoxes, crepuscular and futurist texts can guide twenty-first-century readers to rethink the function of everyday objects and our sense of humanity in relation to the nonhuman environment.

Futurism(s) and Crepuscularism: The Twilight of Modern Humanism

If one mentions the Italian avant-garde, Filippo Tommaso Marinetti (1876–1944) and his founding manifesto of futurism (1909) immediately come to mind. This seminal work exalted the thrilling speed of the modern metropolis, glorified war, and marked a radical break with a stagnant past guided by harmonious beauty and moral values. Ironic as it may seem, the manifesto that affirmed the project to destroy museums and libraries was physically hung on the wall of the Guggenheim Museum, on the occasion of the 2013 exhibition "Italian Futurism, 1909–1944: Reconstructing the Universe." The exhibit testifies to a renewed interest in futurism for both European and North American scholars. Over the last few decades, a number of studies have re-examined the iconoclast aesthetics, political engagement, fascination with technology, and rhetoric of gender of this intriguing movement.[24]

The recent re-evaluation of futurism has emphasized a misconception about Marinetti's movement, namely the predominant identification of futurism with its founder. Undeniably, Marinetti acted as the catalyst for a wave of creative destruction that hit a wide range of fields, spanning literature, music, visual arts, fashion, culinary art, politics, and even religion. Yet, as Geert Buelens and Monica Jansen have proposed in their introduction to the volume *The History of Futurism* (2012), we should speak instead of "futurisms" if we aim to acknowledge the plurality of voices and perspectives garnered by this avant-garde movement.[25] Engaging with the notion of "futurisms," *The Quiet Avant-Garde* discusses Marinetti's experimentalism along with "unorthodox" futurist paths.

Without any pretence of exhaustiveness, my purpose is to pay close attention to the Florentine circle of the "Pattuglia Azzurra" [Azure Patrol], a futurist group that developed between 1916 and 1918 around the journal *L'Italia futurista* [*Futurist Italy*] and saw the participation of many women writers. Unlike mainstream "Marinettism," the Florentine circle expressed a stronger interest in exotericism, turning the techno-vitalism of futurism into a mystical animism that identifies matter with a vibrant living force. Artists related to the Azure Patrol, such as the Corradini brothers, experimented with an artistic language that combined futurism, abstract art, and surrealism in an original fashion. A focus on this group can guide our understanding of the futurist avant-garde beyond its supposed cult of progress. In particular, the works of the Azure Patrol's women writers highlight how the futurist movement was fascinated, yet also deeply frightened, by the socio-political, economic, and ontological changes caused by the Industrial Revolution and the First World War.

The exoteric futurism of the Azure Patrol, as well as Marinetti's portrayal of modern cities as electrical jungles, is far from an Apollonian conception of modernity as rational emancipation. Art history scholar Christine Poggi has illustrated that Marinetti's group "encountered the belated industrialization of Italy and experienced its psychosomatic shocks and jolts … its losses and displacements."[26] Futurist "artificial optimism," as Poggi dubs it, masked a shared discomfort with the fast process of transformation that reshaped Italy at the beginning of the twentieth century. The avant-garde incendiary revolution, set to destroy bourgeois ethics and aesthetics, triggered a much broader "destructive reconstruction" of the universe. This fire endangered the epistemological categories of modernity, first and foremost the idea that nonhuman "things" exist only in relation to the (human) mind that processes them. Once the avant-garde reveals that matter has an independent life and, possibly, even an ungraspable psychology, the domino effect is unstoppable. Many modern pillars begin to shake: the solidity of the "I-subject," the patriarchal authority of the speaking "I," the static nature of the nonhuman. All these reassuring categories creak. Yet Marinetti tried to conceal this crisis though the artificial creation of an all-encompassing mechanical sublime and an affective rhetoric that skilfully moved the focus from the individual "I" to the collectivity that the futurist brotherhood and the experience of war offered.

The revised critical approach that extends our conception of futurism(s) beyond "Marinettism" and challenges any simplistic identification of the Italian avant-garde with a celebration of progress still relies on the assumption that the futurists ignited a fire in Western culture. Yet in 1909, when Marinetti's incendiary message flared up, the crepuscular poets had already sabotaged a golden anthropocentric tradition. They did so by composing humble verses in which petty objects and debased quasi-subjects – sick children, provincial intellectuals, uneducated girls – undermine the poetics of human greatness. Crepuscularism finds its two main voices in two young authors affected by tuberculosis:

the Roman Sergio Corazzini (1886–1907), who is regarded as the "father" of mystical crepuscularism, and the Turinese Guido Gozzano (1883–1916), the main poet of the so-called school of irony. Besides Corazzini and Gozzano, the most relevant crepuscular poets are Carlo Chiaves, Corrado Govoni, Fausto Maria Martini, Marino Moretti, Nino Oxilia, Aldo Palazzeschi, and Carlo Vallini. Each of these authors engaged with the crepuscular poetics in his own idiosyncratic way; for instance, a few of them – in particular, Govoni, Palazzeschi, and Oxilia – experimented with both crepuscularism and futurism at different stages of their literary careers. Overall, the crepuscular "movement" is an exemplary case of fluid poetics that did not formalize either into a group or into a manifesto. Its poetry represents one of the "peripheral vortices" that, according to Italian literature scholar Alberto Asor Rosa, animated the ebullient cultural life of the peninsula in the early twentieth century.[27]

Crepuscularism took its name from the adjective "crepuscular" ["crepuscolare"], denoting the dimming light of dusk, yet also the feeble light of dawn. The term was originally adopted to evoke the crisis of poetic inspiration at the twilight of the Italian Risorgimento (1848–70), a period of political events that "led Italy from [being] a fragmented peninsula to an independent and unified nation-state, under the Savoy king, Victor Emmanuel II."[28] The literary critic Giuseppe Antonio Borgese coined the "crepuscular" moniker in his milestone 1910 article "Poesia crepuscolare" ["Crepuscular Poetry"], in which he analysed – and criticized – the movement within the context of broader reflections on the evolution of Italian literature. Borgese, addressing the void that Giosuè Carducci's lyric passion for liberty had left in the post-Risorgimento scene, argued that the two dominant figures of twentieth-century Italian poetry, Giovanni Pascoli and Gabriele D'Annunzio, represented a form of self-indulgent decline: the former through his ingenuous "humanitarian spirit," and the latter through the "leonine Dionysian sensuality" of his language. In this context of regression, the emerging poetic youth of Borgese's own epoch brought a variety of literary trends – not just crepuscularism but also "skepticism, decadence, futurism, [and] *novecentismo*"[29] – that in his view ought to be condemned as characteristics of a poetry that had abandoned its civic mission. In the context of this analysis, it is interesting to note that Borgese grouped the crepusculars with the futurists, as expressions of a similar wave of change that hit Italian literature and culture.

Borgese argues that, bereft of political engagement and stylistic refinement, crepuscular poetry is relegated to the wasteland of "nothing to say," to a middle earth overpopulated with obsolete objects and disempowered quasi-characters. This critical view was strongly rebutted in the second half of the twentieth century. The spokesman for a re-evaluation of crepuscularism, Edoardo

Sanguineti, identified the parodic function of Gozzano's poetry in overthrowing the dominant aesthetics of D'Annunzio and in originating the "crepuscular lineage," a prosaic and "objective" lineage that shaped Italian post–First World War poetry. Furthermore, scholars like Giuseppe Farinelli and Angela Ida Villa have debunked the myth of crepuscular poetry as the naïve self-confession of sick poets, delineating the philosophical roots of the movement – between Latin Renaissance and Neo-Idealism – its connections with French symbolism, Nietzsche's thought, and mystical irrationalism. From this newly rehabilitated perspective, the term "crepuscular" designates the diaphanous light of the twentieth-century dawn, a dawn still overshadowed by the monumental profile of the nineteenth-century tradition, yet also nourished with the first light of the modernist poetics that the futurist avant-garde would violently illuminate.[30]

From a literary perspective, the anticipatory function of crepuscularism significantly emerged in the 1953 anthology *Lirica del Novecento* [*Poetry of the Twentieth Century*], edited by Luciano Anceschi and Sergio Antonielli. The collection opens with the crepusculars, rather than with the futurists, suggesting another possible starting point for twentieth-century anti-traditionalism. Through their poetic "sabotage" – making the most dignified literary language clash with debased verses – crepuscular authors certainly set the stage for the futurist attack on the antiquated syntax and trite repertoire of the past. However, for Anceschi, placing crepuscular poetry in such a primary position was a way to highlight its complementary role of caesura and suture: the movement polemically emphasized the languid exhaustion of D'Annunzio's and Pascoli's heritage, while marking the rise of an "anti-poetry" of reality. Through its focus on everyday "little things," this poetic lineage created a world of "objective allegories," wherein concrete images stand for a nuanced sentiment of lack, nostalgia, and malaise – an "objective" feeling of crisis that would become central in the modernist poetics of Eugenio Montale's *Ossi di seppia* [*Cuttlefish Bones*, 1925].[31]

In the 1950s, modernism was not a critical category that Anceschi would have adopted to define twentieth-century Italian poetry; and yet, his statement on the precursory function of crepuscularism can be linked to Raffaele Donnarumma's recent critique of the identification of futurism with the propulsive moment of Italian modernism.[32] Donnarumma considers the futurist avant-garde an extremist moment of modernist poetics, a poetics that, prior to Marinetti's founding manifesto of futurism (1909), had come forth in Pirandello's essay on humour ("L'Umorismo" ["On Humour"], 1908), the journal *La voce* [*The Voice*] (founded in 1908), and the crepuscular poetics of Govoni, Corazzini, and Gozzano. The question Donnarumma's overview leaves unanswered is to what extent and in what respect crepuscularism can be considered a precursory movement, liminal to both modernism and the extremist fringe of futurism. The connecting element, as Anceschi implicitly suggested, resides in the poetics of things that crepuscular poetry ushered in, articulating an "objective discourse" on human vulnerability, on a fragility that is reflected and somewhat embedded in the nonhuman. Its unpoetic verses, crowded with quotidian, trivial, and useless "stuff" that appears simultaneously reassuring and uncanny, testify to a pivotal transition in the twentieth-century mindset: namely, a move from the self-celebrating humanistic tradition, which places man in control of things, to the modernist and avant-garde counter-cultures, which defiantly undermine the anthropocentric master narrative of modernity.

As a form of poetry born during the spread of technological progress and bourgeois capitalism, crepuscularism displays the hidden correlation that links modernity with modernism: that is, this poetry manages to depict a "living human who is both the subject and the object of modernization," a "subject-object" that futurism will deform into a proto-cyborg, thrown into a forest of electric wires.[33] If, on one hand, the nineteenth-century Industrial Revolution maximized human labour by using machines on a larger scale, it also produced, on the other hand, a socio-economic apparatus that amplified the mutual influence of human and nonhuman agents. The development in Italy of a pre-capitalist society, in which the bourgeoisie was progressively gaining power while being, in turn, increasingly "controlled" by consumer goods, is indeed a central aspect of the crepusculars' social critique. In short, this quiet liminal movement can be interpreted as anticipating the avant-garde material vitalism and its incoherencies.

Crepuscular poetry works to overcome the positivist understanding of things as goods made by humans for humans. By parodying the aestheticization of objects that was typical of D'Annunzio's hyper-refined descriptions, the movement turned the typical approach, which overlooked the existence of (and our dependence on) objects, on its head, making painfully visible the presence of objects and their irreducibility to tools designed for usage. In the crepuscular texts, objects freed from any practical purpose rise as subjects who question the well-fabricated lie that ties modern progress to human hegemony over the nonhuman. In this way, crepuscular poetry anticipates, but also casts a modernist ironic shadow on, the groundbreaking idea of the "Manifesto tecnico della letteratura futurista" ["Technical Manifesto of Futurist Literature"] (1912), namely that poets should "Sorprendere attraverso gli oggetti in libertà e i movimenti capricciosi la respirazione, la sensibilità e gli istinti dei metalli, delle pietre, del legno, ecc." ["capture the breath, the sensibility, and the instincts of metals, stones, woods, and so on, through the medium of free objects and capricious motors"] (*TIF* 50, *F* 122).

Looking at crepuscularism as the link connecting – and converting – the late nineteenth-century zest for ekphrasis (in)to the futurist vitalism of still life, it is thus possible to reframe this marginal Italian movement within a broader reflection on materiality that crosses both modernism and the avant-garde. Baudelaire's theory of correspondences, the Proustian iconic madeleine, T.S. Eliot's reflection on the objective correlative, the deep deformation of reality typical of abstract art, expressionism, and cubism, all find a common thread in the investigation of what makes materiality a thing, distinct from an object; namely, of what makes a thing a dynamic cluster of human-nonhuman interaction, distinct from the static tangibility of the object. In Kantian terms, this inner discrepancy resides in the distinction between phenomena, which the human mind can access and categorize, and noumena, "things in themselves," which remain inaccessible. In everyday life, this gap in understanding empirically applies to the difference between a consumable, considered in its bare materiality, and the network of economic transactions, power relations, and emotional values embedded in that thing. Yet, what if defining materiality was a much more articulated and complex task?

Under the guise of self-debasing and humble poetry, crepuscularism hides a message of destabilization of the bourgeois order, further eroding the role of the Kantian rational and ethical "I-cataloguer," which Romanticism had already undermined in the nineteenth century. Futurism later magnifies this understated polemic, translating the subtle sabotage indicated by the crepuscular poets into a brazen invalidation of tradition.

After Sunset, before Sunrise: A Brief Overview of the Crepuscular Poetics

As crepuscular poetry is a much less explored movement than futurism, it will be useful to provide an overview of its style and themes, focusing in particular on its "twilight function" as connector between declining nineteenth-century poetics and new literary trends that emerged in the twentieth century.

In one of his most highly regarded poems, "Desolazione del povero poeta sentimentale" ["Desolation of the Poor Sentimental Poet"], Corazzini, speaking in the guise of a whimpering child, declares, "Io amo la vita semplice delle cose" ["I love the simple life of things"] (*SE* 32–3). A few lines later, referencing his tuberculosis, the poet compares the decay of his body to the consumption of quotidian materiality: "E muoio, un poco, ogni giorno. / Vedi: come le cose" ["And I die, a little bit, each day. / You see: just like things"] (*SE* 33–4). The transience of animate and inanimate life, expressed so poignantly by Corazzini in this poem, is a theme that also informs the more ironic poetry of Gozzano. In a

1907 text, "La via del rifugio" ["The Road to Shelter"], the Turinese author compacts his own name into a cluster of lower-case letters: expressing the existential condition of his poetic double, he affirms, "vive tra il Tutto e il Niente / questa cosa vivente / detta guidogozzano!" ["lives between Everything and Nothing / this living thing / called guidogozzano!"] (*TP* 70). These juxtapositions of the human and nonhuman evoke a sense of regression into an inert existence that sickness only intensifies. Yet, observing everyday "little things" and searching for their puzzling meaning also illustrates the emergence of a new twentieth-century poetics that simultaneously wonders about the place of the human and the place of literature.[34]

The twilight, with its dimming lights and melancholic atmosphere, is an image that condenses the richness of the crepuscular wonder in the face of life. In the poem "Crepuscolo" ["Sunset"], Govoni grasps the ephemeral atmosphere of the twilight, through a rhythmic series of images linked by the anaphora "È l'ora in cui" ["It's the time in which"]. The sunset is the time of acrobats and prostitutes, of death and desire, of a declining sun, "rosso e vacillante come un ubbriaco" ["red and wavering like a drunk"], and the rise of a lunar princess. This is the time, the poet concludes, of a spreading sadness that comes from the soul – "È l'ora in cui le viscide tristezze escon dai tetti muffidi dell'anima come dei pipistrelli" ["It's the time in which the viscid sadnesses come out of the mouldy roofs of the soul like bats"] (*P* 110–11). Overall, the sunset that Govoni attempts to recreate in these lines reflects many aspects of crepuscular poetics, in both its mystical and ironic nuances. The twilight evokes a nostalgia for an unrecoverable past, an ineffable sense of indefiniteness, the odd sensation of being human spectators of a nonhuman live performance, and a jarring combination of inescapable rituality and astonishing sublimity. Through material allegories, crepuscularism defines, in Anceschi's words, a "new disposition of the soul," a mode of being that rises from the overwhelming feeling of standing before the end of an epoch.[35]

Crepuscular poetics undermines the anthropocentric foundations of modern humanism while constructing a provocative meta-literary discourse. The main target of this dual polemic is the role of the poet as the gravitational centre of the human and nonhuman world. The examples of this provocation are numerous, but Moretti's "La giostra" ["The Carousel"] offers one of the most paradigmatic cases. In this text, the celebrated poet laureate turns into a ridiculous clown. Moretti's persona is riding a carousel horse, and he suddenly appears for who he is: on that merry-go-round, the poet "sembra il pagliaccio ch'egli è" ["looks like the clown he actually is"] (*TLP* 52). In another text, effectively titled "Io non ho nulla da dire" ["I Don't Have Anything to Say"], Moretti remarks that he, the author, is "l'unico al mondo / che non ha niente da dire" ["the only one in the world / who hasn't anything to say"] (*TLP* 260). Juxtaposing these images, we see the speechless disorientation of a "poetry-carousel ride" where unformed thoughts are spinning, and the real world is present yet somewhat suspended. However, this disoriented poetry that declares it has nothing to say has not abandoned its communicative mission. In the poem "Gli orti" ["The Orchards"], Oxilia compares poets to blind donkeys, who exercise a very useful function: "Come l'asino cieco, noi poeti. / Giriamo intorno al nostro cuore, chimere / traendo perché il mondo si disseti" ["Like the blind donkey, we poets. / We go around our heart, chimeras / pulling out so the world quenches its thirst"] (*PO* 103). The dark chimeras of the twentieth century, its illusions and monstrous fears, are very different from the sunny dreams written about by poets of the previous century.

The polemic message of the crepusculars' humble chimeras is fully revealed when their debased imagery is compared with the personae and allegories created by the great masters of nineteenth-century Italian poetry. Carducci, a celebrated author representative of a tradition inspired by civic and politic values, uses the figure of the craftsman to represent the poet. In his poem "Congedo" ["Furlough," translated as "The Poet"], a strong blacksmith forges verses out of "Love and thought … / All the glories / of his nation and his fathers."[36] In "La poesia" ["Poetry"], Pascoli synthesizes the themes of poetic inspiration and guidance in the symbolist image of the poet, "lampada" ["lamp"]. This anthropomorphized object comforts and guides its readers in their difficult journey.[37] In "Le stirpi canore" ["The Roots of Song"], the aesthete D'Annunzio compared his refined verses to a spider web, a beautiful interweaving of human emotions and nature.[38]

How can we define Moretti's clown and Oxilia's donkey, along with Corazzini's and Gozzano's thinglike personae, in relation to creative artisans, guiding lights, and weaving spiders that take a glorious past and translate it into an inspiring present? Touching on the issue of the crepusculars' self-debasement, Italian scholar Jole Soldateschi has stressed that theirs is a "polemic humility."[39] The bitter humility that Soldateschi highlights emerges more clearly if we recall that, in "Congedo," prior to introducing his master artisan, Carducci defines what a poet is not: "Folk profane, I'd have ye know it / That the poet / Is no merry-andrew … / And still less is he a lazy / Fool … / Nor is he a garden lover."[40] Crepuscularism converts Carducci's anti-poets into provocative new models. Echoing "Congedo," Moretti, in "Il giardino dei frutti" ["The Garden of Fruits"], affirms "Io non sono un giardiniere e nemmen forse un poeta" ["I am not a gardener and perhaps not even a poet"] (*TLP* 235). In "Chi sono?" ["Who Am I?"], Palazzeschi rhetorically asks "Son forse un poeta?" ["Am I perhaps a poet?"], answering himself "No, certo" ["Not at all"], and confessing: I am "Il saltimbanco dell'anima mia" ["the acrobat of my soul"] (*TTP* 71). The poet debases himself to a "lazy fool," to a circus performer who mimics the unpredictable changes of the fleeting human soul. However, the strongest declarations of the crepuscular poetics of debasement and wonder come from Corazzini and Gozzano. In "Desolazione del povero poeta sentimentale," the Roman poet declares to an unnamed "you": "Perché tu mi dici: poeta? Io non sono un poeta. / Io non sono che un piccolo fanciullo che piange" ["Why do you call me a poet? / I am not a poet. I'm only a crying little boy"] (*SE* 30–1).[41] In "La signorina Felicita" ["Felicity"], one of Gozzano's autobiographical personae, Guido the lawyer, contemplates the intriguing idea of abandoning his intellectual engagement and enjoying the simple pleasures of a petty bourgeois life. "Io mi vergogno, / sí, mi vergogno d'essere un poeta!" ["I'm ashamed to be – / yes, I confess, I'm ashamed to be a poet!"] (*TM* 86–7), Guido states, parodying D'Annunzio's ideal of an "inimitable life" with the dream of an uneventful existence.

From a stylistic perspective, the crepuscular *modus poetandi* overturns D'Annunzio's statement that each line of poetry contains a description of the divine beauty of the world – "The verse is everything," he famously stated in a sonnet of *L'Isotteo* (*Isotteo*, 1886). Conversely, the crepusculars' poetic "arte povera" experiments with unadorned free verse – especially the poetry of Corazzini and Govoni – or with a parodic reuse of old-fashioned metre, a strategy that Gozzano often adopts.[42] Traditional metres and strophes, though, are repurposed to contain hilarious jarring images, such as in the lines of "La signorina Felicita," in which Gozzano makes "camicie" ["shirts"] rhyme with "Nietzsche." In the context of this poem, the German philosopher's thought is (mis)matched with the domestic duties of a bourgeois young lady, who is ignorant of philosophy and tailors shirts for her father.

Another outstanding innovation of the movement is the use of a repetitive plain lexicon, which virtually deprives language of its poetic function. Crepuscular poetry uses frantic and dry parataxis, as the incipit of Moretti's "A Cesena" ["In Cesena"] exemplifies: "Piove. È mercoledì. Sono a Cesena" ["It rains. It's Wednesday. I'm in Cesena"] (*TLP* 288). A popular strategy is also the adoption of a "listing poetry" that assembles people, objects, thoughts, emotions, and natural settings as interchangeable pieces of a narrative litany. This modest style, in Gozzano's words, "lo stile d'uno scolare / corretto un po' da una serva" ["the style of a schoolboy / corrected a little by a servant"] ("L'altro" ["The Other"], *TP* 309), mocks the verbosity and formal perfection that had generally characterized poetry up to that point. As Vallini ironically declares, in "Alcuni desideri" ["A Few Wishes"], these are his wishes when making poetry:

Vorrei pure scrivere, senza
fatica, dei versi: ma sparsi
a spizzico, da giudicarsi
con una bonaria indulgenza:
dei versi bizzarri, rimati
secondo la mia prosodía,
con molta malinconía
e quasi niente grammatica (*UG* 61)

[I would also like to write, without
any effort, a few verses, but scattered
and nibbled, to be judged
with kind benevolence:
a few bizarre verses, rhymed
according to my prosody,
with great melancholy
and virtually no grammar.]

It is indeed by experimenting with ordinary simplicity – Corazzini's bare verse or Gozzano's lines overcrowded with lists of petty things – that the crepusculars explore new expressive possibilities to portray the limits of humanity.

However, it is important to emphasize that the crepusculars were fully aware of being (atypical) poets. Their denial of the poetic norm and their sloppy verses without accurate grammar were implemented as primarily rhetorical devices through which their "misfits" and inept alter egos construct a literary counter-culture. Furthermore, as I will discuss in detail in chapter 1, the use of these "misfits" and inept alter egos – Corazzini's crying child and Gozzano's many poetic personae – shows, again, the ways in which the crepusculars played a connective role between tradition and symbolism, on the one hand, and modernism and the avant-garde, on the other. The motif of the author's own disguise and degradation, as opposed to the model of the poet-guide, evolves from symbolist *maudit* writing – one may think of Baudelaire's *Les Fleurs du Mal* (1857) – to Luigi Pirandello's recurrent topoi of the mask and the "I-other," motifs that are widely adopted by other modernist European authors, including Juan Ramon Jimenez and Fernando Pessoa. In a renewed socio-cultural space, transformed further by the First World War, the avant-garde poetic "I" becomes an odd and unsuitable "container" of things that he or she can barely control. In a 1915 letter to Marinetti, Govoni affirmed: "Io stesso sono il centro del mondo sensibile, anzi tutto il mondo intero con tutte le sue propaggini e diramazioni" ["I myself am the centre of the sensible world, or rather, the whole world with all its offshoots and branches"].[43] The switch, emphasized by the interjection "anzi" ["or rather"], signals the (crepuscular) passage from a self-centred cognizing "I–poetic subject" to a relational "molecular I" who rises as a perceiving self only when subjected to other "things."

The crepusculars' retreat into domestic spaces was initially perceived as a sign of their provincial isolation. In 1921, Italian critic Francesco Flora dubbed the crepusculars "poeti provincialeschi" ["provincialish," or "somewhat provincial"].[44] Yet, this provincialism provides a language to represent the middle-class lifestyle and the delicate mechanisms of power and petty revenge that shaped the lifestyle and morals of Chiaves's "cari amici borghesi, / pettegoli e senza mercé, / fin troppo educati e cortesi" ["dear bourgeois friends / gossipy and merciless, / even too well-manned and courteous"].[45] Moreover, although crepuscular poetry features actual places, these places are often set in an evanescent temporality, in a dusty past or fairy-tale time-space. The movement is not actually concerned with describing a particular provincial place; rather, this poetry uses well-known locations and objects to re-create the unsettling feeling of claustrophobia and the ineffable mystery that emanates from the "same old stuff." The ordinary suddenly becomes mysterious, and even exotic. The early work of Govoni, such as the collection *Le fiale* (*The Vials*, 1903), testifies to a curiosity about an "incerto Timbuctù" ["uncertain Timbuktu"] (*P* 6) that often takes the shape of a fantasy-land Japan, evoked through objects: fans and umbrellas, cups from Satsuma, decorations with dragons, and koto music. The overwhelming presence of outlandish or odd objects far exceeds decorative allure and functionality. One may think of Corazzini's uncomfortable churches, abandoned by people, but still filled with forgotten objects. Another very suitable example is Gozzano's incipit of "L'amica di nonna Speranza" ["Grandmother Speranza's Friend"]. The poem opens with a detailed inventory of "things in bad taste," which construe an ineffable, and yet *objectively* perceivable, bourgeois setting.

Crepuscular poetry is not directly related to any artistic movement; however, its fascination with everyday objects, exoticism, and arts and crafts from the past echoes some aspects of Art Nouveau. This style, which in the early twentieth century spread throughout Western Europe and America, had a great impact as a "break-away from the 'historical' style that preceded it," from the naturalism that had dominated nineteenth-century art.[46] Art Nouveau found a new source of inspiration in styles from remote times and exotic spaces. The movement promoted an anti-academic eclecticism and provided a unifying language that could "encapsulate modernity and tradition, anxiety and confidence, decadence and progress, conservative national identities and radical internationalism."[47] Art Nouveau became popular in Italy with the name of "Stile Floreale"

["Floral Style"] and then "Stile Liberty" ["Liberty Style"]. After reaching its apex in France during the 1900 Parisian "Exposition Universelle," this style found its Italian centre in Turin, with the "Esposizione internazionale d'arte decorativa moderna" ["International Exhibit of Modern Decorative Art"] in 1902. It is no surprise, then, that Gozzano proposes a comparison between Art Nouveau poets and Art Nouveau painters in his article "Misticismo moderno" ["Modern mysticism"], arguing that as the modern floral decoration recalls medieval and primitive frescos, so too does contemporary poetry draw its inspiration from figures of the past such as Dante, Petrarch, Botticelli, and da Vinci.[48]

Crepuscularism was also not immune to D'Annunzio's fascination with Pre-Raphaelite art. While D'Annunzio recovered only some formal aspects of this artistic movement, such as the sensual and languid poses, the crepusculars show a deeper connection with the fundamental focus of the Pre-Raphaelites, namely a return to the fourteenth-century "primitive art" as opposed to the academic style of the sixteenth-century artists. Crepuscularism expressed, in poetry, the same anti-academic protest, proposing an anti-classical return to the time of "cultural infancy" and simple poetry.[49] However, crepuscularism also exhibits an openness to forms of synthetic experimental art. *Cronache Latine* [*Latin Chronicles*], the journal of Corazzini's Roman group, published articles on visual art, and painter Guglielmo Genua wrote a piece on the centrality of colour in painting in the journal's last issue (15 January 1906). Genua envisions the possibility of musical chromatism – of colours that modulate sounds – and quotes the British aesthete Walter Pater: "all art constantly aspires towards the condition of music." This perspective draws interesting parallels with Arnaldo Ginna's futurist experimentation with colour. Genua concludes his hymn to the expressive potential of colour, calling for a new chromatic painting that derives from Hans Memling, Gèrard David, Rogier Van der Weyden, and the Pre-Raphaelites:

> Noi oggi, pur con mutati ideali, con anima più fiera e non più religiosa, con pensiero più audace e non più servile, perché non dovremmo far sì che dalle nostre mani esperte fiorissero su le tele anche con soli accordi cromatici, rivelazioni nuove d'un'arte non costretta né pur da esigenze logiche, e non fatta per adornare gli offici di bottegai moderati e benpensanti o i profumati *boudoirs* di vereconde puttanelle cattoliche e intellettuali?[50]

> [Today, although with renovated ideals, with a fiercer and no longer religious soul, with a more audacious and no longer servile thought, why wouldn't we make it possible that from our expert hands blooms on our canvases, even only through chromatic accords, new revelations of an art that is neither constrained by the

needs of logic, nor made to decorate the offices of moderate and conformist shop-keepers, or the perfumed boudoirs of modest little catholic and intellectual tarts?]

Beyond the possible connections with art, the crepuscular attention to practical and decorative objects also highlights sociological aspects of the bourgeois relation with material "still life." This emergent social class, so concerned with utility and profit, was paying to enjoy the symbolic luxury of being "bored" with piles of trivial knickknacks. Crepuscular poetry, through the placid and hypnotizing carillon of its verses filled with useless "stuff," shows objects existing in a state of non-use. This poetry addresses the self-indulgence people gain from filling their lives with material belongings, even when (or precisely because) these objects remain unused, serving only as status symbols. Expressing a precursory wit, crepuscularism makes the subtle power of consumables disturbingly evident. In "La passeggiata" ["The Walk"], Palazzeschi puts the domination of objects over human relations into verse. Although Palazzeschi is not a crepuscular poet *tout court*, his verses creatively blend elements of Corazzini's and Gozzano's poetics, with the iconoclast verve of futurism. "La passeggiata" shows how a quintessential Italian ritual – the evening walk – morphs from a moment of sociality into a depersonalized experience of spectatorship before a live performance of consumables. From line 3 to line 141, the text features a parade of goods in shop windows, promotional claims, and advertising on billboards:

Avviso importante alle signore!
la bellezza del viso!
pelle di velluto,
nuovissimo insuperabile sapone.
Orologeria di precisione.
43
Lotteria del milione.
Antica trattoria
…
fiaschetteria,
…
Loffredo e Rondinella,
primaria casa di stoffe,
panni, lana e flanella.
Oggetti d'arte,
antichità. (*TTP* 295–6)

[Important announcement for the ladies!
the beauty of the face!

velvety skin.
Newest incomparable soap.
Precision clock making.
43
Lottery of the million.
Old trattoria
...
wine shop,
...
Loffredo and Rondinella,
prime fabric shop,
cloth, wool, and flannel.
Artifacts,
antiquity.]

Objects invade relational space, becoming the only tangible grip in a fast-moving world. Items have names or can easily be identified; by contrast, the couple remains unnamed. While things speak on their behalf, the only words these two individuals exchange are the initial invitation to go for a walk: "– Andiamo? / – Andiamo pure" ["Shall we go? – Sure, let's go"] and "– Torniamo indietro? – Torniamo pure" ["Shall we go back? – Let's go back"] (*TTP* 295, 298). In this grey walk animated by items for sale, objects become out-and-out living puppets or allegories of "L'orribile / La dozzinale / Noia / Di tutto" ["The horrible / Cheap / Boredom/ With all of this"], as painter and crepuscular poet Raul Dal Molin Ferenzona writes in his poem "Invernale" ["Wintry Scene"].[51] These objects, taking centre stage, foretell philosopher Mario Perniola's notion of the sex appeal of the inorganic: objects are in fact bearers of alternative forms of sexual satisfaction beyond the notion of intercourse.[52]

Crepusculars offer a "still life poetry" that goes beyond mere reference to everyday objects in poetry. The English expression "still life," rather than the Italian "natura morta" – literally "dead nature" – is a more accurate description of the crepuscular revolution regarding the perception and conception of materiality. Although seemingly inert or asleep, things participate in life in a way that remains mysteriously remote to people. Borrowing from Manuel DeLanda, we can see how, in place of an "essentialist metaphysics, in which the world is already segmented by [human] logical categories," crepuscular poetry moves towards a material and "metaphysical approach in which the world begins as a *continuum of* [human and nonhuman] *intensity*."[53] The reader's task is to approach this continuum and retrace humanity as a hybrid, being open and eager to understand the other sources of intensity that are intermingled with our own.

The Crepuscular "Nonhuman Turn"

In *The Parasite* (1982), a seminal work for posthuman theories, philosopher Michel Serres obliterates the artificial distance between (human) subject and (nonhuman) object, featuring the hybrid category of the quasi-object or quasi-subject. In the chapter "Theory of the Quasi-Object," Serres discusses the dual meaning of the word *furet* to exemplify the function of the quasi-object. As the translator's note explains, in French, *furet* can designate "the animal, the ferret, as well as the marker in a game somewhat like hunt-the-slipper or button, button, who's got the button."[54] Playing on the two accepted meanings of the word, Serres writes:

> [The ferret] is the vampire of the rabbit, following it into its warren; it throws itself on the rabbit, biting its nose or neck, sucking its blood. We have domesticated the ferret and no longer know about the wild variety. We make it run for us, like the buzzard, like the kestrel; we parasite them. We muzzle the ferret before introducing it into the system of the burrow; the crazed rabbit leaves through another hole and is trapped in the net. Once more, a nice diversion of flows in a network.
>
> We have all played the game of hunt-the-slipper or button, button, who's got the button. The one who is caught with the *furet* has to pay a forfeit. The furet points him out. One person is marked with the sign of the furet. Condemned, he goes to the center; he's "it"; he sees, he looks.
>
> What is the furet?

In the hunt-the-slipper game, it is the *furet* and not solely human nature that defines (and redefines) the player. As Serres continues, the *furet* is "the quasi-object and quasi-subject by which I am a subject, that is to say, sub-mitted. Fallen, put beneath, trampled, tackled, thrown about, subjugated, exposed, then substituted, suddenly by that vicariance."[55] Serres's reflection on quasi-objects/quasi-subjects and their pivotal function as subject markers and dynamic constructers of intersubjective relations finds further meaning in socio-cultural discourse. Like the *furet*, minor groups can become major agents in public dialogue, contributing to the diversity and complexity vital to the development of our society. To contextualize this notion in the twenty-first century, we can consider the role of illegal immigrants – barely subjects in their host countries – in the public debate, such as in defining the future face of Europe and the United States, as well as in shaping new geopolitical alliances and material boundaries.

We shall now return to Serres's question – What is the *furet*? – and analyse how the metaphor of "the *furet* quasi-object" can apply to crepuscularism on a variety of levels. This movement acted as the *furet* of tradition. "Creative parasites" of the great nineteenth-century heritage, the crepuscular poets insinuate themselves into a weakening world of literary giants and invade it with a Lilliputian horde of disturbing "little things" and pitiful characters. However, in turn, these poetic objects also play the role of quasi-objects, because, like Serres's *furet*, they serve as important markers. The crepuscular-debased "little things" can be defined only in relation to the literary magnificence they lack or parody; and yet, it is this miserable "stuff" that allows readers to understand the collective crisis of humans, and poets, who have lost their hegemonic position in the world.

The "parasitic" action of the crepusculars' sloppy verses introduces a certain dullness and simplicity, and an overwhelming feeling of melancholic emptiness to the language and imaginary of Italian poetry. Moreover, in both its mystical and ironic nuances, the movement offers a reflection on the barely visible intersubjective relations with material things that shape our being. As a precursory reflection on nonhuman agency, crepuscular poetry pens an innovative message that is still relevant in the epoch of global capitalism, in which material and virtual objects are invisibly ubiquitous. By pulling everyday quasi-objects into poetry, by making them hyper-visible, the crepusculars implicitly ask their readers if it is indeed possible to define what it means to be human without entering into dialogue with barely noticeable object-markers. What, then, is behind the assumed fixity of a "still life" that subtly participates in *ma(r)king* the human? If we consider that many of the crepuscular authors "inhabited" sick bodies, broken machines that existed beyond their functionality, the issue of our relationship with things becomes even more complicated. The body, a quasi-object/quasi-subject, suddenly reveals its quiescent agency. Where is the boundary between a malady consuming the body and the creative mind that writes about that suffering flesh? What is the role of intellectuals in relation to a silent environment filled with agentic "objects"? Are poets representing the surrounding world or rather learning to be ignorant observers who contemplate the mystery of nature's intelligent action? These are a few questions that crepuscular poetry raises, and that futurism, with its frightening parade of mechanical beasts, proto-cyborgs, and vibrant electric wires, continues to explore and revise.

Read in parallel, crepuscular and futurist texts spur reflections on the vulnerability that *being* (*in*) *relation* entails, and draw innovative inter- and *intra*-connections between human and nonhuman. The goal of this book is ultimately to voice the "silent" and thought-provoking questions through which these two movements acted as fastidious "parasites" of the modern mindset, and to argue that they can still act as productive – and problematic – contributors to our changing view of the nonhuman.

A central unresolved issue, for example, is that the revolution of the avant-garde is rarely constructive. As philosopher Maurizio Ferraris has highlighted, "deconstruction without reconstruction is irresponsibility,"[56] and avant-garde movements often do not embrace ethical concerns. But their aesthetic polemics touches upon ethical and environmental issues. For instance, both crepuscularism – in its anticipatory-linking role – and futurism articulate a series of thorny ecological questions, examining the possibilities of reusing outdated objects for new creative purposes or dismantling the nature-culture gap. In addition, the avant-garde fascination with the mingling of organic and inorganic triggers a redefinition of the body as a "feeling thing" in communion with the universe, rather than as a socially negotiated corporeality, or corporeal matter determined by its biological sex. Overall, both movements try, in different ways, to demolish the classic Promethean role of humans. They foster a type of Promethean irony that revises anthropocentrism into a participative humanism, into an ontology of co-belonging.

This book illustrates that, beginning with crepuscularism, we witness a twilight of traditional modern humanism that sets the stage for the futurist revolution and can offer new insights on current nonhuman perspectives. The book opens with a chapter that situates the crepusculars' and futurists' innovative poetics of living objects, while providing a more detailed discussion of the crepuscular movement. The first chapter, "A Matter of Things: Modernity, Modernism, Avant-Garde," maps three discourses on the object that shaped early twentieth-century culture: the objective narrative of bourgeois modernity – say, the human subject in control of the object; the modernist conception of the object as the blurry emanation of the (human) subject; and the vitalistic approach of the avant-garde – objects turning into animate beings. Modernity tries to affirm a dividing paradigm that is unable to deal with cross-category relationships. While criticizing modernity, modernism still proposes human subjects that, although in crisis, use the environment as a projection of their state of mind. The crepuscular poetics of things delimits a transitional "grey area" in which an anti-modern hybridization of the human with things takes shape. Humans transmute into "living things" and, in turn, everyday objects become animated agents. Futurism later formalizes this radical rethinking of "still life" in its bold project of replacing human psychology with the energetic life of matter.

The second chapter, "The Avant-Garde Is Made of Useless Objects," examines the representation of materiality by the crepusculars and futurists in more depth. The analysis focuses on the crepuscular hoarding of useless "little things," showing how these discarded objects, living at the margins of practicality and aesthetic function, act as silent witnesses of human vulnerability. This dusty and forgotten "stuff" also reveals the paradox of the shiny futurists' machines: these fast and unbreakable machines can remain new only while immobile and unused. Anticipating the weak spot in Marinetti's mechanical dream, crepuscular objects become material symbols of the internal incoherence of the avant-garde, of the limitation of its ephemeral and self-destructive nature in confronting the process of becoming. These disturbing "little things" also serve as intriguing material for current theories. Within the contemporary debate, the crepuscular objects, so at-hand and yet so ineffably withdrawn from the experience of being human, provide a literary lens for the exploration of OOO's and new materialism's conflicting notions of being and becoming.

Chapter 3, "Being a Living Thing: Towards a New Notion of Body," examines the crepuscular and futurist recasting of the human body as living and "storied" matter. Overcoming the centripetal model of the "flesh-and-soul" subject, the two movements embrace the centrifugal paradigm of the "open subject" and explore new aesthetic and gender possibilities. Gozzano insisted that he was nothing more than a "living thing" called "guidogozzano" and even described his body as an estranged "sick thing" scrutinized by doctors. In "Toblack," Corazzini represented the sanatorium as the place where the human body is simultaneously "Vita che piange, Morte che cammina" ["crying Life, walking Death"] (*O* 123). These representations of masculinity in pain seem to contrast with the glorified androcentric view of the futurists. The chapter discusses how the crepuscular martyrized bodies can be read as an anticipation of the futurist anthropotechnic project of the mechanical man, constructed of interchangeable parts. Furthermore, in the aftermath of the First World War, the ideal of a techno-masculine corporality evolved with the reality of the veteran's mutilated or prosthetic body in pain. The revised model of masculinity that crepuscularism and Marinettian futurism bring forward is analysed in comparison to the reflection on femininity that the women of the Azure Patrol elaborate on, and through the contemporary lens of ecofeminism. These early twentieth-century proposals involve the exploration of new genders and gender roles, including the hybrid notions of pansexual virility and male motherhood. From a social point of view, these mutant and mutilated bodies overthrow the Promethean model of the modern hero and develop new abilities to adapt to the unpredictable flow of life.

Adopting the frameworks of affect theory and material ecocriticism, chapter 4, "Love and the Grand Solidarity of Sound," analyses how crepuscularism and futurism criticize the bourgeois notion of "love" as a predefined social destiny leading to a respectable marriage. Although the avant-garde reinvention of romance was not as groundbreaking as Marinetti claimed, its provocative view of lover-beloved relationships contributed in fuelling a debate that involved women writers. The latter responded to this iconoclast poetics of love, reshaping their identities as women and lovers. The chapter analyses another pivotal point in the crepuscular and futurist discourse about love: both movements are fascinated with a redefinition of this affective bond beyond the human scale. What would love look like, once transposed beyond our sensorial perception and rational understanding? Reimagined through a decentred human perspective, the avant-garde narrative of love traces uncharted affective landscapes. Love becomes a dispersed "material solidarity," across organic and inorganic life. To express this diffused connection, crepuscular and futurist texts return to the non-verbal language of sound. Through their modulations, silence and noises become media to express the grand "solidarity" – the inhuman love – that interweaves matter and makes it "storied matter," a material space in which human and nonhuman stories intertwine.

The final chapter, "Avant-Garde Immersive Onto-Cognition," focuses on the epistemological switch caused by the crepusculars' and futurists' notion of living animacy. If agency is not uniquely human, knowledge, as a form of cognitive agency, must also be redefined and extended beyond the boundaries of the mind of *homo sapiens*. While the avant-garde epistemological proposals undeniably draw from the irrational wave that characterized early twentieth-century culture, these proposals also contribute to shaping a hybrid view of knowledge, which includes emotional and corporeal elements into the cognitive process. Cognition is portrayed as an immersion in surrounding matter rather than as a process of rational distancing from the object of inquiry. In addition, this rethinking of knowledge implies a complex re-evaluation of the possibilities that ignorance opens, from mystical experiences of rapture to forms of sensorial intuition. The crepuscular and futurist parallel proposals of immersive cognition are also creative attempts to disentangle and re-entangle the human-nature knot. What do we learn by being part of nature, by being nature ourselves? The avant-garde cognitive reflection can be read as a literary precursor to Barad's notion of "intra-action," and her concept of material and discursive inseparability of knowing, being, and doing. This reflection also opens further ecocritical perspectives to investigate, and possibly knit together, nature and culture.

Ultimately, *The Quiet Avant-Garde* aims to reframe our understanding of avant-garde Italian movements beyond the futurist manifestos and their innovations in the art world. Crepuscularism and futurism find an up-to-date reading in their ability to reposition humans as puzzled "things" violently scattered amidst matter. The crepuscular emphasis on human vulnerability and the futurist notion of human hybridity are captivating ideas that we can reconsider from new ethical, environmental, and non-anthropocentric premises. By retracing poetics at the twilight of modern humanism, we may discover we are contemplating, today, the same sunset that the crepusculars and futurists glimpsed in the early twentieth century, and that twilight unfolded "So many sunsets / Facebook and Instagram couldn't contain them."[57]

Chapter One

A Matter of Things: Modernity, Modernism, Avant-Garde

The Question of the Object

In the early twentieth century, the futurist avant-garde shook off stagnant cultural traditions based on harmony and beauty, adopting in their place an artistic language of creative destruction and radical experimentalism. According to the origin narrative recounted in the founding manifesto of futurism (1909), penned by Filippo Tommaso Marinetti (1876–1944), the futurist program of violent palingenesis sprang from a literal collision between a thrilling new machine of the future and a slow-moving, traditional machine of the past. This epochal crash occurred when Marinetti was speeding along the road in his car, chasing Death – a beast "dal pelame nero maculato di pallide croci" ["its black hide stained with pale crosses"] (*TIF* 8, *F* 50) – and was suddenly cut off by two hesitant cyclists. He careened into a muddy ditch. Climbing out from underneath the capsized car, his body covered in dust and mud, Marinetti felt that his heart was "attraversa[to] … deliziosamente, dal ferro arroventato della gioia!" ["being slashed with the red-hot iron of joy"] (*TIF* 9, F 50). As a nearby crowd of fishermen rushed to retrieve the vehicle, which was "simile ad un grande pescecane arenato" ["stranded like a large shark"] in the ditch (*TIF* 9, F 50), the futurist leader watched the car emerge transformed: "La macchina emerse lentamente dal fosso, abbandonando nel fondo, come squame, la sua pesante carrozzeria di buon senso e le sue morbide imbottiture di comodità" ["The car slowly emerged from the ditch, leaving behind in the depths its heavy chassis of good sense and its soft upholstery of comfort, like scales"] (*TIF* 9, *F* 50). Marinetti revivified the beautiful car-shark with one caress, and "eccolo in corsa, di nuovo, sulle sue pinne possenti!" ["there it was again, once more alive, running on its powerful fins"] (*TIF* 9, *F* 50). Prompted by this crucial moment of contact between the man and the machine – a co-mingling of human and nonhuman vitality – Marinetti and his "arsonist brothers," his fellow racers, proclaim the eleven tenets that will come to define futurism.

Marinetti's 1909 futurist manifesto, a seminal avant-garde text, assembles and reinvents elements from medieval bestiaries, mythologies, and biblical texts: a roughly chopped mixture of languages and images, melding advanced technology and primal wildness, organic and inorganic, human and nonhuman. At a linguistic level, this magmatic, materic discourse expresses the ferment that the futurists brought to the twentieth-century cultural scene. Their vital tumult finds its preferred space in the modern metropolises, which in the early twentieth century are animated with "le maree multicolori e polifoniche delle rivoluzioni" ["multicolored and polyphonic tidal waves of revolution"]; "il vibrante fervore notturno degli arsenali e dei cantieri incendiati da violente lune elettriche" ["the vibrating nocturnal fervor of factories and shipyards burning under violent electrical moons"]; "le stazioni ingorde, divoratrici di serpi che fumano" ["bloated railroad stations that devour smoking serpents"]; gigantic locomotives with swollen chests; and flying airplanes that oscillate in the air (*TIF* 11, *F* 51–2). The futurist animated cities, inhabited with techno-animal machines, clash with the paradigm of modernity, understood as a linear emancipatory project, historically tied to the rise and consolidation of Western bourgeois society. Is it possible to argue that the true challenge offered by the 1909 futurist manifesto is its portrayal of a hyper-modern world that regresses into a "primordial soup," wherein human and nonhuman coexist indistinct and intertwined?

To address this query, I advance the hypothesis that the core inquiry of modernity, modernism, and the avant-garde in the early twentieth century is "the question of the object," that is, the necessity of redefining the relation between the human and the nonhuman. At the turn of the twentieth century, the divergent and yet interdependent discourses of modernity, modernism, and the avant-garde all shared a common need to reposition the human within the universe of things. Proceeding from this premise, I examine each of these three narratives of the object: the modern reduction of objects to verifiable phenomena, resources, or consumable goods, with the human hierarchically above the object; its modernist counter-narrative, which preserved the human's superior place but portrayed objects as projections of a (human) subject who faces the challenges of modern progress; and finally, the futurist revolutionary proposition of a holistic material vitalism, in which human and nonhuman are co-mingled. My analysis aims to discuss these three discourses on the object, while offering a more detailed account of how these narratives unfold in the context of early twentieth-century Italian society and literature.

The exploration of the "question of the object" illustrates that Marinetti's founding manifesto was, albeit radical, not as innovative as it claimed to be. Futurism did not suddenly depose *homo sapiens* as the measure of all things; rather, it marked the zenith of a long-running, subtle sabotage of that notion. In the realm of Italian literature, the liminal quiet voice between early modernism and the avant-garde was crepuscular poetry, which articulated a transition from modern anthropocentrism to avant-garde object-oriented vitalism.

The Modern Epic: Constructing Solid Narratives of Human Empowerment

Baudelaire's identification of modernity with "the ephemeral, the fugitive, the contingent, the half of art whose other half is the eternal and the immutable" is a milestone definition.[1] However, in defining modernity, one should also recognize that even the transient "half of art," which emerges from the encounter with the present, eventually *solidifies* into a "rewriting … of previously existing versions or narratives of the past."[2] When modernity is understood, in Jamesonian terms, as a "narrative category," it is seen to have developed through a process of rupture with tradition and palimpsestuous rewriting of the past. Modernity thus acts as an ongoing process of *solidification through storytelling*, through which the fleeting quality of time is fixed into new narratives, which are themselves open to future receptions and rewritings.

From a historical perspective, the term "modernity" has often been associated with a specific period – a modernity *par excellence*, we may say – that spans the sixteenth through twentieth centuries, reaching its acme in the sociopolitical and economic transformations that occurred with the Industrial and French Revolutions.[3] These drastic changes marked the transition from an aristocratic ancient regime, founded on blood legacy and the feudal system, to a bourgeois society that was based on democratic ideals and the capitalist notion of free markets. Modernity, as an ebullient epoch of change and mythopoeic "category," shaped its own discourses and narrative modes by creating its own bourgeois epic, the novel. As Hegel argued in the 1820s *Aesthetics*, the "modern popular epic," which found its elective genre in the novel, presented readers with "the wealth and many-sidedness of interests, situations, characters, relations involved in life, the wide background of the whole world, as well as the epic portrayal of events."[4] The German philosopher did still affirm the pre-eminence of the classical epic for creating a totalizing form of poetry, one founded on the "perfect communion between poet and audience"; and Hegel did hold that the novel could not help but exhibit a prosaically ordered world, an excessive emphasis on individualism, and a missing notion of totality.[5] However, Hegel recognizes the epic-novel as the genre of the modern epoch, a genre characterized by a rewriting of classical and chivalric motives, through which the bourgeoisie can assert its own heroes, quests, and objects of desire.

My adoption of the term *bourgeois epic* does not solely refer to the literary field; it denotes the broader formation of a new set of values, social myths, and practices that were triggered by the process of industrialization and socio-economic transition to the capitalist model. The modern bourgeois *epos*, embracing a choral dimension that is typical of epic narration, moulded a collective mythology wherein a crowd of socio-economic, technological, and cultural actors came into play and transformed one another. To depict the rich intertwining of characters, facts, and places that contributed to the affirmation of a new epic, one might recall Marshall Berman's portrayal of modernity as a maelstrom that "has been fed from many sources":

> great discoveries in the physical sciences, changing our images of the universe and our place in it; the industrialization of production, which transforms scientific knowledge into technology, creates new human environments and destroys old ones, speeds up the whole tempo of life, generates new forms of corporate power and class struggle; immense demographic upheavals, severing millions of people from their ancestral habitats, hurtling them half-way across the world into new lives; rapid and often cataclysmic urban growth; systems of mass communication, dynamic in their development, enveloping and binding together the most diverse people and societies; increasingly powerful national states, bureaucratically structured and operated, constantly striving to expand their powers; mass social movements of people, and peoples, challenging their political and economic rulers, striving to gain some control over their lives; finally, bearing and driving all these people and institutions along, an ever-expanding, drastically fluctuating capitalist world market.[6]

Berman's crowded inventory proceeds through a chain of interactions between human and nonhuman actors, illustrating a fundamental feature of the modern epic: it ushered in a temporality of transience and accelerated progress that strictly depends on complex dynamics of human-nonhuman intermixing and mutual transformation. The *cross-breeding list* of Berman's account depicts the epic polyphony of the modern capitalist apparatus as a network of "discourses, institutions, buildings, laws, police measures, philosophical propositions, and so on," whose "power relations and relations of knowledge" affect human as well as nonhuman bodies.[7] Yet, transposed into Bruno Latour's framework, the mingling of technology, nature, culture, and economics that characterizes modernity also gives rise to its constitutional impasse. Modernity figures humans as the regulators of a series of fundamental dichotomies (culture-nature, human-thing, *homo sapiens*–animal) and, simultaneously, as the generators of phenomena that controvert these dichotomies – such as global warming, natural catastrophes, or bio-technologic advancement. Thus, it is possible to affirm that, underneath the solid narrative surface of an enlightened *homo oeconomicus* in control of nature and its resources, modernity hides a narrative of assemblage, liquidity, and cross-relations.[8] In the attempt to hide this constitutional incongruence, the bourgeois epic developed a discourse of the object that aimed to "solidify" the human and the nonhuman into strictly separate and hierarchically organized silos. In the modern *epos*, the sole authority over the inanimate domain is the human hero, while "things" occupy the periphery as either phenomena to be verified (mere objects of human knowledge) or prosthetic extensions of human power (tools, commodities, consumables, and celebrative items).

An example of the modern "solid narrative" of the object emerges in the historical account that Edmundo O'Gorman offers in *The Invention of America* (1961). In this work, he uses original documents to delineate the European process of geographic "construction" and cognitive (re)mapping of America as the New World. Retelling the history of the first explorers' expeditions overseas, O'Gorman illustrates two different ways of relating to an unknown object, the continent later dubbed America: Columbus, the firm *believer*, adjusts his findings in order not to controvert the commonly accepted cartography of the *Orbis Terrarum*; whereas Vespucci, the *doubter*, relinquishes the common belief and formulates the existence of a fourth land, "a single geographic entity, separate and distinct from the Island of the Earth."[9] In O'Gorman's reconstruction of Columbus's and Vespucci's voyages, the changing discourse of the object is what marks the shift from the pre-modern to the modern mindset. Only by casting doubt on the unquestioned truths of the past can moderns turn the unknown territories and lands of believers into colonial objects of knowledge. Indeed, in the modern epoch, medieval faith in unchallengeable a priori hypothesis gradually gives way to a new cognitive approach that entails direct experience and verification.

Environmental historian Carolyn Merchant, in her seminal work *The Death of Nature* (1980), explores in depth the long-term impact that the modern approach produced not only at a socio-economic and cultural level but also from an environmental and gendered perspective. She highlights that the scientific mindset developed in seventeenth-century Europe marked an epochal transition from an organic view of nature as a vital, animistic, and harmonic macrocosm, which included the human microcosm, to a mechanist and sexualized understanding of nature as a passive machine that (male) rulers, scientists, and traders would fully manipulate and rationally control.[10] In a parallel way,

Val Plumwood has highlighted in her feminist critique of dominant forms of rationality that "reason in the western tradition has been constructed as the privileged domain of the master, who has conceived nature as a wife or subordinate other encompassing and representing the sphere of materiality, subsistence and the feminine which the master has split off and constructed as beneath him."[11] For Plumwood, this hierarchical perspective has negatively affected the Western view of progress and development.

Merchant's and Plumwood's analyses of how mechanical understandings of nature have justified the capitalist exploitation of natural resources and affected Western culture in its construct of nature as a feminized non-agentic matter also suggest that modernity should not exclusively be conceived as a historical period. As Foucault maintained, modernity is more an "attitude" than a period of history.[12] Thus, it is possible to isolate the modern understanding of objects as a peculiar aspect of that attitude: in the modern conception, unknown "things" – including natural elements – are simultaneously conceived as objects of knowledge and as tangible mediators between the mindsets of the past and the present. In this way, O'Gorman's contraposition of Columbus to Vespucci implicitly rewrites Dante's myth of Ulysses. According to the modern discourse, it is the humans' attitude towards the unknown that reveals what Dante's Ulysses calls the species' true "seed," which allows a few humans to distinguish themselves from their peers as well as from the feral instinct of animals. Dante's Ulysses says to his travelling companions in the twenty-sixth canto of the *Inferno*: "You were not born to live like mindless brutes / but to follow paths of excellence and knowledge."[13] With these words, Ulysses spurs his companions to undertake a voyage beyond the Pillars of Hercules, rising as the modern man *ante litteram*, animated by an authentic thirst for knowledge. On one hand, the modern narrative affirms the division between human subjects, who are endowed with reason, and nonhuman objects, which are understood as verifiable phenomena; yet, on the other hand, modernity uses the human attitude towards objects as a criterion to categorize different types of humanity, by dividing those who act critically and approach objects as objects of knowledge (the moderns) from those who remain attached to beliefs and fetishes embedded in objects (the primitives).[14]

What I have defined as the "solid" narrative of the object was first formalized with Descartes's *cogito*, which marked a "rearrangement of subject and object in a specific relationship of knowledge (and even domination) towards each other: the object coming to be only as it is known or represented, the subject only as it becomes the locus and the vehicle for such representation."[15] The gap between human subject and nonhuman object widened during the Enlightenment, when knowledge was promoted as an emancipatory means to escape ignorance and mind-numbing messages: Kant's motto, "sapere aude!" ["dare to know!"] can be interpreted as an exculpation of Ulysses from his presumed cognitive hubris, and as an open invitation to know without reservations. The Dantian Ulysses converts himself into the champion of free, human thought, with an irrepressible will "to strive, to seek, to find, and not to yield."[16] Guided by the autonomy of reason, the Kantian intellect asserts the supreme cognitive authority of the human mind over any worldly phenomenon; being the unique perceiver and cataloguer of the nonhuman, the intellect rises as the true hero of the modern *epos*, a cognitive hero that can know anything except for the *noumenon*, the thing in itself, which can be postulated but remains unknowable. A later step in modern thought's appropriation of the nonhuman is Hegel's reaction against the Kantian philosophy of finitude. Hegel defines Reason as the infinite organic sum of all reality and affirms the perfect identity of reality and reason. Whereas Kant's intellect is a cataloguer of the finite, Hegel overcomes this boundary and "claims that we can, in fact, know Kantian noumena (things in themselves) because our own minds [as individual parts of an organic whole] posited those things in the first place."[17] Thus, in the encounter with the object, the subject ends with encountering its own emanation.

Interestingly enough, the question of the object is also at the heart of the criticisms of the socio-economic apparatus of modernity. The capitalist system is founded on the *homo oeconomicus*'s privileged status as master of human and nonhuman resources. Thus the question of the object draws attention to the "tension between the modern orientations towards autonomy and towards mastery."[18] "The crisis that goes by the name of modernity" relies on a constitutional contrast between production and expropriation; as explained by Michael Hardt and Antonio Negri, "From the Renaissance revolution onward, modernity has been characterized by an extraordinary liberation of productive forces and emancipation from every transcendental destination of human activity, to which was opposed the forces of expropriation, private wealth, and instrumental rationality."[19] This feature of modernity is at the core of Marx's critique of a capitalist system based on market exchange and sale of labour power; such a system turns human relations into relations mediated by commodities. The reification of social relations alienates human beings from their work and from its products, as well as from other human beings and from themselves, thereby eradicating the possibility of autonomy and sovereignty for the economic actors.[20]

Embracing a sociological perspective on the origin of the capitalist system, Max Weber in *The Protestant Ethic and the Spirit of Capitalism* (1905) adopted the powerful "material" metaphor of the iron dwelling. He contended that the ethic of Protestantism, which regards professional and economic success as a sign of divine predestination, shaped the capitalist mindset and imposed a rationalized conduct on its inhabitants. Later, Theodor Adorno and Max Horkheimer illustrated how the Enlightenment ultimately failed in its mission to liberate human beings and install them as masters of nature in a world finally disenchanted by irrational myths. According to the two authors, systems of power can function only through an instrumentalization of reason, which is by creating a "machinery of control" that turns human individuals back into "mere examples of the species, identical to one another [and isolated] within the compulsively controlled collectivity."[21] Thus the selected social groups who control the technical apparatus also gain "a disproportionate advantage over the rest of the population."[22] In their debunking of the Enlightenment under totalitarian regimes, Adorno and Horkheimer made a further point in the criticism of modernity, arguing that Enlightenment ideals relapse into modern mythology when the fear of truth petrifies the search for freedom and truth. They explained:

> The loyal son of modern civilization's fear of departing from the facts, which even in their perception are turned into clichés by the prevailing usages in science, business, and politics, is exactly the same as the fear of social deviation. Those usages also define the concept of clarity in language and thought to which art, literature, and philosophy must conform today. By tabooing any thought which sets out negatively from the facts and from the prevailing modes of thought as obscure, convoluted, and preferably foreign, that concept holds mind captive in ever deeper blindness.[23]

Slavoj Žižek has recently restated this view from a psychoanalytical perspective, contending that, today, science functions as an "ideological institution" that provides certainties and constitutes people's sole firm point of reference. Science has exchanged places with religion and become, in Lacanian terms, "knowledge whose 'truth' is a Master-Signifier." For Žižek, the "shattering impact of modernity" on the symbolic grounding of our identities lies in the melding of capitalism with "the hegemony of scientific discourse."[24]

As seen in this overview, modernity is a multifaceted category: the term usually designates a historical period beginning at the end of the sixteenth century and culminating in the Industrial Revolution in the nineteenth century; yet, broadly speaking, modernity can also be defined as a narrative of human dominance over nature and objects developed within a socio-cultural apparatus in which techno-scientific progress and capitalist economy become hegemonic perspectives. This dominant mindset implies a narrative *solidification* of the fluid relation between the human and nonhuman, so that people would maintain their fixed roles of subjects, and material "things" would always remain objects of knowledge or exploitable resources. However, the modern perspective cannot help but generate a series of issues: first of all, it enforces hierarchies and artificial divides that separate human rationality from supposedly "lower-rank" organic and inorganic matter; second, the modern mindset supports constructs of nature that are environmentally unsustainable and erroneously associated with a feminization of the nonhuman environment, seen as either passive or dangerous. Nature is then regarded as a resource that must be tamed and colonized by (male) reason and power.

Proceeding with my investigation of modernity as a historical, socio-cultural, and mythopoeic category, in the next section I will illustrate through literary texts how the modern narrative of "solid" objects enforces human dominance over materiality, while unfolding a series of unresolved contradictions.

Modern Divides and Contradictions in the Literary Discourse: A Few Examples

The liquid tension between autonomy and mastery that is unmasked by the critiques of modernity is one of the aspects that modern "solidity" tries to conceal when representing the evolution from mercantile to industrial capitalism. In this transitional epoch, a proto-consumer society gradually developed: objects of leisure and luxury items, of the sort that used to affirm the symbolic distinction of the ruling elite, became tangible proofs of bourgeois social empowerment. Writer Giovanni Verga, one of most notable exponents of Italian Verism, represented this social transformation in his novella "La roba" ["The Stuff"] (1883). In this work, Verga tells the story of Mazzarò, a daily worker who, over time, succeeds in acquiring all the possessions of his former employer, the Baron. As a parodic King Midas, the nouveau riche Mazzarò grows morbidly keen on all his new "stuff" and falls victim to his own wealth: he lives far below his means and is constantly obsessed with the threat of being robbed and losing his possessions. The novella ends with the old Mazzarò bursting out in rage at the exhortation from other people to think more of his soul than of his material things. The character rushes outside and begins beating to death his ducks and turkeys, shouting, "Stuff, my stuff, come along with me!"[25] The thought of leaving his hard-earned belongings forever – such an "ingiustizia di Dio" ["divine injustice"][26] – drives him to the insane attempt to bring his "stuff" with him to the grave.

This story, which has been described as a "parable of late nineteenth-century materialism centered on the figure of the peasant entrepreneur in post-feudal

Sicily,"[27] offers a clear example of Verga's bitter determinism and his scepticism towards the social change that modernity has produced. Like many of Verga's other characters, including the Malavoglia family and Mastro Don Gesualdo, Mazzarò fails in his attempts to challenge an unchangeable social destiny. The Sicilian writer also depicts this delicate equilibrium in the novella "Fantasticheria" ["Daydream"]. He does so through the metaphor of the "ostrica" ["oyster"], a mollusc that can stay alive as long as it remains attached to its rock and avoids the threat of the shrimp or the diver's knife; similarly, humble people have to stay together and maintain their modest lifestyles, because if they abandon their roots in search of a better life or just to satisfy their curiosity, the world, being full of sharks, will inevitably eat them.[28]

But Verga offers more than just social determinism in "La roba"; he also offers the possibility that Mazzarò's attachment to his belongings is truly human, yet not in a traditional humanistic sense. As Maurizia Boscagli suggests, "In this image of untranscended matter, and of a man both dominating and dominated by it, the story opens a vista to a traffic between subject and object at odds with the classical dialectical opposition of these terms."[29] That is, Verga's novella reveals a crack in the solid anthropocentric narrative that objects are under complete human control as man's property or tools. In Mazzarò's story, the "work of purification," through which culture splits human subjects from nonhuman objects, collides – and "melts" – with the "work of translation," allowing for these two dimensions to penetrate each other.[30] The novella does not acknowledge this "material" impasse, though: Mazzarò's unwillingness to let go of that which makes an integral part of his human experience – his attachment to his stuff – is relegated to an abnormality, characterized as the pathological outburst of a madman who was never destined to live the life of a baron. Adopting a regulatory practice of exclusion, the novella guarantees, at least temporarily, the preservation of the modern gap between human subject and nonhuman object.

Yet, modernity does not always follow Verga's narrative; it does not always employ normativization to reaffirm human hegemony over goods. In the modern epic's ode to technological progress, Latourian "translation" functions as a triumphant moment of empowerment that allows humans to potentiate themselves through techno-prosthetic attachments. To further explore this concept, one can consider Marinetti's ironic description of a Parisian "modern man" who has identified his "modern lifestyle" with an overflowing repository of technological treasures and luxury items:

> Ecco un Parigino ricchissimo. Egli è *moderno*, tutto quello che c'è di più *moderno*. Circola soltanto in automobile, fa copiare le sue lettere con la macchina da scrivere,

ha un cameriere inglese, va a vedere tutte le sfide di *boxe*, dà del *voi* a sua moglie, giuoca al *bridge*, ecc.

Andate a casa sua: casa nuova, con calorifero, ascensore, luce elettrica, telefono … Evidentemente, questo borghese, non disprezza il progresso. Va col suo tempo: fra poco, si recherà al suo circolo in aeroplano e comunicherà col suo maggiordomo mediante il telegrafo senza fili … (*PF* 38)

[Here he is, a very wealthy Parisian man. He is modern, the most modern [that] exists. He goes around only by car, has his letters copied by typewriter, has an English servant, goes to see all the boxing matches, addresses his wife with "you," plays bridge, etc.

Go to his house: new house, with heaters, elevator, electric light, telephone … Evidently, this bourgeois man does not despise progress. He follows his time: in a bit, he will go to his club by plane and communicate with his butler through the wireless telegraph …]

This twentieth-century King Midas, like Mazzarò, transforms everything he touches into golden, consumable novelties. And like Mazzarò, it is inevitable that he will be *subjected* to those modern objects as he seeks to affirm his identity as a "modern man." Marinetti's parody of a presumed modern life – attained through the ostentatious accumulation of trendy objects and electronic machines – invites a reflection on the peculiar mythology of the "post-human" that was ushered in by modernity. I purposely hyphenate "post-human" in order to emphasize the term's double meanings. As observed by Cary Wolfe, a group of scholars have defined post-humanism (or transhumanism) from a teleological perspective, specifically "in the sense of being 'after' our embodiment has been transcended"[31] or has been overcome through technological mastery; some others have engaged with the posthuman framework as a rethinking of our "taken-for-granted modes of … experience," open to the "entire sensorium of other living beings."[32] This latter view entails a repositioning of the human as "a prosthetic creature that has coevolved with various forms of technicity and materiality, forms that are radically 'not-human' and yet nevertheless made the human what it is."[33] Wolfe's contraposition of these two views clarifies how the modern narrative of technological objects does not embrace the posthuman in its rejection of anthropocentrism, but in its diachronic sense of being "after-human": specifically, post-humans whose bodies have been augmented (albeit not fully transcended) by technology. In the dominant bourgeois epic, technology takes the place once occupied by divine or magic tools in mythology and fairy tales: technological progress acts as a bodily prosthesis that enhances modern heroes by enhancing their human capabilities.

Although the futurist avant-garde in Italy is commonly associated with its provocative idolization of machines, the modern myth of the prosthetic hero was actually shaped by the "backward" nineteenth-century traditions that Marinetti so harshly attacked. The hymn to mechanical progress, opposed to regressive anti-intellectualism, found an early champion in 1863, when the civic-minded poet Giosuè Carducci, with a strong anticlerical tone, invoked Satan as a vital force of intellectual freedom, secularization, and rationality: "O Satana, / O ribellione, / O forza vindice / de la ragione!" ["Hail to thee, Satan! / Hail, the Rebellion! / Hail, of the reason the / Great Vindicator!"].[34] Throughout his hymn to Satan, Carducci alludes to a metamorphic identification of the "demonic" power of human reason with the ebullient energy of the train: "Un bello e orribile / mostro si sferra, / corre gli oceani, / corre la terra" ["A fair and terrible / Monster unchained / Courses the oceans / Courses the earth"].[35] A similar mythicization of technology appears in Mario Morasso's *La nuova arma (La macchina)* [*The New Weapon (The Car)*], published in 1905, from which Marinetti's 1909 manifesto most likely borrowed the association of the car with the Victory of Samothrace. Morasso envisioned his "weapon-car" as a response to "the myths of antiquity as a living, breathing reality, now within the grasp of ordinary mortals. [The car] possesses practical value, easing the flow of persons, commodities, and information; promoting industrial development, cultural exchange, and the advancement of science."[36] The automobile brings back the ancient divine into modern secular life in the form of speed, which humans, as drivers fused with racing cars, can finally seize.

D'Annunzio, the greatest exponent of Italian Decadentism, praised machines by building his public image on the thrilling experience of flying and the cult of the "velivolo" – a word for "plane" that he introduced in the novel *Forse che sì forse che no* [*Maybe Yes, Maybe No*] (1910) and diffused through his public speeches and war endeavours. D'Annunzio, in his role as *vate* ["national bard"], fostered the ideal of the Latin man's heroic destiny, drawing from a world of classical myths, such as Icarus's flight, and reshaping these images into the dream of success for the Latin "post-human" man, who was equipped with flying machines.[37] The poet used an even more refined techno-mythopoeic strategy in the early 1920s, during the occupation and reclamation of Fiume, a territory in Istria that the Treaty of Versailles had not assigned to Italy after the First World War. As Timothy Campbell has contended in his analysis of the "materialities of communication" that were in place at Fiume, D'Annunzio's use of wireless technology to deliver speeches to the crowd affected both the creation and the reception of the message. Wireless communication contributed in popularizing an apocalyptic view of Fiume as a mythical place of sacrifice and liberation, yet it also framed "a new mode of listening in which silence is transformed into a medium of revelation and the *comandante* ["captain"] becomes its agent of disclosure."[38] Wireless technology was simultaneously a visible sign of innovation and the instrument that allowed for D'Annunzio to be lionized beyond his human capabilities as a semi-divine messenger.

In addition to the increasing mechanization of production systems, the socio-economic and technological changes brought by modernity exacted an equally heavy impact on the cultural industry. Between the eighteenth and nineteenth centuries, an epochal shift occurred from a centralized, patronage-based system to a centrifugal system based on the labour force of freelance writers and artists. Artwork now reached a heterogeneous marketplace of consumers rather than an exclusive, longstanding coterie of arts patrons. This shift corresponded to a parallel transformation in the nature and fruition of the aesthetic experience from a tailored to a commodified good. In the early twentieth century, the broader diffusion of non-verbal languages, such as cinema and photography, further altered the new status quo of the bourgeois art world; consequently, literature, music, and traditional visual arts lost their sacred aura, as Walter Benjamin famously stated, and became mass experiences.

Art's loss of its sacred allure was internalized in literature through the use of compensatory mechanisms that left visible traces in the materiality of the "object-book," and that testify to a consumable meta-narrative that is embedded in the novel's text and paratext. In her analysis of the bourgeois novel culture, Giovanna Rosa argues that, in the modern epoch, a novel's beginning became a crucial space in which writers negotiated the terms of their narrative agreement with the readers-buyers. Authors began calculating the openings of their novels to capture the attention of their "customers" and set the readers' expectations of the experience that the book would deliver, in exchange for an investment of money and time.[39] As an example of this practice, Rosa refers to the opening pages of *Tom Jones*, specifically the introductory section entitled "Bill of Fare to the Feast," in which Henry Fielding states that "an author ought to consider himself, not as a gentlemen who gives a private or eleemosynary treat, but rather as one who keeps a public ordinary, at which all persons are welcome for their money." The job of the "author-restaurateur" is thus to provide customers – regular, new, or even occasional clients – with dishes to satisfy their tastes. Fielding aims to please his customers, placing his "menu" in sight so that prospective readers can immediately see his offerings and be lured to stay and "dine." According to the novelist, the only way for authors to cope with the rules of an expanding editorial market, dominated by so many unpredictable needs and desires, was to establish straightforward communication and clear expectations from the outset.

The objects in Fielding's opening to *Tom Jones* proliferate, recalling again the mythical image of Midas, ceaselessly generating gold out of ordinary objects. The writer constructs a fictional world wherein literature functions as a good for consumers to exchange, and the author pretends to regulate his literary catering service through a menu – a quasi-object embedded with a mediating "human" function. While claiming to offer freedom to both writer and reader, the menu is an effective image of an unavoidable process of "contamination" by the non-human dimension – the products, market, and laws embedded in goods – that modernity cannot escape.

Modernity Made in Italy

The "solid" narrative of the object delineated here pertains to a broad and cross-cultural notion of Western modernity. While this notion most certainly applies to Italy as well, one ought to pinpoint a few distinctive traits of the Italian context, to better locate the polemic action of crepuscularism and futurism in its socio-political scenario.

Unlike other European countries, such as Spain, France, and England, in Italy modernity did not immediately overlap with the strengthening of a sovereign national state. Between the nineteenth and the twentieth centuries, the creation of a politically and culturally unified nation-state was still a project under construction. During the Risorgimento, the Italian peninsula was itself the object of a geo-political joining that culminated in the unification of Italy in 1861. Thus, for the newly united Italian people, political modernity featured a further process of "solidification": it involved a laborious consolidation of common policies, as well as the growth of a proto-capitalist economy, and the emerging of a new bourgeois class. The social outcome of the Risorgimento has been interpreted through different perspectives; yet, it is possible to summarize two main views.[40] This transitional phase of Italian history has been identified with a bourgeois revolution that established the socio-political and economic empowerment of this rising class. Yet, according to Antonio Gramsci's definition of the Risorgimento as a missed or passive revolution, the unification process was not a real revolution because it involved only the economic and cultural elite, not the masses. We should in fact recall that the unification process was ultimately led by the Savoia family – the ruling family of the Kingdom of Piedmont and Sardinia – and skilfully orchestrated by their statesman, Camillo Benso, Count of Cavour (1810–1861). As Tomasi di Lampedusa famously stated in the novel *Il gattopardo* [*The Leopard*] (1958), the Risorgimento failed to create a strong new leading power, and it ended by merely camouflaging the old ruling apparatus within the newly unified liberal state.

Political modernity in Italy involved a carefully designed compromise that combined many different, and even opposing, interests: on the one hand was an affirmation of national identity and the enlightened ideals of people's self-determination, and on the other were political pressures to maintain the status quo and avoid the threat of republicanism. From a literary perspective, the different sentiments that animated the Risorgimento and the divergent views of Italy as a new geo-political object emerge if we compare Ippolito Nievo's *Le confessioni d'un Italiano* [*Confessions of an Italian*] (1867) to "Libertà" ["Freedom"], a novella by Verga.

Carlino, the protagonist of *Le confessioni*, completely identifies with the national cause – the metamorphic "Italy-object"[41] – and introduces himself as one who, born Venetian, will die Italian.[42] Nievo's work is both a historic novel and a bildungsroman, in which Carlino's recollection of his patriotic commitment progresses along with his personal maturation and his romance with his beloved lady, Pisana. Yet, as Cesare De Michelis proposes, *Le confessioni* is more than a bildungsroman; it is a "romanzo progettuale" ["a projectual novel"] that brackets the present and the past as preliminary historical conditions for a future project: the creation of the Italian nation-state.[43] Nievo's novel develops a lifelong reflection on the muddled process of *making* Italy and the Italians that partially challenges the nationalist rhetoric, which is tailored on classical myths and civic virtues. In *Le confessioni* the overlapping of political and emotional geographies marks out a jagged, fraught territory wherein converge "the old discourse of *patria* embodied in a female figure, the metamorphosis of *patria* into [an idealized] nation-state, as well as the evolving discourses of nationalism and national character."[44]

However, the modern epic of Nievo's novel, as is typical in the modern discourse of the object, does not raise any question about Carlino's self-identification with alien and virtually untraceable materialities: with Venice, a formally non-Italian city that will be annexed to the Italian Kingdom only in 1866; with an as-yet non-existent Italian nation; and with a mercurial woman, Pisana. These blurry "objects" in fact *construct* the protagonist's lifelong experience of a Venetian who will die Italian, becoming the actual narrative quasi-subjects: Carlino's life, as he declares in the opening, is the effect of the action of time on a man.[45] His existence has been an extension of the Pisana-patria dyad; thus, it is impossible to isolate Carlino from the objects that have driven his life. At the end of the novel, while mourning the loss of his beloved, he even affirms this inextricability: "Sperammo ed amammo insieme; insieme dovremo trovarci là dove si raccolgono gli amori dell'umanità passata e le speranze della futura. Senza di te che sarei io mai?" ["We hoped and loved together; together we will have to find each other there, where one gathers the loves of the past generations and the hopes of the future generations. Without you, what would I ever be?"].[46] Nievo's work poses and simultaneously neutralizes the question of the unreachability of the object and the complexity of human-nonhuman interactions. Rewriting the epic and chivalric motif of the quest, modernity treats objects of desire not as a problematic plot point per se, but as a mere trigger and "material" theme of the hero's adventure. Although this quest, like Carlino's journey, crosses human and nonhuman territories, man's enterprise remains the only focal point through which modernity conveys its narratives.

In a complementary way, this focal practice also informs the writing of Sicilian authors, who were spokesmen of a sentiment of mistrust in the change that the Risorgimento had promised. Novels such as De Roberto's *I Vicerè* [*The Vice-Kings*] (1894) and Pirandello's *I vecchi e i giovani* [*The Old and the Young*] (1913) as well as *novelle* such as "Il Quarantotto" ["The Nineteen Forty-Eighth"] by Sciascia and Verga's "Libertà," all depict the other face of the Risorgimento. Leveraging the bitter pun of its title, "Libertà" retells the bloody "misunderstanding" generated by false expectations surrounding the unification of Italy, which in the Kingdom of the Two Sicilies was conceived as a "liberation" from the oppressive feudal system.[47] Some Sicilian peasants, excited by the arrival of Garibaldi's army, had rebelled against the *cappelli*, the aristocratic landlords. Upon the arrival of the army, the *camicie rosse* [the redshirts] executed the leaders of the revolt, while the other participants in the riot went to trial. The novella ends with an expression of disbelief by a charcoal burner who, while getting handcuffed, asks: "– In galera? – O perché? Non mi è toccato neppure un palmo di terra! Se avevano detto che c'era la libertà?" ["– In jail? – And why? I did not even get a few inches of land! And they said there was freedom?"].[48] The scene makes clear that for peasants, freedom is not a promised national land. The actual liberation from a long-lasting "foreign" dominance entails connecting with an object – the land – which they are equally attached to and detached from. Through the bewildered words of this worker, the narrative of human dominion and intellectual autonomy from objects reveals its artificiality. In Verga's peasant world, human dominance over the nonhuman (and over a "less human" humanity) is enforced, according to a deterministic social "law" that, like an endless vicious cycle, is based on land as property. Read through the perspective of writers from the southern end of the peninsula, the process of sewing Italy together appears to be a joint effort by the socio-economic and intellectual elite from the north, working along with the landlords in the south.

The clashing views of Italy as a "nation-object" are still evident in an early twentieth-century poem of crepuscular poet Marino Moretti, entitled "Ada Kaleh." In this text, Moretti wonders about Italy: "La Patria! Chi è costei? Ha un cuore, un volto? / Sa quel che sono? sa quello che fui?" ["The Nation! Who is she? Has she a heart, a face? / Does she know who I am? Does she know who I was?"] (*TLP* 157). To contextualize this poem, it is important to add that Ada Kaleh is a little island in the middle of the Danube, on the border of Hungary, Romania, and Serbia. This territory is a sort of non-place, forgotten even in the Treaty of Berlin (a revised treaty that ended the Russian-Turkish War [1877–8]). Yet, for the poet, the isle becomes a symbolic place in which anybody is free to rest in peace without needing patriotic glory.

These literary testimonies show that the immediate and long-term aftermath of the unification of Italy was one of political precariousness, struggles with regional heterogeneity, and resistance by old local powers. Yet, in 1903, a new and controversial political era began under the guidance of Giovanni Giolitti, giving further shape to Italian national identity.[49] Although Giolitti ruled over Italian politics until the early 1920s, only the years before the First World War were later labelled the "Giolittian epoch," to highlight the great influence that this statesman had on both Italian life and foreign politics.

Giolitti gained his power through a masterly game of shifting alliances across right and left coalitions (the so-called *trasformismo*), which helped him establish a liberal proto-welfare state. The Giolitti government promoted a series of social initiatives: although maintaining a neutral position on the clashes between workers and industry, the government issued laws to regulate working conditions, nationalized railways and insurance, passed financial reforms, extended the right to vote to all male citizens, and adopted measures in favour of the south. Despite his welfare politics, many Italian intellectuals harshly criticized Giolitti for his corruption, political patronage, and opportunistic strategy of shifting alliances. For example, in an article from 1909, Giuseppe Prezzolini, who at the time directed the journal *La voce*, illustrated the failure of democracy caused by Giolitti's system. For Prezzolini, "[the government] ended by producing … a reaction on the conservative side called nationalism, and on the opposing side called revolutionary socialism."[50]

The "Giolittian epoch" brought Italy a general period of economic growth, industrialization, and social improvement, but the new nation was also the theatre of explosive political and social issues, such as campaigns for workers' rights and massive immigration. The industrial expansion of 1896–1908, with the development of hydro-electricity, represented a first, remarkable spurt of growth. Nevertheless, as Martin Clark remarks, "Italy in 1914 was still '*Italietta*,' an agricultural economy, and her most important industry was still cotton; it was the First World War that provided the real stimulus to the engineering industries."[51] As support for this argument, it is worth recalling that in the first quarter of the twentieth century, 150,000 emigrants left Italy each year (about 2 million in total), and over 1.5 million Italians never moved back.[52] Overall, the immigration experience made even more visible a process that was becoming evident in the Italian context: the ancient-regime distinction between landed aristocracy and peasants was gradually being replaced by the contrast between bourgeois ownership and proletarian labour.

A milestone of Giolitti's foreign policies was the colonial campaign in Libya in 1911. The Italian socio-political setting had created a fertile ground for war that could channel into one imperialistic dream a number of different interests: the nationalistic revanchism for the "unredeemed lands" (i.e., the need to conquer Italian territories that were still not part of the Italian nation), the bourgeois aspiration to expand new markets, and the violent platform of the Sorelian syndicalist fringe. The journal *Il Regno* [*The Kingdom*], founded by Enrico Corradini in 1903, exerted a strong force in shaping common opinion towards an aggressive nationalist ideology. In particular, Corradini was able to create a shared goal for nationalists and socialists, popularizing the myth of a proletarian Italy, founded on a working-class imperialism. The majority of the intellectual class supported the colonial plan: D'Annunzio emphasized the possibility of rescuing Italy from its miserable condition as "museo e affittacamere dell'Europa spendereccia" ["museum and landlady of the spendthrift Europe"], and the futurists saw in the war a "cleanser of the world," a form of regenerative violence.[53] Even Pascoli, who was a socialist sympathizing with the anarchists, hailed war as a heroic enterprise for Italian emigrants in his famous speech "La grande proletaria si è mossa" ["The great proletarian stirs"].

In 1912 the war ended with a new Italian colonial dominion; the campaign contributed to fuelling nationalistic tendencies, shifting the political focus from domestic to foreign policies. Furthermore, it broke the dialogue between Giolitti and the socialist reformers, while the revolutionary left gained power. Giolitti changed his alliances once again, this time looking to the right wing and the Catholics. His government, which had been strongly secular and anticlerical, made a move towards the Unione Elettorale Cattolica Italiana [Italian Catholic Electoral Coalition], and eventually came to an agreement with this group in 1913 (the "patto Gentiloni" ["Gentiloni's agreement"]). The colonial campaign in Libya, along with the Balkan crisis that emerged in 1912, exacerbated nationalist and anti-Austrian sentiments, creating the pre-conditions for the First World War.

To summarize, between 1861 and the First World War, Italy gradually acquired material definition and unified politics through the leadership of Giolitti. In complementary and at times contrasting ways, modernity was for Italy a laboratory of narratives about the *solidification* of a collective identity, entwining patriotism with the rising techno-myth of the modern bourgeois hero, driving fast cars and flying airplanes. What unifies these modern stories is the presence of a normative subject – either the voice of a narrator-witness like Nievo's Carlino, the impersonal and impending "law" of Verga, or the shifting politics of Giolitti – which alternatively adopts (and adapts) narratives of purification or translation to create a reality that resonates with the modern techno-capitalist platform.

The Modernist Tantalizing Gaze

If the modern narrative pivots on a process of solidification that defines and separates human subjects from objects, the modernist narrative ushers in a much more problematic approach to the subject-object relation and, more in general, to the cultural framework of modernity. Modernism is a wide literary and artistic category that embraces a variety of aesthetic experiences and practices developed between the end of the nineteenth century and the the middle of the twentieth century. They include innovative movements like symbolism, expressionism, and vorticism, as well as the works of individual authors – T.S. Eliot, Virginia Woolf, and James Joyce immediately come to mind. In addition, for some scholars, modernism also embraces the more extreme experimentation of avant-garde groups like Italian and Russian futurism, cubism, and dadaism. As a broad category, modernism offers the dialogic possibility of connecting a number of cross-cultural experiences that shared a similar *weltanschauung*: all these works recorded the collapse of the classical epistemological and metaphysical absolutes – Time and Space, God, the notion of Truth – and the crumbling of the cohesive function of the speaking "I-subject." Yet, as Michael Levenson argues, the common thread linking modernist works is ultimately their shared critical attitude towards modernity. Put differently, their search for novelty expressed shocking counter-cultures, opposing the sensibility, values, and ambitions of the bourgeoisie. However, as Levenson also points out, it would be over-simplistic to set in opposition bourgeois culture and tradition, on the one side, and modernism and novelty, on the other, as the bourgeoisie was very intrigued with the ongoing process of scientific progress and modernization. Therefore, he concludes, "the agon of modernism was not a collision between novelty and tradition but a *contest of novelties*, a struggle to define the trajectory of the new" in a fast-changing and disorienting world.[54] In portraying this struggle, modernist art and literature engaged many strategies – irony, sabotage of highbrow poetic language, recovery of myths, shocking images, nonsense, and the destruction of linear plot and meaning.

In order to tackle our central question about modernism – namely, how does it redefine the representation of objects – it is important to draw a few preliminary considerations on the relationship between materiality, reality, and meaning. The ambiguity of this relationship is exemplified in a text that, although not belonging to the modernist period, can help guide our reflections. Ludovico Ariosto's sixteenth-century chivalric poem *Orlando Furioso* (1532) contains a vivid representation of objects that quite literally escape human rational control and assigned meaning. In canto 34, Astolfo, one of the paladins fighting on Orlando's side, flies to the moon in order to retrieve the wit of Orlando, who had gone mad out of jealousy over Angelica. Guiding Astolfo in this endeavour is Saint John the Apostle, who leads the paladin through "a valley shut in between two hills, where everything that is lost on earth (be the fault ours or that of time or fate) fetches up miraculously" (34.73).[55] Astolfo eventually finds "the mighty brain of mad Orlando" in a phial "distinguished from the others by the inscription upon it: 'The wits of Orlando'" (34.83). In this episode, Ariosto depicts the moon as a land of hoarded objects, where lost or forgotten possessions have been accumulating for ages:

> As Astolfo passed among these mounds, he asked his guide about various of them. Noticing a lofty pile of tumid bladders from which seemed to emanate a hubbub of cries, he was told that these were the ancient crowns of the Assyrians and of Lydia, of the Persians and Greeks – once so illustrious, now forgotten almost to their very names.
>
> Next he saw a heap of gold and silver hooks: gifts made in hope of reward to kings, to greedy princes, to patrons. He asked about garlands he saw which concealed a noose: all flattery, he was told. Verses written in praise of patrons wore the guise of exploded crickets.
>
> Love affairs pursued to little purpose had the shape of gilded bonds, jewel-studded shackles. There were eagles' talons – and these were, I am told, the authority which lords vest in their servants. The bellows littering the hillside all around denoted the praise given by princes and the favours conferred upon their favourites, all wafted away with the flower of their years. (34.76–8)

On *Orlando Furioso*'s moon, what is lost is the immediate correspondence between material referents and the meanings that human culture has assigned to them. The piles of junk accumulating on the moon are composed of objects orphaned of their terrestrial purpose, whose names and memories still remain in place on earth, albeit detached from their materiality. To allow the narrative to proceed, Astolfo must artificially reconstruct the mutual relation between the "liquor suttile e molle" ["soft, tenuous liquid"] (34.83) that he finds in the labelled ampoule on the moon, and rationality, the quintessential (yet so precarious) ideal on which modern humanity is founded. The episode of Astolfo's voyage to the moon serves as an essential plot point in the epic, reasserting

Orlando's authority as a hero: the journey to the moon recovers the structural coordinates of a fictional fantasy world, based on the univocal correspondence between an object and its given meaning – a meaning or purpose that in Ariosto's epic is never actually lost, but only misplaced. Using Astolfo's journey to the moon as a guiding metaphor, I suggest interpreting the modernist poetics of things as a rejection of the meaning-mending voyage that the modern epic narrative prescribes to reconstitute the human order on the nonhuman. Thus, what other forms of human-nonhuman interaction does modernism envision as alternatives to the prescriptive relation between rational subjects and their objects of knowledge, consumption, or empowerment?

Tweaking his definition of modernism, in the article "What's the Difference?" Astradur Eysteinsson briefly touches upon the question of subject-object relations in modernist literature. He adopts the term "invironment" to designate the process of internalization through which the modernist "I" turns the external world into an inner space.[56] This frantic subject, in his wandering through scattered thoughts, fragmented memories, and subconscious voices, annihilates any division between inside and outside to create the all-encompassing dimension of "invironment." Thus, as Bill Brown states, the subject's effort is not so much "to accept things in their physical quiddity" as "to penetrate them, to see through them, and to find ... within an object ... the subject."[57] In this respect, the Proustian madeleine stands out as a one of the most quintessential modernist objects: real and thinglike, the tea biscuit serves the first-person narrator as a trigger to release, at the first bite, a flow of buried memories from childhood. The madeleine is the concrete medium for a process that, in stressing the function of things beyond their utility, still reinforces the primacy of the "I" who *subjectivizes* them.

In modernist works, the practice of subjectification adopts a variety of shapes, figures of speech, and narrative modes, but one of the most renowned is the stream of consciousness. Unlike the modern narrative, which is mostly concerned with finding and ratifying the order of things, the modernist discourse – its poetics of things, as we may call it – emphasizes the chaos of the world, as tangible projection of the subject's crisis and the collapse of all-encompassing truths. Measurable notions of time and space shift into a blurry concept of interiorized duration, filtered through memory. This distorted mirroring appears, for instance, in the syntactic structure that opens Woolf's *Mrs. Dalloway* (1925). The entire narration of Clarissa's morning is framed by the parenthetic "thought Clarissa Dalloway." The parenthetical phrase asserts the subject's distorted perception over a sequence of objects piling upon other objects:

> How fresh, how calm, stiller than this of course, the air was in the early morning; like the flap of a wave; the kiss of a wave; chill and sharp and yet (for a girl of

> eighteen as she then was) solemn, feeling as she did, standing there at the open window, that something awful was about to happen; looking at the flowers, at the trees with the smoke winding off them and the rooks rising, falling; standing and looking until Peter Walsh said, "Musing among the vegetables?" – was that it? – "I prefer men to cauliflowers" – was that it? He must have said it at breakfast one morning when she had gone out on to the terrace – Peter Walsh. He would be back from India one of these days, June or July, she forgot which, for his letters were awfully dull; it was his sayings one remembered; his eyes, his pocket-knife, his smile, his grumpiness and, when millions of things had utterly vanished – how strange it was! – a few sayings like this about cabbages.[58]

Once the objects are inserted into Clarissa's stream of consciousness, they detach from both their conventional meanings and any traditional symbolic allusion. They become impalpable: inaccessible through logic and virtually unrecoverable through memory. The repetition of "Was that it?" emphasizes the impossibility and the unimportance of recovering an original relation between subject and object – whether those objects be vegetables, cauliflowers, or a pocket-knife – that has vanished for good and that can only be partially remembered or reassembled in a new chain of thought. As triggers of memories and emotions, all modernist objects are, to a certain extent, objective correlatives of a puzzled state of mind. They are objective correlatives of a sense of tangible bemusement, the opaque mirror images of a question without answer: "What are the roots that clutch, what branches grow / Out of this stony rubbish? Son of man, / You cannot say, or guess, for you know only / A heap of broken images."[59] Material "stuff" thus becomes the concrete avatar of a subject-object relation that can no longer be stated in positive terms or easily retrieved, but only evoked, for "l'apparente univocità dell'oggetto si sfarina nella molteplicità e complessità e ricchezza delle percezioni soggettive … fino a minare ogni certezza di banale oggettivismo" ["the apparent univocity of the object has been chalked in the multiplicity, complexity, and richness of subjective perceptions … to the point of undermining any objective certainty"].[60] Paraphrasing Italian poet Eugenio Montale, in the modernist epoch, there is no word that, resplendent like a yellow crocus in a dusty lawn, is able to manifest our soul. If the apophantic language of modernity proves to be a lie, poets are left with a few words, crooked and dry like tree branches, which can express "quello che non siamo / quello che non vogliamo" ["what we are not, what we do not want"].[61]

The modernist questioning of the objective, univocal relation of meaning that links a human observer to an observed phenomenon originated in the nineteenth century, when symbolism and aestheticism reframed the question of the object from the perspective of the spectator's gaze. French symbolism was an especially propulsive movement for the later modernist and avant-garde radical reconception of the representation of human-nonhuman relations. What is central in the symbolist poetics and will impact the subsequent literary experiences is the practice of turning objects from realistic references into symbols. Things become repositories of a surplus of meaning that trespasses on both the empirical and rational dimensions by triggering sudden epiphanies, analogies, and allusions. Baudelaire formalized the modernist rethinking of subject-object relations in the poem "Correspondences," in which he stated:

> Nature is a temple of living pillars
> where often words emerge, confused and dim;
> and man goes through this forest, with familiar
> eyes of symbols always watching him.[62]

These verses picture the human submerged within living surroundings that cannot be plainly read or explained, but that must be intuitively grasped through instantaneous, alogical, or pre-logical connections. Colours, perfumes, and sounds suddenly generate a random web of analogies. The modern hierarchical model of man in control of inanimate things turns into a system of symbiotic relations within a mysterious, cryptic world. The human observer becomes a *voyant*, a connective agent able to *see* in an intricate forest of symbols, and able to link objects in unconventional chains of new significance. According to Baudelaire's poetics of things, truly "happy is he who wings an upward way" and "whose flight, unchecked, / outreaches life and readily comprehends / the language of flowers and of all mute things."[63] The weakening of the rational discourse in response to a sudden vision implies, as Peter Nicholls notices, a whole reconsideration of poetry as a language that originates "from the point at which the boundaries of the self begin to fry, where subject and object flow into each other. The Cartesian 'I think' dissolves into the fluid condition of 'I am thought.'"[64]

However, it is crucial to note that, through this apparent dissolution of subjective boundaries, the modernist "I" still exercises a hermeneutical – albeit subconscious and virtually passive – magnetism on objects. To become symbols and momentarily reveal an "occasional" meaning, objects need to be captured by the eye of an "I" who is simultaneously a voyeur and a *voyant*. For instance, in his *Illuminations*, Rimbaud, one of the most revolutionary figures of symbolism, acts as a spectator and participant in "visions of totality … over which he has no control, and usually only imperfect comprehension."[65] The poetry of this poet-seer does not aim to offer a rational understanding of objects – which would inevitably be inadequate – but rather adopts a "rational *derangement* of *all the senses*"[66] to go beyond the limits of rationality, reaching a notion of "correspondence" as pure visual evocativeness of images and musicality of sounds.

The modernist inward turn and the associated questioning of modern rationality have implications for a rethinking of materiality as a shell to crack open. This tendency is particularly evident in the symbolist attempt to go beyond the physicality of things. Symbolism, recognizing the inadequacy of human reason for comprehending everyday phenomena, transfigures materiality into a shell that poetry must break in order to fathom the essence of things, that knot of secret analogies. This subtle process of dematerialization equates objects to the pale reflection of their essence, of the Ideal that informs them. The key spokesman for this position was Stéphane Mallarmé, who in the preface to René Ghil's *Traité du Verbe* wrote, "Je dis: une fleur! et ... musicalement se lève, idée même et suave, l'absente de tous bouquets" ["I say: a flower! And ... musically arises, an idea itself and fragrant, the one absent from all bouquets"].[67] In the space-time of the vision, objects-symbols detach not only from their ordinary meanings but also from their referentiality; they transmogrify into pure sounds, bare words, isolated from the systemic coordinates of language, dissolving into an out-and-out process of purification of things-ideas from their materiality. Meaning thus resides in a blurry suggestion, in the absence and untranslatability of the Idea, and poetry becomes the space – the material locus – wherein the Idea can be glimpsed. In Mallarmé's poetry, the materiality of the written word acts as a guiding musical score: "The paper intervenes each time an image, of its own accord, ceases or withdraws, accepting the succession of others, and, as it is not a question, as it always is, of regular sonorous strokes of lines of verse – rather, of prismatic subdivisions of the Idea, for the moment of their appearance and while their co-operation in some exact spiritual setting lasts."[68] The sole "materiality" of poetic meaning is a visual puzzle; in its wording, poetry mirrors an unsolvable rebus, displayed in front of the readers' eyes. In the best exemplar of this practice, Mallarmé's "Un coup de dés jamais n'abolira le hasard" ["A Dice-Throw Will Never Abolish Chance"] effectively renders the chaos embedded into life: the poem, in its printed layout, resembles the unpredictable, elusive assemblage of cases, probability, and concrete circumstances that become visible only when opposed to the white spaces – the silences – of the page.

A Grey Area: Early Modernism in Italian Literature and Culture

Synthesizing the thought of several scholars, Giuseppe Gazzola states that "depending upon who is asked, modernism could variably begin with the symbolist season, or with the crisis produced by Darwin's evolutionary theory."[69]

This problematic aspect is magnified in the Italian literary context. While modernism is a term widely used to define twentieth-century poets and novelists like Eugenio Montale, Umberto Saba, Luigi Pirandello, Federigo Tozzi, Italo Svevo, and Carlo Emilio Gadda, the exact periodization, and especially the starting date, of Italian modernism is still under debate. The issue is that if the category of modernism were equally applied to late nineteenth- and early twentieth-century Italian culture, it would include not the counter-culture embodied by the French symbolists, but acclaimed poet-bards, like Pascoli, who engaged in a "domestic" symbolism of private affections and family bonds; and D'Annunzio, who expressed a type of decadent sensibility fascinated with classical mythology and Parnassian aesthetic refinement. Acknowledging the problematic chronology of Italian modernism, Valentino Baldi has proposed a compromise, stressing that, along with the avant-garde rupture, Italian modernism fuels a lineage of continuity that maintains a dialogue with both nineteenth-century realism and classical tradition.[70] While Baldi makes an important point about the interrelation of continuity and innovation, I agree with Romano Luperini's clear delimitation of Italian modernism within a period that spans from a few years before the First World War to the beginning of the Second. As Luperini stresses, the literary aura of Pascoli and D'Annunzio, their view of Beauty and Art as absolutes, and their highbrow references to classicism openly clash with the criticism of literature as an institution and with the epistemological crisis that emerges in the prose of Pirandello and Svevo, or in the poetics of the crepusculars, futurists, and expressionists. Peter Bürger, in his *Theory of the Avant-Garde* (1984), similarly highlighted this meta-critical attitude of art, although circumscribing it to avant-garde movements. As he states, "with the historical avant-garde movements, the social subsystem that is art enters the stage of self-criticism."[71] Furthermore, Luperini continues, the "patrician-bourgeois" society represented by Pascoli and D'Annunzio is far from the new democratic mass society of the Giolittian epoch. This cultural distance was already evident in the early twentieth century. In *La coltura italiana* [*Italian Culture*] (1906), a book that Giovanni Papini co-authored with Giuseppe Prezzolini, the former wrote a chapter in which he criticized D'Annunzio for thinking that the Italian national crisis could have been solved through aesthetic creation, while not having any real idea on "how to reconnect Italian culture and civilization with its rapid economic development and the spiritual crisis of modernity associated with that development."[72]

As the crepuscular movement was one of the initiators of Italian modernism, my analysis engages with a pre–First World War "grey area," in which late Romanticism, realism, symbolism, and decadent aestheticism gather and briefly overlap, while modernism begins to take shape. We could call this grey area early modernism. Thus, in order to illustrate how crepuscularism, with its innovative poetics of things, veers towards modernism, I will first discuss a few pre-modernist examples that definitely influenced crepuscular authors.

With its "theory" of analogies, fascination with the mysterious allure of things, and rarefication of objects into forms of the Ideal, French symbolist poetry certainly affected the poetics of D'Annunzio and Pascoli, as well as the work of niche groups like the *Scapigliati* [the Dishevelled Ones]. In particular, D'Annunzio's elaboration on the object was born at the crossroads of decadentism and literary aestheticism. As a public figure, he created his own tangible mythography through the accumulation of unique items. His monumental residence near Lake Garda, *Il Vittoriale*, is a material embodiment of D'Annunzio's eccentric exhibitionism, which turned private spaces into self-celebratory museums. Paintings, sculptures, china, designer shoes, and a bronze turtle built in memory of his late pet are a few of the collectables displayed in this site, for ceremonial squander. The celebratory ritual of disinterested aesthetic enjoyment is a central motif in D'Annunzio novel *Il piacere* [*Pleasure*] (1889), whose protagonist, Andrea Sperelli, was raised according to one sole precept: "Habere not haberi" ["to possess, not to be possessed"].[73] This intellectual aesthete embraces the cult of beauty as the hedonist freedom to appreciate objects beyond their utility. He develops an aesthetic sensibility that allows him to redefine canonized art in the name of a personal, sophisticated taste: Sperelli would have given away the grandeur of the Coliseum for the exclusivity of the Roman Villa Medici, with its sumptuous frescos and patrician allure.[74]

The notion of decadent art that D'Annunzio elaborated in his work relies on the identification of beauty with an idiosyncratic practice of squandering. As Nicoletta Pireddu explains, drawing from Marcel Mauss's anthropological theories, decadent beauty is rooted in the symbolic economy of the gift, understood as an ambiguous catalyst of the material and the ideal, of disinterested giving and binding egoism.[75] D'Annunzio conceived of art as a symbolic practice that resists the utilitarian Western approach to consumerism, a sort of unconditional expenditure without any prospect of material reward. To his bourgeois readership, the author offered the gift of a contemplative beauty that succeeded in capturing the attention of *homo oeconomicus* while thwarting his attempt to maximize utility. The utility of D'Annunzio's objects relies upon their evanescent charm, their inscrutable artistic stasis dense with meaning. This aspect of D'Annunzio is pervasive in the opening of *Pleasure*, in which the refined objects in Sperelli's parlour radiate a "special loving care."[76] The furniture, which emanates the emotions felt by the protagonist as he waits for his lover Elena, becomes a memorial embodiment of the woman herself. As the fetish of her gaze and her touch, the objects project their token meaning upon the reader, acting as narrative agents: "From every object that Elena had looked at or touched, flocks of memories arose, and the images of that distant time came tumultuously to life."[77]

D'Annunzio's fascination with objects also finds a central place in his poetic works, through which he portrays the contemplation of a transient beauty to the point of paroxysm. His commitment to aestheticizing materiality through the purifying power of verse extends from the lowest abjection to the most magnificent pulchritude. In "L'inconsapevole" ["The Unaware"], recalling Baudelaire's "A Carcasse," D'Annunzio describes the inner vibrancy of putrid vegetation, the locus where death revivifies into still life, through the medium of poetry:

Come da la putredine le vite
nuove crescono in denso brulicame
e truci piante balzano nudrite
dai liquidi fermenti d'un carname;

s'apron corolle simili a ferite
fresche di sangue, con un giallo stame;
si schiudono crisalidi sopite
ne le rughe del carneo fogliame:

così dentro il mio cuore una maligna
specie di versi germina.[78]

[As from putridity the new
lives grow in a dense swarm
and cruel plants spring out nourished
by corrupted humours of rotting flesh:

corollas flow out like wounds
fresh of blood with a yellow thread
and chrysalises hibernating in the wrinkles
of the fleshy foliage open:

so inside my heart an evil
species of verse germinates.]

While Baudelaire uses the image of a carcass horribly eaten by worms in order to assert himself as the "keeper for corpses of love / Of the form and the essence divine,"[79] D'Annunzio portrays his own writing as a process of putrefaction that creates new life from death, animating still life and infusing it with beauty. The coexistence of allure and revulsion is a central feature in the poetics of things that the *Scapigliati* developed in the late nineteenth century. They recall the French *poètes maudits* with their profligate lifestyles and dark symbolism. Arrigo Boito, one of the best-known personalities of the group, was a writer of poetry and prose, as well as a famous librettist. His work emphasized the notion of dichotomy as the central principle of life. "Dualismo" ["Dualism"], one of Boito's most highly regarded poems, opens with a series of self-defining images that fuse good and evil, sanctity and perversity, beauty and monstrosity:

Son luce ed ombra; angelica
Farfalla o verme immondo,
Sono un caduto cherubo
Dannato a errar sul mondo,
O un demone che sale,
Affaticando l'ale,
Verso un lontano ciel

[I am light and darkness; an angelic
Butterfly or filthy worm;
I am a fallen cherub
Damned to wander over the world
Or a demon who soars on high,
Beating his wings,
Toward a remote heaven][80]

The notion of dualism also constitutes the backbone of Boito's *noir* short story, "L'Alfier nero" ["The Black Ensign"],[81] the account of a chess game that places in opposition a white man, Sir Giorgio Anderssen, and a black man, "Uncle Tom" – a stereotypical representation of the "negro" in the epoch soon after the American Civil War, when black riots were going on in Jamaica. The short story develops through a progressive identification of the two sets of chess pieces with the two players: Anderssen, with his rational pace, becomes identified with the white figurines, while Tom, with his bold instinctiveness, becomes the black figurines. Eventually, Tom comes to embody the black ensign entirely – a sinisterly marked piece that has been glued back together with red sealing wax during the game. Antiphrastically, this game of logic escalates to the point that, when Tom finally wins, the "bloody" black ensign on the chessboard has its human double lying lifeless on the floor. Out of rage, Anderssen has shot his chess rival.

"L'Alfier nero" is undoubtedly a parable of the "paradoxical law of reciprocity" that ties together reason and madness, insomuch that "each of the terms has its mirror counterpart in its opposite."[82] Playing with a socially pre-imposed set of symbolic correspondences – white-black, good-evil, rational-irrational – Boito's short story also blurs the human-nonhuman dichotomy. Albeit through the filter of dark fantasy, the narration detects a parallel impossibility in making a sharp distinction between the chess players and the game being played. Throughout its development, "L'Alfier nero" purposely muddies objects with their human personification, to the extent that the reader can no longer clearly trace where the human ends and the object begins. The story closes with Anderssen, who is not condemned for killing Tom, seeing the ghost of the black ensign every time he is about to play a game: "Tom era sulla scacchiera!" ["Tom was on the chessboard!"].[83] The reference to the phantom of Tom is partially a return to the normativizing tendency of modernity, which pushes the agency of things into the realm of the abnormal; nevertheless, the fact that materiality is an emanation or projection of the mind points to the irrationality of artificially separating human subjects and nonhuman objects.

The evocative charisma of Boito's black ensign is also visible, albeit in a very different context, in the poetry of Giovanni Pascoli, the Italian voice of an intimistic symbolism that elicits domestic and familiar settings. Pascoli's work represents quotidian objects in such a way as to transcend homely realism to create suggestive "invironments" of intimate memories and associations. In the poem "La tovaglia" ["The Tablecloth"], from *Canti di Castelvecchio* [*Songs of Castelvecchio*] (1903), the dining table cover stands for a folkloric belief that leaving the tablecloth on the table after dinner summons the dead, "i tristi, i pallidi morti!" ["the sad, the pale dead!"]. The uncleared dining area turns into a site of memory, where the past comes to remember and revivify itself through its objects:

– Pane, sì … pane si chiama,
che noi spezzammo concordi:
ricordate? … È tela, a dama:
ce n'era tanta: ricordi?[84]

[– Bread, yes … we call it bread,
bread that we broke united:
remember? … This is checked cloth:
there was a lot: remember?]

Italian critic Gianfranco Contini, commenting on Pascoli's use of humble everyday things in his poetry, stresses two fundamental traits of his work: the adoption of *scarabattole* [knickknacks] to create an intimate counter-melody to the traditional high language of poetry, and the poetic reuse of these *scarabattole* as objects of sound.[85] Contini compares Pascoli to an artisan, one who has worked on linguistic objects to elaborate a new language that combines a revitalized tradition, everyday speech, and various dialects. Contini also briefly touches upon an aspect of Pascoli's objects that sets their suggestive use in opposition to the later development of the avant-garde: although Pascoli moves the emphasis of his discourse from the human to things, things speak through the voice of the poet who interprets them: "È Pascoli solo che parla" ["Only Pascoli is speaking"].[86] This process of personification is very visible in "La poesia," the opening text of the *Songs of Castelvecchio*. Using a metaphor, the poet objectifies himself into a lamp, defining his role as follows:

> Io sono una lampada ch'arda
> soave!
> la lampada, forse, che guarda,
> pendendo alla fumida trave,
> la veglia che fila;
>
> e ascolta novelle e ragioni
> da bocche
> celate nell'ombra, ai cantoni,
> là dietro le soffici rócche
> che albeggiano in fila.
>
> [A lamp I am, burning with radiant
> sweetness!
> the lamp, it may be, that, suspended,
> looks down from the smoke-covered rafters
> on the evening group spinning;
>
> and hearkens to tales and conversing,
> from voices
> deep hidden in shadowy corners,
> just back of the softly wound distaffs,
> that gleam in line whitely.][87]

Pascoli's poet-lamp is the witness of a collective memory that he listens to, elaborates on, and retells. Poetry thus shines a new light, making quotidian rural life a source of wonder and transforming objects of memory into evocative objects of sounds. Although the objects exude their mere usability, in fact materiality only *lives* as a projection of the speaking human agent. This core element in the poetics of things of nineteenth-century symbolism is one of the few solid points of reference that remain in high modernism. However, the destructive action of the avant-garde will also tear down this last piece of certainty.

Crepuscular Poetry and Its Protagonists

Before 1909, the founder of futurism, Marinetti, was close to symbolist circles. According to Cinzia Sartini Blum, the writer's literary evolution testifies to "a paroxysmal development, both sclerotic and hypertrophic, of the symbolist style and of the decadent pursuit of extreme experiences and sensations."[88] It is well known that Marinetti's intellectual formation was influenced by his francophone upbringing in Alexandria, Egypt. The futurist leader wrote extensively in French, and his early poetic vein recalls the suggestive tone of symbolist poetry. For example, in the poem "Les vieux marins" [translated as "The Old Sailors"], Marinetti adopts dusky-coloured images to evoke the melancholy of a twilight marine scene:

> One night when it was red
> In a sea-green port, flowering musk and spray,
> The old battered sunset
> Dragged its senile agony down in the shacks,
> And its blood oozed
> Tragically, through the dead windows' hearts.
> – One night when it was red …[89]

If one compares this evocative landscape to the techno-ebullient urban scenery of futurism, Marinetti's evolution cannot appear anything other than sudden and extreme. The futurist conversion of symbolist and decadent elements – such as the use of sudden analogies and the fascination with the horrid side of beauty – into a vitalist language of destructive palingenesis has generally been understood as an abrupt break in literary history and the art world. Yet, to explain this passage as an out-and-out caesura falls into the rhetoric of the "miraculous crash and rebirth" that Marinetti meticulously staged in his 1909 manifesto, to assert futurism as an epochal moment of rebirth. However, no rebirth would have ever been possible without a gestational period, which is to say, without transitional poetics that prepared the ground for the futurist material revolution of living objects. In the Italian literary scene, the articulated reflection on still life that was conducted by crepuscular poetry in the early twentieth century fills the apparent break between the proto-modernist "inward turn," which transformed the environment into a subjective "invironment," and the avant-garde "outward nonhuman turn," which called for humans' immersive participation in the life of matter.

A more detailed overview of Corazzini's and Gozzano's work will provide the context for discussing crepuscularism as a transitional or anticipatory movement. Aldo Palazzeschi, a poet close to the Roman crepuscular group who later joined Marinetti's futurism, explained the difference between the two authors in these terms: "mentre con Sergio Corazzini, e con gli altri crepuscolari, abbiamo un ritorno al misticismo dei primitivi, Gozzano introduce nella lirica italiana la banalità borghese" ["while with Corazzini, and the other crepusculars, we have a return to the mysticism of the primitives, Gozzano introduces bourgeois banality in the Italian lyric"].[90] Oddly enough, the names of these two key figures of crepuscularism do not appear in Borgese's 1910 article that coined the crepuscular moniker, though Italian critic Emilio Cecchi did connect them in his review of Gozzano's collection *La via del rifugio*, stating that Gozzano was the *poeta major* and Corazzini his John the Baptist.[91] According to Cecchi, both poets shared a common agenda that he summarized as follows: "Non crediamo nella vita, nè nell'amore, nè nello spirito, tanto meno poi nel Padre Eterno" ["we believe neither in life, nor in love, nor in the Spirit, and least of all in God"].[92] This invalidating "manifesto" can guide our understanding of crepuscularism as a collective voice of dissent that reinvented poetry out of negative ideals and discarded "quasi-subjects."

Corazzini began his literary career writing satirical poems in Roman dialect. He later embraced the religious imagery that characterizes mystical crepuscularism, with abandoned churches, devotional objects, bigoted women, sorrowful Virgin Marys, nuns, and whispered prayers becoming the idiosyncratic settings and characters of his poetry. Corazzini was the leader of a literary group based in Rome, which saw the participation of many young intellectuals, including Alberto Tarchiani, Antonello Caprino, Fausto Maria Martini, and occasionally Corrado Govoni. Among the occasional attendees of the meetings were also painter Guglielmo Genua, musician Giuseppe Vannicola, and engraver Raoul Dal Molin Ferenzona.[93] The members of this group met regularly at Caffè Sartoris and, after 1906, at Caffè Aragno. They were fond readers of the French symbolists and loved to walk at night around the old churches of Rome. For a brief period, between 1905 and 1906, the Roman crepuscular group also had a journal, *Cronache Latine*. In addition, Corazzini wrote in many literary journals, such as *Il Marforio* [*The Marphurius*], *Roma Flamma* [*Roman Flame*], and *La Vita Letteraria* [*The Literary Life*].

As crepuscular scholar Angela Ida Villa has clarified, the mysticism that inspired Corazzini and his peers was not strictly religious. Caprino effectively defined this poetic style as "a sensuality of religious idealizations,"[94] which transformed religious objects and practices into aesthetic, and even carnal, images. This religious nuance emerged in D'Annunzio's *Poema paradisiaco* [*Paradisiac Poem*] (1883) and *Le vergini delle rocce* [*The Virgins of the Rocks*] (1885), and, with a more melancholic tone, in the symbolist works of Francis Jammes, Albert Samain, Maurice Maeterlinck, and Georges Rodenbach.

However, Corazzini's mysticism was also the result of a peculiar syncretism that combined the poet's fascination with canonized mystical figures with his interest in Nietzsche's "mystique" of nihilism.

Mysticism is one of the key autobiographical components in the creation of Corazzini's poetic persona, the sick "fanciullo poeta" ["child poet"]. The young Roman author viewed his life and literary experience as a sweet martyrdom, in which corporal sacrifice, *imitatio Christi*, and sublime moments of rapture mingled together. The intermixing of spiritual and bodily sacrifice is in line with medieval mysticism, along with its contrasting tendencies towards carnal desire: on the one hand, religious abandonment generated forms of sensual ecstasy; on the other, the pleasure of the flesh was repressed through corporeal sufferings. This blending of spiritual elevation and anguish of the flesh is fundamental in Corazzini's debasement of his autobiographical poetic "I" into an abject "object," masochistically condemned and narcissistically adored.

In the eyes of his peers, Corazzini was a cult figure. This gifted "child," marked by death, represented the messianic – and yet somewhat perturbing – promise of a new poetry to come.[95] This mythologized identity is quite visible in Martini's novel *Si sbarca a New York* [*Let's Disembark in New York*] (1930). In this work, Martini tells of his experience as a member of Corazzini's group, the trauma of his friend's premature death, and the sudden decision to cope with this loss by migrating to New York. Answering the question "Chi era Sergio per noi?" ["Who was Sergio for us?"], Martini describes the crepuscular poet as a demigod:

> l'angelo in esilio per le vie della terra, il semidio, della cui vicinanza ciascuno di noi s'inorgogliva e che avremmo voluto additare continuamente agli uomini frettolosi ed ignari, i quali ci passavano accanto e non s'accorgevano di lui né mostravano di sapere chi fosse il prodigioso fanciullo che camminava in mezzo a noi.[96]

> [An angel in exile through the streets of earth, a demi-god, whose close proximity each of us was proud of and at whom we would have liked to point continuously to the rushed and unaware men, they passed by us and neither noticed him nor showed interest in knowing who the prodigious young man who walked among us was.]

With sincere admiration, Giovanni Papini, a Florentine intellectual who participated in the futurist movement, also dedicated a passage to Corazzini in his collection of memories *Passato remoto (1885–1914)* [*Remote Past (1885–1914)*] (1948). Papini highlights the Roman poet's ability to overthrow literary tradition through his disarming simplicity:

scriveva poesie dove una disperata tristezza sapeva esprimersi con semplicità fanciullesca, in pieno contrasto con la poesia sontuosa e pretenziosa dei carducciani e dei dannunziani. Era una voce sommessa, mesta, patetica, talvolta quasi puerile ma che saliva spontaneamente dal cuore di quel giovanissimo che si sapeva condannato a una morte imminente.[97]

[He used to write poems in which a desperate sadness could express itself through childish simplicity, completely in contrast with the sumptuous and pretentious poetry of Carducci and D'Annunzio followers. His voice was hushed, melancholy, pathetic, sometimes virtually childish, but spontaneously rising from the heart of that very young man that, as everybody knew, was condemned to an imminent death.]

However, Corazzini was not portrayed only as a delicate angelic figure condemned to a premature death. He was also perceived as a rebellious innovator. Maudit artist Dal Molin Ferenzona dedicated to his "brother in art," Corazzini, *La ghirlanda di stelle* [*The Garland of Stars*] (1912), a perturbing collection of poems and drawings. In the "poem-manifesto" that closes this work, Ferenzona celebrates the end of the literary tradition with vehement and violent tones that recall Marinetti's attacks against Romanticism and symbolism. In his hymn of hate for the highest nineteenth-century masters, Ferenzona even proposes to cover poet Giacomo Leopardi's tomb with bloody garlands and to rejoice at his liberating death. The artist writes:

O funebre scheletro del romanticismo, col nostro

piede sprezzante calpestiamo la tua polvere!
Noi non piangiamo più!
Via le stampelle della tradizione e della speranza!
Noi non piangiamo più!
Beviamo al calice, che il presente ci offre,
di un sorso rapido![98]

[O funeral skeleton of Romanticism, with our

scornful foot we step on your dust!
We no longer cry!
Go away, crutches of tradition and hope!
We no longer cry!
We drink from the chalice that the present offers to us, with a quick sip!]

Through Ferenzona's dedication, we can see how Corazzini embodied both the figure of the suffering child and the prophetic persona of an inspiring rebel.

After the young poet's death in 1907, the Roman crepuscular group dissolved. In 1909, his friends edited the first complete edition of Corazzini's work, *Le liriche* [*The Lyrics*].[99] During his brief literary career, the author published five collections: *Dolcezze* [*Sweetnesses*] (1904), *L'amaro calice* [*The Bitter Chalice*] (1904), *Le aureole* [*The Halos*] (1905), *Piccolo libro inutile* [*Little Useless Book*] (1906), *Elegia* [*Elegy*] (1906), and *Libro per la sera della Domenica* [*Book for Sunday Evening*] (1906). He also composed two works of lyrical prose, *Soliloquio delle cose* [*The Soliloquy of Things*] (1905), and *Esortazione al fratello* [*Exhortation to the Brother*] (1906), and a stage play, *Il traguardo* [*The Finish Line*] (1905).

Gozzano, the other iconic figure of crepuscularism, was more of an eclectic intellectual than Corazzini. A law school student at the University of Turin, Gozzano preferred to attend Arturo Graf's lectures on Italian literature, though, because of his precarious health conditions, he never graduated. The poet participated in the meetings of the Società della cultura [Society of Culture], a literary circle that many Turin intellectuals attended. He also worked as a journalist, with his articles appearing in several newspapers and magazines, including *La Stampa* [*The Press*], *Il Momento* [*The Moment*], *Gazzetta del Popolo* [*People's Gazette*], *Donna* [*Woman*], *La Lettura* [*The Reading*], and *L'illustrazione Italiana* [*The Italian Illustration*]. As a poet, he published two collections: *La via del rifugio* [*The Road to Shelter*] (1907) and *I colloqui* [*The Colloquies*] (1911). His incomplete long poem, *Le farfalle* [*Butterflies*], appeared posthumously. Gozzano was quite fascinated with Eastern religions and between 1912 and 1913 travelled to India to seek relief from his tuberculosis and gain direct experience of Eastern culture. After this journey, he wrote a series of articles for *La Stampa* and other magazines, and eighteen of these texts were later collected in the volume *Verso la cuna del mondo. Lettere dall'India (1912–1913)* [*Journey to the Cradle of Mankind: Letters from India (1912–1913)*]. This collection, as Roberto Carnero has noted, shows a sincere interest in Eastern culture, yet it also reveals the poet's own struggle with abandoning a Western perspective.[100] Gozzano's intellectual engagement encompassed a number of fields, beyond poetry and journalism: he wrote children's literature, worked for the cinema, and had a great passion for entomology. As a screenwriter, he contributed to a 1911 documentary about butterflies, Roberto Omegna's *La vita delle farfalle* [*The Life of Butterflies*], and worked on the script of a film on Saint Francis that was never released.

The Turinese author constructed his literary identity by playing on self-pity and ironic bitterness, autobiographical references and fictional narration. Crepuscular writer Marino Moretti, in his memoir *Tutti i ricordi* [*All the Memories*] (1962), describes Gozzano as a poet gifted with the delicate soul of a child, a soul that was simultaneously refined and corrupt like that of a decadent poet.[101] Because Gozzano's verses have a distinct jocular tone, prominent

Italian scholars, including Giuseppe De Robertis, have argued that the poet's style is much closer to nineteenth-century parodic poetry than to crepuscular poetry.[102] A similar criticism comes from Paolo Trompeo and Pietro Pancrazi: for them, the crepuscular label does not exhaust the richness of Gozzano's poetics.[103] François Livi found a compromise, suggesting that although the Turinese author does not engage with typical crepuscular topoi and characters – sad hand-organs, bigoted women, sanatoria, and nuns – he shares the movement's desire to retreat and struggle with enjoying life.[104] In more recent years, the debate around Gozzano's atypical poetics – traditional, crepuscular, and realistically parodic – has focused on whether or not it should be included in the category of modernism. Is Gozzano one of the first Italian modernist poets? Or rather, does his work represent an idiosyncratic case of "illusory modernism," which echoes Nietzsche's thought and only superficially deals with the collapse of the "I's" fixed structure?[105] Yet if we consider crepuscularism as a transitional poetic experience that attests to the early emergence of modernism in Italy, Gozzano's idiosyncratic work definitely contributed in bridging modernism and futurism, through its melancholic twilight and auroral envisioning of avant-garde experimentalism. Hence, Gozzano's ambiguous positioning in the closing line of tradition and outpost of modernism also marks an epochal "crossing point" of nineteenth-century models, while paving the way to the prosaic and realist poetry of the twentieth century.[106]

An enduring term used to define Gozzano's poetics is Marziano Guglielminetti's notion of the "school of irony." Guglielminetti borrowed this moniker from a verse of poet Carlo Vallini, who in "Gli affetti" ["The Affections"] writes, "per me la scuola migliore / è la scuola dell'ironia / … / è quella che ancora ci salva / dal ridicolo verso noi stessi" ["for me the best school is the school of irony / … / the school that still saves us / from being ridiculed by ourselves"] (*UG* 43). The school of irony designates a playful, caustic, and realistic site of crepuscularism that includes Gozzano, Vallini, Moretti, Carlo Chiaves, Ernesto Ragazzoni, and Nino Oxilia.[107] Gozzano's ability to alternate melancholy, elegant humour, and grotesque "realism" constitutes the backbone of this informal "group," which often adopted traditional metrics and forms to engage in a scathing mockery of bourgeois life – its clash of provincialism, grand aspirations, and narrow-minded ideals. Unlike Corazzini, Gozzano even used religion to hit his polemic targets. In the uncollected poem "L'altro," the author plays with a rhyme, and thanks God for making him what he is: the poor and simple "guidogozzano" and not a "gabrieldannunziano" ["a follower of D'Annunzio"] (*TP* 309). In addition to its strong ironic tone, Gozzano's poetry stands out for a storytelling cadence that combines poetic narration with dialogical insertions. This intermixing of dialogues and diegesis creates, at a linguistic level, a blending of everyday vocabulary – kitchen tools and bourgeois décor – Piedmont dialect, and refined references to Italian poetic tradition from Dante and Petrarch to Leopardi. The result is a pastiche of tradition and parodic reinvention of tradition.

The precursory function of Corazzini and Gozzano is based on their poetic ability to contemplate the twilight of an assertive and outspoken humanism and foreshadow the dawn of alternative relations between vulnerable humans and witnessing "things." Their poetry expresses a complex feeling of "perplexity," as modernist writer Scipio Slataper defined it. This feeling takes the shape of an "incomprensione fantastica" ["fantastic wondering"] in Corazzini's poetry and becomes a "cozzo umano, dei mille dubbi" ["human clash of a thousand doubts"] in Gozzano's works.[108] Through the filter of perplexity, readers can access a petty everyday world that reveals itself as enchanted, mystical, and disarmingly grotesque.

Crepuscular Poetry as the Quiet Transition to Avant-Garde Vitalism

As we have seen, crepuscularism delimits a modernist middle ground connecting nineteenth-century tradition to the extreme innovation of the futurist avant-garde. In particular, when crepuscular poetry is analysed in terms of its pioneering discourse on the object, it evinces a gradual ontological shift from a modern, and still modernist, universe that is fully subject to humans, to the avant-garde human-thing constellation wherein a number of co-agents live in close interdependence. Yet, what are the connective elements linking the precursory poetry of crepuscularism and the later development of futurism? And what are the differences?

Unlike futurism, which had its main centres in Milan and Florence, the crepuscular groups were principally based in Rome and Turin. The two movements overlapped for a few years and, in 1910, Federico De Maria, a writer close to Corazzini's circle, expressly stated that crepuscularism was a precursor to futurism. He affirmed that, since 1902, his group had launched a vibrant artistic program that anticipated "quel futurismo che adesso impazza" ["that futurism that now is in full swing"].[109] Furthermore, as Walter Binni affirmed, crepuscularism and futurism are actually two sides of the same coin – of the same reaction, we might add – to the dominant notion of cultural and political "modernity" of their time. Through very different styles, they express an equally "exasperated prosecution" of D'Annunzio's aestheticism and Pascoli's symbolism:[110]

> I crepuscolari hanno per loro vicini immediati i futuristi, da cui, ad un esame superficiale, sembra dividerli un abisso. In realtà futuristi e crepuscolari non sono che uno stesso momento spirituale svolto in due maniere psicologicamente diverse: da una parte, poetica delle piccole cose quotidiane, e quindi scoratezza e rinunzia; dall'altra, poetica del dinamismo, del violento, prepotente accettazione

della realtà: predominio in ambedue i casi della più grezza psicologia, tentativo sentimentale, volitivo, e solo mediatamente artistico.[111]

[Crepusculars are the futurists' closest neighbours, even though, from a superficial examination, an abyss seems to divide the two. Actually, futurists and crepusculars are nothing more than the same spiritual phenomenon, developed in two different psychological ways: on the one side, the poetics of the little quotidian things, and indeed discouragement and resignation; on the other side, the poetics of dynamism, of violent, aggressive acceptance of reality: in both cases [they show] the predominance of the roughest psychology, a sentimental, determined attempt, and only indirectly artistic.]

Binni's binary opposition, which has guided critics for decades, has the undoubted advantage of linking crepuscularism and futurism to the same cultural roots. Yet, the critic unifies these two cultural phenomena under the idea of a gauche and rushed departure from the masters of Italian poetry without acknowledging that the two "pseudo-artistic reactions" radically diverge in their literary outcomes. Crepuscularism invalidated the modern mindset through a regression into unproductive domestic spaces, crowded with trivial objects and disempowered characters. By contrast, Marinetti's futurism rapidly ushered in a hypermodern posterity, envisioning an animalistic techno-world, and the futurist Azure Patrol escaped into esoteric dimensions that challenge the techno-scientific rigour of modernity.

However, while crepuscularism and futurism generally express complementary reactions against early twentieth-century modernity, for a few poets, the threshold between the two movements was more of a gradient than a clear divide. The futurist "conversion" of writers and artists linked to the Roman group, such as Govoni and Palazzeschi, further testifies that these two poetic sensibilities were not at odds. For example, Govoni, in a letter to Marinetti dated October 1910, called himself a "mezzo figliol prodigo" ["half prodigal son"], and openly admitted to having doubts about futurism:

Io sono sempre stato (e tu te ne sarai certamente accorto) poco futurista, almeno nell'intenzione; sono sempre stato riluttante nell'accettare certe tue idee e massime che non mi sembravano del tutto confacenti alla mia indole e cozzanti con la mia educazione.[112]

[I have always been (and you must surely have realized it) little of a futurist, at least in my intention; I have always been reluctant in accepting some of your ideas and maxims that did not seem entirely suitable to my character and were clashing with my education.]

Given his declaration of being an atypical futurist, it is not surprising that, in the iconoclastic anthology *I poeti futuristi* [*Futurist Poets*] (1912), Govoni published a poem, "Notte" ["Night"], "Alla memoria dell'amico indimenticabile Sergio Corazzini" ["To the memory of the unforgettable friend Sergio Corazzini"] (*PF* 267). The same can be said for Nino Oxilia, who included a poem entitled "Il saluto ai poeti crepuscolari" ["Farewell to the Crepuscular Poets"] in a collection, *Gli orti* [*The Orchards*] (1918), which very closely echoes the crepuscular style. Oxilia did not actually say farewell to Corazzini and Gozzano, as he maintained a double crepuscular-futurist identity throughout his literary career. Moreover, critics rarely mention that futurist artists like Gino Severini, Giacomo Balla, and Umberto Boccioni were familiar with the Roman crepuscular group before joining Marinetti's movement. This might further explain why crepuscularism acted as an anticipatory modernist movement to the futurist avant-garde. Such a precursory relation is evident, for instance, in Corazzini's dedications of his poetry collections to the painter Gino Severini, whom the crepuscular leader defined as a "fratello nel puro ideale" ["brother in the pure ideal"] and encouraged in his coming artistic battles (*O* 308). Reciprocally, in Severini's memoir, the futurist painter recalled his friendship with Corazzini and highlighted the avant-garde sensibility of the sick young poet:

> Un altro scrittore che veniva spesso con noi, ma non di notte a causa della sua fragile salute, era il giovane poeta Sergio Corazzini, legato da profonda amicizia soprattutto con me. Morì un anno dopo la mia partenza da Roma, nel 1907, a ventun anni. Mi ricordo sempre questo gentilissimo amico con profondo rammarico per la sua fine prematura. Era un poeta di estrema sensibilità. Come noi per gli impressionisti, egli aveva la più ardente curiosità e la più profonda ammirazione per i simbolisti francesi, in particolare Rimbaud, Laforgue. Verso il 1905–6 aveva già pubblicato tre volumetti di versi: *Dolcezze*, *L'amaro calice*, e *Le aureole*, che erano più che promesse, forse anticipazioni vere e proprie, come fu riconosciuto più tardi. La sua morte mi addolorò profondamente.[113]
>
> [Another writer who often used to come with us, but not at night due to his weak health, was the young poet Sergio Corazzini, linked by an intimate friendship, especially with me. He died after my departure from Rome, in 1907, when he was twenty-one. I always remember this very kind friend with deep regret for his premature end. He was a poet of extreme sensibility. As with the Impressionists, he had the most ardent curiosity and the deepest admiration for the French Symbolists, in particular Rimbaud [and] Laforgue. Around 1905–6, he had already published three little books of verses: *Dolcezze*, *L'amaro calice*, and *Le aureole*, which were more than promises, perhaps out-and-out anticipations, as it was acknowledged only later.]

In order to highlight the latent progression from crepuscular early modernism to the futurist avant-garde, one must abandon the sole identification of the avant-garde with its linguistic and artistic experimentalism. Rather, as Gerald Graff proposes, the aesthetics of the avant-garde is a "refusal of the entire bourgeois view of reality, epitomized by the subject-object paradigm of rationalist epistemology."[114] The avant-garde aesthetic provocation marks a deep ontological and epistemological passage to an object-object or subject-subject paradigm, in which the human and the nonhuman abandon their modern categories and interact in anti-hierarchical terms. The avant-garde verbally and materially performs a destruction of these categories, and it discloses, through its constitutional vocation to hybridity, a world overwhelmed with "quasi-objects" and "quasi-subjects." Pointing at a central characteristic of the modernist and avant-garde discourse on things, Brown has shown that "modernism's resistance to modernity is its effort to deny the distinction between subjects and objects, people and things"; yet "modernism's own 'discourse of things' … is far from consistent in what it reveals as the source of their animation."[115] It is the avant-garde that radicalizes the modernist challenge to modernity, which it does by integrating humans and things in an assemblage of intrinsically "vital materialities," in a "turbulent, immanent field in which various and variable materialities collide, congeal, morph, evolve, and disintegrate."[116]

The avant-garde artistic experiences, adopting a wide range of strategies and languages, recreated a pre-modern Pangea in which the material territories of the human and the nonhuman blend. This tendency towards blending invites further consideration of the avant-garde's *material* erosion of the border between art and ordinary life. Futurism openly breaks the boundaries between the human sublime fabricated by an artist-demiurge and the nonhuman *unsublime*, made of raw life in its many forms. Thus, in the case of Marinetti's movement, early modernism trespasses into the avant-garde when purposely contaminating the purity of art with inartistic elements, reaching the point of a chaotic art–non-art, neither artefact nor quotidian object. To mention a few examples, one may recall the futurist still-life artworks that "randomly" combined newspaper articles and everyday items on the canvas – such as Ardengo Soffici's "Piccola velocità" ["Little Speed"], the art of music-noise with which Luigi Russolo experimented, or Fortunato Depero's "plastic dances" featuring quasi-human marionettes in motion.

If futurism marks the ultimate upheaval of the modern narrative of the object, crepuscularism represents an overlooked link in the transition from the cautious early modernist denial of the people-thing divide to the all-encompassing, Pangean model of the avant-garde. "Il mio cuore" ["My Heart"], the introductory poem of Corazzini's first collection, *Dolcezze*, plays entirely on the symbolist poetics of correspondence and on late Romantic influences. The poetic persona compares his bleeding heart to the ink that nourishes his poetry: "Il mio cuore è una rossa / macchia di sangue dove / io bagno senza possa / la penna" ["My heart is a red / stain of blood where / I restlessly dip / my pen"] (*O* 100). Establishing a symbolic identification between the act of writing and the heart – the locus of intuitive thinking and passion – Corazzini remains fully within the early modernist projective paradigm, wherein all objects, including his pen, are emanations of the human subject. In his third collection, *Piccolo libro inutile*, Corazzini's early poetics of correspondences evolves from the creation of object-like analogies to an actual desire for self-objectification. This desire arises from the alluring power that objects exercise as things "suggestive of knowledge"; however, the crepuscular fascination with the nonhuman also "underscore[s] the irreconcilable separations between all objects," an unbridgeable chasm that is the very limitation of the human.[117] For example, in "Desolazione del povero poeta sentimentale," Corazzini's sick child expresses a yearning to experience the extreme feeling of becoming a sort of living corpse: he wishes to be forgotten by other humans, to become prey, to be sold and beaten. The child's negative egotism shapes an "as-if world," a fascinating yet threatening fantasyland in which the chasm between human subjectivity and inert objects can finally be filled.[118]

Corazzini's proposal of the "child-thing," rejecting the ideal of humanity as the ultimate repository of rationality and subjectivity, anticipates the drastic futurist claim of "**Distruggere nella letteratura l'"io"**" ["**Destroy[ing] the 'I' in literature**"] (*TIF* 50, *F* 122). The negation and dissolution of the perceiving "I" as the sole cataloguer of reality emerges even more strongly within the so-called school of irony – the group of crepuscular poets centred in Turin. Gozzano's first collection, *La via del rifugio*, opens with a nonsensical childish chant, used to determine the seeker in a game of hide-and-seek: "*Trenta quaranta, / tutto il Mondo canta / canta lo gallo / risponde la gallina …*" ["*Thirty forty, / the whole World sings / sings the rooster / answers the hen …*"] (*TP* 69). The poetic persona lies on the grass watching his nieces play, when all of a sudden, by feeling the shape of his skull with his fingertips, he realizes with astonishment that he exists.

The parody of Cartesian philosophy in Gozzano proceeds by turning the notion of man as a rational machine into an inert and mostly irrational "thing." The rhyme of the children leads the "I" to a nihilistic form of eternity wherein bourgeois logic dissolves into an orientalizing, contemplative beatitude, understood as lack of any worldly desire. The "I's" sole remaining wish is to become a gazing stillness: "Un desiderio? Sto / supino nel trifoglio / e vedo un quatrifoglio / che non raccoglierò" ["A wish? I stay / supine on the clover / and see a four-leaf clover / that I won't pick"] (*TP* 74). Similarly, in the poem "La morte" ["The

Death"], Vallini, a poet very close to Gozzano, who most likely introduced the latter to Buddhist philosophy, addressed the "I-pronoun" as the actual issue of humanity: "l'io per ciascuna persona / è come un'amante noiosa / che stanca sopra ogni cosa, / ma che tuttavia non si dona" ["The I, for each of us / is like an annoying lover / who teases a ton / and yet doesn't give herself"] (*UG* 66).

The crepuscular "regressive" poetics of things reduces the agency of human subjects and questions their hegemonic position in relation to the nonhuman. Futurism moves further by launching the anti-modern proposal to redefine human-nonhuman interaction as a dynamic intertwining of living elements. As Luciano De Maria clarifies, "L'adesione entusiastica agli aspetti più esterni della civiltà moderna è l'elemento della modernolatria futurista che è stato in genere isolato per caratterizzare il futurismo stesso" ["the enthusiastic adhesion to the most external aspects of modern society is the element of the futurist modernolatry that has been generally isolated to characterize futurism as a whole"].[119] Beneath the surface of its hymn to technology, futurism nourishes a regressive nature that clashes with an enlightened notion of modernity, understood in Habermas's terms as an incomplete, ongoing project of emancipation. When Marinetti "set[s] out to rework a modest traffic accident into … the birth-scene of a traumatic yet emancipating modernity,"[120] he is rewriting the Promethean topos of fire into a violent pyromania. Rather than celebrating the post–Industrial Revolution Anthropocene as the epoch that ratified *homo sapiens*' sovereignty over the planet, the founding manifesto of futurism depicts an infernal metropolitan landscape, the dominion of monstrous creatures that palpitate with primal life. Indeed, if incendiary futurist modernity is an emancipation, it is an emancipation from modern *humanitas*, conceived as a fine balance between action and contemplation, as embodied by Leonardo's Vitruvian man.

As futurism hymns the "l'entusiastico fervore degli elementi primordiali" ["enthusiastic fervor of the primordial elements"] (*TIF* 10, *F* 51), it is far from providing a mimetic representation of twentieth-century urban culture. But the deformation of modern machines into vitalized or feral objects is not solely a rhetorical device: futurism conceives of machines as animated force fields of sorts, which is to say, as living amalgamations of engineered instincts that humans can intuitively grasp. This is what Marinetti means when he speaks of the "**ossessione lirica della materia**" ["**lyrical obsession of matter**"] (*TIF* 50)[121] that futurism seeks to fathom. As he states in the "Manifesto tecnico della letteratura futurista": "Noi vogliamo dare in letteratura la vita del motore, nuovo animale istintivo del quale conosceremo l'istinto generale allorché avremo conosciuto gl'istinti delle diverse forze che lo compongono" ["We want literature to render the life of a motor, a new instinctive animal whose guiding principle we will recognize when we have come to know the instincts of the various forces that compose it"] (*TIF* 51, *F* 122). One of the Florentine branches of futurism, which developed around the journal *L'Italia futurista*, restated the motif of living machines and cities in Mario Carli's 1916 article "Vulcanizziamo le grandi città" ["Let's Vulcanize Big Cities"]:

> Noi giovani, noi artisti, noi futuristi, noi soldati italiani vogliamo che le nostre città siano dei vulcani, le vogliamo pericolose, fosforescenti, febbricitanti, infernalmente rumoristiche e maliziose, smontabili e disgregabili, le vogliamo veder vivere di vita magica e camaleontica, sprofondarsi e rinascere, cambiar forma e riflessi nelle diverse ore del giorno e della notte, contenere tutti gli istinti i capricci le fantasticherie e le ferocie di una immensa macchina pensante e robusta, sirena di carne di pietra di legno a [sic] d'acciaio deliziosamente promettente e perfidamente ingannevole, formidabile impasto cosciente di umanità, di fuoco, di mare, di belva, e di nitroglicerina.[122]

> [We young people, we artists, we futurists, we Italian soldiers, we want our cities to be volcanoes, we want them dangerous, phosphorescent, feverish, infernally noisy and malicious, able to be disassembled and broken apart, we want to see them live a magical and chameleonic life, sink and be born again, change shape and reflexes in the different hours of day and night, contain all the instincts, the whims, the fantasies, and the ferocities of an immense thinking and robust machine, siren of flesh, rock, wood, and steel, deliciously promising and perfidiously misleading, formidable conscious mix of humanity, fire, sea, beast and nitroglycerine.]

Carli's representation of modern cities as explosive volcanoes that fuse humans, beasts, and uncontaminated nature in their lava flow provides a very effective metaphor of vitalism as a cluster of disparate elements. Moreover, the image of such ferocious volcano-metropolises can help illustrate why futurist urban technology "offers the possibility of vitalizing … by animalizing":[123] the techno-primitive life of such volcanic cities calls for an ancestral form of animal energy, understood as the bare flux of brutal force embedded in matter, a subterranean magma always ready to explosively overflow. The notion of triggering a disruptive-generative impulse that frees materic primordial forces recalls forms of ancient hylozoism, according to which the *hylē* – the Greek term for matter – was alive or was penetrated by a living principle. Marinetti's techno-primitivism thus fuses the most external, ephemeral, and gaudy aspects of technological culture with an ancestral – and in a sense Promethean – impulse to attack the old divinities and create a paradoxical "primitive emancipation." This idea permeates all sub-branches of the movement, and appears, for example, in *Proposte* [*Propositions*], a collection of notes and proposals by Bruno Corra. He articulates his position on the concept of creative disruption as follows:

> Molte volte il distruggere è altrettanto proficuo che il creare – Chi distrugge le idee false dell'oggi fa opera grande: prepara il terreno alla creazione di domani – Tagliar via la cancrena.
>
> Chiedetene ai chirurghi.[124]
>
> [Many times destroying is as productive as creating – Who destroys the false ideas of today does a great work: preparing the ground for the creation of tomorrow – Chopping off the gangrene.
>
> Ask the surgeons.]

From the perspective of this scorched-earth strategy, it is possible to contextualize the definition of the futurist artists as "i Primitivi di una nuova sensibilità completamente trasformata" ["Primitives of a new sensibility that has been utterly transformed"] (*MDF* 33, *F* 67) featured in "La pittura futurista. Manifesto tecnico" ["Technical Manifesto of Futurist Painting"] (1910). This programmatic text stakes the claim that, in order to innovate, futurists have to be "primitives" of a new mindset that anti-hierarchically repositions the human as a living element, merged in a field of human-nonhuman interpenetration. As the manifesto declares, to think of a portrait as a human figure detached from or framed by a surrounding environment is an undesirable goal:

> Per dipingere una figura non bisogna *farla*: bisogna farne l'atmosfera … Chi può credere ancora all'opacità dei corpi, mentre la nostra acuìta e moltiplicata sensibilità ci fa intuire le oscure manifestazioni dei fenomeni medianici? Perché si deve continuare a creare senza tener conto della nostra potenza visiva che può dare risultati analoghi a quelli dei raggi X? (*MDF* 30)
>
> [To paint a human figure you must not paint it; you must render its surrounding atmosphere … Who can still believe in the opacity of bodies, since our sharpened and multiplied sensibilities have already grasped the obscure manifestations of mediums? Why should we continue to create works that don't take into account our growing visual powers which can yield results analogous to those of X-rays?] (*F* 67)

Futurism thus reshapes the commonly accepted notion of surrounding atmosphere into a force field in which disparate elements intertwine and co-participate in the creation of a living picture.

A Pioneering Material Vitalism

The modern discourse of the object, which is founded on the human-to-world relation, poses *homo sapiens* as the reference point, the ultimate distributor of natural resources, manager of the production and circulation of goods, and implementer of new technologies. According to this modern paradigm, objects exist as *solidifications* of our thoughts and representations: they are either objects of knowledge (like Vespucci's America or Nievo's Italy) or objects of consumption, placed in front of our eager eyes as in the opening of *Tom Jones*. Although modernity postulates the limited capability of the human intellect, it treats reason as the measure of our encounter with things – be they physical phenomena, organic elements, or inert matter. Challenging the dominant narrative of modernity, modernism finds its origin in the symbolist attempt to blur the dividing line between human perceiver and nonhuman perceived. Yet in doing so, the modernist discourse still falls into the practice of reducing objects to extensions of the human mind: the observer's inner life projects into inanimate things and dissolves their materiality into pure ideas, sudden Baudelairian correspondences, and alogical associations.

Both the modern and modernist narratives of the object are premised upon a colonization of the nonhuman, whose agency is negated by and replaced with human will, thoughts, and feelings. The avant-garde breaks this correlationist model, specifically "the idea according to which we only ever have access to the correlation between thinking and being, and never to either term considered apart from the other."[125] The avant-garde gives back to things what both modernity and modernism, albeit in different fashions, relegated to the off-limits land of human thought or displaced into the realm of the subconscious. As a transitional poetic experience at the boundary of nineteenth-century tradition, early modernism, and the avant-garde, crepuscularism begins to question the artificial human sovereignty over the nonhuman, preparing the ground for the futurist understanding of matter in terms of vital energy. However, in redefining the traditional subject-object dichotomy and freeing "the (still) life of things" from total human control, crepusculars and futurists explore quite different paths. Both movements affirm that objects exercise agency in the world, but the two movements assert very different paradigms of human-nonhuman relations. As we will see more in depth in chapter 2, while crepuscularism wonders in front of the inaccessible mystery of things, futurism challenges that mystery and reclaims new possibilities for living co-interaction.

Chapter Two

The Avant-Garde Is Made of Useless Objects

A Pervasive Uselessness

Ever since Baudelaire, Massimo Fusillo suggests, poetry has been intrigued with objects that exceed their physical materiality: objects loaded with sacred and epiphanic values or pervaded with enigmatic ambiguity.[1] The crepuscular Lilliputian cosmos of "piccole cose" ["little things"] and the futurist cutting edge of shiny new machines certainly echo the fascination of symbolism with material landscapes oozing with meaning. Yet, what meaning? Shifting from the encoded symbolist landscapes towards the avant-garde poetics of vibrant matter, crepuscular poetry puts into verse a lingering sense of wonder at the estrangement embodied by objects. What do humans look like when seen through the eyes of things? Adopting this reversed perspective, crepuscularism and futurism engage in complementary attempts to grasp the life of things outside human laws and portray our vulnerability in the face of objects.

Before exploring these themes further, a preliminary digression on the notions of *object* and *thing* is due. Although, in everyday language (and, often, even in this book), the two terms tend to overlap, a thing is irreducible to an object, when the latter is exclusively understood as a tool to use or a good to consume. Bill Brown has meditated on the thing-object distinction in his seminal article "Thing Theory" (2001). Engaging with Heidegger's philosophy, Brown has argued that we can "look through objects because there are codes by which our interpretive attention makes them meaningful, because there is a discourse of objectivity that allows us to use them as facts."[2] By contrast, a thing quite literally breaks this norm and emerges from a disturbance of the usability code; thus "We begin to confront the thingness of objects when they stop working for us: when the drill breaks, when the car stalls, when the windows get filthy, when their flow within the circuits of production and distribution, consumption and exhibition, has been arrested, however momentarily."[3] Summarizing this concept, Raymond Malewitz, in his account of the practice of misuse, concludes that "a thing appears [to us] when the object no longer can appear."[4]

In *Tool-Being* (2002), object-oriented philosopher Graham Harman has proposed a quite different interpretation of Heidegger's discourse on things, and, in particular, of the analysis of the broken hammer featured in *Being and Time* (1927). Scholars (including Brown and Malewitz) have generally interpreted Heidegger's discussion of non-functional tools as the claim that equipment gains visibility only when it stops serving our purposes. By contrast, Harman has embraced an object-oriented perspective to explain why "being a tool" exceeds the human concept of usability. He contends that, if examined from the viewpoint of the object, Heidegger's claim would lead us to a more compelling thesis:

> Equipment is not effective "because people use it"; on the contrary, it can only be used because it is *capable of an effect*, of inflicting some kind of blow on reality. *In short, the tool isn't "used" – it is* [my emphasis]. In each instant, entities form a determinate landscape that offers a specific range of possibilities and obstacles. *Beings in themselves* are ready-to-hand, not in the derivative sense of "manipulable," but in the primary sense of "in action." The tool is a real function or effect, an invisible sun radiating its energies into the world before ever coming to view.[5]

To summarize Harman's view along with more traditional interpretations of Heidegger's broken hammer, we could affirm that a thing, in its active or agentic being-in-the-world, comes to include its (human-given) purpose *and* an unknown depth, which resides beyond the taken-for-granted notions of usability and availability. Put in other terms, a thing retains a halo of impenetrability and an inaccessible surplus of meaning; as philosopher Remo Bodei maintains, a thing conjures content and significance for its users but remains inexhaustible in its depth.[6] Diana Coole and Samantha Frost express a similar view in their account of vital materialism, a type of new materialism that posits matter as lively or agentic. Commenting on the continuous action of subatomic particles, they assert that the comforting static nature of "the empirical realm we stumble around in does not capture the truth or essence of matter in any ultimate sense."[7]

Moving beyond theoretical perspectives, we can also see that the intrinsic inexhaustibility of things emerges even in colloquial language; for instance, when the term "thing" is used as a generic substitute for a more specific object. The possibility of this linguistic substitution intuitively exemplifies how a thing is more than an object. A similar "hiatus empirically applies to the difference between a consumer good, considered in its bare materiality, and the network of economic transactions, power relations, and emotional values imbedded in that thing."[8] Things mobilize systems of relations that extend far beyond the specific purpose of single objects. Finally, the irreducibility of the thing reveals further empirical evidence if we look into the "afterlife" of material objects. Objects do not cease "living" when they stop functioning for us or serving our needs. Garbage and discarded "stuff" long survive their dismissal; and the Great Pacific Plastic Patch, a massive collection of marine debris in the North Pacific Ocean, is perhaps the most exemplary case of this survival. As Serenella Iovino argues:

> L'incorruttibilità del polietilene, infatti, non è un'incorruttibilità di "forma" ma di "sostanza." Gli oggetti si dissolvono, ma le molecole che li compongono persistono. È stato addirittura calcolato che, per ogni particella di plancton, negli oceani ve ne siano sei di composti plastici derivati dal petrolio.[9]

> [The incorruptibility of polyethylene is indeed not an incorruptibility of "form" but of "substance." Objects dissolves themselves, but the molecules that compose them persist. And it has been even calculated that, for each particle of plankton, in the oceans, there are six of plastic compounds derived from petroleum.]

Such non-degradable materials abandoned in the oceans – Iovino remarks – eventually return, through the food chain, to their human "creators."

To conclude this digression, it is important to highlight that, although twenty-first-century theoretical approaches, such as OOO (object-oriented ontology) and new materialism, seem to have interchangeably adopted the terms "thing" and "object," the distinction between the two terms – one actively asserting meaning beyond its usefulness, the other passively receptive to the human use imposed upon it – is often implicit. This difference, I contend, is actually crucial in the contemporary reassessment of nonhuman life beyond the modern anthropocentric perspectives of exchange value, functionality, and socio-cultural constructions.

We shall now return to crepuscularism and futurism, and their complementary poetics of things. The crux of the question is not simply the fact that these two movements call attention to the inner life – the agentic "thingness" – of what in the modern mindset is solely understood as inert matter. Rather, their poetics assume a distinctive connotation if one considers that crepuscular and futurist works are equally overpopulated with useless "stuff" or with objects that, once used, lose their brand-new appeal, to become trivial yet "irreducible" garbage. In this chapter, my goal is to examine the crepuscular and futurist reflections on materiality both as meditations on the objectification of literature in bourgeois culture and as theoretical discourses on the object-thing distinction, which offer insights on the scholarly discussion on the nonhuman.

At a meta-literary level, the pervasive and hyper-cumulative uselessness that affects the literary object – the text in its materiality – stands as a tangible reference to the worthlessness of artistic goods in an epoch of cultural commodification. To cite Walter Benjamin, crepuscular and futurist works are "art that begins to doubt its task and ceases to be 'inseparable from … utility,'"[10] an art-aftermath of the bourgeois "false consciousness" that mistakes the idolatry of the new for the evolution of cultural history, making "novelty into its highest value."[11] The question is whether an escape from this vicious cycle of production-consumption is possible. Dealing with this question, crepuscularism and futurism react very differently to the pressing demand of the bourgeois market, as well as to the common feeling of being left with the debris of the nineteenth-century tradition. The divergent ways in which the two movements portray useless objects exemplify the different outcomes of their poetic experimentalism: the crepuscular "eco-literature" of humble bricolage versus the futurist incendiary disposal of old-fashioned chaff. Futurism remains caught in its spiralling process of consumption and destruction; its scorched-earth strategy ends up perpetuating a demolition that regenerates itself without releasing any constructive energy. Conversely, crepuscularism engages in a creative reuse of out-of-fashion paraphernalia and obsolete machines by repurposing this old stuff into "recycled" poetry.

However, at a theoretical level, the lumbering presence of discarded or residual materiality poses a further interrogative to its observers: what are objects that live suspended between anti-functionalism and oblivion, between missed usage and unattainable aesthetic contemplation? Lingering outside the human order of things, crepuscular stuff denounces the modern mystification of a world that must conform to *homo sapiens's* mind and thus must be sized down to fit the human-world gap. Through their poetics of purposeless things, crepusculars and, later, futurists experiment with a speculative aestheticism that detaches ordinary materiality from its identification with tools destined for human usage. They do so by portraying objects as objects of wonder, watchful witnesses, or out-and-out animate beings.

The complementary features of crepuscularism and futurism, testifying to the trailblazing views of these two movements, are central to contemporary debates over the agency of the nonhuman. Passé knickknacks and vibrant animal-machines, which are simultaneously so ready-to-hand and so ineffably far from the experience of being human, offer a literary lens for the exploration of OOO's and new materialism's conflicting notions of being-becoming and withdrawal-relation. Moreover, as cultural experiences that engaged with massive socio-economic changes, political transitions, and conflicts, crepuscularism and futurism also raise questions about human social responsibility in the disposal and accountability of material "life."

Literature as a Sellable "Anti-Good"

Crepuscular poetry was born at the dusk of the nineteenth-century "high" poetic tradition, in an epoch when artistic mercantilism was taking over a bourgeois cultural market increasingly concerned with satisfying a crowd of avid new readers. By that time, the political inspirations that animated the Risorgimento had exhausted their verve, insomuch that in "Pioggia d'agosto" ["August Rain"] Gozzano could cram the three main pillars of civic engagement into the space of one verse, as useless words empty of value: "La Patria? Dio? L'Umanità? Parole / che i retori t'han fatto nauseose! ..." ["Humanity? God? Country? Rhetoricians / have mouthed the words so much they've made them / nauseous! ..."] (*TM* 160–1). Addressing this void of ideals with a more radical attitude, Corazzini in his poem "Bando" ["Announcement"] stages the ultimate abandonment of a literary world that has debased itself to a flea market. Acting as a street vendor, his poetic persona tries to sell off his own ideas: "Avanti! Chi le vuole? / Idee originali / a prezzi normali" ["Come on! Who wants to buy? Original thoughts / at not much over cost"] (*SE* 60–1). However, he does not sell to make money, but to get rid of his thoughts, curl up in the sun like a cat, and sleep until the end of time. Corazzini dreams of a lethargic inanity, a silent life outside the economic mechanisms that treat literature as a good while trying to conceal its commercialization under the claim of aesthetic independence.

In its double-edged sabotage and exploitation of the bourgeois cultural system, the crepuscular movement can be considered a harbinger of the criticism of artistic commodification that futurism will later bring to the extreme. The self-aware "misuse" of literature – rebellion, radicalization, and even nonsense – is one of the fundamental components of the avant-garde, along with its ability to catalyse the attention of readers to unfamiliar or shocking products. In his essay "Sopra l'avanguardia" ["On the Avant-Garde"], Edoardo Sanguineti touches on this controversialism, locating the structural origin of the avant-garde in "la prostituzione ineluttabile del poeta, in relazione al mercato come istanza oggettiva, e al prodotto artistico come merce" ["the unavoidable prostitution of the poet, in relation to the market as an objective phenomenon and to the artistic product as a good"].[12] On one hand, the avant-garde strives to create an uncontaminated artistic good that, being "commercialmente impraticabile" ["commercially impracticable"], challenges the supply-demand system of the bourgeois literary market; but on the other hand, this iconoclastic cultural phenomenon exhibits "il virtuosismo cinico del persuasore occulto" ["the cynical virtuosity of the hidden persuader"] who sneakily launches a new and provocative artistic product to beat the offerings of the competition.[13] As Sanguineti concludes, this constitutional contradiction finds its complement in the conservative behaviour of bourgeois culture: while treating art as a commodity or a mere moment of entertainment, the economic elite tries to compensate for this process of commodification by institutionalizing a disinterested contemplation of art in the space of the museum. The avant-garde function of demystification – which is still latent in crepuscularism – resides in the ability to commercialize the uncanny feeling in front of a concealed process of commodification, to which the bourgeois audience was tacitly accustomed.

The trade-off between conforming to the siren call of the market and using literature as a space of counter-attack emerges vividly in Corazzini's and Gozzano's private writings. Although the infantile tone that Corazzini adopts in his poetry has fostered the myth of the naïf "poet child," it is essential to recognize that the young poet was quite aware of his literary rebelliousness. In a letter to Palazzeschi, he defines his group as those "che comprendono interamente certe arti 'fuori della legge' e se ne deliziano" ["who can fully understand some 'outlaw' arts and are delighted by them"] (*O* 299), foretelling the futurist theme of brotherhood founded on the goal of making outlawed art. Yet, writing to Moretti, Corazzini wonders whether a victory in the literary battlefield will be ever attainable:

> Vinceremo? Io nel l.p.l.s.d.d. [*Libro per la sera della domenica*] rompo le dighe e atterro molte case vecchie ... Potrei annegare anch'io! Ho molti nemici. E ne avremo insieme, moltissimi! (*O* 304)
>
> [Are we going to win? In the *Book for Sunday Evening*, I break the dams and knock down many old houses ... I could drown, myself! I have many enemies. And, together, we will have a lot of them!]

At times, the Roman poet cannot help but to contemplate the possibility of surrender, in the form of an escape. As he admits to Moretti:

> un convegno di poeti, imaginato in una *intimità infrangibile*, evocatore di canzoni per il meraviglioso Agro o lungo i viali di una villa muta, sarebbe, in verità, una assai bella e dolce figurazione. (*O* 302)
>
> [a meeting of poets, imagined in an *infrangible intimacy*, eliciter of poetic songs alongside the wonderful Pontin Marshes or the boulevards of a silent villa, would be, in all truth, a very beautiful and sweet depiction.]

Compared to Corazzini, Gozzano rises as a much more pragmatic actor in the modern literary system. Not by chance, Giorgio De Rienzo defines the letters that the Turinese poet exchanged with his friend Carlo Vallini as an out-and-out "carteggio d'affari" ["business correspondence"].[14] The correspondence offers a lucid analysis of the unavoidable process of hybridization between ideas and things, a process through which literature emerges in all its material tangibility. As a real businessman, Gozzano discusses the importance of paratextual "packaging," comments on advertisement strategies, and underlines the pivotal role of editors and reviewers in channelling the opinion of the readers. In one passage, the poet gives a lecture in his *ars* of mediation, disclosing the networking and the web of power relations behind a literary work. Commenting on his review of Vallini's *Un giorno* [*A Day*], which appeared in the Genoese newspaper *Il Caffaro*, he writes:

> Ti prego, ti prego, non essermi riconoscente! Sono riconoscente io a te, che mi hai dato un pretesto per contropelare un po' questi signori. E non essermi riconoscente, anche, perché la critica che t'ho fatto, potrà benissimo non piacere. Prima di tutto non è una critica: è un articolo piuttosto lungo, tra il letterario e il borghese, che potrà certo fruttarti molti acquisitori (le copie le hai firmate?) perché a Genova in fatto di "letture," signore, signorine, giovanotti eleganti stanno a quanto "n'u l'ha dito u' Caffaru." E comperano. Per questo ho intitolato il tuo articolo "*Filosofia che diverte*."[15]
>
> [I beg you, I beg you; do not be grateful to me! I am grateful to you, 'cause you gave me the pretext to rub these gentlemen the wrong way a little bit. And do not be grateful to me, because people could, conceivably, not like the critical piece I wrote for you. First of all, it isn't a piece of criticism: it is a rather long article, between literary and bourgeois, that could win you many customers (did you sign the copies?) as in Genoa, regarding readings, ladies, young ladies, elegant young men conform to "what Caffaru said" [in dialect in the original]. And they buy. For this reason, I titled the article about you "*Philosophy That Entertains*."]

Albeit in his distinctive ironic tone, Gozzano recognizes that, under the claim of aesthetic independence, the modern literary market frees authors from the tyranny of patrons but leaves them dependent on an audience that demands to be pleased and entertained. Able to encounter a wider audience, literature can potentially speak any language and reach everybody, and yet this sense of unlimited potential makes the fear of being heard by no one even more unbearable. Although Gozzano manoeuvres deftly within an intricate literary world, he cannot help but express his frustrations with a market in which the purest literary inspiration melts under economic and personal turmoil. In an outburst, he admits to Vallini, "Oh! mio caro e povero amico! La stampa, i letterati, i critici, le ambizioni, la poesia, merda, merda, merda" ["Oh! My dear and poor friend! Press, intellectuals, critics, ambitions, poetry, shit, shit, shit"].[16] Literature itself becomes a residue, the basest encounter between pure thoughts and waste products: something that has been expelled, but in being "outside" still retains the most ineffable and abject form of intimate otherness. Thus, we should not be surprised that in a later letter, the same Gozzano-businessman rejects the consumable aspect of literature. He declares his fear of seeing his name published, his terror of having his name attached to a product that will circulate among unappreciative readers:

> Eppure – lo crederesti – io non ho affatto piacere di vedervi il mio nome! O per meglio dire il piacere è molto inferiore al panico che mi dà l'idea di essere giudicato da una falange di lettori malevoli. Tu sai quanto la N.A. [*Nuova Antologia*] sia letta e da quanti idioti … udita.[17]

> [Though – would you believe it? – I am not pleased at all to see my name on it. Or better, the pleasure is much inferior to the fear that I have of the idea of being judged by a phalanx of malevolent readers. You know how many people read the N.A. (*New Anthology*) and how many idiots … listen to it.]

The only alternative between regurgitating trite clichés and selling out "original thoughts at not much over cost" is a self-condemnation to literary isolation. The icon of this bittersweet compromise is Gozzano's alter ego Totò Merùmeni, an intellectual without distinguishing qualities, who is indeed "il vero figlio del tempo nostro" ["the true child, in a word, of these our modern times"] (*TM* 124–5). Totò was too inept to become a "word-vendor" or to capture a prestigious job in the literary field; thus, he became the modern parody of the exiled intellectual. His name, a play on words on "Heauton Timorumenos," the self-tormentor, expresses the status of living like a forgotten object, a waste of the grandiose literary empyrean, exiled to the realm of the nonhuman, with his three companions: "una ghiandaia rôca, / un micio, una bertuccia che ha nome Makakita …" ["a screeching jay, / a tom-cat, a Barbary ape whose name is Little Margot …"] (*TM* 126–7). Nevertheless, through this *ingaglioffimento* [process of decivilization] – to borrow a Machiavellian term – Totò rediscovers the more practical and paradoxically less mercantile value of his literary education: helping children with compositions and writing letters of reference for emigrants. Living the passive existence of one who "Un giorno è nato. Un giorno morirà" ["One day … was born. One day … [wi]ll die"] (*TM* 128–9), Totò actually gains an "active" engagement with literature and finds a renewed pleasure in poetry, becoming finally almost happy and self-content.

Through their poetry and meta-literary reflection, the crepusculars express the acute self-awareness of being the unwilling heirs of a devalued literary estate. They are "master artisans" who can only reassemble discarded pieces of junk left behind by the nineteenth-century tradition. Even their muse is degraded, a scrap merchant who loves "schlock," or useless junk – that "ciarpame / reietto, così caro" ["outcast / schlock, so beloved"] to Gozzano's muse (*TP* 173). In Govoni's poem "Alla musa" ["To the Muse"], the muse is debased even further to the status of prostitute, "seller and sold in one."[18] She scandalizes people not by being sexually promiscuous, but by keeping her own "leftovers": "tu i tuoi miseri aborti / non costumi gettarli dentro le latrine / o ravvolti in un sudicio giornale / nasconderli nell'immondizie" ["you, your miserable abortions, / are not used to throwing them in the latrines / or wrapped in dirty newspapers / to hiding them in the garbage"] (*P* 99). The pervasive references to material schlock express very concretely the crepusculars' nostalgia for a literary golden age that tarnished before they could enjoy it. This worthless debris stands as a material metaphor for the assertive language and the solid ideals of the poetic tradition, which, though unusable, are still pointlessly preserved. The crepuscular "spleen" resides in this complex feeling of regret for what is lost, mingled with ironic relief over the loss. Exemplary of this resigned – and yet always covertly smug – spleen are Gozzano's "Sonetti del ritorno" ["Sonnets of the Return"]. In this sequence of six sonnets, the protagonist recounts a visit to his grandfather's house. The place exhales a sad smell of quince and mould, a "smell" of good old coziness. The "I" searches for himself in the outdated objects that fill the house: the fake flowers, the broken mirror, the yellowed daguerreotypes, the outmoded decor (*TP* 99). But while experiencing again "tutto ciò che fu" ["everything that used to be"] (*TP* 101), he realizes that the past, along with his childhood's gods, remained trapped in that site of memory, within its objects: "Mi specchio ancora nello specchio rotto, / rivedo i finti frutti d'alabastro ... / Ma tu sei morto e non c'è più Gesù" ["I look at myself in the broken mirror once again, / I see the fake fruits made of alabaster ... / But you are dead and Jesus is no longer here"] (*TP* 101).

Once the childhood idols are gone, the crepuscular "heir-poets" have to deal with the debris of their grandfathers' world and with a decrepit "nonna letteratura" ["grandmother literature"] who, as Vallini ironically puts it, regards as a poet even someone who does not have anything to say (*UG* 40). Their poetics of nostalgia, or what we might call "tactile nostalgia," develops through a programmatic practice of creative reuse: "useless" artefacts from the past are reassembled into new poetic materiality. Used poetic "stuff," deprived of its use value, returns to poetry disguised as humble, prosaic verses. From Gozzano's "patchworks" of transtextual references to Corazzini's melancholic chant of poetic ineptitude, the crepuscular "secondhand verses" offer both a form of polemic innovation and a language of mourning. In its material texture, Corazzini's and Gozzano's poetry is an early twentieth-century form of *arte povera* that makes verses out of unconventional literary materials. Poetry thus becomes a sanctuary of recycled "uselessness" that mocks the inconsistency of the modern conception of art as pure aesthetic resort – a sellable good that must preserve its unsellable purity.[19]

The crepusculars' commitment to a rebellious recycling of the high tradition's waste comes through the titles of their books, among which are Corazzini's *Piccolo libro inutile* (1906), Govoni's *Gli aborti* [*The Abortions*] (1907), Vallini's *La rinunzia* [*The Renunciation*] (1907), and Moretti's *Poesie scritte col lapis* [*Poems Written with the Pencil*] (1910). To a bourgeoisie that was seeking socio-cultural empowerment, crepuscular poetry promised a mediocre if not totally empty reading experience, based on everyday petty life and unexciting dramas. According to Vittorio Spinazzola, in modern times, the qualification of "reader" can be attributed to anybody who freely decides to read a written work, with the self-interested goal of gaining some advantage from this experience.[20] In this context, crepuscular poetry challenges the expectations that associate books with leisure, intellectual enjoyment, and escape into fantasy, and proposes instead a polemic repurposing of literature. An extreme case of repurposing appears in Carlo Chiaves's time-travelling poem, "Nel secolo duemila trecento" ["In the Twenty-Third Century"]. In the poem, a child of the future rummages in an abandoned library and finds the last remaining copy of a poetry book. The child does not even know what the word "poet" means, so his father explains: "O figlio, vuol dire una razza inquieta / di gente, che è scomparsa da quasi un'eternità!" ["Oh son, it means a restless race / of people, who disappeared almost an eternity ago!"].[21] The boy does not fully understand; he grabs the book, pierces it with thread and needle, and makes a toy out of the senseless object. The book is destroyed, but at least it has served an unexpected purpose:

> Indi, dispersi, laceri, i fogli, e calpesti, nel foco
> consumerai, più presto di quanto saremo già noi
> in terra consumati, poeti inutili o eroi,
> tu che un istante almeno avrai servito ad un gioco.[22]
>
> [Thus, dispersed, ripped apart, your papers trodden, in the fire
> you, book, will be already consumed sooner than we will be
> consumed on earth, we useless poets and heroes,
> you that for an instant will at least have served as a game.]

The need to attack bourgeois literature by making painfully evident its "uselessness" is likewise a central theme for the futurist avant-garde, but the solution envisioned by Marinetti and his companions is much more drastic: books must be burnt along with their library-catacombs. Old volumes are denounced as a "mezzo assolutamente passatista di conservare e comunicare il pensiero" ["a totally passé tool to save and communicate thoughts"] (*TIF* 138), and, in the founding manifesto, the futurists are arsonist brothers in the act of warming their hands by the fires of books (*F* 53). Futurism exacerbates the early twentieth-century cultural twilight by kindling a massive funeral pyre. Surrendering to the flames, old books "ripugnan(ti) come cadaveri di vecchi amici" ["repugnant like corpses of old friends"][23] allow those within the movement to fill the modern gap between the static status of art and the intrinsic dynamism of life. The burning of books also provides a decisive escape from an inevitable process of literary commodification; as Paolo Buzzi declares in "Le paure" ["Fears"], the sole certainty about his "poetic soul" is that:

> ... domani, se muori, i tuoi fratelli
> piuttosto che bruciarla,
> la venderanno al chilo
> come carta.[24]
>
> [... tomorrow, if you die, your brothers,
> rather than burning it,
> will sell it at the pound
> like paper.]

One could also argue that literary uselessness – understood as the inability to produce positive values – is not just a target of the futurist rebellion, but is in fact the core (dis)value of avant-garde poetics. As Renato Poggioli explains, the avant-garde is animated by an antagonistic attitude that manifests itself in the "taste for action for action's sake" and "finds joy ... in the act of beating down barriers, razing obstacles, destroying whatever stands in its way."[25] Nevertheless, Poggioli continues, in its obsession with making a clean sweep of tradition, the avant-garde "can reach the point where it no longer heeds the ruins and losses of others and ignores even its own catastrophe and perdition." This tendency often emerges in the creation of a self-reflective discourse, in which destroying significances and deconstructing language become the only *pars construens.* Unlike futurism, which generates the new by destroying the old, crepuscularism succeeds in repurposing the burdensome waste of tradition while questioning the role of art, the notion of aesthetic usage, and the commerce of cultural goods. Interpreted through Francesco Orlando's psychoanalytical framework, the recycled objects of crepuscularism are "anti-merci" ["anti-goods"] because they embody a mode of return of what has been repressed, and they exercise the quasi-autonomy to disturb the functional capitalist order in which the ego operates.[26] An exemplary case of obsessive accumulation of anti-goods is the first stanza of Gozzano's "L'amica di nonna Speranza." The poem opens with a long list of useless knickknacks and decor crowding a bourgeois 1850s parlour:

Loreto impagliato ed il busto d'Alfieri, di Napoleone
i fiori in cornice (le buone cose di pessimo gusto),

il caminetto un po' tetro, le scatole senza confetti,
i frutti di marmo protetti dalle campane di vetro,

un qualche raro balocco, gli scrigni fatti di valve,
gli oggetti col monito *salve*, *ricordo*, le noci di cocco,

Venezia ritratta a musaici, gli acquarelli un po' scialbi,
le stampe, i cofani, gli albi dipinti d'anemoni arcaici,

le tele di Massimo d'Azeglio, le miniature,
i dagherottipi: figure sognanti in perplessità,

il gran lampadario vetusto che pende a mezzo il salone
e immilla nel quarzo le buone cose di pessimo gusto,

il cùcu dell'ore che canta, le sedie parate a damasco
chèrmisi ... rinasco, rinasco del mille ottocento cinquanta!

[Pol parrot stuffed and the bust of Napoleon, of Alfieri,
the flowery moldings (the very good things in terrible taste),

the dark fireplace, the collection of boxes without any candy,
the clusters of marble fruit standing under the bell jars' protection,

the odd toy, the coconuts there, the box made of seashells, the warning
of *Pray* or *Remember* adorning the keepsakes that lie everywhere,

the albums with painted archaic wildflowers, an engraving or two,
the pale watercolors, the view of Venice done all in mosaic,

the miniatures there in profusion, a painting or two by D'Azeglio,
daguerreotypes (just a bit yellow) with figures in dreamy confusion,

the splendid old chandelier placed in the center, above the great hall:
a thousand reflections of all the good things in terrible taste,

the red damasked chairs, in the corner the cuckoo clock ...
All of them lift me out of myself: I'm reborn in the year eighteen hundred and fifty!]
(*TM* 98–101)

The question is whether these "anti-goods" are a subconscious disturbance or rather a hyper-conscious criticism of the bourgeois cultural system. What ought to be emphasized is that these dissident "anti-goods" occupy a no-man's land, located between the aesthetic reservation of the museum and the mass-market consumption of artistic entertainment. The anti-goods in Grandmother Speranza's parlour are repurposed poetic objects that challenge the system from within by smugly controverting its laws. The crepusculars' poetic practice of misuse and reuse of the poetic tradition seems to prefigure a peculiar consumer behaviour that Malewitz dubbed "rugged consumerism." Living in a culture "in which the only readily available platform for collective action [was gradually turning into] a network of consumer behaviors" – namely what bourgeois readers expected and what the literary market produced for them – the crepusculars "respond[ed] by reimaging consumption as an idiosyncratic, productive, and critical enterprise."[27] Through their incorporation of seemingly useless stuff into "recycled poetry," the crepusculars invalidated the bourgeois cultural system, offering a form of poetic consumption that redefined the idea itself of "high" literature and aesthetic enjoyment. This aesthetic redefinition can be connected to an economic transition that Matei Calinescu discusses in *Five Faces of Modernity* (1987), commenting on the clash between novelty and kitsch in bourgeois modernity. As Calinescu explains, the presence of kitsch objects – their trivial banality and serialized production – is "an unmistakable sign of 'modernization.' Once kitsch is technically possible and economically profitable, the proliferation of cheap or not-so-cheap imitations of everything – from primitive or folk art to the latest avant-garde – is limited only by the market."[28] The market, with its ability to regulate mass production and scarcity of goods, determines their aesthetic value.

If read through the lens of the crepusculars' critical reuse of anti-goods and kitsch artefacts, Poggioli's challenging statement that "the genuine art of a bourgeois society can be only antibourgeois"[29] makes actual sense, as it expresses the conflict between a sense of belonging to bourgeois society and a material denial of its own values, which are revealed to be fictitious, pretentious, and purposeless. Both the crepusculars and the futurists articulate an unsolved "confrontation between writer and commercialism," between the classic ideal of "autonomous 'high' literature" and the realization that, in modern times, "literature [has been] given over to the ideological reproduction of society."[30] Yet, if reinvented as a practice of recycling, literature can still provide a heterotopia, namely, a space within the bourgeois cultural system in which the hegemonic rules of productivity, usefulness, and profit are suspended, ignored, or explicitly turned upside down.

Another important point separates the crepuscular poetics of recycling and the futurist poetics of rapid disposal: the fascination of the former with démodé objects expresses a resistance to the mechanism of rapid obsolescence that regulates the capitalist production cycle. Their reaction to such decay is a key reason why this "weak" movement survived the futurist avant-garde, founding a long-lasting poetic lineage – what Sanguineti named "linea crepuscolare" ["crepuscular lineage"].[31] The futurist movement called for a rebirth, attainable through a eugenic process of denunciation, purging, and destruction, which culminated in the identification of war as the sole cleanser of the world. Marinetti himself began his career as intellectual saboteur when he succeeded in publishing the first futurist manifesto on the front page of *Le Figaro*, the French conservative organ of bourgeois culture. On that occasion, art vilified an idle life, fixed in the columns of a newspaper, and fostered a violent regeneration. Engaging in a wake-up call, futurism took on an aggressive role with a disturbing purpose. As Marinetti clarified in "Il poeta futurista Aldo Palazzeschi" ["The Futurist Poet Aldo Palazzeschi"], his movement was a "school" with a distinct "pedagogical" mission, "[una] scuola nella quale s'insegna a ribellarsi, a essere originali, indipendenti. Una *scuola* che mi fa pensare a una certa caverna di Belgrado, dove vidi un capo Macedone dare quotidianamente delle lezioni di lancio di bombe" ["a school in which one is taught to rebel, be original, be independent. A *school* that reminds me of a certain cave in Belgrade, where I saw a Macedonian leader giving daily classes on how to launch bombs"] (*TIF* 63).

The futurist "re-education" aimed to dismantle the traditional ways in which art had detached itself from real life, becoming a medium of pure aesthetic evasion. In doing so, futurism used a model of mass and viral communication that rapidly branched out, conquering all new languages of early twentieth-century modernity – cinema and radio. Marinetti and his companions envisioned with extraordinary clairvoyance the hidden psychological power that modern technology and media would exert on average consumers. As the futurist leader affirmed in "Distruzione della sintassi – Immaginazione senza fili – Parole in libertà" ["Destruction of Syntax. Radio Imagination. Words-in-Freedom"] (1913):

> Coloro che usano oggi del telegrafo, del telefono e del grammofono, del treno, della bicicletta, della motocicletta, dell'automobile, del transatlantico, del dirigibile,

dell'aeroplano, del cinematografo, del grande quotidiano (sintesi di una giornata del mondo) non pensano che queste diverse forme di comunicazione, di trasporto e d'informazione esercitano sulla loro psiche una decisiva influenza. (*TIF* 65–6)

[Those people who today make use of the telegraph, the telephone, the gramophone, the train, the bicycle, the motorcycle, the automobile, the ocean liner, the dirigible, the airplane, the cinema, the great newspaper (synthesis of a day in the world's life) are not aware of the decisive influence that these various forms of communication, transportation, and information have on their psyches.] (*F* 143)

Thus, the cataclysmic "aesthetics" of the movement attacked the bourgeois "concept of art as an institution" while exploiting "the distribution apparatus on which the work of art depends."[32] However, in fomenting a destructive novelty, the movement succumbed to the very process of cultural commodification that it had denounced. With their love for the extreme, futurists volunteered themselves as the first victims of obsolescence:

I più anziani fra noi, hanno trent'anni: ci rimane dunque almeno un decennio, per compier l'opera nostra. Quando avremo quarant'anni, altri uomini più giovani e più validi di noi, ci gettino pure nel cestino, come manoscritti inutili. – Noi lo desideriamo! (*TIF* 13)

[The oldest of us is thirty: so we have at least a decade left to fulfill our task. When we are forty, others who are younger and stronger will throw us into the wastebasket, like useless manuscripts – We want it to happen!] (*F* 53)

In foretelling the death of the "thrown-away object," the futurist avant-garde exemplifies Walter Benjamin's reflection on modernity as a specific temporality of things as consumable goods: the capitalist temporality of the "truly new" that quickly turns into the decrepit "picture of the obsolete."[33] Futurism embodies the destiny of any new good that, under the capitalist economy, must become obsolete soon after its purchase in order to fuel the fast turnover of the production cycle. The true economic value of "the new" relies paradoxically on its potential for aging, in the possibility of its replacement. What counts, more than the actual utility, is the time an item takes to turn into worthless waste. By contrast, the crepusculars' ironic poetics of recycling escapes the trap of obsolescence by being baldly obsolescent. Their useless junk does not have any "counterparty," as it lives declaredly outside the circuit of modern production. From such a privileged position, crepuscular reused stuff can indeed embody a positive critical alternative to consumption.

The crepuscular useless old things represent the constitutional limit embedded in the avant-garde: they are its fuel, but also its ghost in the closet. In emphasizing the mission of renewal at the heart of Marinetti's movement, the critics have generally overlooked that many futurist works, for example the poems collected in the anthology *I poeti futuristi*, swarm with "crepuscular" bric-à-brac – old accordions, pale flowers, melancholic marionettes, votive candles – expressing the need to expedite an end that the sped-up time of technology makes even more imminent. As Timothy Campbell contends, in order for futurism to guarantee the ruling power of its "technological sovereign," it constructs "an unbreakable link between the past and the future … such that the past is continuously seen as contagious."[34] Marinetti's pyromaniac ebullience of the present time finds vitality in the connection with a rapidly aging past, one that futurism has purposely never dropped; so, the present provides more and more waste material to its hyper-modern funeral pyre. The futurist poet Luciano Folgore illustrates this concept in a poem expressively dedicated to coal: "Sali, o carbone, luminosamente / e abbaglia col fiato dei forni / i piccoli giorni / del nostro esiguo presente" ["Rise, coal, luminously / and blind with the breath of furnaces / the little days / of our exiguous present"] (*PF* 252).

A text that renders explicit the vicious cycle of past and present is Oxilia's "Il saluto ai poeti crepuscolari." A sui generis crepuscular, this poet celebrated "healthy vitalism" and cautiously experimented with the avant-garde poetics of "words in freedom." Discussing Oxilia's eclecticism, which originally combines D'Annunzio, the crepusculars, and the futurists, Roberto Tessari has proposed the definition of "critical" or "moderate futurism."[35] Yet, Oxilia's eclectic compromise struggles in finding a poetic language that can balance nostalgic hoarding with euphoric disposal. His poetic farewell to the crepusculars is indeed exemplary of this struggle. The poem proceeds through a visual evocation of crepuscular paraphernalia: puppets, bells, worm-eaten furniture, daguerreotypes, coaches, crinolines, and a piano playing an out-of-tune gavotte. What is really striking in this farewell is the speaker's visceral need to remember a material past in order to announce a future that, in 1918, should have already been present. Why are those things returning? And why do they need to be remembered, if they have never even been buried? One may wonder whether Oxilia's run "in un mondo / più vasto; in un ciel più profondo, / dentro a un più profondo mare" ["in a wider / world; in a deeper sky / in a deeper sea"] is rather a retelling of Orpheus's run to rescue Eurydice, which can only succeed if he does not turn back (*PO* 187). Under the guise of sprinting, Marinetti's avant-garde does linger to look back at those obsolescent, useless things, which stand still in their *memento mori*. Being the weak spot in the futurist dream – its "banana peel," as Guido Oldani ironically puts it[36] – the crepuscular objects are the repositories of the avant-garde's internal incoherencies: its vital need for old junk to destroy, and its inability to confront the process of becoming without succumbing to self-destruction.

Crepuscular Objects as Living Witnesses and Doors to the Beyond

Ordinary "stuff" has the curious quality of being able to remain virtually invisible when confined to its usual settings; only when placed in an extraneous context – say, on a written page – does it become perceptible to reader-spectators as a collage of disturbing "good things in terrible taste." As neither commodities nor beautiful artefacts, crepuscular "little things" seem to translate into poetry the conceit with which Marcel Duchamp was experimenting almost simultaneously in the creation of his "ready-mades": to have quotidian objects randomly removed from their functional settings and reassembled in a subversive work that was perhaps not technically a work of art. In a similar way, in their ugly tangibility that "refuse[s] to be [fully] assimilated to the mechanisms of representation,"[37] the ordinary-things-out-of-place of crepuscularism stand between the readers and their aesthetic fruition, like an inconvenient "something" that occupies the interstitial space between functional tool and sublime artwork. By converting everyday objects into alien accent pieces, the crepuscular poetics of things turns this overlooked interstitial space into an exclusive territory of observation. While exploring this early twentieth-century poetic territory, in this section, I will also draw further parallels with the reflection on materiality developed by OOO, and briefly illustrated in the Introduction.

The crepuscular "ready-made poetry" can be understood as a dowdy literary reinvention of the still-life painting. Immortalizing ordinary items in their lingering stillness, the movement puts into verse a barely visible world that suddenly comes to light, taking over the poetic canvas. Govoni's "Le cose che fanno la domenica" ["Things That Make Sunday"] is a vivid example of crepuscular still life. The text crowds a random list of human and nonhuman "objects," turning an establishing shot of a Sunday scene into the main subject:

> L'odore caldo del pane che si cuoce dentro il forno.
> Il canto del gallo nel pollaio.
> Il gorgheggio dei canarini alle finestre.
> L'urto dei secchi contro il pozzo e il cigolìo della puleggia.
> La biancheria distesa nel prato.
> Il sole sulle soglie.
> La tovaglia nuova nella tavola.

Gli specchi nelle camere.
I fiori nei bicchieri.
Il girovago che fa piangere la sua armonica.
Il grido dello spazzacamino.
L'elemosina.
La neve.
Il canale gelato.
Il suono delle campane. (*P* 115)

[The warm smell of the bread that cooks in the oven.
The crowing of the rooster in the coop.
The warble of the canaries at the windows.
The banging of the buckets against the well and the squeak of the pulley.
The sheets lying on the grass.
The sun on the doorsteps.
The new tablecloth on the table.
The mirrors in the rooms.
The flowers in the glasses.
The wanderer who makes his harmonica cry.
The shout of the chimney sweep.
The alms given.
The snow.
The frozen gutter.
The sound of the bells.]

Govoni's poem is overpopulated with micro-details that dissect the impalpable atmosphere of an ordinary Sunday into defined units. In its careful recording of each single element that makes Sunday, this listing-poem performs an *ontography*, namely "a general inscriptive strategy, one that uncovers the repleteness of units and their interobjectivity."[38] Proposing this definition, Ian Bogost – one of the OOO theorists – argues that the stylistic device of the list isolates and underscores the "inherent partition between things … turning the flowing legato of a literary account into the jarring staccato of real being."[39] Bogost has effectively explained the OOO approach to reality in a video in which he discusses Garry Winogrand's photographs of mid-twentieth-century American life. Using the work of Winogrand, Bogost contends that these photos do not offer a comprehensive synthesis of American society, but a particular world view; they allow us "to see the world of things as things in a world, rather than our world with things in it."[40] Bogost's image of a non-anthropocentric "world of things" can be connected to a statement by Graham Harman, in which the latter affirms that reality draws "a world-system, one that has swallowed up all individual components into a single world-effect." However, "It is only from out of this system that specific beings can ever emerge. *The world of tools is an invisible realm from which the visible structure of the universe emerges.*"[41] Ultimately, to get a sense of the "carpentry of things" – another key term of Harman's philosophy – it is necessary to consider each item in its singularity and "carnal reality," detached from any system.[42]

Govoni's listing-staccato provides us with a view on a "world of things," virtually independent from human presence and from each other. However, the poem still succeeds in creating a "material atmosphere" – a poetic picture – out of disassembled material pieces: its scattered Sunday's things fix on the page the tangible melancholy that each single human and thing emanates. The text exhibits a sad "carnival of things," laying bare their Sunday solitude.[43]

In its attention to the details that construct – yet cannot be reduced to – a certain "world-system" or a material feeling, crepuscular poetry diverges from the "ready-made *poetry*" of Walt Whitman.[44] Although Corazzini particularly admired the American poet for his "impetuous lyric,"[45] his own poetry – and crepuscular poetry in general – expresses something far from Whitman's "celebratory relation" with things.[46] Corazzini rather focuses on catching the uncanniness of still life, and the crepuscular still-life scenes are devoid of the vibrant vitality that emanates from the verses of *Leaves of Grass*:

> The blow, the quick loud word, the tight bargain, the crafty lure,
> The family usages, the language, the company, the furniture, the yearning and
> swelling heart,
> Affection that will not be gainsay'd, the sense of what is real, the thought if, after all,
> it should prove unreal,
> The doubts of day-time and the doubts of night-time, the curious whether and how,
> Whether that which appears so is so, or is it all flashes and specks?
> Men and women crowding fast in the streets, if they are not flashes and specks what
> are they?[47]

Once Whitman's items are transposed into the crepuscular claustrophobic microcosmos of magnified details, these objects – with their "family usages," "language," "company," and "furniture" – become tokens of a renewed sense of wonder at what the moderns assume they materially and cognitively own. Magnifying ordinary things to the point of unrecognizability is a way for the crepusculars to challenge the modern presumption of immunity from the entropic flow of life, from the capacity of life to lie still and yet escape fixed categories.

As both leaders of crepuscularism spent long periods of time in sanatoria and died young of tuberculosis, their poetic gazes embody quite literally the spiritual condition of the artist as a convalescent, described by Baudelaire: "The convalescent, like the child, is possessed in the highest degree of the faculty of keenly interesting himself in things, be they apparently of the most trivial."[48] The convalescent's vision brings into focus that foggy still life that is usually overlooked or taken for granted. Humble triviality is often ignored because its empirical evidence is obvious: things are always there, self-evident in their inert materiality. Yet, when looked at through the unconventional convalescent gaze, inert matter loses its cortex of obviousness and appears in its puzzling substance: albeit visible, things always maintain an obscure backside.[49] While we barely notice their existence, we constantly expose ourselves to the silent eyes of things.

In his lyric prose *Soliloquio delle cose*, Corazzini describes some pieces of furniture left behind in an abandoned house as "le eterne ascoltatrici … il silenzio che vede e che ascolta: il visibile silenzio" ["the eternal listeners … the silence that sees and listens: the visible silence"] (*O* 232). Throughout his representation, Corazzini reverses the modern visual perspective that fashions the role of observer as solely a human role. If we stop to look at the "visible silence" of things, then we realize that everyday "stuff" has always been observing us and that this mutual vision has impacted us all along: while we mould our humanity by constantly meshing with things, things are "incrusted into [our] flesh."[50] In the words of philosopher Maurice Merleau-Ponty: "vision happens among, or is caught in, things – in that place where … there persists, like mother water in crystal, undividedness [*l'indivision*] of the sensing and the sensed."[51] Merleau-Ponty's "carnal" phenomenology – as Harman defines it – and his attention to the gaze of things are aspects that OOO re-evaluates, although criticizing phenomenology for relying on the relational medium of the human perceiver and observer.

The presence of an observing materiality in Corazzini's poetry shows that, when looking at ourselves, we cannot avoid falling under the gaze of things. This sense of reciprocity and "undividedness" especially emerges in the verses of Corazzini's "Elegia" ["Elegy"], in which the poetic persona exhorts his "piccola cara" ["little beloved"][52] to let go of her sadness in a liberating cry. The cry of the little friend is made of the same fabric as her small crepuscular world and cannot be separated from the objects that are wet by her tears. Tears and objects dovetail in a complex visual game, which reminds one of trompe-l'oeil techniques adopted in Flemish and Dutch still-life paintings:

> Piangi pur anche la malinconia
> mortale di una piccola bottega
> nera, di vecchi mobili, di vecchi
> abiti, in una triste via, nell'ora
> crepuscolare, e tutte quelle cose

imagini che sieno per morire
in uno specchio, simili a dei fiori
obliati in un vaso? … (*O* 156)

[Cry even the deathly
melancholy of a small dark
shop, of old furniture, of old
clothes, in a sad street, at
dusk, and all those things,
do you imagine are about to die
in a mirror, like flowers
forgotten in a vase? …]

According to Merleau-Ponty, in the act of viewing, the body of the artist extends and opens to the world. "Visible and mobile, [the] body is a thing among things."[53] Thus, the visual relation between perceiver and observed mainly depends on the fact that "the world is made of the same stuff as the body," and "Since things and my body are made of the same stuff, vision must somehow take place in them; their manifest visibility must be repeated in the body by a secret visibility."[54]

If things somehow have vision, then what do they see of us? Embracing a displaced visual perspective, crepuscular poetry turns dormant objects into active voyeurs of all the contradictions that the modern age exposes but pretends to hide under the myth of rational progress. In "La chiesa venne riconsacrata …" ["The Church Was Reconsecrated …"], Corazzini represents objects as those unseen eyes that spy on humans: the poem describes the macabre death of a sacristan, who hangs himself in a church. The only "witnesses" of this extreme action are the sacred ornaments – the stoup, which looks like a weepy eye; the sleepy confessionals; a rosary at the feet of the crucifix, whose beads look like drops of blood – and, in particular, a forgotten book of prayers (*SE* 18–19). Repository of an unmentionable human truth, the open book "è l'unica bocca che parli / nella chiesa silenziosa, / è l'unico occhio che veda, / nella chiesa oscura, / la morte della creatura" ["is the only mouth to speak / in the silent church, / is the only eye to see, / in the dark church, / the death of the poor wretch"] (*SE* 20–1).

Gozzano's "school of irony" uses its visual discourse on things as a criticism of the bourgeois social code: objects act as a hidden photographic eye and overexpose all those thorny details that the bourgeoisie would rather conceal. As Daniel Miller affirms, "objects are important … precisely because we do not 'see' them," ignoring how they can "determine our expectations by setting the scene and ensuring normative behavior."[55] Gozzano's and Vallini's poetry unmercifully unmasks the normative behaviour that things guarantee by staying in place. As perfectly camouflaged paparazzi, home décor and furniture are, so to speak, the negative of modern society, reversing the socially constructed positive image of the bourgeois *homo faber* [man maker]. All of a sudden, the productive maker of wealth appears as a bored collector of futilities. In "La noia" ["Boredom"], Vallini mocks the bourgeois ethics of labour and proposes to celebrate inutility instead:

> Inutilità! Se la fatua
> credulità delle masse
> umane non me lo vietasse,
> vorrei farti fare una statua. (*UG* 55)
>
> [Uselessness! If the fatuous
> credulity of the human
> masses didn't forbid me
> I'd like for you to have a statue.]

Vallini's celebration of inutility testifies to a broader social phenomenon. The passage of the bourgeoisie from a subaltern to a dominant class involved, as Pierre Bourdieu maintains, a parallel passage from the ethics of duty to the ethics of fun, creating a need for the appropriation of "distinctive signs in the form of classified, classifying goods or practices" that could testify to a new position on the social ladder.[56] The exemplary case of Gozzano's "L'amica di nonna Speranza," previously mentioned, can provide further insight, if one analyses the syndrome of obsessive accumulation that affects the 1850s bourgeois parlour from a sociological framework. Like a set of Chinese boxes, the jumble of furniture, collectables, and exotic souvenirs that fills the tacky room is framed within one more object: a picture, the "novissima cosa" ["latest invention"] that makes it possible for the poetic narrator to travel back in time. Indulging in a campy ekphrasis, Gozzano resurrects a beloved material world that has vanished along with its ideals, heroes, and antagonists: the wars for Independence, General Radetzky, Verdi, Mazzini, Foscolo, and the *Novelliere Illustrato* [*Illustrated Tales*]. Bringing back the frivolous life of this chatty nineteenth-century drawing room, in which history debases itself to juicy gossip, the poetic narrator offers a bittersweet snapshot of his own bourgeois identity, an identity that depends on the tangible sentiment of self-reassurance that material accumulation provides.

Objects are witnesses of the human and retain something of us; likewise, we humans do get imbricated with the "life" of things that surround us. Yet, crepuscular "still-life poetry" raises the question of whether this reciprocal vision and corporeal revelation is more of an oblique look than an open manifestation. What mystic crepuscularism represents through its delicate poetic nuances is the opacity of things, the enigma of vision as a renewed wonder in front of that "old stuff," standing in front of us, so ready-at-hand and so deeply inaccessible. This is why, especially in Corazzini's poetry, objects appear in an estranged guise: being forgotten or abandoned, crepuscular things are materiality that, albeit "encrusted" with the human, lives independent from us and remains untouched by our presence or reasoning. A recurrent theme in Corazzini's work is the representation of deserted chapels, in which "corone d'oro, manti di broccato, / cuori trafitti, bocche dolorose, / occhi con occhi in adorazione" ["golden crowns, brocade mantles, / stabbed hearts, agonizing mouths, / eyes with eyes in adoration"] consume themselves "ne la tetra rovina de le cose" ["in the dusky ruin of things"] (*O* 107). Corazzini had a particular fascination for these liminal places, abandoned by their congregations and inhabited by the quasi-sacred:[57]

> Santa Prassede, convegno di beghine tristissime. Santa Sabina, adornata di muschio e di orto, maravigliosamente, San Clemente, lungo una strada di conventi e di piccole pensioni cristiane! E poi tante ancora, sacre a un nome ignoto, perdute nel suburbio, sconsacrate e riconsacrate per delle umili funzioni annue, povere, che ti senti morire entrando, antiche e abbandonate senza pianto. (Letter to Palazzeschi, 4 December 1906; *O* 298)
>
> [Saint Praxedes, gathering of very sad beguines. Saint Sabina, marvellously adorned with musk and orchard, Saint Clement, along a street of convents and little Christian hostels! And many other churches, sacred to an unknown name, a name lost in the suburbs, deconsecrated and reconsecrated for humble yearly functions, poor churches – that you feel you are about to die entering – ancient and abandoned without crying.]

Within the sacred space of the church, religious ornaments are acts of *poiesis* with a symbolic praxis; yet what about missals, reliquaries, statues, votive candles, and vessels lingering in deconsecrated chapels? The loss of the symbolic renders this materiality not only quintessentially useless but also cognitively problematic, marking a passage from the empirically "obvious" – the object as functional tool – to what is rationally "abvious" ["off route"] – the object as a separate living entity.[58] Remote and detached, this equipment "acting" outside the realm of human practice and intentionality illustrates the ontological status of "tool-being," as described by Harman. According to the OOO philosopher, even when material things are exposed to our gaze, they present a "sensible and explorable profile" and an "irreducibly veiled activity."[59] Tool-being is indeed this veiled activity, a "vacuum-sealed" dimension or an unexplored planet, which remains invisible and alien, always withdrawn into its own depth.

Going back to the crepuscular "abvious objects," we can see, through the parallel with Harman's object-oriented philosophy, how this inaccessible materiality is strictly related to an understanding of the life of things as a living mystery, a receded off-limits space. Non-functionality and apartness are powerful crepuscular metaphors to illustrate that, either as useful tools or useless junk, things cannot be fully exhausted by human perception or by their supposed relation with humans, as, in Harman's words, they "will always be dependent on their primary reality as tool-beings."[60] Representing a tangibility that cannot be accessed but only contemplated in its otherness, crepuscularism transcribes into verses a peculiar *pothos* – the regretful nostalgia for an unreachable beloved – which is experienced in front of everyday objects, physically reachable and withdrawn at the same time.

The allure of objects relies precisely on the fact that they are tangible materiality "retreated into its own depths."[61] Commenting on this aspect, Steven Shaviro, a speculative realist scholar close to the OOO milieu, has compared the experience of the allure emanated by objects to the experience of the sublime "because it stretches the observer to the point where it reaches the limits of its power or where its apprehensions break down. To be allured is to be beckoned into a realm that cannot even be reached."[62] The sublime of the crepuscular junk is a kitsch sublime that opens the possibility of seeing ordinary objects as a territory of daily acquiescence with the world, wherein human vulnerability to the world gets inevitably exposed. Being allured by things implies a return to childhood, when wondering in front of objects, being bewitched, intrigued, or comforted by them, was a genuine practice of "enchanted materialism."[63] Gozzano expresses this rediscovered sense of enchantment in these verses of "L'assenza" ["The Absence"], in which the roses and geraniums suddenly become a source of childish puzzlement, but also a reassuring point of reference – a solid grip in a slippery world:

E non sono triste. Ma sono
stupito se guardo il giardino …
stupito di che? non mi sono
sentito mai tanto bambino …

Stupito di che? Delle cose.
I fiori mi paiono strani:

ci sono pur sempre le rose,
ci sono pur sempre i gerani ... (*TP* 152)

[And I am not sad. But I am
surprised if I look at the garden ...
surprised at what? I have never
felt so much like a child ...

Surprised at what? At things.
Flowers seem strange to me:
and yet here are still the roses,
here are still the geraniums ...]

In the poem "Gli affetti," Vallini restates this feeling of infantile wonder in front of things. The poetic "I" returns to childhood and lives once again the time "quando tutto era grande" ["when everything was big"] and the best thing ever was the thrilling simplicity of a morning ritual: drinking a *caffelatte*, that "caffé e latte che ancora / serba un profumo di cose / rimaste oneste ed intatte" ["coffee and milk that still / preserves a smell of things / remained honest and untouched"] (*UG* 39).

In the crepuscular poetic universe, the alluring sense of wonder in front of things is a pathway to experiencing a renewed *sympatheia* with things, understood in the ancient Greek meaning of "feeling together." Unlike the notion of *transfer*, that of *sympatheia* – think for example of sympathetic magic – is founded on the assumption that things can be linked to or participate in human feelings. In the uncollected poem "Chiesa" ["Church"], Corazzini asserts the sympathetic voice of materiality, stating, "Prossime al fine hanno una voce anco / le cose" ["When close to their end, even things have / a voice"] (*O* 191). Portraying "l'agonia misteriosa de le cose" ["the mysterious agony of things"] in a church in decay, the poet constructs a series of human analogies that pivot on the experience of corporal passion – a distinct topos of Corazzini's mystic crepuscularism:

Era come un morir di silenziose
Vergini, cui da le ferite buone
sfuggisse il sangue puro a stilla, a stilla. (*O* 191)

[It was like a dying of silent
Virgins, from whose good wounds
a pure blood escaped, drop by drop.]

Corazzini adopts the analogy as a device through which the human can get closer to the mysterious alterity that things embody. If, as Bogost asserts, anthropocentrism is relatively unavoidable for us, still "There is a considerable difference between accepting the truth of human accounts of object perceptions and recognizing that, as humans, we are destined to offer anthropomorphic metaphors for the unit operations of object perception."[64] Extending anthropomorphic qualities to what is generally understood as inert matter is another rhetorical device through which crepuscular poetry tries to render the life of things. In "La tipografia abbandonata" ["The Deserted Print Shop"], the humble objects of an abandoned printing house perform an act of *écriture automatique* that is outside the control of human reason, morality, or aesthetic canon:

> nel silenzio le lettere si unirono,
> composero parole, versi, canti
> interi, per quel sole tanto bello
> e tanto buono ...
>
> [in the silence the letters came together,
> composed themselves in words and lines and whole
> songs, thanks to that sun so beautiful
> and so good ...] (*SE* 12–13)

The crepuscular poetics of things developed by the Roman circle reveals its mystical character in the exploration of a living *sympatheia* that embraces everything into the all-encompassing *anima mundi* or "over-soul." The notion of *anima mundi*, an over-worldly yet also immanently "shared" soul, is a key concept that testifies to the openness of crepuscularism to cross-cultural thoughts. In particular, the idea of the "over-soul" can be connected to the distorted reception of Ralph Waldo Emerson's essays in Italy. Like many intellectuals of their epoch, what the crepusculars admired in Emerson were his mystic qualities, broadly construed. Emerson's immanent god, with its "indwelling property of human personhood and physical nature, not located in some otherworldly realm,"[65] was understood as a divine, living principle embedded in matter. This mystic perspective of connection with everything and among everything finds another strong model in Maurice Maeterlinck. The crepusculars were great admirers of the Belgian writer and dramatist, and in this passage from his "The Tragic in Daily Life" it is possible to notice a connection between Maeterlinck's intimate experience of the divine and the humble objects of crepuscularism. From obvious to *abvius*, objects become doorways to a deeper reality:

> I have grown to believe … that an old man, seated in his arm-chair, waiting patiently with his lamp beside him, giving unconscious ear to all the eternal laws that reign about his house, interpreting without comprehending the silence of doors and windows and the quivering voice of the light, submitting with bent head to the presence of his soul and of his destiny, – I have grown to believe that he, motionless as he is, does yet live in reality a deeper, more human, and more universal life, than the lover who strangles his mistress, the captain who conquers in battle, or the husband who avenges his honor.[66]

This yearning for the universal life that exudes from quotidian things appears in Gozzano, as well. Toying with Eastern conceptions of human-nonhuman relations, even a sceptic and fine sophist like the Turinese poet catches himself wondering about an immanent force that "pulsates everywhere." In one of his letters from India, he writes,

> E se fosse vero? Se veramente noi non fossimo il Re dell'Universo come la nostra religione ci promette? Se veramente il verme, il cane, l'uomo non fossero che graduazioni varie dello spirito, della stessa forza immanente che palpita ovunque, esitando incerta verso una mèta che ignoriamo e che non è forse se non la pace dell'Increato?
>
> [What if this were true? If we were truly not the masters of creation, as our religion promises? If indeed the worm, the dog, and man are nothing but different gradations of the spirit, of the same immanent force that pulsates everywhere, hesitantly moving toward an unpredictable goal of which we are ignorant and that is perhaps nothing more than the peace of the Uncreated?][67]

The possibility of returning to the "uncreated," on which Gozzano occasionally speculates, is a much stronger leitmotif in Corazzini's mystic crepuscularism. In *Soliloquio delle cose*, the speaking things are only materialized through their own voices, which temporarily pull them out from their shady "nothingness," as they declare, "Noi non siamo che cose in una cosa: imagine terribilmente perfetta del Nulla" ["We are things in a thing: terribly perfect image of the Nothing"] (*O* 232). Although their materiality keeps them in a space of domestic seclusion, these things are a tangible, silent reminder of what is beyond them. The key to this interpretation relies on a sibylline sentence that the friend who abandoned them in the house used to say: "Una porta chiusa è figurazione di gran gioia" ["A closed door is a prefiguration of great joy"] (*O* 233). Things are the mysterious doors that must be opened and entered to pass from the limited sight of phenomenal perception to the unlimited mystic vision, where the human perspective is annulled into all-encompassing matter.

The ultimate resort of Roman crepuscularism – which Corazzini's poetry identifies with the extreme experience of death – is the corporeal "dissolvimento" ["dissolution"]. Giuseppe Vannicola, a violinist close to the Roman circle, borrowed the notion of dissolution from music and used it to synaesthetically define the possibility of dispersing the form of things into the flow of matter. In the article "Vagamente" ["Vaguely"], published in the crepuscular journal *Cronache Latine* in 1906, Vannicola describes music as the "fluid" that binds together human and nonhuman, visible and invisible, in a cohesive melody:

> La musica, questa fluidità di tutte le arti, non esprimerebbe forse la vera presenza nascosta, l'eucarestia simboleggiante l'occlusione del Dio, *claritas caritas,* eterno archetipo del ritmo interiore in tutte le cose?
>
> Ogni fremito di melodia è un altare su cui il visibile parla segretamente con l'invisibile e si ciba della divina transustanziazione.[68]
>
> [Music, this fluidity of all the arts, wouldn't it perhaps express the actual hidden presence, the Eucharist symbolizing the occlusion of God, *claritas caritas*, eternal archetype of the inner rhythm of all things?
>
> Each thrill of melody is an altar on which the visible secretly speaks to the invisible and feeds itself with the divine transubstantiation.]

Through a more elusive concept of the divine, Vannicola recalls Dante's literary elaboration of the doctrine of God the First Mover by Saint Thomas Aquinas: human and material things are merged in a spiritual rhythm that allows them to participate in the invisible divine. Yet, Roman crepuscularism trespasses on the rational structure of Saint Thomas's *Summa Theologica*; the movement embraces Neoplatonic positions, oriented towards a pantheistic monism that hinges on a unifying divine principle embedded in human as well as nonhuman matter. Sixteenth-century mystic naturalism, for instance, relies on the theory of *mens insita omnibus*, namely on the presence of a divine soul that pervades material life. In this context, the myth of Actaeon by Giordano Bruno provides an interesting connection for understanding the crepuscular exploration of things as doors to an "immanent beyond" or, in Vannicola's words, as integral parts of the "inner rhythm" that pulsates in everything.[69] After looking at Diana nude, Actaeon is transformed into a deer, as the ultimate degree of philosophical contemplation is attained by reaching a magic communion with nature, through a moment of over-human inebriation and identification with the whole universe.

The yearning for an immersion and supreme dissolution into a nonhuman realm that – not without irony – comes to include everyday junk can be conceived as a twentieth-century adaptation of Brunian naturalism. This revised naturalism is particularly present in the Turinese group: in Gozzano's long poem, *Le farfalle*, he wonders whether the "spirito moderno" ["modern spirit"] should rather return to "poche forme prime" ["a few original forms"], to inquire of them, meditate on them, and worship them. These original forms end up coinciding with a "Spirito immanente" ["immanent Spirit"] that informs Nature and humanity at once (*TP* 446). In a similar fashion, in "Lo scoglio" ["The Rock"], Vallini describes human beings as integral parts, albeit unaware, of an all-encompassing whole: "l'uomo [è] una parte / del Tutto, che ignora … / un mistero / di cui egli stesso fa parte" ["man [is] a part / of the Whole who ignores … / a mystery in which he himself takes part"] (*UG* 34). This whole, in Vallini's re-elaboration of Buddhist philosophy, is a cycle of continuous transformations, of dissolving and reassembling; as he explains in "Il teschio fiorito" ["The Blossoming Skull"], whole in fact means also nothingness, means the falling of the worlds towards the unknown, means matter and vacuum. It is "quello che vedi / e che non vedi" ["what you see and don't see"] "che credi / e che non credi" ["what you believe and don't believe"] (*UG* 37).

Far from providing a coherent system of thought, crepuscular poetry portrays a visual conundrum: on the one hand, things are represented as inaccessible units, which live estranged from the human in their withdrawn cocoons; yet, on the other hand, materiality is also treated as the overlooked entry door to an all-encompassing "tangible transcendence" that connects everything. Whether as withdrawn tool-beings or binding agents, material things remain the boundary of an ultimate experience that resides outside human cognition. Objects act as barely visible reminders of a world that cannot be exhausted by human experience, a world that, in Nietzsche's words, is "neither perfect nor beautiful, nor noble, nor does it wish to become any of these things; it does not by any means strive to imitate man."[70]

Futurist Assemblages in Movement

In its melancholic reiteration, the domestic setting of crepuscular poetry displays the quotidian mystery of "tool-being," leaving a material enigma open before its spectators. In a way, by turning ordinary objects into hyper-visible still-life poetry, crepuscularism accentuates the dividing line between human and nonhuman. Yet, the visual emphasis on a ubiquitous material world that goes virtually unnoticed triggers the repositioning of humans from absolute controlling agents to puzzled observers of their own vulnerability – a vulnerability somewhat "encrusted" with things, in the sensual and limited experience we have of them. Futurism accomplishes a similar repositioning, but adopts a different strategy: by programmatically breaching the boundary between human and nonhuman, this avant-garde movement promotes a precursory notion of vital materialism that "acknowledge[s] the existence of correlations and symmetries in the field of existence, and thus subvert[s] the previous illusions about the nature of reality as a field of separately existing elements."[71]

Vital materialism, as we have briefly seen in the Introduction, is a twenty-first-century interdisciplinary approach that recasts our understanding of materiality, asserting that matter is gifted with agency and possibilities for self-transformation. This reconfiguration, as Coole and Frost explain in their Introduction to the edited collection *New Materialisms* (2010), implies a critique of constructivist and idealist assumptions that separate inert matter from the "immaterial" and dynamic realm of language, subjectivity, consciousness, and, broadly speaking, culture. The new materialist wave has reconnected embodied humans to a vital material world that unfolds an arena of mutual interactions and interlocking systems – global flows of capital, biotechnological engineering, the impact of virtual technologies. These interconnected realities are in fact corporeal and biological as much as cultural, ethical, and political. According to this revised lineage of materialism, matter shapes "choreographies of becoming" in which assembling and disassembling forces forge transformative patterns: "objects forming and emerging within relational fields, bodies composing their natural environment in ways that are corporeally meaningful for them, and subjectivities being constituted as open series of capacities or potencies that emerge hazardously and ambiguously within a multitude of organic and social processes."[72] The analysis of this human-nonhuman material assemblages is the lens through which new, or vital, materialism examines reality as an immanent field of interacting and evolving networks.

The new materialist proposal can indeed be connected to the futurist rethinking of life as an active territory of material entanglements. The avant-garde redefinition ranges from conservative re-adaptations of the poetic practice of the "landscape-state of mind" to more daring experimentations with the conceit of dynamic "plasticity" as a mingling platform where humans and things share the trauma of modernization and war. In some cases, the vital materialism of futurism veers towards forms of animism and spiritual fascination with a material world penetrated by living forces.

An example of "avant-garde conservatism" can be found in the anthology *I poeti futuristi*. The collection does not propose any radical innovation, yet it marks an important passage from the static poetics of the object-symbol to the poetics of the object in movement, or the "object becoming." This shift appears in Libero Altomare's poem "Insonnia fantastica" ["Fantastic Insomnia"], in which everyday "crepuscular" things abandon their torpor and are animated with the same ferment that keeps the poetic persona from sleep:

> – Ma chi batte là,
> telegrafista occulto, sovra il tavolo
> piccoli colpi ...?
> Le mie scarpe
> si urtano come navi, ed i vestiti,
> quali flàccidi automi s'incamminano
> cautamente verso il grande specchio
> ch'è la visione di un cinematografo
> bizzarro ... (*PF* 65)
>
> [But who beats there,
> hidden telegraphist, on the table,
> little bangs ...?
> My shoes
> bump into each other like ships, and my clothes,
> walk cautiously like flabby automatons
> towards the big mirror
> which is the vision of a bizarre
> cinematograph ...]

The impression is that, following a traditional strategy of projection, Altomare injects objects with a feverish vitality that, albeit shared, emanates from the human subject. Embracing a more direct strategy of personification, in the poem "Le case parlano" ["The Houses Speak"], the author gives voice to houses, turning them into messengers of the futurist exhortation to embrace life in its dynamic potential: humans must abandon traditional dwellings to live in "Dimore aeree" ["aerial dwellings"], "case nomadi" ["nomadic houses"], and "pagode-volanti" ["flying-pagodas"] (*PF* 80). From a more general perspective, the nomadism of objects and people predicated by the speaking houses is strictly related to the futurist notion of movement as the final awakening from a conception of the world based on static routine, attachment to roots, and the need to anchor life to a solid "order of things." As Marinetti explains in "Guerra sola igiene del mondo ["War, the Only Cleanser of the World"], futurists – unlike the anarchists, who "s'accontentano ... di assalire i rami politici, giuridici ed economici dell'albero sociale" ["are content with attacking the political, legal, and economic branches of the social tree"] (*TIF* 291, *F* 85) – want to completely extirpate what constitutes the status quo. Namely, they reject:

> desiderio del minimo sforzo, quietismo vile, amore dell'antico e del vecchio, di ciò che è corrotto e ammalato, orrore del nuovo, disprezzo della gioventù, venerazione del tempo, degli anni accumulati, dei morti e dei moribondi, bisogno istintivo di leggi, di catene e di ostacoli, paura di una libertà totale. (*TIF* 291)

> [desire for the least possible effort, vile quietism, love for the old and the aged, for whatever is worn out or ill, horror in the face of the new, contempt for youth, veneration of time and the years which have accumulated, of dead and moribund people, the instinct for laws, chains, and obstacles, fear of total freedom.] (adapted from *F* 85)

Movement, as opposed to the notion of stasis, becomes a futurist synonym for progress, which, according to Marinetti, "ha sempre ragione, anche quando ha torto, perché è il movimento, la vita, la lotta, la speranza" ["is always right even when it is wrong, because it is movement, life, struggle, hope"] (*TIF* 316, *F* 100). Conceived quite literally – from the Latin *progredi* [to move forward] – futurist progress is a fast-forward movement, an ongoing process without beginning or end, which manifests itself in "la … ardente passione pel divenire delle cose" ["[the] burning passion for things under development"] (*TIF* 316, *F* 99). As the futurist leader explains in "Guerra elettrica" ["Electrical War"]:

> l'armatura di una casa, col ritmo delle carrucole, dei martelli e dei cuori, e di tanto in tanto, – sia pure – il grido straziante e il tonfo pesante di un muratore che cade, grossa goccia di sangue, sul selciato! (*TIF* 316)

> [The frame, with its rhythms of pulleys, hammers, and from time to time the harrowing cry and heavy thud of a fallen construction worker, great drop of blood on the pavement …] (*F* 99)

is the raw image of this ongoing violent progression in which human and non-human "things" breathe with potential, are destroyed, and yet proceed forward.

Motion, in the broader sense of living energy and interaction, is a key concept of the futurist poetics of things, which encompasses all the artistic experience of this eclectic avant-garde: from literature to art, from theatre to cinema, and beyond to dance and fashion. Yet, if movement is the trigger of the futurist revolution, war is the bonfire capable of regenerating vital dynamism. In Buzzi's "Canto di guerra" ["Chant of War"], war is represented as an essential element that has been artificially expelled from the "necessario bellissimo cerchio energico della Vita" ["necessary, very beautiful, energetic circle of Life"] (*PF* 113). War is in fact a primal space wherein the human and nonhuman fight for life, potentiated by the incumbent possibility of death. Buzzi's war chant evolves into the rewriting of a Homeric catalogue of weapons; the poem develops through a pressing list that marks the accelerated rhythm of war: "Clava, mazze, dardi, bipenni, aste, pili, turcassi, / alabarde, colubrine, bombarde, cannoni, / obici, bombe, fucili, sciabole, baionette, mitragliatrici" ["club, maul, darts, two-edged axes, poles, javelins, quivers, halberds, culverins, bombards, cannons, / howitzers, bombs, rifles, sabres, bayonets, machine guns"] (*PF* 113). The descriptive fussiness of the catalogue culminates in a direct invocation of animated weapons: "armi, armi, armi / … / tornate alle mani degli uomini" ["weapons, weapons, weapons / … / return to the hands of men"] (*PF* 113).

A similar strategy appears in Marinetti's "Battaglia Peso+Odore" ["Battle Weight+Smell"], in which the futurist author conjures up a medley of weapons, food, board games, animals, planes, and random items of all sorts. In Marinetti's listing medley, the identity of things contained in each single world spills over, creating an undefined heap of matter that buzzes with energy. While this uncontrollable flux flattens anything to a basic materic status, it also makes each item decisive: even a single drop of water that in the drought warns "serba-questa-goccia-d'acqua" ["save-this-drop-of-water"] or a pinch of sand that obstructs the way out ("bisogna-arrampicarsi-3-centimetri-per-resistere-a-20-grammi-di-sabbia-e-300-grammi-di-tenebre" ["you-have-to-lift-yourself-3-centimetres-to-overcome-20-grams-of-sand-and-300-grams-of-shadows"]).[73] By making the relation between man and machine so vital and decisive, war becomes the ultimate moment of human-nonhuman cohesion. War moulds its own assemblages; as Folgore writes, in battle "Uomo e cannone … / son tutta una cosa, / e l'anima del metallo / è nell'anima del soldato" ["Man and cannon … / are all one thing, / and the soul of the metal / is in the soul of the soldier"] (*PF* 247–8).

Through the interrelated notions of living movement and "war assemblage," futurism fosters an innovative platform of life that recalls the animistic views of the world that were typical of pre-modern societies. Drawing a parallel with the animistic societies of the Amazons, described by anthropologist Eduardo Viveiros de Castro, the iconoclast "anti-modernity" of futurism particularly emerges in the proposal of an artistic universe wherein "Everything is animated" and the soul is "the most common thing in the world."[74] This conception implies a new understanding of subjectivity, as a mode of being that can interchangeably apply to human, nonhuman, or human-nonhuman clusters. In this passage, from *Spezzature* [*Enjambments*], futurist artist Fortunato Depero describes his existence as a multifarious zone of random interlacing, in which the "I" can even become "un niente materiale" ["a material nothing"], penetrated by cells and atoms of anybody and anything:

> … quest'è la mia esistenza, la mia solitaria, nuda di esteriori, tutta densa di penetrazioni ed incarnazioni. Cellule ed atomi di tutti e di tutto. Anima mia succhiatoio, assorbitoio ad alta tensione. Pompa elettrica a moto perpetuo. Camino enorme ad imbuto, nel quale precipitano tutte le piogge, le tempeste, gli uragani. Il mio cervello per brevi istanti mi pare il centro di gravitazione degli universi circolanti a gran vertigini e paraboli negli spazi …
>
> e sono un nulla, un niente materiale che si stiracchia bighellonando per ogni dove.[75]
>
> [… this is my existence, my solitary [existence], nude of exteriors, all dense of penetrations and embodiments. Cells and atoms of anybody and anything. Soul of mine, sucker, high-tension-absorbing place. Electrical pump in perpetual motion. Enormous funnel-chimney, in which all the rains, the storms, the hurricanes fall. For brief instants, my brain seems to me the centre of gravity of universes going around with great vertigos and parables in the spaces … and I am nothing, a material nothing that stretches wandering everywhere.]

The anticipatory challenge that futurism launches through its poetics of things is, in a nutshell, the attempt to record the intrinsic dynamism that pervades matter, in its human and nonhuman morphism: "i suoi differenti impulsi direttivi, le sue forze di compressione, di dilatazione, di coesione, e di disgregazione, le sue torme di molecole in massa o i suoi turbini di elettroni" ["its different governing impulses, its forces of compression, dilation, cohesion, disintegration, its heaps of molecules massed together or its electrons whirling like turbines"] (*TIF* 50, *F* 122). As Marinetti explains in the "Manifesto tecnico della letteratura futurista," what intrigues the futurist avant-garde is not the possibility of anthropomorphizing matter; rather, its ambition is to render the unintelligible and palpitating density of molecules and electrons:

> Non si tratta di rendere i drammi della materia umanizzata. È la solidità di una lastra d'acciaio, che c'interessa per sé stessa, cioè l'alleanza incomprensibile e inumana delle sue molecole o dei suoi elettroni, che si oppongono, per esempio, alla penetrazione di un obice. Il calore di un pezzo di ferro o di legno è ormai più appassionante, per noi, del sorriso o delle lagrime di una donna. (*TIF* 50–1)
>
> [There is no point in creating a drama of matter that has been humanized. It is the solidity of a steel plate which interests us as something in itself, with its incomprehensible and inhuman cohesion of molecules or electrons which can resist penetration by a howitzer. The heat of a piece of iron or wood leaves us more impassioned than the smile or tears of a woman.] (*F* 122)

The animistic (not anthropomorphized) conception of matter delineated in these lines is the core element of the 1912 literary manifesto. The futurist leader envisions the process of writing itself as an out-and-out living entity, an object virtually independent from man's action, albeit related to it. This view clearly emerges in the prologue to the manifesto, in which Marinetti reshapes the traditional relation between writer and literary artefact, embracing a radical nonhuman narrative. While flying his airplane, "fila[ndo] a duecento metri sopra i possenti fumaioli di Milano" ["spe[e]d[ing] along at two hundred meters above the powerful smokestacks of Milan"], Marinetti hears the voice of "l'elica turbinante" ["the swirling propeller"] (*TIF* 46, *F* 119), the mechanic "muse" who will dictate the manifesto of futurist literature to him. This hybrid text, written by a man under dictation of a machine, states the need for literature to go beyond its traditional dominion and engage with "[i] movimenti della materia, fuor dalle leggi dell'intelligenza e quindi di una essenza più significativa" ["the movements of matter which are beyond the laws of human intelligence, and hence of an essence which is more significant"] (*TIF* 51, *F* 123). Adopting "uno stile orchestrale, ad un tempo policromo, polifonico, e polimorfo" ["an orchestral style, at once polychromatic, polyphonic, and polymorphous"] (*TIF* 48, *F* 120) futurist literature aims to use "l'immaginazione senza fili" ["wireless imagination"] to intuitively express sensorial, kinetic, and synaesthetic elements, including "1. **Il rumore** (manifestazione del dinamismo degli oggetti); 2. **Il peso** (facoltà di volo degli oggetti); 3. **L'odore** (facoltà di sparpagliamento degli oggetti)" ["1. **Noise** (a manifestation of the dynamism of objects); 2. **Weight** (the capacity for flight in objects); [and] 3. **Smell** (the capacity of objects to disperse themselves)"] (*TIF* 51, *F* 123). The outcome of this new literary language is to achieve human-nonhuman unity: namely, "penetrare l'essenza della materia e distruggere la sorda ostilità che la separa da noi" ["to penetrate the essence of matter and destroy the mute hostility that separates it from us"] (*TIF* 52, *F* 123). Annulling any ontological separation between the realm of man and that of things, Marinett's avant-garde envisages a literary universe in which the "soul" of matter is simultaneously the "seat of otherness" – namely, what is not strictly ours, as it universally shared with other living entities – and "what connects us, bring[ing] us together with the rest of the world."[76]

The poetics of things that the futurist manifesto of literature calls forth reimagines matter as a cross-breeding alliance in continuous transformation. Borrowing from Gilles Deleuze and Félix Guattari – theorists who have greatly inspired vital materialism – we can define this 1912 poetics as quintessentially rhizomatic: it connects human and nonhuman "points" in an anti-hierarchical flow of transversal interactions and "directions in motion," delineating a "map that is always detachable, connectable, reversible, modifiable, and has multiple entryways."[77] The idea of rendering the object as a knot of branched-out connections appears very vividly in futurist art as well; in his meta-artistic reflection, Boccioni affirmed that the purpose of a work of art was "concepire e delimitare in una forma la relazione plastica che esiste tra la *conoscenza* dell'oggetto e la sua *apparizione*" ["to conceive and delimit in a form the plastic relation that exists between the *knowledge* of the object and its *apparition*"].[78] According to the futurist artist, the ultimate goal of defining a "plastic relation" does not imply dissolving the form; rather, it leads to the creation of an "oggetto-ambiente" ["object-environment"]: the object is no longer static in its form, but becomes a "nucleo di *direzioni* che appaiono come forma" ["nucleus of *directions* that appear as a form"].[79] The object manifests itself as a centre for dynamic impressions and deformations, as a form in movement, which dynamically interacts with the artist. In the futurist universe, feeling and movement are intertwined concepts: "cumulative emotions," we may say, that develop through a reciprocal exchange of energies between observer and observed. The observer is open to receive the life of the object, and the object reveals itself to its observer through a mutually engaging relation that is always susceptible to change. As the futurist artists affirmed in the catalogue of the first exhibition of futurist painting (1912), their works focused on highlighting an underexplored aspect of the inner animation of objects:

> ... nessuno si accorge che tutti gli oggetti cosiddetti inanimati rivelano, nelle loro linee, della calma o della follia, della tristezza o della gaiezza. Queste tendenze diverse danno alle linee di cui sono formati un sentimento e un carattere di stabilità pesante o di leggerezza aerea. Ogni oggetto rivela, per mezzo delle sue linee, come si scomporrebbe secondo le tendenze delle sue forze.
>
> Questa scomposizione non è guidata da leggi fisse, ma varia secondo la personalità caratteristica dell'oggetto, che è poi la sua psicologia e l'emozione di colui che lo guarda.[80]

> [What is overlooked is that all inanimate objects display, by their lines, calmness or frenzy, sadness or gaiety. These various tendencies lend to the lines of which they are formed a sense and character of weighty stability or of aerial lightness.
>
> Every object reveals by its lines how it would resolve itself were it to follow the tendencies of its forces.
>
> This decomposition is not governed by fixed laws but varies according to the characteristic personality of the object and the emotions of the onlooker.] (*F* 107)

If, for the futurists, matter is intrinsically sentient and interactive, Marinetti uses his experimental theatre to offer his audience the possibility of experiencing the overlooked agency that even domestic tools and furniture exercise upon the human. In the "drama of objects" entitled *Vengono* [*They're Coming*], Marinetti creates a synthesis of animated objects to show how eight chairs and a large armchair, rearranging themselves in space in preparation for guests' arrival, express their disappointment to the trembling servants by projecting on them "ombre spiccatissime" ["very vivid shadows"].[81]

It is ironic that such a controversial movement, which ultimately froze its turbulent vitality in the biopolitics of Fascism, articulated such a fascinating view of materic intentionality, multiplicity, and collective subjectivity, through which the traditional relation between the subject and the human recedes, as "the subject [becomes] an objective function that one can find deposited on the surface of everything."[82] Borrowing again from Viveiros de Castro's analysis of Amazonian animism, we can trace the anti-modern avant-gardism of futurism in its conception of "subjectivity [as] a fusion of multiplicity, not of unity," a fusion that produces "not a unity of consciousness or a function of integration" but a function of energetic dispersion – a "disjunctive synthesis." The type of animistic ontology that extends subjectivity to nonhumans – mainly animals and plants, but occasionally also artefacts[83] – certainly applies to the living platform that futurism drafts in its manifestos and cutting-edge works. However, it is important to underline that, while "the notion of matter as a universal substrate seems wholly absent from Amazonian ontologies,"[84] for the futurist avant-garde, the idea that the base of the real is the soul – or more precisely, matter steeped in soul – does not exclude the notion of an immanent over-soul or a universal matter in which "everything breathes, and everything conspires in a global breath."[85]

In the futurist universe of things, transcendence is integral to matter because it is embedded into matter: if matter is energy in movement, then it can ultimately be dematerialized into a pure flow of energy. The celebration of speed, for example, is a way to link material and immaterial, visible and invisible, worldly and unworldly, in the realm of immanent "things"; the same can be said for the extra-sensorial nature of electricity, whose effects are as powerful as they are impalpable. This interest in linking the material and immaterial sheds light on the futurist fascination for occultism – a fascination that, while rather concealed in Marinetti's group, is very distinct in other futurist circles, like the Florentine Azure Patrol. In his manifesto "Pittura dell'avvenire" ["Painting of the Future"] (1915), the painter Arnaldo Ginna, one of the spokesman of the mystical fringe of futurism, exposes the need to abandon physical perception in order to experience the presence of those vibrating forces that, similar to electricity or Hertz's waves, propagate through the ether invisibly and silently.[86] In the form of kinetic force or electromagnetic waves, energy becomes the interconnecting agent of a "molecular animism,"[87] to borrow Jeffrey Schnapp's definition, through which every particle lives independently yet is also integrated in a plurality of material-immaterial networks.

The discourse of "molecular animism" and subjectivity as a function of organic dispersion is particularly preponderant in the artistic experimentalism of the women writers who collaborated on the journal *L'Italia futurista*. Unlike other futurist groups, this Florentine circle included several women, among them Maria Ginanni, Rosa Rosà, Fanny Dini, and Irma Valeria. The group and its publications became the locus for an artistic and spiritual search that involved a broader reflection on the social role of women in the early twentieth century. Furthermore, being decentred from Marinettian futurism, the Azure Patrol constitutes a niche artistic laboratory that offers an ideal bridge between the quiet retreat of the crepuscular poetics of things and the rambunctious manifestos of the futurist avant-garde. Through their work, the writers and artists of the Azure Patrol experimented with a type of "enchanted materialism" that – readapting an expression of Jane Bennett – portrays the modern world outside its mainstream narratives of rationality and disenchantment.

Ginanni, one of the most active women in the group, expressed her holistic vision of the "universe of things" in the work *Il poema dello spazio* [*The Poem of Space*] (1919). Echoing Roman crepuscularism, Ginanni postulates the existence of a shared living principle that inhabits everything. According to her, a totalizing mystery embeds every single atom: any individual organism is part of a vibrating whole, and any particle "*deve* dare alla totalità vibrante dell'universo il ritmo della propria pulsazione isolata" ["*must* give the rhythm of its isolated pulsation to the vibrant totality of the universe"].[88] In order for this vibration to propagate, human flesh must be envisioned as a permeable "thing," a porous substance that can absorb life while being immersed in a universal flow of life. Existing thus equates to coexisting in a space wherein subjectivity percolates, incorporating other living elements.

In Irma Valeria's writing, the distinction between human and nonhuman even becomes superfluous because, as she affirms in "Occultismo e arte nuova" ["Occultism and New Art"], "l'atomo occulto del nostro essere e quello del mondo si unificano, si confondono perché non sono che la stessa cosa" ["the occult atom of our being and that of the world unify themselves, confuse themselves, because they are indeed the same thing"] (*SF* 199). Given this deep interconnection, art ultimately aims to penetrate objects and vivify them not by projecting human feelings onto things, but by transferring into words "[del]la vita propria dell'oggetto" ["the very own life of the object"], its rich soul (*SF* 198). In her interest in occultism, Valeria also proposes a reflection on human vulnerability that very closely recalls the crepuscular undermining of traditional anthropocentrism. In "Dialoghi inutili" ["Useless Dialogues"], she emphasizes the limitation of the human, compared to the infinity of the universe in which we are immersed; in her view, being human is rather a confinement than a privileged position, as "La porzione minima da noi occupata nello spazio ci impedirà sempre di immaginare l'illimitato" ["the minimal portion that we occupy in the space will always prevent us from imagining the unlimited"] (*SF* 201).

From things self-animated by kinetic energy to things connected through the inner movement of a universal "molecular animism," futurism conducts an investigation into materiality that, in rejecting the notion of inert matter, also rejects the idea of placing humans as spectators of the living mystery of things. In all its forms and languages, art is the futurist means of accessing the vibrant plasticity that informs the world, to enter "direttamente nell'universo e fa[re] corpo con esso" ["directly ... into the universe and become one body with it"] (*TIF* 53, *F* 124).

The Aesthetic Encounter with the Alterity of Things

In the introduction to the July 2012 issue of *e-flux*, which was entirely dedicated to animistic conceptions of the world, Anselm Franke provides a captivating definition of animism. This "anarchic ontology" takes the semblance of a "ghost ... haunting modernity," a ghost who "awaits us everywhere when we step outside modern reason's cone of light, outside its firmly mapped order, when approaching its frontier zones and 'outside.'"[89] By adopting Franke's view, we can apply the term "anarchic ontologies" to crepuscular and futurist representations of the world, to their complementary attempts to loosen the solid and dualistic logic of coherence that characterizes the modern mindset and then, from the scrapheap of reason, to shape a vibrant aesthetic universe. We can also apply the label "anarchic ontologies" to those contemporary frameworks that, although far from avant-garde animism, have tried to offer an alternative to the biased thinking that equates nonhuman beings to inert objects. Many of these alternative proposals have been central in the twenty-first-century scholarly debate: from new materialism to OOO (and, more broadly speculative realism), including the ecocritical approach of environmental humanities, the attention to waste of discard studies, and the more traditional socio-criticism of what Maurizia Boscagli labelled "stuff-theory." The common thread that links these heterogeneous theories is the refusal to relegate the nonhuman to a passive function of framing the human or to a fully controllable and separate "otherness." Yet, the issues under debate are to what extent things exercise their agency as subjects and what types of interaction, if any, exist between human and nonhuman materialities. These queries offer the grounds on which to retrace the key points of the crepuscular and futurist poetics of things, in relation to a set of new dichotomies – consumable-recyclable, withdrawal-assemblage, being-becoming – that surprisingly emerged from these non-dualistic theoretical discourses on the nonhuman.

Both crepuscularism and futurism call into question the modern identification of objects as consumable items that can be conveniently discarded. Their objects – and the avant-garde itself, as the hyper-object that contains them – are disturbingly dysfunctional "inconsumables," old pieces of junk and feral mechanic chimeras that live at the outskirts of bourgeois consumerism. The crepuscular and futurist "underworld" of "anti-goods" unveils the self-deceiving nuts and bolts of an economic system that can (unsustainably) sustain itself only by accelerating a fast-forward production cycle and becoming submerged in its own waste. As Walter Benjamin affirmed, the avant-garde shows how the "mechanisms of the capitalist process reveal themselves fully only in their waste products – in that which no longer serves a purpose and is thus free from the mechanisms of ideological control so pervasive elsewhere."[90]

However, the two movements deal very differently with the waste management challenge that modernity poses. Futurism exaggerates the metamorphosis that modern progress fosters, transforming Italian cities into monstrous forges of new "stuff," inhospitable techno-jungles inhabited by automatons and burning machines that exhale harmful emissions. Unaware of depicting a realistic twenty-first-century dystopia, Marinetti engages with an ontological transformation that, while stressing the interdependence of human and nonhuman, welcomes an apocalyptic industrialization that will destroy both. Commenting on this aspect of uncontrolled advancement from an ecocritical perspective, Serenella Iovino has contended that Marinetti's anathema "Contro Venezia passatista" ["Against Passéist Venice"] (1910) can in fact be read as a precursory discourse on the "cannibal mechanism of the 'development narrative.'"[91] Such a magnification of industrial development would lead to the creation of the industrial area of Porto Marghera in 1917, altogether reducing human and nonhuman to disposable consumables. As Iovino notes, the futurists foster their myth of savage industrialization in part by replacing the image of "old Venice," "cloaca maxima of passéism," with a renovated Venice, deformed by a robust "cure" of mechanic innovation that eradicates any sign of tradition:

> Noi vogliamo preparare la nascita di una Venezia industriale e militare che possa dominare il mare Adriatico, gran lago Italiano.
>
> Affrettiamoci a colmare i piccoli canali puzzolenti con le macerie dei vecchi palazzi crollanti e lebbrosi.
>
> Bruciamo le gondole, poltrone a dondolo per cretini, e innalziamo fino al cielo l'imponente geometria dei ponti metallici e degli opifici chiomati di fumo, per abolire le curve cascanti delle vecchie architetture.

Venga finalmente il regno della divina Luce Elettrica, a liberare Venezia dal suo venale chiaro di luna da camera ammobigliata. (*TIF* 34)

[We want to prepare the birth of an industrial and military Venice that can dominate the Adriatic Sea, that great Italian lake.

Let us hasten to fill in its little reeking canals with the ruins from its leprous and crumbling palaces.

Let us burn the gondolas, rocking chairs for cretins, and raise to the heavens the imposing geometry of metal bridges and factories plumed with smoke, to abolish the cascading curves of the old architecture.

Let the reign of divine Electric Light finally come to liberate Venice from its venal moonlight for furnished rooms to let.][92]

By contrast to the futurist arson, the crepuscular lingering before what is old, useless, and forgotten allows for a re-evaluation of passé things, reimagining them as living materialities smeared with human residue. What is lost of the human inevitably attaches to things; not by chance, the mirror is a recurrent object in crepuscular poetry and performs a revelatory function. In the act of mirroring, things reveal their magnetic and frightening power by capturing something of the human and retaining it within their nonhuman materiality. It is by looking at the mirror in his grandfather's house that Gozzano's poetic "I" finds the death of his former idols in his own living flesh. Corazzini provides an elaboration on this "retaining mirroring" in the poem "Stazione sesta" ["Sixth Station"], highlighting how the absence of the beloved person has soaked the things she left behind. She is indeed in those used things: "La cerchi nelle sue cose? / Ritrovi le sue dita in quelle rose / di carta gialla o lungo la tastiera / di quel suo vecchio pianoforte a coda?" ["Do you look for her in her things? Do you find her fingers in those roses / of yellow paper or along the keyboard of that old grand piano of hers?"] (*O* 164).

Staring at Gozzano's mirror and Corazzini's decrepit paper flowers is uncomfortable because this old stuff "looks back," evoking a hidden threat: "to detonate the unrealized future contained in the past, to expose in the objects themselves the realizations of the utopias of generations past."[93] What are the ideals of the Risorgimento, embodied by the objects in Grandmother Speranza's parlour? What are the ebullient futurist cities and bloody machines when seen through the trauma of the First World War and later, through more than twenty years of fascist rule? Jumping into contemporary history, what are the material vestiges of colonization, if seen through the lens of material networks wherein religious beliefs, arms trafficking, disposal of energetic resources, and the flow of immigrant bodies are twisted and interlocked into physical and symbolic assemblages? The only way to deny these tangible interconnections is to rid ourselves of their memory: namely, to incorporate reified memory into a process of rapid production and even more rapid disposal. Futurism tries to accelerate this process in order to annihilate any trace of the past; to this purpose, it tailors a new concept of memory, which painter Gino Severini presents in the manifesto "Le analogie plastiche del dinamismo" ["Plastic Analogies of Dynamism"] (1913). Futurist memory, "indipendente da ogni unità di tempo e di luogo" ["independent of any unity of time or place"], turns into an enhanced experience of the present; memory "agirà dunque nell'opera come *elemento d'intensificazione plastica* ed anche come vera e propria causa emotiva" ["will act in the work of art as an *element of artistic intensification* and as a true emotive source"] (*MDF* 112, *F* 165). Remembrance becomes detached from history, in the name of the atemporal synchrony that the work of art displays. By enclosing the entire universe in its dynamic materiality, the painting replaces the conceptions of diachronic time and spatialization with the interwoven continuum of the spacetime that the work of art embodies. As Severini argues, "soltanto il ricordo dell'emozione persiste, e non quello della causa che l'ha prodotta" ["only the memory of the [present] emotion remains, not the memory of the cause that produced it"] (*MDF* 112, *F* 165). Emotions burn out and disperse in an intense, instantaneous moment of connection with the universal vitality that the painting contains.

By contrast, crepuscular poetry idles amid the inconvenient inheritance of the past. Under the guise of passively waiting, the movement gives voice to a poetic ecology that calls for a critical reuse of what has been discarded – including the "missed" past, what might have happened but did not – into new material artefacts. These recycled poetic patchworks tell the story of past things as co-agents: how they participate in forging material and symbolic relations, redefining human landscapes, and delineating different literary "onto-cartographies" in which the old is critically rewritten and reinserted into the new.[94]

The contours and dynamics of the material and symbolic relations in which human and nonhuman become co-agents, equally subject and object, represent an intricate knot in both crepuscular and futurist poetics, and are similarly a controversial point in the twenty-first-century debate on the agency of things. What does it mean for humans to enter into relations with things, and how do these relations evolve? Crepuscular poetry shows the negative side of a relation that is nourished with wonder at what is tangible but humanly inaccessible; by contrast, futurism puts greater emphasis on the positive moment of vital mingling, entanglement, and intuitive grasping of nonhuman life. The two movements usher in polarized discourses that can be compared to the opposing views of OOO and new materialism: that is, to the assertion that a "tool *is* in the mode of executing itself"[95] and the affirmation that "'matter becomes' rather than 'matter is.'"[96]

Summarizing a few key arguments discussed in this chapter, we can remark that, in the investigation of materiality proposed by OOO, relationality occupies a very limited space. Harman elaborates on Heidegger's concept of readiness-to-hand [*Zuhandenheit*], a concept that for the object-oriented theorist is not exclusively applicable to useful tools but can be extended to "*all* entities, [all 'tools'], no matter how useful or useless they might be."[97] The OOO scholar identifies "tool-being" not only as a realm of existence independent from human perception, but also as a withdrawal from the view of any other object. As he explains:

> Like the giant squids of the Marianas Trench, tool-beings are encountered only once they have washed up dead on the shore, no longer immersed in their withdrawn reality. It is impossible to define tool-being as a linguistic network or culturally coded system of "social practices," as many commentators do. Tool-being is that which *withdraws* from all such networks ...[98]

Tool-being is a territory of exposed alterity. Hence, Harman argues that, through the concept of "readiness-to-hand," Heidegger does not designate human praxis – the practical usability of tools – as opposed to the theoretical understanding of objects, but rather constitutes "a mysterious capital 'X,' a brutal subterranean realm which we can glimpse only at second hand."[99] Thus, it appears that any given object is not going to be exhaustively defined through the relations in which it takes part; an object therefore remains "a unified reality not exhausted by any relation to it from the outside."[100] Relations are accidental and, at most, asymmetrical encounters that cannot go much further than a superficial grasping of sensual qualities. In an essay entitled "Objects, Matter, Sleep, and Death" (2009), Harman clarifies this point, using the concrete example of a man looking at a tree:

> I never fuse homogenously into a tree in a blinding flash of light. The tree always remains separate from me, standing over against me. Moreover, this twofold is also *asymmetrical*, since here the *real* me encounters a merely *phenomenal* or *intentional* tree. When by contrast the real tree encounters the phenomenal caricature of me, as it must in all cases when it comes into contact with me, this must result in a different but closely related object.[101]

Harman's view is radically opposite to futurist poetics, which posits the notions of hybridity and transformative motion as the very substance of futurist things. Marinetti's avant-garde, in its rendering of velocity, creates a vibrant fusion of all forces in movement, representing the energetic synthesis that results from the dynamic interpenetration of human and nonhuman forces. For futurism, as Boccioni states, absolute motion is a dynamic law, "inherent in an object"; and dynamism is indeed the "plastic potential" that any human or nonhuman object already possess in its substance (*F* 187). This idea of plastic fusion is restated, from a human perspective, in the manifesto "La danza futurista" ["Futurist Dance"] (1917). Here Marinetti postulates the possibility of dance imitating mechanical movement by transferring the life of the motor into the dancing body. He affirms:

> Bisogna imitare con i gesti i movimenti delle macchine; fare una corte assidua ai volanti, alle ruote, agli stantuffi; preparare così la fusione dell'uomo con la macchina, giungere al metallismo della danza futurista. (*MDF* 183).
>
> [Our gestures must imitate the movements of machines assiduously paying court to steering wheels, tires, pistons, and so preparing for the fusion of man with the machine, achieving the metallism of Futurist dance.] (*F* 236).

Exemplifying this practice in his "danza dello shrapnel" ["Shrapnel Dance"], Marinetti employs the corporeal language of dance to express multisensorial synthesis:

> la fusione della montagna con la parabola dello shrapnel. La fusione della canzone umana carnale col rumore meccanico dello shrapnel. Dare la sintesi ideale della guerra: un alpino che canta spensierato sotto una volta ininterrotta di shrapnels. (*MDF* 183–4)
>
> [the fusion of a mountain with the parabola of shrapnel. The fusion of carnal human song with the mechanical noise of shrapnel. To render an ideal synthesis of the war: a soldier in the mountains who carelessly sings beneath an uninterrupted vault of shrapnel.] (*F* 237).

The issue of interdependence is a point from which Harman's speculation also greatly diverges from contemporary theories of network and assemblage, which assert co-dependency and interactions as the essential mode of being – or more properly, of becoming – shared by the agents in a network. Relationality among objects is a point in which Levi Bryant's "onticology" also strays far from Harman; for Bryant, who was initially an active member of the OOO group, "Given that objects often do unleash forces in other objects, it thus appears that objects must somehow be capable of perturbing one another, while the virtual proper being of an object forever remains in excess of this encounter and is nonetheless closed."[102] In Gozzano's ironic verses of "La signorina Felicita," the world itself is the arena of chaotic perturbations, in which infantilized "human-thingies" get unwittingly entangled with other "things": "il Mondo: quella cosa tutta piena / di lotte e di commerci turbinosi, / la cosa tutta piena di quei 'cosi / con due gambe' che fanno tanta pena ..." ["a mad affair / of struggle and whirling trade and eternal change / they call the World: a thing filled up with strange / 'two-legged things' that spread pain everywhere ..."] (*TM* 78–9). In the realm of crepuscular poetics, relations are unsettling and somewhat transformative, but the objects involved in the experience of encounter always maintain a certain degree of apartness and opacity.

Illustrating Harman's view of relations, Peter Gratton offers a perspective that serves as a bridge between object-oriented ontology and the crepuscular poetics of things. Gratton argues that the philosophical model of Harman's theoretical approach is not Heideggerian, but rather is Levinas's reflection on "the Other." According to Levinas, "the Other ... is irreducible to the qualities we give it"; similarly, for Harman, the "'alterity of the thing' ... is irreducible to its representations or, indeed, any of the modes through which humans, animals, or anything else encounters it."[103] The notion of the irreducibility of the "otherness" that emanates from things is certainly a fundamental point in crepuscularism, along with the idea that we can never scratch the surface of the real qualities of an object, which thus remain withdrawn. Yet, for crepuscularism, comprehension of otherness ultimately seems to descend from a holistic conception of matter that trespasses into animistic beliefs: Corazzini's mystical poetry, the crepuscular nuanced works of the Azure Patrol, and Gozzano's interest in the living mystery of nature all share a "conjunction of transcendence and immanence."[104] Consequently, even though the inner substance of things remains baffling, their palpable "otherness" is comprehended – in the dual meaning of being grasped and being contained – through a "universally promiscuous ... sense of relations among entities."[105]

It seems that what is at odds, both in the avant-garde poetics of things and in the OOO contemporary discussion of materiality, is not so much the possibility of forging human-nonhuman relations but rather the possibility of delineating crystalline "see-through" relations that can overcome the opacity of things. As Harman himself refers to phenomenology and its human-centred limitations, it might be useful to draw a parallel with the writings of phenomenologist Enzo Paci on the opacity of things. In a few entries of his *Diario fenomenologico* [*Phenomenological Journal*] (1961), Paci meditates on the "dura ed impenetrabile alterità dell'oggetto" ["hard and impenetrable alterity of the object"]; yet he also highlights a possible conjunction between human and nonhuman when he affirms that "noi e le cose siamo legati da un misterioso piacere" ["we and things are linked by a mysterious pleasure"].[106] Unlike OOO, which "brackets" the human to focus its speculation on an ultimately unreachable object, Paci's phenomenological investigation brackets the object, maintaining that the human subject is the one who awakens the dormant significance within things, who uses his or her intentionality to discover their hidden truth. From his "humanistic" yet not fully anthropocentric view, Paci offers an interesting reflection, stating that the link between human and nonhuman resides in a "mysterious pleasure," namely, in the achievement of an aesthetic experience in which rationality is not the primary modality of relation.

Even though the "otherness" of things – their reverse or impenetrable hardness – cannot be exhausted through the encounter we have with them, the notion of aesthetic encounter opens a range of relational possibilities that go beyond the power relation between consumer and consumable, subject and object, *homo sapiens* and object of knowledge. Even ordinary things, when aesthetically encountered, can disclose a surplus of meaning and reveal, albeit partially, what we do not see of them and of ourselves. This, in a nutshell, is the message that the crepuscular poetics of objects develops, debasing the human to "un essere medio, che vale / né più né meno del resto" ["an average being, that is worth / neither more nor less that the other beings"] (*UG* 66). And this is where we can find in crepuscularism a poetics of humility and respect before the "rappresentazione pura dell'oggetto" ["the bare representation of the object"],[107] before the object lying bare, delimiting with its uncanny presence a space of meaning, yet also of human inaccessibility. Through crepuscular poetry, we experience a world that, as new realist philosopher Maurizio Ferraris contends, is "recalcitrant to our will and exerts a friction against it," a world whose positivity relies on the principle "'it exists, therefore it resists.'"[108]

Marinetti's avant-garde hubris rejects the crepuscular contemplative attitude, turning the field of resistance that objects occupy into the ultimate challenge of futurism. The futurist leader fosters a notion of relationality as penetration of the otherness that things embody; hence, the futurists' desire to fuse dynamically with the universe, blending humans and things, is undoubtedly a violent desire to win over the resistance of the world. At a linguistic level, this abusive coercion shows through the use of a metaphorical terminology that evokes sexual violence; for example, in "Lo splendore geometrico e meccanico e la sensibilità numerica" ["Geometrical and Mechanical Splendour and the Numerical Sensibility"] (1914), Marinetti justifies the use of onomatopoeia as an extreme desire to deflower material "bodies" of their secrecy: "Il nostro amore crescente per la materia, la volontà di penetrarla e di conoscere le sue vibrazioni, la simpatia fisica che ci lega ai motori, ci spingono all'**uso dell'onomatopea**" ["Our growing love for matter, the will to penetrate it and know its vibrations, the physical sympathy that connects us with motors – these impel us to the *use of onomatopoeia*"] (*TIF* 105, *F* 178–9).

In both the crepuscular and futurist aesthetic universes, things are relational hubs and create the material trestle wherein human and nonhuman come together and continually transform each other. Yet, for the two movements, relations are intrinsically vulnerable as they are constantly at the mercy of unpredictable changes. Exemplary of this relational precariousness are crepuscular malady or futurist war. These networks unravel a web of extremely unstable human-nonhuman vital interconnections: the body lives at the threshold of death, at the turning-point of becoming a corpse; objects, like medicines or weapons, are indispensable to survival and yet are often only futile placebos that help us cope with impending death. Avant-garde poetry itself is a vulnerable relational space: it is the seat of a self-referential commitment to seclusion from the modern audience and is also an eccentric gesture born from a narcissistic need for visibility.

Investigating human-nonhuman relations as territories of transition and inevitable change involves a parallel reflection on the notion of being itself, as the experience of the possibilities that are opened by the encounter with the world. A text that exemplifies this conceit and that can be imagined as the suture point between the crepuscular lingering before the object and the futurist thrilling movement towards the object is "La morte di Tantalo" ["The Death of Tantalus"], Corazzini's last poem, composed a few days before his death. Rewriting the Genesis myth of Adam and Eve, the poem tells the sibylline story of a transformative encounter that sets the groundwork for defining a new notion of "imperfect" yet vital relationality with the world. In an enchanted garden that recalls the terrestrial Paradise, a couple breaks the impending ban that keeps them frozen in an everlasting spell: they dare to eat the marvellous grapes of the golden vineyard and drink the water of its fountain. The man and woman fall asleep and awaken in an utterly transfigured setting: the vineyard is no longer golden, and they are free to leave. The text closes with the poetic "I" exhorting his "dolce amica" ["sweet girlfriend"] to confess her sin to a mysterious "viandante" ["wayfarer or wanderer"]. The random wayfarer is a key figure, embedded with trans-textual references: in Nietzsche's writings, the wanderer is often associated with the liberating capability of finding joy in change and transience.[109] The final confession thus contains a programmatic "manifesto" that identifies death with immobility and life with eternal wandering through the possibilities that the relation with the world discloses: "E aggiungi che non morremo più / e che andremo per la vita / errando per sempre" ["And add that we will die no more / and that we will wander / through life [erring] forever"] (modified from *SE* 64–5).

Erring through life, in its ambiguous double meaning of the Italian "errare" (wandering and making errors), is the commitment to a nomadic, flawed, and fragile relationality that Corazzini embraces through this profane myth. "La morte di Tantalo" tells the story of a life-changing encounter with things that breaks a long-lasting isolation and condemnation to immobility. In classic mythology, Tantalus is a demigod condemned to stand in a pool of water beneath a fruit tree, cursed so that he is unable to drink the water or grasp the fruit suspended from the low branches of the tree. Commenting on Tantalus's death – a metaphor for the end of a relational seclusion – it is worth recalling that the motif of the encounter is a crucial aspect in Heidegger's later speculation on things. In *What Is a Thing?* (1954) the philosopher designates the "thingness of the thing" as "the basic way (model, approach, framework) in which we meet … things," namely "the mode of being of these things around us, how they are."[110] Heidegger then defines a person as "a having things given" and a thing as "something that encounters." Returning to Corazzini's text, we can see how the encounter with things – the wonderful fruits, the golden water, the enchanted fountain in which the moon reflects its rays – is a liberating event that cannot be enjoyed merely cognitively or bodily. Encountering the alterity of things is an experience that, in itself, is a co-mingling of bodies and sensations, a tactile, emotional, symbolic, and cognitive experience. In Shaviro's words, "I feel a thing when it affects me or changes me, and what affects me is not just certain qualities of the thing but its total and irreducible existence."[111]

However, as I will explore more in detail in the next chapters, the all-encompassing experience of encountering *other* things problematizes the very notion of being that is so central in the speculation of OOO. First of all, although Bogost's and Harman's accounts of the "world of things" dislodge human hubris, their shared view remains deeply problematic. When the theoretical attention shifts from epistemology to ontology, the problem is whether being is conceived, as OOO seems to suggest, as an immutable and ahistorical realm, or as a historicized process of relational becoming, as vital materialism proposes.

From an environmentalist perspective, the lack of historical context undermines, for instance, Harman's acknowledgment of the inner activity of nature, which Timothy Morton endorses in his personal blog, "Ecology without Nature." In *Guerrilla Metaphysics*, Harman writes that "nature is not natural and can never be naturalized … *Nature is unnatural*, if the word 'natural' is meant to describe the status of slabs of inert matter."[112] Undoubtedly, this claim highlights the importance of nonhuman life, and Harman proceeds by asserting that "The life of gravel and sandpaper is every bit as troubled by inner ambiguities as human existence ever was."[113] Yet, if nature has been troubled, many of its troubles are historically connected to human action and, ultimately, to a Western mindset that, according to Val Plumwood, has identified the realm of nature with a different realm of being, which is inferior and antithetical to male reason.[114] Too often matter has been debased to a dominated space, neglecting that nature is the locus where our "freedom to act" is enabled, as Elizabeth Grosz contends.[115] From a different perspective, Plumwood's and Grosz's critiques emerge in Morton's attack against the "agrilogistic" modern approach, which has exploited natural resources to the extreme of turning agriculture from a source of survival into a global-scale economy of exploitation and pollution. Ultimately, this is the unresolved point of OOO: how can "natural objects" simultaneously be withdrawn "subterranean realms" and historical agents, whose own being has been transformed and jeopardized by human action and culture, as the evolution of Venice's lagoon proves?

The question of historization becomes even more controversial if we *realistically* observe people and material things in the social world. The idea that everything exists equally may be ontologically sound, but it raises a number of questions when examined from a materialist and feminist standpoint. Things in the world convey their agency through a "carnal" appearance that has, or has been attributed to, class, gender, and race. As this appearance is neither equal nor purely existential, anything exists by bearing meanings through its embodiment and through the transformative encounters that such appearance enables.

Concluding on a literary note, we can also see that the transformative encounter narrated by Corazzini in "La morte di Tantalo" is, in turn, encountered by its readers across epochs, through the material medium of the text, a human-nonhuman "thing." Irreducibility is thus a category that extensively applies to all texts, in their ability to mix the categories of "[e]ssence and existence, imaginary and real, visible and invisible ... laying out [their] oneiric universe of carnal essences, of effective likeness, of [opaque] meanings."[116] Birthed and transmitted as a palimpsest, any literary work is an idiosyncratic "*distributive network* of bodies,"[117] a work in progress wherein a number of different body-texts converge and interact on paper or in electronic materiality: authors, editors, publishers, designers, readers, critics, paratextual elements, words, facts, figures, and transtextual references all create a material and interwoven subjectivity by bricolage. Thus, the practice of (re)writing and (re)reading – the inner vibrancy embedded in textual corporeality – unfolds through a "constant encounter with external, different others."[118]

Thinking of a text as a human-nonhuman evolving ecosystem – or as a peculiar type of "storied matter"[119] – it is also possible to reimagine the role of humans in their relationship with things, whether they are artefacts or natural elements. Texts offer a platform of encounter, by unspooling a network of material and symbolic relations; within the textual network, humans act as readers, or in Arjun Appadurai's words, as "mediants, [namely] mediators among other mediators." As Appadurai proposes, this mediating role comes with a "special responsibility" for humans, that of acting "as trustees of a larger world of mediants." Further, being "mediants who have cost the planet … much more than all the mediants that surround us," we "owe to the planet some special consideration in return."[120] Apparadurai's view can be linked to the crepuscular ecocritical poetics of recycling, in its recovery of that "old stuff" for whose presence we must account. If human beings are mediants, Gozzanian (yet more responsible) things among other things, corporality is indeed the concrete and historicized locus of encounter with material reality. Humans can mediate because they are corporeally immersed in matter, because they are quite literally "erring" through matter's own *text*-ure – through a living materiality that shapes stories. Moreover, humans are constantly defined by the things that make humans what they are. Acknowledging that one lives in a dimension of corporeal immersion in matter necessitates a reconsideration of subjectivity as a shared, participative, and distributive quality of networks.

Chapter Three

Being a Living Thing: Towards a New Notion of Body

Mutant Bodies and Multiplying "I's"

Gozzano insisted that he was nothing more than a "cosa vivente" ["living thing"] called "guidogozzano," a clump of lowercase letters scattered amidst other words (*TP* 70). In a similar fashion, Vallini describes his poetic persona using the "neuter epithet" of "cosa umana" ["human thing"] (*UG* 38); and Corazzini compares the slow agony of his body's consumption to the decay of an object, albeit one wishing for dissolution (*SE* 33–5). Whether conceived as breathing materiality or decomposing corpse, the body is the territory wherein the co-mingling of human and nonhuman is most visible: a dense interweaving of tissues, organs, and clusters of cells, all immersed in matter, composed of matter, and affected by external matter. Yet, the body, in its rich hybridity, is also a text of its own.

In chapter 2, I proposed to rethink literary texts as an arena of material and symbolic encounters. Here I proceed with my analysis by examining human and nonhuman bodies as matter that can be read as a text. In *Material Ecocriticism* (2014), editors Serenella Iovino and Serpil Oppermann argue that bodies are the "'middle place' where matter enmeshes in the discursive forces of politics, society, technology, biology … and symbolic imaginaries. Whether performing their narratives as statues in a square, teachers in a classroom, plankton in the ocean, fossils trapped in a stone wall, or chickens in industrial factory farms, bodies are living texts that recount *naturalcultural* stories."[1] Engaging with the founding theoretical premise of material ecocriticism, my goal is to analyse how the bodies narrated by crepuscular and futurist texts unfold corporeal stories in which nature and culture encounter and combine their voices.

Both movements rework the image of the human body as a functional machine, which is a central theme of modern scientific culture, from Descartes onwards. Crepuscular poets focus on the broken gears of their dysfunctional human machines. The futurists, on the other hand, attempt to assemble a mélange of mechanical cogs and human clay into a new Adam. The outcome of the futurists' genetic experimentation is a revolutionary, prototypical cyborg that belies the traditional understanding of the "flesh-and-soul" human as the sole corporeal model. Similar to Lego constructions that can be continually pieced together, disassembled, and reassembled with other units, avant-garde bodies overcome the centripetal model of the "feeling and thinking body-subject" to propose the centrifugal paradigm of the "loose subject": one that is open to assimilating the world into its flesh, and to being assimilated by the world.

The redefinition of the body in terms of mutant living matter involves a parallel re-envisioning of the speaking persona or speaking "I." In its liminal position between early modernism and the avant-garde, crepuscularism develops a bitter denunciation of the deceptive nature of subjectivity as a fixed, embodied category. Luigi Pirandello will later examine this theme in his modernist masterpiece, *Uno, nessuno, centomila* [*One, No One, and One Hundred Thousand*] (1926), a novel in which the protagonist's wife's comment on his bent nose triggers a deep identity crisis. Corazzini, anticipating the high modernist concern with identity and appearance, substance, and form, represents sick bodies as bits of corporeal materiality estranged from human will. Similarly, Gozzano ironizes on his debilitated body, an ambiguous "subject-object" that hardly even belongs to him anymore; rather, the doctors, the drugs, and the invasive procedures seem to own his body, as they daily and painfully violate his flesh. In "I sonetti del ritorno," the Turinese poet wonders whether the subject-pronoun "I," which we commonly associate with our own body, is merely "una sola virtù dell'Apparenza" ["only a virtue of Appearance"] (*TP* 102), a tricky linguistic device – the "I," the "me" – that can serve the purpose of subject or object interchangeably. The futurist avant-garde also targets the soundness of the "flesh-and-soul character," ungluing the artificial joints that allow the Vitruvian man to stay fixed and act as the rational balance point of his microcosm. Yet, the dismantling of the human "I-embodiment" and of the body-soul pairing is not as radical as Marinetti makes it seem. Rather than succumbing to its demolition, the avant-garde "I" evolves into chameleonic forms: it takes new physiognomic semblances and fluidly embodies a polymorphous and participative bodily subjectivity.

Both the crepuscular and futurist renewed bodies are, in appearance, ugly deformations of classical beauty: sick, disproportionate, and undignified, they are even vivisected into raw, loose parts – inner organs, fluids, discharges, mutilated limbs. This desecration involves a parallel destabilization of the gender and social identities attached to such dismembered bodies. If crepuscularism deals with a masculinity threatened by illness, futurism tries to revitalize the undermined virility of First World War veterans. Both movements end with rejecting traditionally codified gender normativity, questioning the commonly accepted divisions between femininity and masculinity, and between the roles of *mater* and *pater familias*. Nevertheless, this gender redefinition finds its impasse in the inability to portray a positive role for women outside a farcical mimicking of male virility.

Can women have their own gender, cultural, and (pro)creative identity in the avant-garde transgressive world? This issue surprisingly remains unresolved also in the progressive works of futurist female writers, including Valentine de Saint-Point's "Manifesto of Futurist Woman" (1912) and the contributions published in the journal *L'Italia futurista*, between 1916 and 1918.

Overall, futurist women, including Maria Ginanni, Rosa Rosà, and Enif Robert, contributed in affirming female agency and reshaping the notions of gender, female beauty, and acceptable social behaviours. Their redefinition of femininity found an especially suitable context during the First World War, when many Italian women enjoyed for the first time the opportunity to work outside the home, earn a salary, and feel independent from institutionalized male control.[2] From a cultural perspective, their reflection on gender is pivotal in reassessing the ambiguous stance of futurist misogyny. Marinetti, while attacking the countless faults of average women, praised the exceptional work of his female fellow artists and encouraged their literary endeavours. For example, he co-authored the book *Ventre di donna. Romanzo chirurgico* [*A Woman's Womb: A Surgical Novel*] (1919) with Robert. Furthermore, as Lucia Re highlights, Ginanni's "'brain' as well as her authoritativeness in literary and political matters became one of the … recurrent themes" of *L'Italia futurista*.[3] Marinetti described Ginanni's unique brain as "la più grande miniera di radio" ["the biggest mine of radium"].[4] In an article published in the journal, on 4 March 1917, she is celebrated by Emilio Settimelli as "prima grande scrittrice italiana" ["first great Italian woman writer"] able to express "tutta la genialità, la bellezza, la poesia, l'ardore della divina donna italiana" ["all the geniality, beauty, poetry, ardor of the divine Italian woman"]. Settimelli equally emphasized Ginanni's talent in his preface to *Montagne trasparenti* [*Transparent Mountains*] (1917).

However, if these women were at the forefront of their time, they also seem to have fallen into the contradiction of a "feminism of uncritical equality," which is typical of a first-wave feminism that is mainly concerned with achieving equal rights for women.[5] They were very innovative in portraying gender as a spectrum rather than as a strict binary and in endorsing a message of sexual liberation. Yet, in many cases, their groundbreaking notion of gender aligned with an undifferentiated model, based on virility, pro-war propaganda, and the overcoming of an (allegedly weak) female nature. As Stacy Alaimo explains in *Undomesticated Ground* (2000), one of the problems that feminist movements have faced throughout history has indeed been to recast a more balanced view of the association between women and nature, avoiding the two extremes of denying women's participation in nature and asserting an essentialist connection between female nurturing function and Mother Earth.[6] In the writings of feminist women, female nature is often superseded through an empowering cerebralism, or is counterpoised to the liberating achievement of male lifestyle and culture. Adopting an ecofeminist perspective, we can then see that, while futurist women authors worked to erase the male-female dualism, they still endorsed the divide between an inferior feminized nature, which debases both men and women, and a superior futurist culture of virility and rapid modernization that can rescue the whole of humankind.

Beyond the discourse on gender, female identity is problematic for futurism and crepuscularism because both movements fuel homoerotic fantasies that seek to obliterate women's biological – and metaphorically cultural – potential and creative difference. While Marinetti, in *Mafarka il futurista* [*Mafarka the Futurist*] (1909), portrays the dream of generating a son without female mediation, crepuscular authors obsessively explore the image of the aborted fetus or the possibility of a "chaste creativity" that bypasses the (pro)creative function of women. The natural inventiveness that inhabits women's bodies is revealed to be a threat to the autonomy and uniqueness of male genius.

From a broader socio-literary perspective, the crepuscular and futurist mutant and gender-fluid bodies succeed in overthrowing the Promethean model of the bourgeois hero. The odd characters that the two movements depict stand out for a distinctive skill: their "gift of fire," a symbol of ironic resilience amidst the chaos of life.

By exploring human bodies as mutant and bizarre machines hosting a number of poetic personae, conflicting gender identities, and troubled social roles, we will examine how crepuscularism and futurism problematize the modern mechanistic notion of the body and foster alternative embodied narratives.

Overcoming the "Flesh-and-Soul" Individual

The characterization of nineteenth-century fictional personae, especially in historical and bildungsroman novels, relies on a tacit agreement between authors and audience: based on a process of identification, the bourgeois reader is willing to develop either an antithetic or a sympathetic relationship with the narrated personae. The reader's horizon of expectations thus hinges on an automatic response that identifies a human or humanized character with a corporeal entity endowed with psychological traits – which is to say, endowed with a soul.

Crepuscular works cautiously begin eroding this assumption, adopting borderline poetic personae who do not fit with readers' expectations for identification. In the poem "La pietà" ["The Pity"], Vallini portrays the human as a scrap of matter that serendipitously comes to life, albeit lost and unaware. Reworking the myth of Genesis, the poet depicts the first man as the dumb Man-Misery:

L'uomo era un po' di materia
che nulla vedeva e sentiva:
un soffio improvviso l'avviva
ed eccoti l'Uomo Miseria:
s'abbranca – il perché non lo sa –
a un lembo rotondo d'ignoto,
e via che parte nel vuoto
a tutta velocità:
il tempo di dire: – Son qui –
senza capir ciò che dice
e di gridar ch'è infelice …
poi, zitto. Tutto finì. (*UG* 52)

[Man was a little bit of matter
that saw and felt nothing:
a sudden breath vivifies him
and here you have Man-Misery:
he clings – doesn't know why –
to a round hem of unknown,
and there he goes in the void
at great speed:
the time of saying: – I'm here –
without understanding what he's saying
and of screaming that he's unhappy …
then, silent. Everything ended.]

In Vallini's myth, embodied subjectivity is a random occurrence that this miserable new Adam passively receives, while being thrown into the world. Subjectivity – the voice of the "I" and the material corporeality that hosts it – transforms from a solid given into a random accident, as expressed in the puzzled "I'm here" of Man-Misery.

Rethinking the category of embodied subjectivity as an abrupt result of serendipity involves questioning the relation between body and selfhood. What if, because of an accident similar to that which occurred to Man-Misery, a number of "I's" came to reside in the same flesh? Or what if that flesh contained "I's" and non-"I's" in equal parts? Palazzeschi's "Il pappagallo" ["The Parrot"] can be read as an exploration of these inquiries in a purposely aseptic and impersonal fairy-tale setting. This text was originally published in the collection *I cavalli bianchi* [*The White Horses*] in 1905. At the time, Palazzeschi was very close to the Roman crepuscular circle, but also ready to move away from Corazzini's style and explore themes – such as the disappearance of the "I" – that would become central for the futurist avant-garde. The poem portrays a parrot that is atypically silent: a cryptic animal-totem, stared at by the people passing by. The bird embodies the unexplored possibility of a corporeal identity, one that is traceable outside the coordinates of the modern *animal rationale* that is gifted with language. The enchanted parrot roosts on a window, keeping watch for a century, quietly contemplating a life that is displayed before his eyes:

> Su quella finestra egli sta da cent'anni
> guardando passare la gente.
> Non parla e non canta.
> La gente passando si ferma a guardarlo,
> si ferma a chiamarlo,
> si ferma parlando fischiando cantando:
> ei guarda tacendo. (*TTP* 13)
>
> [On that window, he has been for one hundred years
> looking at the people passing by.
> He does not speak and does not sing.
> The people passing by stop to look at him,
> stop to call him,
> stop and speak, whistle, sing:
> he looks on in silence.]

The parrot and the crowd emerge from a desert of selfhood: the immobile animal-spectator observes the anonymous pedestrians, while himself being looked at as a senseless attraction without a name. In Palazzeschi's enchanted void, the marvellous, speechless animal and the undefined horde of quiet human figures are body-subjects that sabotage the cult of individuality – the cult of the "I" – that bourgeois culture has fostered. The identities that the poem delineates seem to come together from a clumping of grey amorphousness; they develop not as speaking "I's" but as collective embodiments of silent negativity.

Characterization within crepuscularism and the futurist avant-garde offers an early twentieth-century perspective on topics that remain controversial even today, such as to what extent personal identity is derived from biological individuality, and where the dividing line might be between the substantial individual (the "person") and the functional individual (a biological and physiological entity), or between the flesh-and-blood individual and its electronic avatar. If identity can emerge even from an undefined, shared subjectivity – Palazzeschi's grey crowd – or from a sphinx-parrot, then identity must not reside exclusively in the "flesh-and-soul individual." As Walter Benjamin argues in his reflection on the concept of crowd, in modern times, subjectivity can even be displaced in "the man of the crowd,"[7] in the material impersonality that people typify, or in the interactions between the individual and the blurry contour of Vallini's "quel mare / vivente detto folla" ["that living sea / called crowd"] (*UG* 44). In the words of Marinetti, subjectivity becomes an artificial "add-on feature" injected into laboratory creations. Announcing the possibility of giving life to mechanical humanoids, the futurist founder proudly declares,

> Dopo il regno animale, ecco iniziarsi il regno meccanico. Con la conoscenza e l'amicizia della materia, della quale gli scienziati non possono conoscere che le reazioni fisico-chimiche, noi prepariamo la creazione dell'**uomo meccanico dalle parti cambiabili**. Noi lo libereremo dall'idea della morte, e quindi dalla morte stessa, suprema definizione dell'intelligenza logica. (*TIF* 54)

> [After the reign of the animal, behold the beginning of the reign of the machine. Through growing familiarity and friendship with matter, which scientists can know only in its physical and chemical reactions, we are preparing the creation of the **mechanical man with interchangeable parts.** We will liberate man from the idea of death, and hence from death itself, the supreme definition of the logical mind.] (*F* 124–5)

Futurist post-humanity, an imbricated, living matter that overcomes the physical and logical limitations of *homo sapiens*, locates itself beyond the realm of the speaking "body-I." Through its proto-cyborgs, futurism approaches questions of identity from a new perspective: a persona is the embodiment of a broad and loose corporeal territory, one that is individually recognizable but also merged into an invisible network of embodied relations, which can easily trespass into the animal and techno-mechanical realms. The innovative "ethico-aesthetic paradigm" of futurism can be interpreted as a precursor to Félix Guattari's view of assembled subjectivity. In his investigation, he highlighted how human "Subjectivity does not only produce itself through the psychogenetic stages of psychoanalysis or the 'mathemes' of the Unconscious, but also in the large-scale social machines of language and the mass-media – which cannot be described as human."[8] In its embodiment, the futurist proto-cyborg proves to be the bio-product of a collective process of natural and artificial evolution.

The cyborg, a hybrid of the animal and mechanical kingdoms, challenges the common assumption that subjectivity can be solely identified with the notion of human embodiment. The issue becomes where to locate humanity once the bodily space of the enabled *animal rationale* has proven to be too tight-fitting. As Maria Ginanni explains, the question is indeed very broad: yes, we talk about humanity all the time, but "noi che cosa siamo? Ci conosciamo?" ["what are we? Do we know ourselves"], and, above all, "Chi conosce le radici del nostro senso di umanità?" ["Who knows the roots of our sense of humanity?"].[9] The Italian avant-garde, embracing a much wider category of humanity than the nineteenth-century tradition, investigates unexplored dimensions of our human experience, such as the fluid conditions of the shared body-subject and of the mutant body.

In parallel ways, crepuscular and futurist works represent what Guattari would define as "schizoanalytic modelisation, [namely] … a machinics of existence whose object is not circumscribed within fixed, extrinsic coordinates; and this object can, at any moment, extend beyond itself, proliferate or abolish itself with the Universes of alterity with which it is compossible."[10] For example, in Ginanni's literary works, subjectivity becomes an embodied yet mobile category: subjectivity is the open possibility of maintaining the same flesh while becoming somebody different. According to the Azure Patrol writer, retaining a unique embodied "I" is impossible, as the body is a space inhabited by a number of clandestine personalities:

> c'è sempre dentro noi un estraneo che si muove e si agita per proprio conto, sentiamo il tormento del nostro "Io" sottoposto alle mosse sbilenche e rovescianti d'un "altro."[11]
>
> [There is always, inside us, a stranger who moves and agitates on his own; we feel the torment of our "I" subjected to the lopsided and overthrowing moves of "Another."]

Ginanni's view of subjectivity as the jouncing and clashing of many identities all aboard the same flesh is similarly stated in a letter written by Gozzano to Giulio De Frenzi. The poet writes that the process of gradual decay that affects his body has inspired him with a new type of poetry, infused with a Socratic serenity – the poetry of the one who "si sente svanire a poco a poco, serenamente, e sente il suo io diventare *gli altri*" ["feels himself vanishing little by little, peacefully, and feels his 'I' becoming *the others*"].[12] The idea of the body as pure potential for an infinite process of transformation and proliferation into otherness is enunciated by Prince Zarlino in Palazzeschi's novel *Il codice di Perelà*

[*Perelà's Code*] (1911).[13] This eccentric character, who speaks the voice of madness for the sake of madness, has overcome the idea of being "something" for good. The prince continuously morphs from human to nonhuman identities, experiencing the endless possibilities of nomadic becoming that his body offers:

> Mi piace di spogliarmi nudo innanzi a tutti, poi sono re, sono fabbro, sono ragno, sono tavola, sono il sole, sono la luna sono tutto quello che mi fa piacere. Una notte io fui cometa … e mi sentii veramente cometa, io non fui più uomo, nulla, io fui astro …
>
> Raccolsi tanto di sensazioni che sono nella mia mente come un poema che si intitola: La Cometa.[14]

> [I like to get undressed until bare naked, in front of everybody; then I am king, I am blacksmith, I am spider, I am table, I am the sun, I am the moon, I am everything that pleases me. One night I was a comet … and I felt I really was a comet, I was no longer a man, not at all, I was a celestial body … I collected so many sensations that are stored in my mind as a poem entitled: The Comet.]

Expressing the concept of the body as a "potentially everything," the prince's bold statement seems incompatible with the definition of bodily consciousness as a set of properties that allows an individual to have subjective awareness about his or her surroundings and self-reflecting awareness about self-consciousness.[15] Zarlino nullifies any idea of surroundings or boundaries, achieving a completely absorbing and metamorphic corporeal experience. The chameleonic vitalism of Palazzeschi's prince seems to provide an alternative to the problem that George Bataille poses in his aphoristic affirmation: "man is only man: to be nothing but man, not to emerge from this – is suffocation, burdensome ignorance, the intolerable."[16] What is intolerable for Zarlino is precisely a static existence attached to the same suffocating flesh. This intolerance of subjectivity also appears in Gozzano's poem "Ah! Difettivi sillogismi!" ["Ah! Defective Syllogisms"], in which the Turinese author expresses his terror at thinking of a life trapped within the asphyxiating cage of the "I": "Come pensare senz'abbrividire / tutta l'eternità chiusa nell'io / in questo angusto carcere terreno? ["How to think without shivering / all eternity closes within the I / in this narrow terrestrial prison?"] (*TP* 319). Escaping this eternal imprisonment implies the acknowledgment of a faulty reasoning: the "I" is simultaneously a subject of knowledge and its self-mirroring object. The "I" reflects the "me," perpetuating an elusive game of mirrors:

> Ohimè! L'essenza che rivibra in noi
> non può per intelletto esser compresa

da poi che l'io solo con se stesso,
soggetto, oggetto della conoscenza,
come uno specchio vano si moltiplica
inutilmente ed infinitamente
e nel riflesso è prigioniero il raggio
di verità che l'occhio non discerne. (*TP* 320)

[Dear me! The essence that reverberates in us
cannot be understood through the intellect
as the I alone with himself,
subject, object of knowledge,
like a vain mirror multiplies
uselessly and infinitely
and in the reflection the ray
of truth that the eye does not discern is imprisoned.]

The only possible way to avoid Gozzano's labyrinth of reflections is a radical one: to free subjectivity from the cage of the individual "I." Futurist writer Irma Valeria dreams of an escape into interstellar space, an escape that could only succeed by eroding the traditional link between body and soul. In *Morbidezze in agguato* [*Softnesses in Ambush*] (1917), she affirms:

> Io voglio questo: questa diabolica logica cosa, che tutti chiameranno assurdità o pazzia; che la mia stessa anima roda lentamente, segretamente, con tragica volontà, i ferri della sua arrugginita prigione, ed evada in silenzio nei liberissimi spazi interstellari, preparati dalla sua attesa magnetica.[17]
>
> [I want this: this diabolical, logical thing, which everyone will call absurdity or foolishness; that my own soul would erode slowly, secretly, with tragic will, the iron bars of its rusty prison, and evade in silence in the very free interstellar spaces, prepared by its magnetic waiting.]

The painter Arnaldo Ginna also engages with the possibility of escaping the self. Through his pioneering abstract art, he communicates a vision or an intuitive perception that can only be accessed in a state of detachment from conscious subjectivity. His work *Occhi sul mondo* [*Eyes on the World*] (1911) represents this alternative form of interaction with the world: a large, disembodied eye in the centre of the canvas, rays shining from its eyelashes and intersecting with sea and sky. The iconography of the single eye – the so called "Occhio-Mente" ["Eye-Mind"] or the eye of the angel – was adopted by esoteric circles to symbolize a clairvoyant vision that could see through and beyond human reality, permeating the invisible.[18] The notion of a permeable, porous "body-soul" embraces, in Ginanni's works, the possibility of turning the corporeal dimension into an impalpable powder or evanescent breath: "Il mio corpo si è totalmente trasformato in respiro" ["My body has totally turned into breath"], she writes in *Montagne trasparenti* (*MT* 115). Her statement brings to mind a letter of Corazzini to Giuseppe Caruso, in which the Roman poet comments on the spiritualization of his flesh: "Io credo essere divenuto anima" ["I believe I have become soul"] (*O* 292). The idea of dematerializing the body-subject, while keeping the impalpable trace of its essence, finds a more ironic adoption in Palazzeschi's characterization of the man of smoke, the protagonist of *Il codice di Perelà*. This unconventional "man" has an inconsistent body; he is made of a pile of smoke that accumulated in a chimney: "– Fui ammassato e composto da quella spira di fumo, cellula per cellula, come le pietre di un edifizio?" ["– Was I amassed and composed by that spiral of smoke, cell after cell, like the stones of a building?"], he asks, still in disbelief.[19]

Perelà is a "divine" incarnation, gravitationally incompatible with terrestrial life; but he is still something, he is at least smoke. The ultimate step in the disassembling of the flesh-and-soul corporeal entity is its translation into a numerical formula. The "I" can be equated to zero: this is what the Sicilian dada-futurist Alfio Berretta proves through his *Autoequazione* [*Autoequation*] (1916). Berretta's "logical hall of mirrors," as Jeffrey Schnapp defines it, dematerializes the human persona through mathematical language, demonstrating that "the square root of the square root of I whose kinetic energy is multiplied thanks to an erotic triangle involving a *him* on the bottom of a *her* on top equivalent to zero … is *zero*."[20] Berretta's equation does not simply exhaust itself in a logical inconsistency; by adopting mathematical language to invalidate any rational explanation of the "I," Berretta playfully shows how any univocal definition of human selfhood – even the most scientific one – ends with being illusory. His equation-joke proves solely that "the question of the 'I'" is destined to echo unresolved. This is indeed the only "truth" that Marino Moretti gains from his investigation of the question "Chi sei? Chi sono?" ["Who are you? Who am I?"]:

> … *chi sei*?
>
> …
>
> ma quando ascolto il suono
> tristissimo al cuore mio
> solo e tremante anch'io,
> dico e ridico: *chi sono*? (*TLP* 25)

[who are you?
...
but when I listen to the sound
very sad to my heart
lonely and trembling
I say and resay too: who am I?]

If the "I" proves to be undefinable – an impalpable echo, a zero, a volatile piece of scrap, an airy breath – poets can only strive to express subjectivity in negative terms, as a "fulfilling deprivation." Being can thus mean a loss of individual consciousness and embodiment. From this perspective of primal lack, the act of existing falls back into the indistinct dimension of the "Es spricht" ["It speaks"] – in Michel de Certeau's words, the locus in which a "non-subject (stranger to all individual subjectivity) demystifies consciousness, its clear surface muddied by the stirred waters of the deeps."[21] This oxymoronic motif of liberation of the individual subject into the depth of the non-subject springs up vividly in the image of the fetus in Moretti's "Il ricordo più lontano" ["The Furthest Memory"]. The poem portrays developing cells as the unwilling aggregation of a much-awaited unknown, one who (or that?) speaks in first person:

io mi formavo senza una parola
della mia stessa arcana volontà,
ero come la docile bestiola
che nulla teme e nulla cerca e sa. (*TLP* 103–4)

[I was developing without a word
of my own arcane will,
I was like a docile beast
that fears nothing and searches for and knows nothing.]

In crepuscular poetry, the status of fetal life, with its peculiar indistinctness – an "I" enclosed within the maternal uterus – expresses the ontological privilege of a participative being that stops with the emergence from the "carne che dolora" ["flesh in pain"] (*TLP* 104). The fetus is the point at which life does not fully know human individuality and subjectivity. Moretti's little beast that neither fears nor knows anything can live the inclusive dimension of existing inside "the other."

Futurism, moving further, rejects the stuffy notion of bourgeois subjectivity by denying even its gestation and birth. Palazzeschi's man of smoke comes from a "utero nero" ["black uterus]" that, while recalling the feminine organ, actually denotes the dark chimney that expelled the mass of smoke that is Perelà. The fantasy of an extra-uterine birth finds its futurist archetype in Marinetti's *Mafarka il futurista*,[22] a novel that tells the story of a genetic experiment that triggers "a technological shock against the old syntax of the bourgeois subject – its culture, experience, and sense."[23] In it, an African Doctor Frankenstein, King Mafarka, artificially gives life to his son, Gazurmah, bypassing the need for the feminine reproductive organs. Mafarka's son, a flying creature with metallic wings, is a mechanical beast whose unique body transgresses human and natural boundaries at once. Gazurmah seems to fill the abyss that Nietzsche describes in his definition of mankind: "a rope fastened between animal and overman – rope over an abyss."[24] To cross this chasm, Mafarka designs a cyborg-chimera that, while maintaining an anthropomorphic semblance, has violently distorted the physical and moral profile of the bourgeois "flesh-and-soul hero": soon after his creation, this over-human creature kills his father and flies away unscathed. Now, more than a century later, *Mafarka il futurista* reads as a parable on the sinister allure of bio-technological advancement and genetic modification. Mafarka's fatal experimentation leaves open the question of the delicate balance between the need to respect bodily boundaries and the possibility of crossing them. What is the human willing to sacrifice to trespass its own limits? This is the thorny issue that the novel poses even today, presenting Mafarka's ultimate achievement – the overcoming of procreative laws and bodily limitations at once – as a suicide.

The transgressive body of the cyborg finds a more ludic adoption in the artist Fortunato Depero's theatrical world of automatic cyber-puppets. The futurist artist transposes the theme of mechanical humanity in a robotic circus of cloned dancing marionettes, affirming that the highest artistic expression is the creation of "l'essere vivente artificiale" ["the artificial living being"]:

> CONGEGNO GRANDIOSAMENTE GENIALE VIVENTE NELLO SPAZIO
> VITALISSIMA FUSIONE
> **ARTE + SCIENZA**
> pirotecnica varia improvvisa trucchi meccanici fisici chimici RUMOREGGIATORI ESSERI AUTOMATICAMENTE GRIIIDANTI DANZANTI COMICAMENTE TRASFORMANTISI.[25]
>
> [GRANDIOSELY BRILLIANT DEVICE LIVING IN THE SPACE
> VERY VITAL FUSION
> **ART+SCIENCE**
> Various sudden pyrotechnic physical chemical mechanical tricks NOISEMAKER BEINGS SCREEEAMING AUTOMATICALLY DANCING COMICALLY TRANSFORMING.]

Depero's dancing automatons are a divertissement, a humorous take on what Marinetti claims in the manifesto "Noi rinneghiamo i nostri maestri simbolisti" ["We Abjure Our Symbolist Masters"], namely,

> Con noi comincia il regno dell'uomo dalle radici tagliate, dell'uomo moltiplicato che si mescola col ferro, si nutre di elettricità e non comprende più altro che la voluttà del pericolo e l'eroismo quotidiano. (*TIF* 304)
>
> [With us [futurists] begins the reign of the man whose roots are cut, the multiplied man who merges himself with iron, is fed by electricity, and no longer understands anything except the sensual delight of danger and quotidian heroism.] (*F* 94)

Once humanity's roots have been severed, bodies can finally adjust to the "biorhythm" of speed. "La pittura futurista. Manifesto tecnico" (1910) describes this new state of things:

> I nostri corpi entrano nei divani su cui ci sediamo, e i divani entrano in noi, così come il tram che passa entra nelle case, le quali a loro volta si scaraventano sul tram e con ess[o] si amalgamano. (*MDF* 31)
>
> [Our bodies penetrate the sofas upon which we sit, and the sofas penetrate our bodies, just as the tram rushes into the houses which it passes, and in their turn the houses throw themselves upon the tram and are merged with it.] (*F* 65).

In the "Manifesto tecnico della scultura futurista" ["Manifesto of Futurist Sculpture"] (1912), Umberto Boccioni proposes something similar:

> Rovesciamo tutto, dunque, e proclamiamo l'**assoluta e completa abolizione della linea finita e della statua chiusa. Spalanchiamo la figura e chiudiamo in essa l'ambiente**. (*MDF* 55)
>
> [Let's turn everything upside down and proclaim the **absolute and complete abolition of finite lines and the self-contained statue. Let's open up the figure and let it enclose the environment**.] (*F* 117).

The futurist body comes to include its surroundings, and vice versa, through the creation of an "object-environment." From this perspective of bodily participation, which denies any hierarchical tree-model, futurism defines its avant-garde body type as a plastic entity that elastically expands or retracts to retrace "l'io integrale cantato, dipinto, scolpito indefinitamente nel suo perpetuo divenire"

["The whole 'I' sung, painted, and sculpted indefinitely in perpetual becoming"] (*TIF* 305, *F* 95).

Branching out to mingle with life, the body performs a perpetual and immersive "vertigine della vita" ["vertigo of life"], transforming itself into a vortex of perfume and light; as futurist writer Fanny Dini writes in her lyric prose "Danzatrice" ["Female Dancer"] (1917), the tensions of such an exhaustive dance have penetrated her very flesh: "M'è nella carne la vertigine d'ogni profumo: nell'anima la febbre d'ogni follia" ["in my flesh is the vertigo of any perfume: in my soul, the fever of any foolishness"] (*SF* 265–6). Crepuscularism and futurism, casting doubt on the possibility of attaching subjectivity to a unique body-soul individual, invite us to explore a new corporeal "dancing frontier," borderline human subjectivity: in Vallini's words, the possibility of "esser l'uomo scomposto nella materia; / non essere più l'universo / nell'universo, ma un fiato / imponderabile, un atomo / labile in aria disperso" ["being the man disassembled in matter / no longer being the universe, / in the universe, but a weightless / breath, a labile / atom dispersed in the air"] (*UG* 34).

Sick, Deformed, Masked Bodies

The crepuscular and futurist propositions of anti-traditional corporeal dimensions provide the basis for new bodily aesthetics. Both movements disregard harmonic bodies as meaningless simulacra from the past – one may think of Gozzano's anachronistic statues of gods and heroes on the decrepit façade of Villa Amarena or Marinetti's static Victories of Samothrace, which "un automobile ruggente" ["a roaring automobile"] surpasses in beauty (*TIF* 10, *F* 51). Challenging the canonical aesthetic paradigm, crepuscularism and futurism develop a magnetic attraction for abnormal corporeality in all its shades: illness, physical deformities, mutilations, and other extraordinary features. Yet, this iconoclastic aesthetics does not exhaust its verve in the definition of an anti-canon. The poetics of the sick and the deformed fosters a pre-modern connection between suffering flesh and redemption; moreover, the emphasis on the abnormal plays a central role in unmasking the mechanisms through which bourgeois subjectivity develops.

In crepuscular poetics, malady is much more than an (anti-)aesthetic "device."[26] As Moretti shamelessly admitted later in his career, malady provided a unifying identity for both the sick and healthy members of the crepuscular group: "Ma sì, confessiamolo che siamo stati tutti malati, dolcissimamente malati, malati, come si conviene, di 'non si sa bene che cosa'" ["But, let's confess that we were all sick, very sweetly sick, sick, conveniently sick, from 'what one does not really know'"].[27] The idea of sharing a distinctive twentieth-century plague becomes a fundamental tool of poetic self-awareness and an attack on the modern biopolitics of psychophysical and socio-cultural normativity. The eugenic conflict between normalcy and divergence generated a broad debate in the late nineteenth century, especially after the publication of Max Nordau's *Degeneration* (1892), in which the physician discussed, among other themes, the pathological effects of degenerated art on the social body. In response to this "manifesto" of corporeal and intellectual prophylaxis, malady presented itself as a form of collective subjectivity that offered an alternative to the modern cult for healthiness. As in archaic rituals, in the crepuscular pre-modern world, sickness and physical pain potentiate the body even while consuming it.

Sick bodies acquire the potentiated corporeal cognition of those who live at the threshold of terrestrial life, wherein the body experiences a status of porousness, being fully alive and yet soaked in the eternal mystery of death. In Corazzini's works, sick flesh becomes the frontier between the spiritual wish to die and a primal instinct for preservation. In the poem "Toblack," named for a sanatorium in northern Italy, the infirm residents of this twentieth-century city of Dis are besieged by death and yet still, illogically, dying to survive. As Corazzini writes, Toblack is a place wherein "tiene i lividi tuoi tubercolosi / un desiderio di convalescenza" ["a desire for convalescence, / holds your livid tuberculars"] (*O* 124). The ambiguous coexistence of life and death within the sick body is a theme that also appears in Corazzini's letters. Emulating the human weakness of Christ at Calvary, the poet plays at joining the desire to die – "Io penso ogni giorno a morire" ["I think every day about dying"] (*O* 296) – with his will to be spared. Writing to Palazzeschi, he admits: "Se resisterò ti dirò quello che sto soffrendo … Perché, non vorrei morire, ancora …" ["If I survive, I will tell you what I am suffering … Because I wouldn't want to die, yet …"] (*O* 299).

Like Corazzini, Gozzano also expresses the conflicted status of illness as the estranged experience of inhabiting his own flesh in pain. In "Alle soglie" ["At the Thresholds"], the poetic voice laughs at the therapeutic persistence of the doctors who have deprived him of any remaining pleasure: no more smoking, sex, or writing in the dead of night. He wonders about the purpose of all these visits and treatments, if the only outcome seems to be paying medical bills for having his body violated. Gozzano describes the invasive X-ray screening – the first such description in poetry – specifically highlighting the abuse performed on his ravaged chest:

> Un fluido investe il torace, frugando il men peggio e il peggiore,
> trascorre, e senza dolore disegna su sfondo di brace
> e l'ossa e gli organi grami, al modo che un lampo nel fosco
> disegna il profilo d'un bosco, coi minimi intrichi dei rami.
> E vedon chi sa quali tarli i vecchi saputi … A che scopo?
> Sorriderei quasi, se dopo non fosse mestiere pagarli.

[Through my thorax a fluid unrolls, through the less malign and the malign,
without sorrow it starts to design on a background of hot glowing coals
all the pitiful organs, the bones, lightning across a dark night
outlining a forest with tight tiny branches and twigs overgrown.
The old know-it-alls watch the playing of who knows what worms in their traces.
And for what? I could laugh in their faces, if not for the bill I'll be paying.] (*TM* 44–5)

Gozzano's insistence on bodily violation exemplifies how crepuscular poetry represents self-perception as a withstanding of such a violation. The poetic persona feels itself to be a body-in-pain, because s/he embodies the perception of occupying (and thus *being*) a space under siege – a peculiar network of conflicting encounters in which the human body expands to incorporate bacteria, healthy and sick cells, the scrutinizing eyes of doctors, chemical substances, and the pervasive radiations of X-rays.

The intertwined theme of malady and corporal siege migrates to futurism, becoming the leitmotif of the chapter "Il the" ["The Tea"] in Palazzeschi's *Il codice di Perelà*. In this section, the man of smoke meets the ladies of the court for tea, and during the meeting, each woman tells him a private story. Physical abuse and sexual nonconformity constitute the common thread of this series of nestled narratives: Countess Cloe is a nymphomaniac, Lady Giacomina has been repudiated because of a deformity of her feminine organs, Countess Rosa must observe her marital duties after being forced to leave a convent, Baroness Gelasia has to spend her youth having sex with an old and repulsive husband, Princess Bianca has caused the death of her sick beloved during their only sexual encounter, and, finally, the violinist of the court hints at her lesbian liaison with an actress. Interpreted in Foucaldian terms, Palazzeschi's rakish harem of "respectable ladies" shows the extent of the proliferation of the discourse about "sick" sex, under the guise of its repression. The women, channelling their desire through the restrictive code, turn sexual taboos into perverse voyeurism, and turn Perelà into the improvised confessor of their profane "confessions of the flesh." Under the pretence of needing to avoid any "healthy" bodily urges, the group explores an *ars erotica* of sexual pathologies and marvellous events, narrated in a feuilleton style, as in this description by Countess Carmen:

Un'aspettativa bestiale, feroce, di dieci anni, una lacerazione lunga, interminabile, occulta di tutto il mio spirito, che si chiuse all'ultimo grido di dolore alla lacerazione della mia carne, col disgusto supremo di tutti i miei sensi.[28]

[A bestial, ferocious expectation of ten years, a long, endless, occult laceration of my whole spirit, which closed itself to the last scream of pain for the laceration of my flesh, with supreme repugnance of all my senses.]

The morbid atmosphere that pervades Perelà's tea reception seems to offer the ideal background for Rosa Rosà's "tavola paroliberista" ["table of words in freedom"] "Ricevimento-thé-signore-nessun uomo" ["Reception-Tea-Ladies-No Man"], a work that originally appeared in *L'Italia futurista* on 9 December 1917 (*SF* 167). The work reproduces a maze of tensions in a bourgeois parlour, wherein a group of ladies is enjoying an afternoon tea. Rosà's table traces a map of the parlour, developing chains of words that, like tentacles, reconstruct the material and emotional profiles of these mundane conversations: ugly family pictures on the walls, whispered phrases, dissimulated boredom, yawning, hostilities, and gluttony. Women's corporality is deformed into a "gynaeceum body" of small talk. This tentacular she-monster embodies the distorted perspective of a male-dominated society that has expelled women, segregating their silly conversations and whispered complaints against men – those "bestie puramente materiali" ["purely material beasts"]. As Mirella Bentivoglio argues, Rosà's futurist table condemns the social alienation of women, typical of the social rituals of the early twentieth-century Italian bourgeoisie.[29] The sentence placed near the parlour's exit door, "io mi pare che ne ho abbastanza" ["I, it seems to me, I had enough"], marks an alternative identity, highlighted with an asterisk and an arrow that points at the door. Through the "I" standing at the door, Rosà expresses the urge to leave a space wherein women disappear, tantalized by their own social isolation into such "gynaeceum body-subjects."

Enif Robert proposed a parallel reflection on the motif of the abnormal female body, adopting a strategy that is far more direct than Rosà's metaphor of women's "deformed" sociality. In the introduction to the novel *Ventre di donna. Romanzo chirurgico* [*A Woman's Womb: A Surgical Novel*] (1919), which she wrote with Marinetti, Robert criticizes both the sentimental languor of the "letteratura-fremito" ["literature-tremor"] and the snobbish spiritual attitude of the "Azure female writers." (*SF* 230–1). Her goal is rather to lay bare the true force of women's affirmation, exploring a reality that is neither pretty nor comforting.[30] In her work, Robert uses a realistic combination of diary and epistolary style to retell the psychosomatic drama of an autobiographical character, Enif, who suffers from an unknown disease. The novel pictures the female body as tortured flesh, a flesh that only when surgically martyred can attain a new symbolic value. Enif's woman's womb, cut apart and sewn together, brings the visible scar of an ideal female body that no longer exists: the ideal storybook identity has been rejected, along with the blood the protagonist lost during surgery. By reading Marinetti's healing letters, Enif gradually embraces the courage to react to her malady and develop a renewed attachment to life; this rediscovered participation in life is an out-and-out "embodiment" of futurist poetics. The avant-garde hybridism of life and art becomes a practice that

Marinetti-the-healer prescribes to his sick friend. As the founder of futurism explains, death is a lack of desire for life; "Bisogna dunque, per guarire, stringere dei nuovi legami con la vita, mediante forti nodi" ["Therefore, to heal, one needs to tighten new bonds with life, through strong knots"] (*SF* 239). Knotting her suffering flesh with her desire to be alive – to be among the things she desires – will symbiotically create a new "*massa di desiderio*" ["*mass of desire*"], namely a new healthy "massa di vita" ["mass of life"] (*SF* 241). Reconciled with her mutilated corporeality, Enif comes to equate her new bodily identity with the "therapeutic experimentalism" that has strengthened her body: being a futurist woman ultimately means to embody an "energetica cura di CORAGGIO + VERITÀ" ["energetic cure of courage and truth"] (*SF* 229).[31]

The anti-aesthetics of the repulsive, what Marinetti ultimately summarizes in his claim "**Facciamo coraggiosamente il 'brutto' in letteratura**" ["**Let us boldly make 'the ugly' in literature**"] (*TIF* 53, *F* 124), was not novel to the literary *Bohème* of the nineteenth century, from French *maudit* literature to the Italian Scapigliatura. Yet, for crepuscularism and futurism, unsightliness opens a richer reservoir of literary and artistic possibilities that reveals anagogical meanings – meanings that are open to a spiritual interpretation. Although crepuscularism does not openly declare an iconoclastic aesthetics of the ugly, its fascination with repulsiveness is noticeable. In mystical crepuscularism, physical aberration becomes a sign of redemption, marked on the suffering flesh, and the "abjection of self" turns "into the ultimate proof of humility before God."[32] Embracing the principle of redemptive debasement, Corazzini tailors a series of poetic counter-figures who achieve divine election through bodily defacement. The poetic reinvention of the motif of martyrdom harks back to a wide range of sources, spanning from the Gospels to Spanish female mystics of the sixteenth and seventeenth centuries, such as Saint Teresa of Avila and María de Ágreda. Adopting the topos of the mortification of flesh, the Roman poet ambiguously degrades his body to a disfigured object while also elevating it as the medium of a divinization attained through extreme suffering and violent ecstatic rapture. Furthermore, in his poetic adaptation, Corazzini plays a subtle game that intertwines the discourse of redemptive corporality in pain with the meta-literary discourse on his textual body, which suffers a "martyrdom" of misunderstanding and despair.

The dual narrative of the stigmatized body and the equally mistreated poetic *corpus* particularly emerges in Corazzini's last collection, *Libro per la sera della domenica*. In this testamentary book, the poet uses the biblical figure of the leper to highlight the irrational contiguity between the stigma of the flesh and spiritual beatitude, playing – at a meta-literary level – on the Gospel teaching that those who are last shall be first. Recalling Erich Auerbach's typological interpretation of the *Divine Comedy* in *Mimesis* (1946), we can see how the self-torturing little boy who wants to die in "Desolazione del povero poeta sentimentale" is a prefiguration of the later "piccolo vecchio lebbroso" ["little old leper"] of "Elemosina del sonno" ["Handout of Sleep"]. In Corazzini's last book, the repellent leper discloses the meaning of willing debasement in his revelatory dream: "Piccolo vecchio lebbroso / tu sogni … sogni / che ti hanno incoronato re dei re!" ["Little old leper you dream, / you dream … that they crowned you king of the kings!"] (*O* 161). The leper rises as condemned yet sacralized flesh, a contaminated corporeal materiality destined to greatness in the unworldly kingdom.

By insisting on the topic of corporeal torment – malady, crowns of thorns, hearts pierced with swords, bleeding, sweat, and tears – Corazzini creates a "spirituality *in* the flesh," as Robert Fuller defines this constitutive grounding of religion in human embodiment.[33] The corporeal mysticism that the Roman poet weaves into his poetry expresses the "embodied hope"[34] for salvation of his own "literary flesh," a textual corporality that Corazzini envisions as eternally alive, albeit residing in his liminal body. Through his mystic poetics of the flesh, the crepuscular poet translates in literary terms the paradox of eternal life that Caroline Walker Bynum illustrates, noticing that "there is a contradiction implicit in the idea that eternal (perduring) salvation is lodged in the historical (hence momentary) event of Calvary."[35] For Walker Bynum, the contradiction is even starker, when considered from the perspective of material flesh: "life, which can be understood only by analogy to the organic and thus changeable, must, if eternal, never undergo the change of generation and corruption that, however, defines it."[36] In a similar way, the literary "martyrdom" of crepuscularism resides in the self-contradiction of wanting to use malady as a transformative and corrosive poetic language of change, while wishing to deform the literary Body *ad aeternum* and make Corazzini a worshipped poetic Messiah.

The two polarities of deformation and eternal redemption – or retention – shape Gozzano's profane understanding of domestic beatitude, as well. In the provincial settings of the Turinese poet, "eternal" bliss can be found in the daily deformation of that which invisibly adapts yet never visibly changes. Advancing this wry hypothesis, Gozzano represents the average ugliness of his beloved Signorina Felicita [Felicity] as her "unique" beauty, her sole redeeming quality. This plain bourgeois lady allures the poet's persona with her naïve homeliness:

E rivedo la tua bocca vermiglia
così larga nel ridere e nel bere,
e il volto quadro, senza sopracciglia,

tutto sparso d'efelidi leggiere
e gli occhi fermi, l'iridi sincere
azzurre d'un azzurro di stoviglia …

[And I can see your bright red mouth again
(when you laughed or when you drank, how wide it grew),
your square face with no eyebrows and a thin
sprinkle of light freckles, and these two
bright steady eyes of yours, as pure and blue
as pots and dishes of blue porcelain …] (*TM* 72–3)

Felicita is the embodiment of everyday plainness; her own name, as Gozzano states in an earlier poem, "L'ipotesi" ["The Hypothesis"], "è come uno scrigno di cose semplici e buone, / … è come un lavacro benigno di canfora spigo sapone …" ["is like a trunk of simple and good things, / … is like a benign bath of camphor lavender soap …"] (*TP* 265).[37] This unpretentious young woman lives like a servant in her empty mansion, now that the old days of Villa Amarena are past and gone. The once exciting life of the villa has gradually descended into a dusty routine that covers objects and bodies with its thick layer of ordinariness. Felicita's physiognomy seems to mirror this process of deforming acquiescence: her face has the resigned yet comforting feeling of homey "stuff," and even her eyes are of an unsublime blue, blue like earthy flatware. This prosaic portrait is intriguing for its subtle caricature of the fantasized femininity that is proposed in literary and visual cultures. This Flemish-looking woman is a "domestic diva," who controverts both the sensual cinematographic imaginary of the *femme fatale* and the equally intriguing magnetism of women affected by mental illness, like Ugo Tarchetti's hysterical Fosca. By contrast, in her sound provincialism, Felicita offers an account of a "blessed" contagious destiny: she is a fallen *donna angelo*, secluded in the opiate atmosphere of her mansion.

An even more grotesque subversion of female beauty appears in Bruno Corra's eccentric novel, *Sam Dunn è morto* [*Sam Dunn Is Dead*] (1915). This futurist "romanzo sintentico" ["synthetic novel"] equates bodily abnormality with prodigious beatitude through the miraculous story of Peppona, the hostess of the Hotel Portorosa. Another bourgeois "diva by chance," she stands out solely for being an obese fool:

Essa aveva una grossa faccia da beduina scoppiante di salute, felicissima di essere completamente idiota e portava in giro con beata disinvoltura i suoi ottantaquattro chili di carne salda e sana.

> [Peppona … had the massive head of a peasant; she carried with serene confidence her 84 kilos of healthy, solid flesh, with her weight so well balanced and consistent that it was plain to see where she swelled or narrowed.][38]

Yet, this gigantic blob of flesh has been gifted with extraordinary healing powers in her enormous posterior, "la parte più autenticamente *mascotte* della padrona di casa" ["the most authentically *bewitching* part of the mistress of the house"].[39] Her staggering deformity becomes a hub of happiness and occult energy, and all the hotel guests seek to benefit from its thaumaturgic effects:

> Bastava sfiorare con la mano quella magica carnosità per sentirsi subito più leggeri e più ottimisti, bastava pizzicarla appena con due dita per guarire da qualunque malessere e non vi era *guigne* che non venisse istantaneamente dissipata da un buon colpo dato con la mano aperta.
>
> [It was enough to caress with one's hand that magical carnality to feel suddenly lighter, more optimistic, enough to pinch it between thumb and finger to be cured of any illness whatever, and there was no stroke of ill-luck that was not instantaneously destroyed by a good slap with the palm.][40]

Corra represents Peppona's blessed deformity as the hub of an irrational force – "frenesia pepponica" ["the *Pepponic* craze"][41] – that seizes the city of Paris for twelve whole hours, compelling the Parisians to pinch each other's posteriors. Corra's depiction of the magnetic quality of Peppona's deformity can lead to a comparison with another alluring female monstrosity: the degraded Coletta of Palazzeschi's poem "Comare Coletta." This old lady, who was once an admired dancer, is now a tattered monster:

> Ricurva, sciancata,
> provandosi ancora di reggere alla piroetta,
> s'aggira per fame la vecchia fangosa;
> trascina la logora veste pendente a brandelli,
> le cade a pennecchi di capo il capecchio
> fra il lazzo e le risa,
> la rabbia le serra la bocca
> di rughe ormai fossa bavosa. (*TTP* 440)
>
> [Round-shouldered, crippled,
> still trying to hold the pirouette,
> begs out of hunger, the muddy old lady;

drags around her filthy and shredded loose dress,
her shaggy hair falls in plumes from her head
among mocking and laughing,
the anger tightens her mouth
with wrinkles, by now a dribbling ditch.]

Although the sight of her is unpleasant, the passers-by cannot help but look at Coletta and assail her with insults. Her repulsive body emanates a deadly attraction: those offences and maledictions sound like the modern actualization of ancient apotropaic rites, betraying a visceral need to acknowledge the hag as a mythical primal goddess. Coletta keeps dancing in silence, as if she has sprung out of a pre-linguistic abyss – an unknown, infamous, wordless Hell. Through her unstoppable twirling, the "vecchiaccia d'inferno" ["hag from Hell"] guides people over the threshold of abjection to keep their puritan bourgeois bodies alive. This tempting attraction for degraded, consumed, or rotten flesh opens a digression on the cognitive experience that Palazzeschi's text triggers in its reader-spectators. The poem displays an intriguing "object of knowledge," Coletta, that, borrowing from Julia Kristeva, is neither an easily namable and imaginable "*ob-ject*," nor an "*ob-jest*," namely "an otherness ceaselessly fleeing in a systematic quest of desire."[42] Coletta embodies Kristeva's definition of "abject," something whose knowledge lies outside and beyond the cognitive "rules of the game," maintaining an unclassifiable and loathsome status of uncanniness.

Kristeva's notion of abject can lead us to consider Coletta as a scary body-threshold that ambiguously undermines yet also reinforces the modern division between human mind and monstrous bodily nature. The experience of abjection described by Kristeva entails physical and emotional repulsion, and this reaction is triggered by the threatening breakdown in meaning that a temporary loss of the distinction between subject and object or between self and other provokes. Thus, the liminal experience of the "abject" provides a unique occasion for self-recognition, acting as the catalyst that lets the bourgeois "I" assert its corporal entity, an identity acknowledged from that "border, the place where I am not and which permits me to be."[43] By staring at Coletta's monstrosity, bourgeois spectators artificially construct their (masks of) fixed subjectivity, in opposition to the threat that Coletta's uncontrollable dancing body represents.

If modern Western subjectivity is constructed in opposition to repulsive bodily matter, we can see how the hag is ultimately monstrous as she displays the fear of falling back into a pre-linguistic chaotic nature or an entropic Hell – Corra's Paris during the *Pepponic* craze – wherein social codes and respectable personae are meaningless. The character of Coletta recalls the figure of the witch and the social ban applied to this female character, able to summon spirits and connect with nature. As Carolyn Merchant contends, "From the perspective of the male, the witch was a symbol of disorder in nature and society, both of which must be brought under control … But from a female perspective, witchcraft represented a form of power by which oppressed lower-class women could retaliate against social injustice, and a source of healing through the use of spirits and the regenerative powers of nature."[44] By being positioned in the space of the abject and the socially threatening, Coletta symbolically "guards" a subject-object, or mind-body, threshold that modern culture cannot trespass to preserve its order.

Yet, how solid is this threshold? Beyond its social function in the formation of a "safe" and fixed bourgeois identity, the experience of abjection delimits a perturbing locus where subject-object borders are blurry and threatening changes are possible. Deformed and deforming bodies are the corporal arena of an ongoing process of metamorphosis, symbolized by Coletta's unstoppable dancing or the feeling of frenzy that subverts the order of Corra's Paris. The effect of this uncontrollable movement is the puzzling sensation that we can be aware only of our own process of becoming and constant displacement. The body, in its corporal spatiality, occupies a shaky territory of transformation, conflict, and even eviction. In crepuscular poetry, this conception emerges as a rewriting of the thirteenth- and fourteenth-century poetics of courtly love. In "Asfodeli" ["Asphodels"], Corazzini adapts a common medieval archetype, presenting his literary alter ego as a humble servant of Love, who offers his bleeding heart to a beloved lady. The topos of the merciless lady who disregards or devours the proffered heart is a recurrent image in courtly literature, and appears, for example, in the third chapter of *La vita nuova* [*The New Life*], in which Dante dreams of Beatrice eating his heart from out of the hands of Love. In Corazzini's rewriting of this topos, the graphic episode of anthropophagy is omitted in favour of an unexpected metamorphosis: as the lady rejects the heart, "Tutte le sue gocce rosse / caddero a terra, mute" ["all its red drops fell on the ground, silent"] (*O* 116) and magically turned into mourning flowers, the sad asphodels that give the poem its title. This story of metamorphosis embraces a pre-modern understanding of the human body as a dispossessed corporeal space, a locus of pathological dividedness and exposure to change, from which the "I" and its will have been virtually evicted.

The theme of abjection and its relation to an uncontrollable – yet deeply fascinating – process of bodily metamorphosis also appears in Gozzano's work, albeit in a very different context. In a scattered poem, alluding to his renowned passion for entomology, the poet defines himself as "l'amico delle crisalidi" ["the chrysalises' friend"], addressing a butterfly's larva – "quell'esserino / che non mi parla" ["that little being / that does not speak to me"] (*TP* 279). This chrysalis of a *Vanessa Atalanta* – a species of butterfly – rises as a body suspended, progressing towards a transformation, from caterpillar into chrysalis and ultimately into winged butterfly. The reflection on the peculiar transitional corporality that this insect embodies returns in the posthumous long poem *Le farfalle*, in which Gozzano lingers in his description of the life of a caterpillar. He frames this as the bodily possibility of "uscire di stessi" ["getting out of one selves"] to become "il novo mostro / inquietante ambigüo diverso / da ciò che fu da ciò che dovrà essere" ["the new monster / disquieting ambiguous different / from what it was and from what it will be"] (*TP* 459).

Gozzano is captivated by this "cosa rimorta" ["thing twice dead"], this "minuscolo drago" ["minuscule dragon"] that encloses in its metamorphic body a plurality of bodily identities: a potential butterfly, a natural "work of art," and the mask of a hunchbacked and horned satyr (*TP* 459). Throughout the process of becoming a butterfly, the chrysalis evolves as a stratification of dead bodies of the past and concealed identities of the future, all of which encounter each other in the corporeal temporality of the "non essere più, / del non essere ancora" ["no longer being, not being yet"] (*TP* 461). In its beautiful monstrosity, the chrysalis is the true, natural embodiment of what Zarlino, in Palazzeschi's novel *Il codice di Perelà*, dreams of: a body that lives suspended in the time of potential otherness.

The emphasis on reimagining the body as a territory of metamorphosis culminates in the futurist pulp vivisection of human corporeality into defunctionalized or re-functionalized parts. Organs without a body, fluids, drops, and excrement take on an independent life, expressing the subtle social threat of "matter out of place,"[45] of embarrassing residue that has escaped the bourgeois Pandora's box of respectability. In Marinetti's writing, the disassembly of the body fulfils a sadistic pleasure of violent breakage. A stronger fascination with the dismembered body, which subtly preannounces Mafarka's own end – "sprawled … like a damp cloth" (*MF* 197) – emerges in the chapter "Il ventre della balena" ["The Womb of the Whale"]. This episode of *Mafarka il futurista* presents a graphic description of extreme torture for the sake of macabre enjoyment. Marinetti pictures the torment that King Mafarka inflicts on his enemies as a means of affirming his own regal supremacy through their corporal suffering and annihilation. The victims, Gandakatale and Acacia, are thrown, still alive, into an aquarium to either drown or be devoured by famished sharks, while the king and his guests observe in amusement:

> Il più forte dei tre si accaniva contro Gandakatale, a cui addentò il ventre enorme, con tanta violenza che per un momento fu sommerso dall'erompere delle viscere …
>
> Aciaca seguì suo padre da vicino. Lo si vide stendersi su un fianco, affondando, con la bocca spalancata e con le gambe inghiottite dal secondo pescecane … il cranio di Aciaca si ruppe come un uovo contro il cristallo. (*M* 110–11)

> [The most powerful of the three [sharks] ripped into Gandakatale, savaging his huge belly so violently that for a moment it was submerged in a stream of intestines … Acacia followed close behind his father. They saw him lying sideways as he dived, his mouth wide open and with his legs swallowed by the second shark … Acacia's skull burst open like an egg against the glass.] (*MF* 98)

Here, engaging with Elaine Scarry's reflection on torture, we can see how in this passage torture acts on Mafarka's victims as an "annihilating negation":[46] the presence of physical pain, accentuated by the suffocating agency of water, monopolizes human language to the paradoxical point of creating a non-verbal language of pain. The sole overpowering "language" of the scene is the speechless body in the aquarium, torn apart by sharks. The bodies' skin barriers broken, they are penetrated fully by the external world – the water and the sharks – and, through their silent screams, exhibit the fragility of human life in its overwhelming encounter with the most animalistic, wordless creatures.

Unlike in Marinetti's works, in Ginanni's writing bodies abandon their organic functionality to explore mystical dimensions. Human limbs become elastic units that fluctuate outside the body-subject, in a universal space whose consciousness is outside the individual soul. Through a combination of futurist techno-language, corporeal images, and spiritual references, in *Montagne trasparenti*, the author describes the gap between the "corsa-locomotiva" ["run-locomotive"] of her soul, launched towards the infinite, and her own physical corporeality, anchored to earth (*MT* 52). To fill this physical gap, Ginanni can only imagine the possibilities for rearranging her bodily shape according to the restless activity of her brain. As she declares, retelling an experience of "disembodiment": "Stanotte la mia testa staccatasi dal mio corpo è restata per lunghe ore sul mio cuore agglomerando con le sue vertigini di pensiero universi innumerevoli" ["Tonight my head, detached from my body, remained for long hours on my heart, agglomerating countless universes with its vertigos of thought"] (*MT* 53).

The desire to go beyond the boundaries of the human can be attained not only by disassembling its traditional corporeal frame, but also by masking or camouflaging the body – another strategy to undermine the crystal-clear notion of "I-embodiment." Corazzini and Gozzano play with creating a number of characters who are very close to their own autobiographical profiles – from the many unhappy "fanciulli" ["boys"] of the Roman poet to Gozzano's fictional quasi-clones: the self-exiled Totò Merumeni; Paolo, the unhappy lover of "Paolo e Virginia"; the lawyer and "cold sophist" with whom Felicita falls in love; the veteran-gardener; and the "friend of the chrysalises." Yet, this over-exhibited role game belies the presence of fixed roles and social "ritual masks," revealing the inauthenticity of the identity models that modern society tries to impose. This mechanism of denunciation is very visible in Govoni's poems entitled "Il trio delle maschere moderne" ["Triptych of the Modern Masks"]. Three of the most traditional masks "unmask" themselves and reveal their actual roles in modern society: Pierrot is a tubercular man, Colombina a prostitute, and Arlecchino a beggar. Closing this grotesque carnival, in "La gran mascherata" ["The Big Masquerade"], Govoni describes an obscene carriage in which the divide between reality and masquerade is purposely blurred:

> Un carro che conducono degli uomoni truccati a buoi
> chiude il cortèo, pien di puttane che si scoprono le natiche
> da cui pendono tanti grappoli di cuori di cartone. (*P* 93)
>
> [A float led by men dressed up like bulls
> closes the parade, full of whores who reveal their posteriors
> from which many bunches of paper hearts hang down.]

This carriage that emblematically closes Govoni's parade questions the very possibility of ending the masquerade, once such debasement has been reached: what is at the end of this indecent collective carnival? Or better, is there an end to the masquerade, or is this *the* reality thrown at the moralist eyes that look at the parade behind their bourgeois masks?

The end of the masquerade is a metaphor that perfectly suits Mafarka's destiny. Like Govoni's degraded triptych, the futurist African king is nothing more than an exotic shell of a hero, who has been reduced to a puppet. Marinetti deforms, inflates, and exaggerates the classic hero-model to the breaking point. In the initial description, Mafarka appears as an invincible Homeric character, perfectly in line with the aesthetic and ethical paradigm of *kalokagathia*, namely the coexistence of external beauty and moral goodness, or rightness:[47]

> Egli aveva la disinvoltura e la robustezza di un giovane atleta invincibile, armato per mordere, per strangolare e per atterrare. Il suo corpo troppo compatto, troppo vivo e quasi frenetico sotto una peluria fulva e una pelle chiazzata, come di serpente, sembrava dipinto coi colori della fortuna e della vittoria, al pari dello scafo

> di una bella nave. E la luce lo adorava certo appassionatamente, poiché non cessava d'accarezzargli i pettorali ampi, tutti a groppi d'impazienti radici, e i bicipiti che parevan di quercia, e la muscolatura inquietante delle gambe, alla quale il sudore dava luccicori esplosivi. (*M* 10)
>
> [He had the ease and broad shoulders of an invincible young athlete built to bite, choke and fell. His body – too compact, too lively and almost frenetic under a tawny down and snakish patterning – seemed to be painted in the colours of good fortune and victory, like the hull of a fine ship. And the light adored him madly, no doubt, for it never ceased to caress his pectorals knotted with impatient roots, his oaken biceps and the disturbing musculature of his legs, explosively highlighted by sweat.] (*MF* 8)

While Mafarka's body-type recalls the *kalos kagathos* [handsome and rightful] profile of Homeric models, this comparison breaks down if we take into consideration the value attributed to the king's body throughout Marinetti's novel. In Homeric epics, the heroic body is bearer of an idiosyncratic sacredness that needs to be either preserved or sacrificed to the gods, not killed by chance; to rage about a corpse or fail to properly bury it are among the worst sacrileges in pre-modern cultures. Moreover, in classical epics, the body is often a locus of recognition: this is the case in the *Odyssey*, in which the true recognition of Odysseus does not occur because of his cunning or resourcefulness, but through his body. Even though Odysseus is dressed as a beggar, when he returns home after decades away, his dog Argos immediately identifies his master. Similarly, his old wet nurse, Eurycleia, recognizes Odysseus when, giving him a bath, she sees a scar he got during a childhood boar hunt. Odysseus's body allows for him to be recognized as a hero and opens the door to his recovery of power, with the cooperation of his son, Telemachus, the only one to whom Odysseus actually declares his identity. Conversely, through Gazurmah's missed acknowledgment of his father, Marinetti stresses the fact that Mafarka's corporal model lies outside the realm of the futurist feral cyborg. The novel stages the destruction of the king's body as a symbolic rite of passage – a ruthless patricidal sacrifice – that marks the advent of a hero-cyborg. Soon after his birth, Gazurmah, the "infuriated bull," throws his father on a rock and kills him. Mafarka is reduced to a lifeless pulp: classic *kalokagathia* disintegrates under the force of an avant-garde Minotaur, who fatally deforms and deeply destabilizes the characterization of the traditional hero. Beauty and harmony are (too) human bodily features that the avant-garde character no longer needs in order to emerge as a hero.

Fluid Genders or Chameleon-like Masculinity?

By destroying the unity, solidity, and harmony of the "flesh-and-soul" character, crepuscularism and futurism conduct a parallel demolition of its fixed gender identities. However, beneath their renewal of gender roles, both movements hide a hypertrophic masculinity in disguise and replace the traditional male-female dualism with a different, yet equally androcentric, view of gender. In investigating this aspect, my analysis centres on the work of futurist women and aims to illustrate a rather unexplored point: namely, how both the crepusculars' and the futurists' representation of gendered bodies involves a discourse on nature and culture.

It is worth recalling that gender has been a main topic in recent studies on futurism. Many scholars have highlighted the complexity of the gender rhetoric that this avant-garde brought forward. Silvia Contarini has illustrated that the positive characterization of masculinity and the negative connotation of femininity constitute the biased perspective that the movement adopts to dissociate gender from biological sex.[48] Commenting on the work of futurist women, Contarini has highlighted another key point: in the pre-war period and throughout the First World War, these writers meditated on their bodily and intellectual metamorphoses; yet, their re-envisioning of female identity was mainly based on male values. Ultimately, futurist women deceived themselves that futurism could voice their fight for emancipation, but this did not happen.

Lucia Re tends towards another view, suggesting that war did create the ideal context for women's emancipation. As she explains, Rosa Rosà's writings – especially the two articles entitled "Le donne del posdomani" ["Women of the Near Future"] – identify wartime work as the "activity that manifested the indivisibility of mind and body, passion and reason, private and public, even male and female."[49] For Rosà, work was a way to affirm women's social agency, a way "to be fully 'human' and equal to men"; this perspective, as Re further clarifies, echoes the egalitarian view of feminist writer Anna Kuliscioff. Yet, was the transformation into men the sole possible strategy for women's emancipation? Paola Sica, in her analysis of Ginanni's work, touches upon this question, illustrating that the writer's conception of a new woman ambivalently responds to the overpowering figure of the futurist male. Ginanni's work indeed finds its limitations in portraying the "image of a super woman who embraces the new possibilities offered by technology, strives to provoke events, and even aspires to dominate time and space. The impetus of this woman, however, tends to be curbed when she comes to terms with the world of men. At that point, she often becomes an imperfect man, or a matrix of virility."[50]

The arguments of Contarini, Re, and Sica can guide our parallel reflection on the dichotomies of male-female and culture-nature in crepuscular and futurist texts. In the common understanding, futurism is associated with the cult of masculinity and crepuscularism with a de-potentiated "feminization" of the masculine; nevertheless, this popular view does not take into account how the myth of the male body-in-pain deeply impacts both these poetics. Crepuscularism and futurism engage in a complementary, and at times strikingly similar, praise of hurt masculinity, which develops into a unique gender model that can be characterized as pansexual.

Valentine de Saint-Point, an eclectic French writer who was also an artist and choreographer, is the author of "Manifesto della donna futurista" ["Manifesto of the Futurist Woman"] (1912). She wrote this work in response to the misogynist claims of Marinetti's founding manifesto. In her work, De Saint-Point proudly declares, "**È assurdo dividere l'umanità in donne e uomini**; essa è composta soltanto di **femminilità** e **mascolinità**" ["IT'S ABSURD TO DIVIDE HUMANITY INTO WOMEN AND MEN; it is composed only of FEMININITY and MASCULINITY"] (*MDF* 46, *F* 110). In her view, humanity consists precisely of an androgynous combination of these two principles; thus,

> Ogni superuomo, ogni eroe, per quanto sia epico, ogni genio per quanto sia possente ... è composto, ad un tempo, di elementi femminili e di elementi maschili, di femminilità e di mascolinità: cioè un essere completo. (*MDF* 46)
>
> [Every superman, every hero to the extent that he has epic value, every genius to the extent that he is powerful ... is simultaneously composed of feminine and masculine elements, femininity and masculinity: which is to say, a complete being.] (*F* 110).

As we shall see in more detail, this perspective of gender contiguity brings forth a transgressive "statute of difference"[51] between masculinity and femininity that similarly shapes the futurist and crepuscular representation of gender. This statute of undividedness supersedes biological determination and identifies gender as a chameleon-like experience, which seemingly challenges bourgeois heteronormativity.

This strategy is especially evident in the futurist manifestos and in many other literary works: Marinetti's proud eulogy of the virile warrior and De Saint-Point's later adaptation both foster a gender narrative that is still present today, and widely represented in the dominant discourse of, for example, action movies. Kent Brintnall argues that "action films ... are constructed through the juxtaposition of spectacular violence and the spectacle of the male body"; hence, although such movies portray suffering masculinity, their overarching message always exemplifies and reinforces "the cultural standard of the solid and impenetrable male body."[52] Thus, the spectacularization of physical suffering, which finds its archetype in the Homeric fighting hero, asserts "admiration and veneration" for a male body that "emerges victorious even though it has been beaten, bruised, made to bleed."[53] This practice of spectacularizing the heroic body in pain is, at the core, the narrative of virility that futurism embraces in the period that spans from the 1909 founding manifesto to the end of the First World War, and that futurist women apply to the female body. Promoting a pro-war culture that gives rise to a loud interventionism, Marinetti develops a virtually hagiographic narrative of sacrifice, identifying virility with a strenuous resistance to the languor and temptation of the flesh that femininity embodies. As the futurist founder argues in "Uccidiamo il chiaro di luna!" ["Let's Murder the Moonlight!"] (1909):

> Sì, i nostri nervi esigono la guerra e disprezzano la donna, poiché noi temiamo che braccia supplici s'intreccino alle nostre ginocchia, la mattina della partenza! ... Che mai pretendono le donne, i sedentarî, gl'invalidi, gli ammalati, e tutti i consiglieri prudenti? Alla loro vita vacillante, rotta da lugubri agonie, da sonni tremebondi e da incubi grevi, noi preferiamo la morte violenta e la glorifichiamo come la sola che sia degna dell'uomo, animale da preda. (*TIF* 15)

> [Yes, our nerves demand war and disdain women, because we fear that supplicating arms will entangle our knees on the morning of departure! ... What do they want – women, sedentary people, invalids, the sick, and all counselors of prudence? To their vacillating lives, broken by dismal agonies, by fearful dreams and burdensome nightmares, we prefer a violent death and we exalt it as the only one worthy of man, that beast of prey.] (*F* 54)

As beasts of prey and potential prey themselves, futurist men display their bodies gloriously, animated with electrified nerves and "orgoglio temerario" ["fearless pride"] (*TIF* 16, *F* 55). The thrilling sensuality of their corporality exposed to death thus derives from their willingness to be wounded, to be immolated as sacrificial animals of war. These men launch their vigorous bodies into the flames against the enemy, an enemy that, in Marinetti's words "si dovrebbe inventare se non esistesse!" ["we would have to invent if it didn't exist!"] (*TIF* 16, *F* 55). This last statement addresses a fundamental point in the futurist rhetoric of virility across sexes: war is an integral element to the cult of the virile body. Marinetti, intermixing classical and Christian images, sacralizes the body of the soldier as a new *figura Christi*, ready to make the ultimate sacrifice:

> agili soldati dalle baionette aguzze, glorificano la forza del pane, che si trasforma in sangue, per sprizzar dritto, fino allo Zenit. Il sangue seppiatelo, non ha valore né splendore, se non liberato, col ferro o col fuoco, dalla prigione delle arterie! (*TIF* 17)
>
> [agile soldiers with sharp bayonets glorify the power of bread that is transformed into blood which shoots straight up to the Zenith. You must know that blood has no value or splendor unless it has been freed from the prison of the arteries by iron or fire!] (*F* 55).

The wounded body of the soldier, and later the veteran's prosthetic body, become popularized versions of the over-man that futurism had earlier celebrated and eroticized through the hybrid Gazurmah. In *Come si seducono le donne* [*How to Seduce Women*], a manual of seduction that Marinetti composed in 1916 on the war front, the spokesman of futurism praises mutilated bodies as champions of a virility that has been engraved in their scars. Addressing women directly, he exhorts them to prefer the glorious mutilated males over the "maschi intatti" ["intact males"], whose bodies exude cowardice. The war veterans will give Italian women "figli d'acciaio, precisi, veloci, carichi di elettricità celeste, ispirati come il fulmine nel colpire e abbattere uomini, alberi e ruderi secolari" ["sons of steel, precise, fast, charged with celestial electricity, inspired like lightning in hitting and tearing down humans, trees, and centuries-old ruins"].[54]

The discourse of the eroticized, mutilated body interweaves with the broader futurist narrative of human-nonhuman mingling; the veteran's virility in fact appears materially in a carnal assemblage of steel and flesh that has the power to grant eternal life:

> Fusione dell'Acciaio e della Carne. Umanizzazione dell'acciaio e metalizzazione della carne nell'uomo moltiplicato. Corpo motore dalle diverse parti intercambiabili e rimpiazzabili. Immortalità dell'uomo![55]
>
> [Fusion of Steel and Flesh. Humanization of steel and metallization of flesh in the multiplied man. Body engine with different interchangeable and replaceable parts. Immortality of man!]

Virility attained through the prosthetic body of the veteran ultimately implies a profane divinization of man into an immortal creature, a demigod who has survived the challenge of war and has metabolized this experience within his redeemed, metallic body.

De Saint-Point extends Marinetti's concept of the virility of war to women's bodies, creating a rhetoric of gender performativity based on the unisex practice of brutal masculinity: "**Ciò che manca di più alle donne come agli uomini è la virilità**" ["WHAT WE MOST NEED, WHETHER MEN OR WOMEN, IS VIRILITY"] (*MDF* 47, *F* 110). She argues that women will abandon the feminine attitude that subdues them into "octopuses of the hearth" only if they evolve into savage women-beasts, namely, "**donne bestialmente amorose, che distruggono nel Desiderio anche la sua forza di rinnovamento!**" ["WOMEN BESTIALLY AMOROUS, WHO DESTROY THEIR POWER OF RENEWAL IN DESIRE!"] (*MDF* 47, *F* 111). By calling for a metamorphosis of women into bestial warriors – "Erinyes and Amazons, Semiramides, Joan of Arcs, Jeanne Hachettes; the Judiths and Charlotte Cordays, the Cleopatras and the Messalinas" (*F* 111) – De Saint-Point ambiguously plays on promoting, yet also recasting, the traditional association between femininity and nature. Being "guerriere che combattono più ferocemente dei maschi ... amanti che incitano ... distruggitrici che spezzando i più fragili contribuiscono alla selezione" ["warriors who fight more ferociously than men ... lovers who incite ... destroyers who contribute to racial selection by smashing the fragile"] (*MDF* 47, *F* 111), the women depicted in De Saint-Point's manifesto are animal bodies stripped of centuries of cultural "taming" and let loose to unleash their passionate instincts. However, the return to nature that she calls forth is very far from the taken-for-granted relation between women's corporality and nature. In opposition to the commonly shared view of women as "naturally" disposed to their nurturing role, De Saint-Point plays on the myth of the untamed and chaotic feminine nature – a narrative that classical mythology and the imagery of the witch had fostered for centuries. She affirms that "per istinto, la donna non è saggia, non è pacifista, non è buona" ["by instinct, woman is not wise, is not pacifist, is not good" (*MDF* 48, *F* 111). In its bloody extremism, the "Manifesto della donna futurista" envisions the possibility of redefining gender while recasting "the notion of biology as destiny."[56] Nevertheless, by liberating women from a pre-imposed sexual and "social nature," the manifesto dictates its adherence to a violent "state of nature," according to which, to be virile, all women must be instinctively cruel and violent like nonhuman animals and natural catastrophes:

> **Riacquisti la donna la sua crudeltà e la sua violenza che fanno ch'ella si accanisca sui vinti, perché sono vinti**, fino a mutilarli. Cessate di predicarle la giustizia spirituale che invano s'è sforzata d'acquistare.

Donne, ridiventate sublimemente ingiuste, come tutte le forze della natura! (*MDF* 49)

[LET WOMAN REACQUIRE THE CRUELTY AND VIOLENCE THAT LETS HER FLY INTO A RAGE OVER THE DEFEATED, PRECISELY BECAUSE THEY ARE DEFEATED, up to the point of mutilating them. Stop preaching spiritual justice to women, who have tried to acquire it in vain. WOMEN, ONCE AGAIN YOU SHOULD BECOME SUBLIMELY UNJUST, LIKE ALL THE FORCES OF NATURE.] (*F* 112)

Rather than liberating women through a positive re-envisioning of their relationship with a multifaceted and self-determined nature, De Saint-Point anthropomorphizes nature as "unjust" and identifies women with the restrictive role of warrior-beasts. This naturalization of women into virile animals returns, albeit in mitigated tones, in Ginanni's "Cannoni d'Italia" ["Cannons of Italy"], a lyrical prose piece that was originally published in *L'Italia futurista* and later included in *Montagne trasparenti*. In this work, Ginanni sings the praise of war as the arena of liberation, extending the narrative of First World War irredentism to the question of women. Combining these two motives, Ginanni delineates the model of a virile *mater familias*, a futurist Cornelia, whose only *ornamenta* [jewels] are the weapons she forges:

Voglio che da me, dalle mie mani che odiano la loro fragilità ed anelano il dominio, scoppi l'urlo selvaggio di gioia ai cannoni che presero Gorizia. (*SF* 105)

[I want that from me, from my hands that hate their fragility and yearn for dominion, explode the savage scream of joy of the cannons that conquered Gorizia].

Bearer of a culturally mediated "second nature," which allows her to reject the natural fragility of her female hands, Ginanni praises the mechanical artificiality that has empowered her with a new procreative role. Her maternal attachment is now for the cannons she "generated" in the steelworks: "ho sentito come la loro vita e la mia pulsassero lo stesso ritmo, ho sentito per loro la forza di ardore di una donna dinanzi all'essere creato dal suo sangue" ["I felt how their life and mine were pulsating at the same rhythm; I felt for them the force of ardour of a woman before a being created by her blood"] (*SF* 107). Through this maternal comparison, Ginanni demands to see women as bodies moulded with the same steel that they are capable of moulding into metallic bodies. These women can exercise their generative power outside the domestic sphere and confront all of their social enemies, not just the invaders.

Rosa Rosà's short story "Una donna con tre anime" ["A Woman with Three Souls"] (1918) provides a further reflection on the virile transformation of women. In this work, Rosà recounts the metamorphosis of Giorgina, a bourgeois housewife who begins experiencing her hidden "souls" through a personality disorder. She is suddenly capable of instinctive and immoral actions, and is discovered to have amazing intellectual capabilities as well as rhetorical and writing skills. However, the story ends with a medical intervention that forces Giorgina to return to her previous "normal" and tranquil lifestyle – or to transition back from a (male) liberating identity to her imprisoning (female) nature. Through this work, Rosà suggests that bourgeois society treats the emergence of women's agency as an unhealthy irregularity, as an anomaly caused by illness. Yet, her "healthier" approach to Giorgina's transformation ultimately reveals the hierarchical divides and contradictions that underlie "Una donna con tre anime." In her first article entitled "Le donne del posdomani [I]," which was published in *L'Italia futurista* on 17 June 1917, Rosà envisions the renewed women as those who have been radically transformed by the experience of war. Thus, soldiers, returning home,

> troveranno ... non la passione delle bambole vanitose ma quella di compagne temprate dalla grandiosità del tempo, creature coscienti del loro compito presente e futuro: di mantenere cioè viva l'energia del paese.[57]

> [will find ... not the passion of conceited little dolls but that of companions tempered by the greatness of the times, people conscious that their present and future task is to keep alive the energy of the nation.] (*F* 234)

The issue, as previously noticed for De Saint-Point and Ginanni, is that Rosà's transformation is similarly predicated on the metamorphosis of women into men. As Contarini argues, discussing "Le donne del posdomani [II]," Rosà wishes for women's evolution towards a superior masculine type, so that they can finally "diventare uomini" ["become men"].[58]

Once again, we can see how the futurist separation of the virile gender from the biological sex ultimately fosters a universal yet hierarchical view, which denies the recognition of a variety of identities. Rather, Rosà's works imply that women should reject the attributes of their debasing female "nature" – passivity, attitude of "little dolls," and emotionality – to turn into virile and encultured futurist companions. Her perspective, although it is advanced as an emancipatory plan, for which "le femministe le più femministe potevano sperare" ["the most feminist of feminists could have hoped" ("Le donne del posdomani [I]," *F* 234), highlights a fundamental problem that ecofeminist Greta

Gaard has effectively summarized, namely, that "the way in which women and nature have been conceptualized historically in the Western intellectual tradition has resulted in devaluing whatever is associated with women, emotion, animals, nature, and the body, while simultaneously elevating in value those things associated with men, reason, humans, culture, and the mind."[59] Futurism in fact elevates bodily and animal instincts only insofar they are perceived as virile qualities.

Furthermore, Rosà's image of Giorgina trapped in her bourgeois apartment exclusively identifies the home with a cage or, in "Le donne del posdomani [I]," with a masculinized "paese" ["fatherland"] that must be defended from enemies. Her work does not consider alternative definitions of home and community that imply a different way of recasting gender roles, for instance definitions that give men nurturing and caring roles, without assigning these functions exclusively to women or feminized bodies. Home – Gaard has affirmed in a more recent contribution – needs to be understood as "'a set of relationships, a series of contextual experiences,' and a place of connection where one lives physically, where one is emotionally connected, and where one is part of a [diverse] community of [human and nonhuman] beings."[60] This ecofeminist perspective can help us fully understand, beyond Contarini's acute criticism, why De Saint-Point's Amazon, Ginanni's "metallic" woman, and Rosà's virile (wo)*man* are not truly emancipatory images, since they are based on the main futurist assumption that female nature is an inferior gendered space without culture, or a sort of "privative alpha" that futurist culture can remove from any female body.

Moving to crepuscularism, we can notice that, at a glance, the movement's obsession with sick male corporality seems to occupy the opposite extreme of the futurist fluid virility, which applies to the male warrior as well as to the combative Amazon. Yet, if one considers how futurism manipulates the motif of the male body-in-pain to construct the myth of the mutilated hero, the crepuscular gender narrative of the "fanciullo malato" ["sick young man"] comes very close to – and virtually anticipates – the futurist pansexual virility of the body at war. In crepuscular poetry, the dismantling of the association between healthy body and powerful masculinity involves a hidden process of renegotiation, through which the vulnerable male body becomes the new, venerable *ecce homo* of modernity. However, as seen for futurism, the inclusive gender ambiguity of crepuscularism also overlooks the issue of women's identity.

The ecce homo, namely the image of Christ crowned with thorns and exposed in all his human fragility to the crowd, is peculiar for its transgressive representation of the divinity: Jesus becomes "a freak to be publicly displayed and mocked."[61] As Michael Worton explains, the iconography of the ecce homo – from Caravaggio's painting (1605) to twentieth-century adaptations, such as Elisabeth Ohlson's provocative exhibition *Ecce Homo* (1989) – has either hinted at the androgynous nature of Christ's beheld body or openly proposed the association between this exposed body and the forced exposition of homosexual identity. In the more traditional iconography of Caravaggio's panting, ambiguity is inherent in the universal redemptive message that Jesus incarnates through his visible corporality: "his head is most definitely male, his torso, his arms and especially his hands are very feminine, thereby making of him an androgynous figure who symbolises all humanity."[62] The androgynous universality of the ecce homo is a fundamental component in the crepuscular rendering of young men and women who embody the exposed vulnerability of a body in transformation, a body that puts into crisis the very possibility of distinguishing between masculine and feminine. This tendency towards gender hybridity can be further compared to the works of Pre-Raphaelite painters like Edward Burne-Jones (for example, *Phyllis and Demophoon* and *The Golden Stairs*) and to William Morris's *The Bathers*. Evoking a similarly nuanced imagery, Corazzini plays on gender equivocality by depicting adolescent characters who stand as symbols of immature identity and delicate anguish. In the poem "Il fanciullo" ["The Boy"], an ephebic ecce homo declares his wish to die through an oneiric fantasy. Crowned with flowers like a pagan god reminiscent of Dionysus, this sweet adolescent abandons the earthly dimension, leaving behind a group of grieving virgin sisters – faded figures of the Virgin Mary, *mater dolorosa*, who endlessly search for him:

> Tu vuoi morire, ecco, tu vuoi dormire,
> solo, per sempre, con le tue corone
> sfiorite e chiudi le pupille buone,
> dolce, così, che sembra ti vanisca
> l'anima, desolato pellegrino.
> E sogni … e nella tua casa in un tetro
> crepuscolo, le pallide sorelle
> vanno inquiete per l'assente, il loro
> dolce fanciullo che le consolava
> con l'innocenza delle sue parole,
> e ti cercano e guardano le stelle. (*O* 138)
>
> [You want to die, indeed, you want to sleep,
> alone, forever, with your faded
> crowns, and close your good pupils,
> sweet, so that you seem as if your soul
> is vanishing, you desolate pilgrim.
> And you dream … in your house a gloomy
> twilight, the pale sisters
> restless are looking for you absent, their

sweet little boy that used to console
them with the innocence of his words,
and they look for you and at the stars.]

The similarity between the poem's main character and the Greek god Dionysus is pivotal to our discussion of the ambiguous figure of the *fanciullo* within the uncategorized inclusiveness of the queer gender. The Greek god is known for his mysterious, polymorphous nature, which embraces the possibility of experiencing a wide spectrum of gender identities and sexualities. In the form of Dionysus Zagreus, the god appears as a pre-pubescent boy who has been killed by the Titans while still a child. However, in his more popular form, Dionysus is a nocturnal hunter and foolish inspirer of orgiastic rites. In *The Bacchantes*, the god uses his gender ambiguity to trick Pentheus into a scandalous death and punish the king for not worshipping Dionysus's divinity. Pentheus dresses up as a woman to spy on the horrific activities of the Maenads, a group of Dionysus's followers that his mother Agave has joined, and is ultimately killed by his possessed mother-bacchante. In the context of his twentieth-century poetry, Corazzini borrows the iconography of Dionysus as the crowned wanderer who emanates gender chaos, thus underscoring a fascination with childhood, adolescence, and malady as peculiar states of undefinition and transition into a corporeal unknown. In Corazzini's poetry, young boys and girls live in an androgynous state of primordial completeness, embodying a Dionysian spectrum of sexualities, through which the notion of gender assumes the form of chameleonic clothing "made of many types of fabrics juxtaposed and interwoven among themselves."[63]

In a parallel yet inverse way, Gozzano adopts gender ambiguity to delineate the physiognomy of Ketty, a masculine American girl whom the poet met during his travels in India. Ketty captures Gozzano's attention with her virile frankness and impudent arrogance; this "vergine folle" ["foolish virgin"] – a parodic reference to D'Annunzio's novel *Le vergini delle rocce* (1896) – lives as if her body were a thing that did not belong to her. And "come una cosa / non sua" ["like a thing not hers"] (*TM* 240–1), her virginal femininity has been promised to her cousin in Baltimore. The libertine "Miss Ketty," who smokes, whistles, and spits, cannot escape from the merciless definition of "signorina" ["unmarried woman"] that Gozzano articulates in a letter to Amalia Guglielminetti:

> Signorina: figura triste; o che inconsapevole della sua miseria, vive beata, intellettualmente impoverita dalla secolare mediocrità borghese, o che, cosciente, rivoltandosi alla "saggezza di antiche norme": cerchi per sè e per le sorelle un sentiero di salute, o che, più ribelle ancora, voglia rivendicarsi in libertà e contendere la sorte agli uomini derisori, o che si strugga nel sogno di un'attesa vana.[64]

[Unmarried young lady: sad character; either unconscious of her misery, she lives blessed, intellectually impoverished by secular bourgeois mediocrity; or consciously rebelling against the "wisdom of ancient norms," she may find for herself and her sisters a healthy path; or, even more rebellious, may want to vindicate herself in freedom, and challenge the destiny of the men who mock her, or pine away in the dream of vain waiting.]

Ketty is the foil of Felicita, who is similarly "ugly-ish" and caged within her social destiny. This bourgeois American "signorina" can express a brief rebellion only through the impetus of her masculine body: "Cerulo-bionda, le mammelle assenti, / ma forte come un giovinetto forte" ["A blue-eyed blonde, her breasts too slight to mention, / but spunky as a boy at any rate" (*TM* 236–7). The "figlia della cifra e del clamore" ["daughter of ledgers and the scandal sheet"] (*TM* 240–1) is a short-term sexual libertine who takes advantage of her pubescent body to pose as a man and explore a world that will soon be closed to her by a respectable marriage. The image of a repressed body that seeks its last leap of rebellion in the form of an exotic escape, Ketty provides an ideal bridge to a deeper understanding of the futurist contempt for women. Associating femininity with a "pathological, renunciatory attitude toward reality,"[65] Marinetti – along with many futurist women – equates the "feminine" to a weakened fantasy-land, one fraught with disempowering sickness, languid love, and adultery. As Claudia Salaris has explained, the notion of women's inferiority was not a futurist invention; rather, it was a widespread cultural panorama at the turn of the century, with intellectuals from various fields, including Schopenhauer, Nietzsche, Moebius, and Weininger, making similar discriminatory statements.[66] Yet, unlike other misogynist voices, the futurists addressed the social constraints and influences that contributed to creating a distorted, gendered image of women. As De Saint-Point argues in a letter to Marinetti, society plays a substantial role in taming the public image of women:

la société contraint les femmes à se transformer d'êtres supérieurs en personnages languissants et sentimentaux que je déteste autant que vous, tout comme je déteste ces rôles d'ouvrières anonymes que les féministes tiennent tant à promouvoir.[67]

[Society forces women to transform themselves from superior beings into languishing and sentimental characters, whom I hate as much as you do, just as I hate those roles of anonymous workers that the feminists care so much to promote.]

The futurist aversion to women becomes a more general attack against the middle-class gendered order, based on the image of the family as a "nest of love and restorative domesticity," whose tutelary goddess was a good wife and caring mother.[68] The question, which I will further explore in the next section, then becomes: Why cannot Ketty and Giorgina maintain both their female identity and their transgressive behaviour? Why can they only evade their gendered destiny by flirting in a displaced India or by being affected by an illness? Futurism handles "Ketty and Giorgina's question" by seemingly dissociating the slippery notion of chromosomal sex from the rigid social construction of gender.[69] However, in many cases this disconnection falls into a "performative" gender paradigm that has, at its core, a chameleon-like masculinity. For futurism, this pansexual gender is founded on virility – a brutal katabolic force that both men and women warriors must enact to be worthy of respect; for crepuscularism, it is based on the sacred allure that ephebic male bodies in pain exude. For both movements, though, women and their threatening nature-outside-culture do not emerge as positive bodily subjects, capable of self-determination.

Maternal Potential and Male Creativity

In *Futurist Virility* (1996), Barbara Spackman has stressed how procreation is a soft spot in Marinetti's virile fantasy. In *Mafarka il futurista*, the futurist founder depicts the male dream of reproduction without copulation, as well as the cultural appropriation of female organs: "the novel's project, in its own terms, is to bypass the 'vulva' and impregnate the 'ovary' that is the male spirit."[70] However, as Spackman demonstrates, in order to achieve an alleged male autarky – a self-sufficiency that is sexual, cultural, and economic – Marinetti must resort to the mediation of women characters, as the opening of the novel implies. The opening scene, in which male soldiers rape a group of African women, symbolizes the sexual colonization of a feminized land, while revealing that the "xenophobic fantasy of cultural and economic autarky can do without the foreign only by annexing it."[71]

The issue with procreation that Spackman effectively illustrates unveils further impasses. What does it mean to envision autarkic men, able to procreate without female companions, men who are independent from a function that is biologically feminine? As Re has observed in a detailed overview of the motif of maternity in futurist works, the movement was both attracted to and repelled by maternal power – and the same could be said for crepuscularism and its obliteration of maternity. Crepuscular authors were in fact more interested in the experience of abortion or in mystical chastity than in the theme of procreation.

In her analysis, Re refers to feminist theorist Adriana Cavarero, who, in *Nonostante Platone* [*Despite Plato*] (1990), argues that "the mystery and power of procreation, guarded by women in their bodies, long ensured the absolute symbolic power of motherhood before the value of the male function"; yet, the power of procreation, as well as the techniques of midwifery, were eventually "transformed into a male right of expropriation and of absolute power of signification."[72] This dialectic between expropriation and appropriation is a central topic in discussing how futurist and crepuscular male authors attempt to use the power of their artistic word to capture the generative creativity of women or to affirm their independence from a living mystery of nature they can never fully appropriate.

As we have previously examined, by reshaping the traditional opposition of feminine and masculine in terms of coexistence within the paradigm of virility, futurism pushes its gender criticism to the extreme of negating the act of copulation that joins men and women. Marinetti envisions new reproductive possibilities for his futurist metallic "cyborgs":

> In nome dell'Orgoglio umano che adoriamo, io vi annuncio prossima l'ora in cui uomini dalle tempie larghe e dal mento d'acciaio figlieranno prodigiosamente, solo con uno sforzo della loro volontà esorbitante, dei giganti dai gesti infallibili ... (*M* 5)

> [*In the name of the human Pride that we adore, I tell you that the hour is near when men with broad foreheads and chins of steel will give birth prodigiously, by one effort of flaring will, to giants infallible in action* ...] (*MF* 3)

Oddly enough, *Mafarka il futurista*, the novel that seems to most emphasize virile masculinity, is also the futurist work that most dilutes and "corrupts" the traditional social role of the bourgeois *pater familias*, envisioning motherhood for a warrior king, as well as homoerotic relationships. Through its brutal episode of heterosexual violence, the novel initially states the idea of masculinity as dominative power that overcomes the biological and cultural otherness of feminine bodies. Later on, the narration insists on the identification of Marfarka's virility with the primary driving force of his regal power. As a long *mise en abyme* reveals, when the king was still a horse trader, the devil tricked him into eating the *zeb* [penis] of a marvellously well endowed horse; after that magic meal, Mafarka acquires the animal's sexual strength, growing an eleven-metre-long member and an uncontrollable desire to copulate with all women. But the *zeb* also opens the door for homoerotic advances. After Mafarka arrives in the kingdom of Boubassa, the king asks to experience the prodigious virile organ. Mafarka takes advantage of the weakness of the king, and while the latter is in a prone position, steals his sceptre and usurps his reign. However, this is not the novel's only instance of sexual deviance from the masculine type of the bourgeois father. Mafarka obtains procreative self-sufficiency, giving life to his mechanical son through an incestuous kiss that borders on the homoerotic:

> Gazurmah! Gazurmah! Gazurmah! … Eccoti la mia anima! … Tendimi le labbra e apri la bocca al mio bacio! …
>
> E saltò al collo di suo figlio, e premette la propria bocca sulla bocca scolpita.
>
> Il formidabile corpo di Gazurmah sussultò subito violentemente, e le sue ali possenti scattarono, infrangendo le pareti della gabbia … (*M* 218)

> ["Gazourmah! Gazourmah! Gazourmah! … Here is my soul! … Offer me your lips and open your mouth for my kiss!" He jumped on his son's neck, and pressed his lips to the sculptured mouth.
>
> At once, Gazourmah's formidable body gave a violent start, and his powerful wings unfurled, bursting the walls of the cage.] (*MF* 196)

Paradoxically, Marinetti's hyper-virile narrative becomes exemplary of the problematic pangender masculinity that is central in the futurist rhetoric of gender: Mafarka "performs" in a male body but conceives a son through a homoerotic kiss, and so becomes a maternal caretaker. *Mafarka il futurista* pictures a case of a male mother who ultimately gives up his virile warrior nature and turns into the weak prey of his son's ferociousness. In the novel, the contrast between Mafarka's social role of king-warrior and his maternal vocation remains unresolved and problematically open: Mafarka is the prototype of a virile masculinity that can equally seduce men and women, but he also embodies a passive surrendering to motherhood and death.

Reaching its saturation point, the novel implicitly highlights the futurist gender incoherence in striving for an autarkic virility that can erase the procreative function of women only by erasing the whole of humanity. As Margaret Wynne Nevinson stated in an open letter to Marinetti, the impasse of futurism is to look forward to an unattainable "machine-governed and womanless world – a world in which even the human race may be generated by mechanism, and where everybody will be of masculine gender" (*F* 74). What Mafarka leaves unaccomplished is the dream of the cyborg as "a creature in a post-gender world," a creature that, according to Donna Haraway's definition, "has no truck with bisexuality, pre-oedipal symbiosis, unalienated labour, or other seductions to organic wholeness through a final appropriation of all the powers of the parts into a higher unity."[73] And yet, can this higher unity be fulfilled by estranging our continuity with nature into a mechanical species? Put differently, can this unity be possible without envisioning new, and unbiased, alliances across genders, and between the creativity of nature and that of art and technology?

The motif of the unaccomplished or misconceived project, along with the dream of subtly erasing the reproductive role of women, is present in crepuscularism as well. The recurrent image of the miscarriage and the dream of a chaste life are symptomatic of this unsolved conflict with male – and broadly speaking, with poetic – self-sufficiency. In "Piccola storia scandalosa" ["Little Scandalous Story"], Moretti's poetic voice tells the story of a child who witnesses his mother's miscarriage and, many years later, catches himself envying the "piccolo feto nel vasetto trasparente" ["little fetus in the see-through vial"], whose brief larva-like existence stopped when it was still possible to be unaware flesh.[74] In "Il Palazzo dell'anima" ["The Palace of the Soul"], Govoni exhibits an eerie collection of "Aborti nelle fiale, / rachitici e verdastri" ["Abortions in vials, / scrawny and greenish"], to which the poet expresses a visceral attachment (*P* 101). In the poem, the vials containing the miscarried fetuses are displayed near a collection of feminine yet infertile dolls, representing all those suppressed voices – anxieties, frustrations, fears, and the collective war hysteria – that virile poetry would prefer to keep hidden in its secret room of horrors, in the dark space of the unconceived, the unborn, the absent.[75]

However, the crepuscular collections of abortions are not secured in a vacuum-sealed space, divided from the realm of the rational (male) human. Rather, they represent a disquieting hybrid area where humans mingle with the feminized chaotic nature that generates them. If we recall Govoni's "Alla Musa," a poem briefly discussed in chapter 1, we can highlight further ambiguous aspects related to this disturbing uterine image. In the text, the Muse-prostitute saves her abortions instead of throwing them away. The need to preserve this flesh, in which potential human matter has devolved into bodily discharges, illustrates the fact that the unconceived – and unconceivable – is a scary place in which masculine culture and feminized matter show their common roots and interdependency. Living outside the (pro)creative power of nature that the female body embodies is indeed a fantasy that does not reflect the interconnectedness and creative intentionality that informs both natural and cultural matter.

For both Roman crepuscular poetry and Gozzano's "school of irony," another strategy to avoid the blurry realm of procreative matter is to imagine an asexual world that, unlike the hyper-sexualized universe of futurism, is committed to absolute chastity. A renunciation of the pleasures of the flesh often implies the sublimation of carnal desire into an object of sacrifice. Ideally speaking, the "manifesto" of crepuscular chastity is Fausto Maria Martini's "Elogio della castità" ["Praise of Chastity"] in which the poetic "I" proclaims his vow to reject sensual love: "oggi ho sepolto in un cofano d'oro / l'ultimo bacio suo, senza lamento ..." ["Today I buried in a golden box / her last kiss without a lament ..."].[76] In making a human sacrifice, which recalls ancient religious traditions and the biblical episode of Abraham nearly immolating Isaac, the poetic persona envisions the transformation of the lover's body into an altar on which he offers his libido: "Null'altro io chiedo: o santa castità / ... fa / della tenera amante una sorella ..." ["I ask nothing more: oh saint chastity / ... make / the tender lover a sister ..."].[77] The beloved woman turns into a sister, an ambiguous term that can indicate both a sibling and a nun, confirming the asexuality of this heterosexual relation.

Although it may seem that, by turning the Dannunzian sensual body into a cold piece of marble, crepuscularism weakens lust, in fact it is more accurate to speak of allusive eroticism. The "atroce gioia" ["atrocious joy"] that Martini immolates returns in the guise of spiritual ardour. Replacing the climax of intercourse with the sensation of ecstasy in "L'ultimo sogno" ["The Last Dream"], Corazzini treats carnal agony as a moment of sublime rapture that does not imply the risk of procreation:

Io mi allontano
e la mia veste bianca
se la dividono i rovi,
e la mia ghirlanda s'è mutata
in una corona di spine,
le mie piccole mani sanguinano
senza fine
e l'anima è triste come
li occhi
di un agnello che sia per morire.

[I draw away
and the brambles start to rend
my white garments,
and my garland is transformed
to a crown of thorns,
my little hands are bleeding
without end
and my soul is as sad as
the eyes
of a lamb that is about to die.] (*SE* 52–3)

The crepuscular erotic sanctification of the male body-in-pain is, paradoxically, not so far from De Saint-Point's proposals in "Manifeste Futuriste de la

Luxure" ["Futurist Manifesto of Lust"] (1913). In this seminal work, the writer describes the experience of religious exaltation as a form of diverted sexuality. In her view, lust conveys an energetic force that can lead to finding the Unknown in the carnal union: "**La lussuria è la ricerca carnale dell'ignoto**, come la Cerebralità ne è la ricerca spirituale. La Lussuria è il gesto di creare, ed è la Creazione" ["LUST IS A CARNAL SEARCH INTO THE UNKNOWN, just as thought is the mind's search into the unknown. Lust is the act of creating, and is creation"] (*MDF* 71, *F* 130). The intercourse that Marinetti denies through Mafarka's sexual self-sufficiency – and that crepuscularism repels through the image of the aborted fetus or sublimates through carnal sacrifice – becomes, in Saint-Point's "Manifesto of Lust," a bodily cognitive experience of intersubjectivity, which is an experience of symbiotic subjectivity outside the boundaries of the flesh-and-soul territory. Bare lust, as the purest and most vital source of energy, allows for an experience of trans-corporal excitement and enthusiasm. In its original meaning, the Greek word ἐνθουσιασμός [*enthusiasmós*] designated the experience of being possessed by the Other, specifically a divinity; the crepuscular sensuality of martyrdom recovers the religious connotation of the experience of lust, as the ultimate experience of living in a dispossessed, ecstatic corporeality, where masculinity can be cognitively "impregnated."

In exploring different male fantasies on autonomous procreation and sublimation of the female body, crepuscular and futurist authors leave two main questions unresolved. The first and foremost question is whether their maternal function is an attempt to deprive both women and nature of their intentional and generative potential. The next issue is that their attempt to deny femininity as a creative force per se cannot help but foster threatening images – like the one of the miscarriage – that undermine this denial.

Traumatic "Heroes": Anti-Promethean Freaks and Modern Hermits

Crepuscular and futurist personae are those of social outsiders: rebels, powerless victims, fools, and pariahs. Exoticism and diversity are the fundamental traits of these characters, whose journey of self-knowledge starts with rejection, either in the form of social banishment or conscious solipsism. The banishment of the "hero" is one of the basic narrative structures of many myths and folktales, in which the main *dramatis persona* must be expelled from his or her native environment in order to mature into a heroic personality through a perilous quest. As Vladimir Propp states in *Morphology of the Folktale* (1928), estrangement serves as a trigger for development towards the final social reintegration and personal victory of the hero. By contrast, in the crepuscular and futurist adaptation of this narrative pattern, the traumatic expulsion of the protagonist generates a counter-action that never reaches a reconciled happy ending. The quest of the hero expands into an everlasting series of unanswered interrogatives, continuous fights against personified or figurative villains, and a helpless waiting for a *deus ex machina* who will never appear. Corra's *Sam Dunn è morto* provides an exemplary case of this spiralling narrative. This "synthetic novel," which one might expect to provide a dry modern narration, lingers instead suspended on the sibylline prophecy of an upcoming revolution of "energie fantastiche" ["creative energies"], thus conveying the uncomfortable feeling that humanity lives "*sopra una polveriera di fantasia che non tarderà a scoppiare*" ["*astride a powder keg of imagination that sooner or later will explode*"].[78] Sam Dunn does not reveal anything more through his death:

> E chissà? Forse egli non ha voluto affaticarsi per tramandarsi delle verità che erano in cammino *e che si sarebbero per forza rivelate da sole*. Tutti conoscono le poche righe incomprensibili che egli scrisse pochi minuti prima di morire: "**Io** sono un attimo bizzarro galleggiante nella pazzia dell'esistenza. **Me** ne sto sulla poltrona sbalordito ed incerto di fronte alla realtà tranquillamente vivente. **Ne** ho una impressione di vertigine non pericolosa in fondo. **Frego** un cerino ed accendo, vivaddio, una buona sigaretta." (87–8)

> [Perhaps he did not care to tire himself out by bequeathing to us some of the truths that we were about to be revealed, *truths which inevitably would have revealed themselves to us without his intervention*. Everybody knows the handful of extremely peculiar lines that he wrote just a few moments before he died: "**I** am a brief, strange moment floating in the madness of existence. **Don't** you see me, in an armchair disconcerted and uncertain in the face of a reality that continues to exist peacefully? **Give** way, I tell myself, to that feeling of dizziness that is not in essence dangerous. **A damn** good cigarette, by God, is what I'll light, once I've struck this match."] (81–2)

At the end of his journey, Sam Dunn knows nothing more about his life or about existence; he can only look on in amazement and "not give a damn." The case of Corra's character opens the way for further consideration of the typology of "heroes" that is proposed by crepuscularism and futurism. Both movements deny any final reconciliatory moment or active return to society, and thus permanently destabilize the modern Promethean model, with its heralding of progress for the community. Instead, these movements intend to proclaim the failure of humanism in the creation of unique personalities, emphasizing the tragic side of the enchained titan's myth in its narrative of intellectual sacrifice.

Restaging the Promethean martyrdom of intelligence is a recurrent strategy in Corazzini's poetics of divine childhood. The "sacred" and "divine" *puer* is a powerful figure in pagan mythology, Christian tradition, and popular folklore.[79] The Roman poet recapitulates the cross-cultural archetype of the chosen child in opposition to the modern cultural canon of the bourgeois "average man," who lives in the age of unique progress but is destined to a petty bourgeois life. Corazzini's innocent "poet boy" recalls Prince Myshkin from Dostoevsky's *The Idiot* (1869). Scornfully rejected for being sick and naïvely saintly, Corazzini's child – along with his many body doubles – finds in the exile of malady the proof of his misunderstood messianic mission. Like the Dostoevyskian prince, the little boy is an *idiot*, in the Greek meaning of being isolated in his own private sphere and lacking the right to participate in socio-political life.

Corazzini plays on autobiographical identification with the chosen child of his poetic works, and in his letters, defines himself as a "Dio scacciato" ["banished god"] (*O* 297) who conflates the unintelligibility of the banishment with the mystery of the divine. In other passages, echoing the Gospels, the poet talks of himself as a divinity on earth: he defines his convalescence bed as his "trono in questo mondo" ["throne in this world"] (*O* 298) and often alludes to his own resurrection as a messianic return (*O* 304). Rather than solely being an expression of "idiotic" candour, Corazzini's choice of a sick child as his main poetic persona can be interpreted within a broader project of self-divinization. Not by chance, in "Stazione sesta," the poet modulates his personal Calvary on Christ's stations of the cross, and points out an overlooked identification:

> Nessuno imagina che il tuo volto
> piangevole e doloroso
> in quel piccolo specchio polveroso
> somigli quello di Cristo sul lino
> della Veronica!
>
> [No one imagines that your face
> streaked and sorrowful
> in that little mirror overrun with dust
> looks like the face of Christ
> in Veronica's veil!] (*SE* 51–2)

When a childhood of sickness is analysed from the perspective of a divine election based on "otherness," such a banishment becomes an out-and-out ritual of spiritual martyrdom. As Amy Hollywood has noted, according to Georges Bataille, pre-modern religious communities use the sacrifice of another, whether human or animal, to allow the subject to vicariously dissolve and to encounter immanence and radical continuity without dying – namely, without experiencing the discontinuity of transcendence, or in Bataille's words, the discontinuity "of being human without being a thing and of escaping the limits of things without returning to animal slumber."[80] In Corazzini's private and poetic works, he enacts this pre-modern practice of sacrifice: the poet immolates the flesh of his alter egos to attain a vicarious unworldly experience of completeness through his writing – a writing that is simultaneously "subjective" and "objective," autobiographical and fictional, poetic and mystical, sensual and religious, cryptic and apparent.

The lumbering sensation of inauthenticity – of living vicarious lives in order to "survive" a drab bourgeois existence – conveys Gozzano's denunciation of the Promethean failure. Unlike Corazzini's poetry, the literary and individual experience of Gozzano's alter egos follows a clear narrative progression. In *La via del rifugio*, the poet delineates a bitter path of "self-discovery": from juvenile abandonment in literary fantasies, to the realization that such high ideals as Love and Death are only a Dannunzian "favola bella" ["beautiful tale"]. As a veteran of illusions – bereft of his own dreams – in the second collection, *I colloqui*, the narrative voice seeks a new balance, conjugating literary vocation with a "vita piccola e borghese" ["little (bourgeois) life without pretenses"] (*TM* 156–7). Throughout *La via del rifugio*, the protagonist realizes that literature is the fictional "safety net" that has prevented him from living to his full potential. Yet, the desire to evade this shelter only draws the poetic persona into a labyrinth where all possible avenues of escape, including religion, are closed off. Even the regression into childhood ends with bringing about the Leopardian lesson: we can enjoy only our own illusions and projections. The child alter ego of "Parabola" ["Parable"] proposes this motif again, illustrating the unfillable gap between his expectations at the view of a juicy apple and the actual experience of eating it: "'Non sentii quasi il gusto e giungo al torso!'" ["'I barely tasted it and get to the core!'"] (*TP* 109). Towards the end of *La via del rifugio*, Gozzano turns towards a sceptical solipsism, which characterizes the most mature poetic persona of the second collection:

Rido nell'abbandono
o Cielo o Terra o Mare,
comincio a dubitare
se sono o se non sono! (*TP* 125)

[I laugh in abandonment
oh Sky oh Earth oh Sea,
I start to doubt
if I am or I am not.]

Reminiscing about Petrarch, Gozzano opens *I colloqui* with a section entitled "Il giovenile errore" ["The Juvenile Error"], which marks the transition from juvenile illusions to the mature "knowledge of irony." The protagonist jumps back and forth among many different but related roles, in an endless game of travesty. The performative nature of Gozzano's poetic persona(e) sows the modernist doubt that being is a mirage, or the acting of a routine. The humour of the second collection is a deforming mirror through which the poet stages a collective performance, told in the first person by the unreliable voices of countless puppet-narrators. Gozzano touches upon a theme that, from a different perspective, is still central in our current era of social media sharing: he presents us with a world in which our only profane resurrection is the possibility of living again and again through avatars. As the poet affirms in "Il più atto" ["The Fittest"]: "Sulle soglie del Tempo e dello Spazio / è pur dolce conforto rivivere in altrui" ["On the threshold of Time and Space I find / sweet comfort to think we live in others once again"] (*TM* 48–9).

Gozzano's untrustworthy poetic narrators, victims of their inability to live authentically, partially repurpose Corazzini's victimized narcissistic heroes. While the "fanciullo" of Corazzini is a chosen sacrificial lamb, Gozzano and his alter egos – first among all the "gelid sophist" of "Felicity" – are the intellectual martyrs of bourgeois culture. Nevertheless, their poetic inspiration comes from that bourgeois world, so mocked and rejected. The real Promethean trait of these complex and continually cloned characters is a rediscovered ability to survive, which Gozzano's *sui generis* "post-humanist" gardener embodies. In the last section of *I colloqui* – "Il reduce" ["The Veteran"] – Gozzano's poetic persona seems to find balance, assuming the role of "bourgeois Epicurean master." He develops a modernized *tetrapharmakos* (the Epicurean four-part remedy) based on ironic detachment and self-acceptance, which makes it possible to cope peacefully with the defeat of his life. Paradoxically, only through this ultimate "renunciation" can Gozzano's persona reassert his privileged position as intellectual. This lonely and wise "veteran-poet," who cultivates the *hortus conclusus* of his own villa, reinvents – in the figure of the "borghese onesto" ["honest bourgeois"] – the Latin topos of the virtuous farmer. One may think of the old Corycian in Virgil's *Georgics* (4.103–48), who owned a few acres of unfertile soil and still, in his opinion, had riches to equal the kings:

> Sono felice. La mia vita è tanto
> pari al mio sogno: il sogno che non varia:
> vivere in una villa solitaria,
> senza passato più, senza rimpianto:
> appartenersi, meditare … Canto
> l'esilio e la rinuncia volontaria.

[I'm happy there. My life's a perfect fit
with my dream, a dream without a deviation:
my villa in its splendid isolation,
a life without a past, without regret,
doing what suits me, musing … I celebrate
exile and free-willed renunciation.] (*TM* 142–3)

The conversion of the Promethean spirit in a free-willed renunciation constitutes a dominant motif in the development of futurist characters, who feel embarrassed for the humanist role of traditional intellectuals. In the poem "Autopsia" ["Autopsy"], Paolo Buzzi translates Gozzano's "ultimate renunciation" into a violent self-confession of isolation:

La carne mi si consuma nel pensiero.
Sono una rete di nervi sospesa sull'abisso.
Fui nel sole
fino ai trent'anni.
Amici avevo ed amiche. Or sento l'ombra
che d'ogni parte m'invade.
Tento d'essere ancora il mio bel sole, io solo.
Ma, spesso, ho notti prive pur della luna.
Adoro i vecchiarelli miei, che m'hanno fatto
così diverso e strano e pieno d'ubbie per la testa:
e, in fondo, ho la vergogna d'essere un Poeta.[81]

[My flesh consumes itself in my thought.
I am a web of nerves suspended on the abyss.
I was in the sun
until I was thirty.
I had male and female friends. Now I feel the shadow
that invades me from everywhere.
I still try to be my beautiful sun, sole.
But, I often have nights without even the moon.
I adore my old parents, who made me
so different and strange and full of groundless fears:
and, deep in my heart, I am ashamed of being a Poet.]

None of the futurist personae embody an educative approach towards the human genre. They rather express revulsion at those who are unable to foresee the violence of a jarring primitive-modernization that creates distinctiveness by dehumanizing the human. Marinetti's Gazurmah is the most blatant case of heroic uniqueness disconnected from any Promethean mission of collective emancipation. By killing his father and Colubbi – Mafarka's lover – Gazurmah rises as a superhuman solipsist hero, careless and self-sufficient owing to his powerful body and exceptional mind. The episode of Colubbi's death seems to restate the "natural" association between woman and Mother Earth that futurist women sought to erase – "uccidendomi, hai uccisa la Terra … la Terra!" ["It is the earth you've killed in killing me!"] she whispers with her last breath (*M* 224, *MF* 202). If Colubbi embodies the natural human, bound to the nourishment of earth, then through his act of murdering his primal mother, Gazurmah pushes the paternal dream of denying the procreative role of women to the final repudiation of the human species as a whole.

This futurist "mechanical god," who flies away, followed by flocks of condors, can only laugh at the ineptitude of the creeping humanity:

> Io non sono un uomo strisciante che si sforza, durante la notte, di spingere la sua piccola testa di tartaruga fuori dall'immenso guscio del firmamento! … Il firmamento? … Io ne sono padrone! (*M* 228)
>
> [I am no crawling man who strives at night to push his puny tortoise head outside of the immense carapace of the firmament! … The firmament? I am its master!] (*MF* 205).

Gazurmah leaves earth and founds a celestial colony beyond the human, asserting a *libido dominandi* that transposes his father's terrestrial dream of power to a wider colonial enterprise that embraces the entire firmament. In this façade of change that reasserts the paternal will of power, Gazurmah becomes a parodic Prometheus by chance. While flying away, he suddenly realizes that his metallic wings are "più vive e sonore di due arpe" ["more alive and resonant than two harps"] and can produce beautiful music (*M* 228, *MF* 205). Music – "la grande speranza del mondo, il gran sogno della musica totale" ["the great hope of the world, the great dream of total music"] – is the accidental "gift of fire" that the unwilling Gazurmah leaves to humanity (*M* 228, *MF* 205). In its intermixing and modulation of human and nonhuman bodily sounds, silences, air, and vibrations, this "music bio-product" is the only actual autonomous agent in Marinetti's fantasy of (unattained) self-sufficiency. The harmonic fluidity compensates for the disharmony that Gazurmah's birth produced and will probably affect humans positively, pushing them to lift up their heads and contemplate beauty.

Palazzeschi's poem "L'incendiario" ["The Arsonist"] offers another twentieth-century Prometheus by chance, a Prometheus who still brings flames but in the form of a wild act of arson. In this avant-garde rewriting of the fire bearer's myth, the chained demigod is a merciless arsonist who has been imprisoned in an iron cage in the middle of a square, while the crowd accuses and insults him. The situation suddenly changes with the arrival of a poet who triggers a counter-action; he celebrates this pyromaniac Prometheus-Jesus as a divine messiah and frees him to set the world on fire:

Uomini che avete orrore del fuoco,
poveri esseri di paglia!
Inginocchiatevi tutti!
Io sono il sacerdote,
questa gabbia è l'altare,
quell'uomo è il Signore! (*TTP* 183–4)

[You creatures afraid of fire,
miserable men of straw!
On your knees, all of you!
I am the priest,
this cage the altar,
this man the Lord!][82]

Once again, the recognition of the hero does not involve any social reconciliation, but rather emphasizes the gap between the poet – the only one able to grasp the deep meaning of the arsonist's pyromania – and the "miserable men of straw" who look but do not understand. In this altered perspective, modern people are afraid of fire, as they can recognize neither the revitalizing power of the arsonist's flames nor his heroic mission. Palazzeschi's unpopular hero is a "Dionysian Prometheus" who has turned the progressive function of fire into a destructive burst: the only purifying antidote against a numb humanity, too serious and too unimaginative. Equally odd, the man of smoke in the *Il codice di Perelà* is an ironic messiah who descends among humans with no redemptive mission, an unaware hero-puppet thrown into the scene to perform a grotesque reenactment of the Passion. Although he brings no message of salvation, Perelà is initially celebrated as a redeemer for no logical reason, and then, in the same illogical way, is indicted for murder and imprisoned as a public enemy. Similarly, Corra's Sam Dunn also surrenders eventually to a senseless delirium: "più forte e più elegante di Cristo" ["stronger and more elegant than Christ"], he moves "resolutely towards his crucifixion," maintaining a truly divine indifference.[83]

Crepuscular and futurist "heroes" are unheard prophets, destined for intellectual solitude and rejection. Yet the defeat of these "saviours by chance," unlike the tragic divide between Romantic heroes and the rest of society, is always accompanied by humour or narcissistic masochism. Through their experiences of martyrdom, the crepuscular and futurist heroes seem to recapitulate Sam Dunn's realization: "la vita è un pasticcio, abbastanza grande, abbastanza complicato e molto confuso, in cui non si capisce niente e in cui si può ficcare tutto ciò che si vuole senza peggiorarlo e senza migliorarlo" ["the world is chaotic, rather large and complicated and very confused … one understands nothing about it and … it is possible to pack everything one wants into it without either making it worse or improving it"].[84] Thus, while Sam Dunn does not have any faith in the world – a faith that for Corra is "the necessary quality" of any heroic mission – he has a great sense of humour and, before dying, is seized by a fit of laughter. This fallen hero accepts the failure of his mission and dies ingloriously in the most tragicomic of accidents: he is suffocated by the giant buttocks of a clumsy maid. The hero is ultimately defeated by the illogical unpredictability of life; nevertheless, his death maintains an intellectual allure, the insatiable need to seek an understanding that might never be attained in this world or in human terms. As the futurist writer Fanny Dini writes in her lyrical prose "Ubriacature" ["Drunkennesses"], her own destiny is to wander through life: "Vado per tutte le vie della terra – con gli occhi di cielo e la bocca di sete: vado – e non mi disseto" ["I wander through all the streets of earth – with eyes of sky and mouth of thirst: I go – and I don't quench my thirst"] (*SF* 267). Echoing the Nietzschean image of Corazzini's wanderer, Dini restates the idea that exceptional personalities cannot be measured by their accomplishments; the only measure of an avant-garde hero is his or her tortuous, haphazard, and even purposeless journey.

Celebrating through these modern fallen heroes that which humans do not comprehend and cannot even project into saviour demigods, crepuscular and futurist literature provides an apophatic theology, namely a description of its terrestrial gods *via negationis*. This literature thus affirms what heroes are *not* when opposed to the "ineffable positivité" ["ineffable positivity"] of life.[85] The "negative positivity" that emerges from torn bodies and degenerated protagonists is the complex redefinition of a *gnōthi seauton* ["know thyself"] formula that – under the masks of humour and sarcasm – cautiously embraces uncertainty, hybridity, and even failure. Immersed in a fear of change that was brought to the fore by the First World War, with its bodily, social, and rational "mutilations," crepusculars and futurists reacted by imagining a complex world of "lived social and body realities in which people are not afraid of their joint kinship with animals and machines, not afraid of permanently partial identities and contradictory standpoints."[86] The beauty of their complementary reflections on the body indeed relies on deconstructing the rationalized image of the body as a perfectly functioning machine and recounting twisted *natureculture* stories, in which material, gender, and socio-environmental issues intertwine.

Chapter Four

Love and the Grand Solidarity of Sound

Love and Its Many Sounds

In the poem "Identificazione" ["Identification"], collected in *L'inaugurazione della primavera* [*The Inauguration of Spring*] (1915), Govoni recounts a unique walk around Milan, in which his poetic "I" echoes the voices, secret emotions, and sufferings of the people around him – a young priest, a sickly old man, a poor bricklayer, and a beautiful woman. The encounter with this woman particularly affects the poetic persona, altering his relationship with a transformed Milan: the young lady's indefinable allure shines through the city's lights, her movements pulsate into the cars, her elegance has informed the houses and surrounding objects. Yet, when the woman eventually disappears, blending into Milan's topography and sounds, her vanishing highlights a hidden relational map that interweaves the urban space. The body of the city, which fuses with the woman's evanescent body, is revealed to be pervaded with affects – the potential for interaction, embedded in anything – and emotions – affects "captured" in an individual form.[1]

Govoni's metamorphic urban setting suggests a transmutation of private interactions into a complex network of transformative events. And yet, these events, triggered by the encounter with the beloved, seemingly produce an uncanny bewilderment. Wondering about his relational identity, Govoni's poetic "I" formulates a question that breaks the silence:

> Sono dunque solo e diminuito,
> con due gambe sole
> due braccia sole
> due occhi ed una unica bocca.
> Gli altri dove saranno mai? (*P* 179)

[So I am sole and diminished,
with two legs solely
two arms solely
two eyes and one only mouth.
Where, then, will the others be?]

Govoni's open query – "Where, then, will the others be?" – offers a leading thread to analyse how crepuscular and futurist works reinvent one of the closest human connections and the most prolific poetic topos: love. Engaging with this traditional motif, both movements dislodge the bias that identifies love with a perilous journey to a safe destination, to a final social accomplishment sealed by marriage, or to the achievement of perfect harmony. They provocatively transmute love into its disorienting "reverse," exploring the emotional potential of love's own incongruences, tics, and violent spasms.

Through a variety of sensorial images, I examine how both crepuscularism and futurism explore the cacophonies and unexpected silences that come to disturb or affect relationships. Deprived of its pacified imagery, love becomes a destabilized (and destabilizing) locus of derangement. Yet, while crepuscularism investigates this derangement as a potential for "rerouting" – for discovering the productivity of love's dead ends, communication gaps, and silences – futurism turns this destabilization into the blaring message of a liberating "politics of love."

However, as previously seen for the redefinition of gender identity and the notion of pangender virility, the discourse about love is also not exempt from incoherencies. By originating a position of resistance to the bourgeois courtly rituals and foundational institutions like family, the two movements betray their continued dependence on such regulated systems. Marinetti's progressive call for free love maintains "passéist" stereotypes of women, who are often eclipsed or depicted as complicit prey. Moreover, under the guise of a fight for emancipation, the futurists' libertine proposals evolve into a biopolitical management of procreation. What I suggest, though, is that the truly affective potential of the avant-garde reinvention of lover-beloved relationships resides not so much in its pseudo-transgressive contents as in its overall capacity to act as a sounding board for dynamics of social change. Through their provocative propositions on sexual and marital life, crepuscular and futurist male authors established a dialogue, or in the case of futurism an intense debate, with women writers, who, in turn, reacted by voicing their own view of love and sexual practices.

As Jeanne Heuving has contended, in modernist and avant-garde poetics, reinventing love does not exhaust its action upon a socio-cultural process of change; it is "By discovering a different way to write love – shifting their erotic energies away from a poetic speaker as lover and onto their poems' others and languages – [that] the poets create a changed love."[2] In the case of crepuscularism and futurism, this shift involves a radical repositioning of love beyond the human scale. Govoni's text serves once again as an example: in his poem, the murky whole of a tentacular Milan encompasses a shrunken poetic "I," who observes his beloved "other" dissolving into the city's body. This image reveals a relevant problem for modernism and the avant-garde: in the fugitive multitude of the modern world, "there is no human account of the whole … And it's a problem of scale."[3] Embracing the whole – its inhuman totality – entails capturing and encompassing a dimension of love that cannot be reduced to the human sensorial scale. What does love look like, beyond human measure? The challenge for both crepuscularism and futurism is to explore this deranging territory, where love transmutes, and even disperses, into an impalpable yet immanent communion of disparate elements. The hurdle is to try to represent love not from the traditional perspective of the lover-subject who chases an object of desire but rather from the inter-subjective or inter-objective space of this chasing – namely, to grasp love in its unfolding in-betweenness. Reimagined through a decentred human view, the avant-garde narrative of love traces uncharted emotional landscapes, where it is possible to simultaneously "touch a multitude of fugitive things, to bring them within reach of inner space," to affect and be affected by them.[4] Love becomes a dispersed "material solidarity," across organic and inorganic life. To express this diffused interconnection, crepuscular and futurist texts adopt the non-verbal language of sounds. Through their modulations, silence and noise turn into the media to express the restless and incommensurable "solidarity" that interweaves the whole.

Focusing on the motif of love and its many "sounds," this chapter retraces the sensorial routes that crepuscular and futurist texts draw while exploring affective connections among people and between human and nonhuman agents.

Crepuscular Silence and the "Rerouting" of Love

Love defines a corporeal, gendered, cognitive, and socio-political site, wherein affect – the capacity of affecting others and being affected by others – is particularly intense. If, as Lauren Berlant has stated, incoherence is a condition of affect, love further emphasizes such constitutional incongruity, as this feeling develops from the combination of two antithetical qualities, "repetition and uniqueness."[5] We might say that love, rather than developing through harmonic sounds, modulates its unique dissonance. Engaging with this intrinsic incoherence, with what Alain Badiou had dubbed love's "agenda of contradictions and violence,"[6] the crepusculars reinvent this overused poetic topos by exploring its "reverse." When "auscultated" carefully, love resonates its numerous inconsistencies, becoming a musical score of missed interactions, miscommunication, and glacial silences. However, what if these interferences were unfolding an equally binding capability that creates love's own "sound"?

Venturing into a path dotted with interferences, we will indeed explore the sensorial map drawn by crepuscular authors. One might rightly affirm that the crepuscular poetic universe is a microcosm deprived of love, as this poetry brackets the crucial moment of the encounter with the beloved. Yet, crepuscularism also testifies to the affective potential that non-encountered love exercises. Proceeding from this premise, we will see that crepuscular texts trace an unconventional map – a sort of photographic negative – whose borders emerge from productive non-encounters, from missed opportunities that, barely noticeably, triggered sudden "reroutings" and alternative paths. An exemplary case of this affective redirection that the not-encountered generates appears in Gozzano's uncollected poem "La più bella" ["The Loveliest"]. The text plays on the idea that the most intriguing object of desire is an unfound island. This wonderland exists to tease humans with the fascinating virtuality of its presence-absence. The navigator has heard fabulous stories about her, can smell her, as if she were a perfumed courtesan, and yet when he moves closer "rapida si dilegua come parvenza vana, / si tinge dell'azzurro color di lontananza" ["rapidly she'll vanish like a vision on the wind, / hiding herself in the azure colors of faraway"] (*TM* 224–5). By displaying an inaccessible "cluster of promises,"[7] the isle guides the navigator to explore unfolding routes, which trace alternative cartographies of encounter and self-discovery. Borrowing again from Berlant, we can state that Gozzano's unfound island anchors our "sense of endurance in [a potential] object"; and, in doing so, this constantly missed locus enables people to access actual routes.

This reflection on the potentiality released by the non-encountered object of love leads us to briefly pinpoint connections between crepuscularism and futurism, while further highlighting the idiosyncratic grey area of the turn of the century, in which poetic tradition, symbolism, early modernism, and the avant-garde hybridize. Gozzano's vanishing island and Govoni's love for a disappearing woman can be linked to a statement by Italian symbolist poet Gian Pietro Lucini. In his 1909 work *Revolverate* [*Revolver Shots*], Lucini affirmed: "*Io amo la verità, che, come le stelle nascoste tuttora al telescopio e ricercate dal suo obbiettivo, esistono ma non sono ancora disegnate dalle carte del planisfero*" ["*I love the truth that, like the stars hidden to the telescope and searched for by its lens, exist but have not been drawn by the world maps yet*"] (*TIF* 31). Interestingly, Marinetti uses this passage in his preface to Lucini's *Revolverate* to show how, in this work, the symbolist poet fostered the futurist love of the unexplored, locating the mission of art in its "*cammino indefinito*" ["*indefinite route*"] (*TIF* 32). Like the futurists, Lucini was fascinated with techno-scientific discourse, and, through his poetry, he investigated the virtuality that informs modern life, from the potential of electric power stations to the living force of steam engines. Discussing the notion of liberating potential that poetry needs to grasp through free verse, the symbolist author mentions radium – "la condensazione degli elettroni irradiati" ["the condensation of irradiated electrons"] (*TIF* 32). This element, discovered in the late nineteenth century, is matter, soaked in its radioactive potential, which keeps transforming throughout its life. To describe the extraordinary potential for change in radium, Lucini adopts the term "entelekeja" ["entelechy"] – a philosophical term that designates the process of "becoming actual" in the materiality of its unfolding.[8] According to Lucini, capturing this unfolding is the objective of poetry. This brief overview must emphasize that what intertwines symbolist, crepuscular, and futurist poetics is the centrality of the topos of potentiality as a substitute discourse for the actuality of love.

Recasting love as a love for the richness of the virtual – for the unheard voice or for the encounter that keeps slipping away – crepuscularism rewrites the literary tradition. In "La più bella," Gozzano can openly play with the topic of the missed encounter because this motif historically constitutes a crucial plot point. One might think of works like Dante's *Vita Nuova* and the *Commedia* [*The Divine Comedy*], Petrarch's *Canzoniere*, Shakespeare's *Romeo and Juliet*, and Manzoni's *I promessi sposi* [*The Betrothed*], which all pivot on an impeded, unfulfilled, or dramatically unachievable encounter. Yet, these traditional works, especially those by Dante and Petrarch, present us with a further incoherence: their love becomes fruitful only in the lover's silence and absence. For instance, only after the death of Beatrice and Laura do Dante and Petrarch move from a self-referential discourse to a dialogue that produces interaction. The loss of Beatrice sets the stage for Dante to experience a plethora of interactions in his journey through the *Commedia*'s *cantiche*. Likewise, in Petrarch's prayer to the Virgin, which closes the *Canzoniere*, he "leav[es] behind all previous attempts to converse with himself and the earthly other outside himself" to embrace a true dialogic nature of speech as an "*in praesentia* conversation" with God.[9]

The crepusculars maximize this aspect of incoherence of a love that can only produce interaction *in absentia*. In their poetics, the love encounter is crucial precisely because it never happened, or because it derailed the poetic persona and triggered a rerouting outside the domain of lover-beloved relationships.

The encounter becomes an ellipsis, an out-and-out narrative silence or vacuum. An exemplary case of this repurposing is Corazzini's poem "Follie" ["Follies"], in which the poetic "I" chaotically recollects the death of his unnamed "Madonna" and, in a haphazard delirium, mourns and gradually assembles a beloved who has never existed – the lips he never kissed, the hands he never touched, the voice he never heard (*O* 111–12).

What Corazzini is celebrating is love as an emotional drive that acts through absence and desire. Crepuscular poetry unveils the "productive incoherence" of a poetics of love that is transformative and relationally constructive, as long as it remains a virtuality – as long as love is an enticing cluster of promises. In "Follie," Corazzini defines the worthless circularity of his feelings, declaring that his "inutile" ["useless"] love is the obsession of a madman who restlessly chases the sun (*O* 112). This statement could be interpreted as an ironic debasement of love from a sublime spiritual redemption to a pointless terrestrial damnation. Yet, the endless movement of Corazzini's "I," who is madly chasing the sun, rewrites the "unproductivity" of courtly love to subtly challenge the bourgeois politics of love, which pivots on "a rhetoric of resting, of coming to terms" with a predefined social destiny.[10] This criticism of love as a "safe space" emerges very bitterly in Moretti's poem "A Cesena." The text represents the fossilization of love into domestic role-play. The poetic narrator describes the final metamorphosis of his newly married sister into a dreadful bourgeois housewife. In only six months of marriage, she has turned her spontaneous smile into a fake "sorriso … di nuora" ["smile of … a daughter-in-law"] (*TLP* 289). Set in opposition to this performative happiness, crepuscular love marks the arousal of "surprise, vivid particularity, and extreme qualitative intensity," stressing how love restlessly resides in the rerouting that unsettles the poetic "I's" journey.[11]

In their reinvention of love from the perspective of its incoherent "reverse" and enticing silences, crepuscular authors often switch the narrative focus from the lover to the pursued non-lover. Viewed through this estranged lens, love does not generate a "(de)compositions of mutual in-compossibilities,"[12] but rather shapes dissonant relations that rise from "in-compossibilities." This oxymoronic status of relational separation emerges in Corazzini's "Dialogo di marionette" ["Dialogue of Marionettes"], a poem that stages the dialogue between two puppets, a detached queen and a passionate poet. The exchange parodies the distortions that the romantic view of love has caused. The poet asks his beloved to let him climb onto her balcony while the king is asleep. Nevertheless, as the realist queen points out, this naïve plan is unfeasible: the papier-mâché balcony would not hold them, her oakum braid cannot serve as a rope, and – even worse – she cannot feel any pain for him, as her heart is made of wood. In this crescendo, the pressing stichomythia provides a camp "experience of the sublime, but seen from the perspective of the ridiculous."[13] While the realist – or ontology-oriented – queen magnifies any pragmatic issues, the idealist – or constructivist – lover minimizes the material fragility of their paper world, to remain loyal to the cultural representation of his Eros-and-Thanatos script. His pathos can only push the queen's realism to the breaking point of caustic irony:

– Non mi dite una parola,
io morirò ...
– Come? Per questa sola
ragione?
– Siete ironica ... addio!

[– You don't speak to me, so
I will die.
– What? you will die for that
alone?
– You are ironic ... Goodbye.] (*SE* 48–9)

As Sianne Ngai has contended, irony is not an emotion per se, but is a "rhetorical attitude with a decidedly affective dimension."[14] The queen's ironic tone exercises a liberating power on the love poet, freeing him from a literary sentiment that his culture has constructed and imposed on him. He can finally depart from those constrictions, whereas his realist queen of irony remains trapped in her role of victim and victimizer. For her, there is no catharsis. Her wooden heart even prevents her from lamenting her lover's departure. Trapped in the ambivalent affective dimension of irony – in its intellectual detachment and self-torturing awareness – the queen, like Gozzano's Totò Merumeni (mentioned in chapter 3), recalls Baudelaire's figure of "L'Héautontimoroumenos," or the man who tortures himself. As it does for the Baudelaireian character, malign irony has taken over her agency:

It's in my voice, the raucous jade!
It's in my blood's black venom too!
I am the looking-glass, wherethrough
Megera sees herself portrayed!
I am the wound, and yet the blade![15]

Irony is similarly the venom and antidote for Gozzano's poetic "I." This character – a self-torturer of many faces – has used literature as a screening filter, so literature has eventually robbed him of his ability to affect and be affected. For

Gozzano, irony translates into a practice of eternal "renunciation." As the poet affirms in "I colloqui," the text that opens the eponymous collection, his life was a beautiful novel that he did not enjoy, a life that his "silent brother" lived, acted, and felt in his behalf:

> Io piansi e risi per quel mio fratello
> che pianse e rise, e fu come lo spetro
> ideale di me, giovine e bello.
>
> [I cried and laughed to see that brother
> who cried and laughed and acted the ideal
> ghost of myself, young and well put together.] (*TM* 6–7)

Gozzano's poetic persona is giving voice to a traumatic separation of mind and body, which has ultimately let irony overpower his human agency. This fictional impasse recalls Baruch Spinoza's reflection on the "parallel interdependence" of mind and body. Clarifying this interrelation, Michael Hardt has explained that although Spinoza's *Ethics* states that mind and body are autonomous, we should not think of them as separate entities – the former concerned with receptivity to external ideas, the latter with sensitivity to other bodies.[16] They should rather be conceived as a continuum, wherein the notion of affect intervenes by straddling any strict divide between the two; consequently, "the greater our power to be affected ... the greater our power to act." Engaging with Spinoza's perspective, we can see how, by completely delegating his power to be affected to literature, Gozzano's persona feels that his power to act is diminished. Yet, his experience of estrangement – his sensation of having been the inept spectator of his own life – is not unique to literature, and can be extended to other forms of "connecting separation" that emerging media of the time, like cinema and radio, were popularizing. For instance, the spectatorship in cinema pivots on the identification between silent spectators and moving images on screen, and yet it is the gap between spectators and action on screen that allows for the emotional transfer. Transposed into our era, Gozzano's replacement of lived life with *lived spectatorship* can be compared to the second-degree experience of affect that social media offers. Is being affected by our own profile, (re)watching pictures or videos that we have posted, getting emotional about them, about what happened and could have happened, not experiencing the "ghost of ourselves," following the traces our silent sibling leaves? And is such virtual or relived experience not indeed the result of our body and mind interacting, as though springing from our projected "shadow"? Gozzano's poetry can be located precisely in this shadowy area of "ghosted agency," which the poet turns into a privileged emotional observatory.

Gozzano's "syndrome" of self-denied action particularly informs his poems about love. If, as Martha Nussbaum remarks in her analysis of Proust's *Research*, "love denied and successfully repressed is not exactly love,"[17] in the case of Gozzano's poetry it would be more accurate to speak of a nuanced quasi-love, barely distinguishable from regret. Gozzano's relationships are always set in a lost past, in a time of missed opportunities and haunting memories. Consequently, his "beloved" women are clones of an Ur-woman, the one he could have loved but never did. This female archetype whom the poet has recurrently met and metaphorically killed is epitomized in his poem "Una risorta" ["A Woman Resurrected"], from the last section of *I colloqui*. Through the character of the resurrected, Gozzano momentarily brings back to life all his female "co-protagonists" – Graziella, Felicita, Virginia, Cocotte – all the women he can finally "love" through the filter of regret.

In a quatrain from "Cocotte," Gozzano states a constitutive feature of his poetics of ghosted love, which comes to complement his poetics of material nostalgia embedded in things past. What Gozzano's "I" loves is the intense virtuality of the experiences he did not live but used to inform his life as a spectator. Not by chance, in the Italian original text, the passage in which he enunciates this affection for missed relationships pivots on a reiteration of double negations – "non amo che le rose che non colsi" – which the English translation partially renders:

> Il mio sogno e nutrito d'abbandono,
> di rimpianto. Non amo che le rose
> che non colsi. Non amo che le cose
> che potevano essere e non sono
> state ...
>
> [Abandonment and fond regret are still
> the nurturers of my dream. I love only that
> rose that I never plucked. I love only what
> could once have come to be and never will ...] (*TM* 118–19)

Living his own life as a "silent spectator," Gozzano can only recapture love as a trauma, tattooed in his memory, as the ghosted life that he did not experience and that yet haunts him. Corazzini, on the other hand, reinvents love as the poetic possibility of what did not happen, mourning the death of a beloved who never existed. Yet, in parallel ways, this non-loved love, through its silences and gaps, still produces relational ties, tracing alternative emotional routes that mark an innovative view onto the traditional poetics of the encounter, while dislodging the bourgeois institutionalization of love as a praxis of social legitimation.

Noise and the Futurist Politics of Love

If crepuscularism explores the rerouting that love's absence triggers, futurism loudly glorifies the affective potential of such absence. According to Marinetti, love is a paranoid obsession that prevents action, an artificial narcotic that must be demystified. In "Contro l'amore e il parlamentarismo" ["Against Love and Parliamentarism"] (1915), he declares:

> Noi siamo convinti che l'amore – sentimentalismo e lussuria – sia la cosa meno naturale del mondo. Non vi è di naturale e d'importante che il coito il quale ha per scopo il futurismo della specie.
>
> L'amore – ossessione romantica e voluttà – non è altro che un'invenzione dei poeti, i quali la regalarono all'umanità ... E saranno i poeti che all'umanità lo ritoglieranno ... (*TIF* 292–3)
>
> [We are convinced that Love – sentimentality and lust – is the least natural thing in the world. There is nothing natural except the perpetuation of the species. Love – romantic, voluptuary obsession – is nothing but an invention of the poets, who gave it to humanity. And it will be the poets who will take it away from humanity.] (*F* 86)

Yet, as Alberto Toscano states, Marinetti does not fully dispose of this "unnatural" sentimentalism. He rather engages in a much more complex operation. The futurist founder sublimates love into a "*personal, sensual* relation" with animated machines. This process of disposal and mechanical sublimation presents a twofold dynamic: on the one hand, Marinetti creates an "anthropomorphic affective transfer that posits 'a new sensibility of the machine' and a kind of machinic-organic continuum"; on the other, this spiritualization of the metallic apparatus allows an "escape from the 'heaviness' of woman" and dialogic relationality, in general.[18] By creating much ado about romantic love and its downfalls, Marinetti succeeds in shifting affective ties from the human to the nonhuman; and this shift is indeed pivotal to recast male sovereignty as an elitist relationship with the machine. "Noise" thus becomes a strategy to advance a vision of love that hides a quite conservative agenda.

Futurism's incoherent process of love's disposal and mechanical sublimation provides an interesting perspective on the role that affect plays within social structures. The avant-garde discourse of love – transgressive and yet deeply reactionary – demonstrates that affective ties should not be naïvely equated to a revolutionary "passion for difference." Futurist politics evolved from the 1909 heated "declaration of love" – "Noi vogliamo cantare l'amor del pericolo, l'abitudine all'energia e alla temerità" ["We intend to sing the love of danger, the habit of energy and fearlessness"] (*TIF* 10, *F* 51) – to the 1919 calcification of this love of change into a totalitarian sociality, in which pregnant women symbolically represent "la proprietà di uno Stato" ["the property of a State"] (*TIF* 378). As Clare Hemmings has contended, affective ties can act "as a central mechanism of social reproduction in the most glaring ways."[19] In their introduction to *The Affect Theory Reader* (2009), Melissa Gregg and Gregory Seigworth have similarly acknowledged that "there are no ultimate or final guarantees – political, ethical, aesthetic, pedagogic, and otherwise – that capacities to affect and be affected will yield an actualized next or new that is somehow better than 'now.'"[20] Ultimately, Brian Massumi, in his *Politics of Affect* (2015), has illustrated the ambiguous action of affect in contemporary Western society, where people are "in-formed by capitalist powers of production," so that their "whole life becomes a 'capitalist tool.'"[21] However, any socio-political system retains spaces of manoeuvrability, where counter-movements to the dominant logic – sudden crepuscular "reroutings" – can develop. In the futurist politics of affect, we can in fact detect the puzzling consistency of an authentic "passion for difference" – a transformative love – intermingled with a male fear of social change.[22]

According to Marinetti, extirpating the "invention" of love is primarily a matter of human emancipation – wherein emancipation should always be understood, in futurist terms, as an elusion of the present, namely, as a simultaneous return to the primal status of the animal and as a projection into a mechanical future. As the futurist founder explains in "L'uomo moltiplicato e il regno della macchina" ["The Multiplied Man and the Reign of the Machine"] (1911), if love is reduced to copulation for the preservation of the species – "semplice funzione corporale, come il bere e il mangiare" ["a simple bodily function, like eating or drinking"] – its action will finally be detached from its literary and cultural narratives (*TIF* 301, *F* 92). Unlike the crepusculars, who conceive love as the emotional surplus of a virtual life that was never actualized, the futurists actualize this surplus in the energetic and truly physical "synthesis" of the intercourse. In the poem "Alcool" ["Alcohol"], anthologized in *I poeti futuristi*, Mario Betuda maintains that sexual pleasure is the "Unica dea ed unica certezza dell'amore" ["unique goddess and certainty of love"] (*PF* 99), the tangible reality of an idealized myth.

The violence of a physical and energetic love, deprived of any poetic "invention," particularly emerges in Paolo Buzzi's work. In the poem "Fine di due gatti" ["End of Two Cats"], also collected in *I poeti futuristi*, the author narrates the self-destructing story of "due gatti che si amavano / e protestavano al mondo l'amore" ["two cats who loved each other and protested their love to the world"]

(*PF* 162). The two animals, a black male and a white female, chase each other until they finally encounter. Their clashing vital energies come together so powerfully that they condense in a tangle of fur and explode "nel foro del Nulla / in una detonazione vocale / di bomba di carne" ["in the hole of Nothing / in a vocal detonation / of a fleshy bomb"] (*PF* 164). The theme of love's conflicting synthesis – its dangerous detonation – is also central in Buzzi's novel *L'ellisse e la spirale* [*The Ellipse and the Spiral*] (1915), both from a genre and content perspective.[23] This work strives to create a new futurist epic, through a clashing medley that combines science fiction, movie script, avant-garde "words in freedom," and esoteric writing. Through this cross-genre mix, *L'ellisse e la spirale* celebrates the birth of a new humankind, emerging from the fight between the masculine and feminine principles. These two primal forces are embodied respectively by the emperor Naxar and the queen Deliria. Echoing Marinetti's *Mafarka il futurista*, Buzzi foretells a social subversion that pivots on an alchemical process of regeneration. During this process of transformation, the metamorphic collision of masculinity and femininity generates new living matter. Under the guise of a fictional displacement into a cosmic "otherness," through this novel, Buzzi endorses the necessity of war, conceived as an alchemical mutation of the human into a potentiated hybrid of clashing forces. Yet this encounter does not promote any dialogical interaction between disparate elements. It brutally compresses constructive difference into a martial construction of unity.

The violent process of creating unity through noisy collision appears in a more grotesque fashion in Palazzeschi's poetry. In "Le beghine" ["The Beguines"], the poet describes bigoted women – their old clothes, décor, behaviour, dated coquetry – and wonders whether they renounced sexual love or fully experienced pleasure before embracing chastity: "Ecco il mistero / che m'interessa in voi. / L'amore!" ["Here is the mystery / that interests me about you ladies. / Love!"] (*PF* 392). Thus, the poetic "I" retells a sadistic dream, in which he possesses these old ladies, in the grip of perverse desire – "Gobbe, torte, mostruose / farvi rinascere per un instante solo / un brivido del più orribile desiderio" ["Hunchbacked, curved, monstrous / to have you revive for just one instant / a shiver of the most horrible desire"] (*PF* 393). His obscene dream is to deflower and contaminate the beguines' untouched flesh with the carnal energy of his twenty years. Yet the poetic persona suddenly appears in front of his grandmother and, regressing to childish behaviour, swears he has never touched the beguines. He simply enjoys fantasizing about them. While Palazzeschi's sudden denial is symptomatic of a fear of the mother – a symbolic epiphany of woman's threatening "heaviness" and confrontational relationality – the sadistic joy of using these old bodies is equally problematic. The libidinal drive to possess the past is charged with guilt and immediately repressed because is incompatible with the futurist eugenic ban of contagious passéist "things," which equates woman "with a calcified, indolent past." Deliverance from the family, "specifically the love of the mother," is thus "the precondition for a successful future aesthetic," which cannot be disconnected from its politics of affect.[24]

The futurist rejection of the pathology of love aims to immunize the human species, through a preventive separation of emotional attachment from sexual practices. For Marinetti, in "L'uomo moltiplicato e il regno della macchina," this vaccination against love is necessary to achieve the dream of new males, able to preserve their "genital power until death":

> i giovani maschi contemporanei, finalmente nauseati dei libri erotici e del duplice alcool sentimentale e lussurioso, essendo finalmente immunizzati contro la malattia dell'amore, imparino metodicamente a distruggere in sé tutti i dolori del cuore, lacerando quotidianamente i loro affetti e distraendo infinitamente il loro sesso con contatti femminili rapidi e disinvolti. (*TIF* 301)

> [young males of our time, at last nauseated by erotic books and the double alcohol of sentimentality and lust, finally immunized against the sickness of love, must learn to destroy all sorrows of the heart within themselves, every day lacerating their feelings and distracting their sexual organs and their minds.] (*F* 92)

From a social perspective, this "laceration of feelings" ushers in an epochal social transformation of bourgeois social institutions. As the futurist founder affirms, free love implies liberation from the "family's suffocating grip" and its socio-cultural entourage of stereotypical figures, such as the abhorred triad of the cuckold, the woman wife-and-mother, and the Don Juan (*F* 92). Prior to the official foundation of futurism, Marinetti had offered "a scathing look at the institution of marriage" in *Poupées électriques* [*Electrical Dolls*], a theatrical piece written between 1905 and 1907.[25] In this work, Marinetti stages the drama of a modern couple, John Wilson – an engineer who makes "electrical dolls" – and his wife, Mary. To affirm their unconventionality, in the key scene, Mary and John have sex in front of two prudish electric dolls, Monsieur Prudent and Mother Prunelle. This act reawakes the couple's sexual drive, while suggesting possible new territories of proximity between human and nonhuman: John compares his wife to one of the electrical automata he produces and asserts that, like the dolls, it is "electricity that makes her nerves vibrate like conducting wires of voluptuousness."[26]

According to Minsoo Kang, in this pre-futurist theatrical work the dolls have a dual value: they are products of modern technology but also denounce the "conformist bourgeois machine" that marriage perpetrates.[27] The symbolic role of the automata becomes even more complex if one considers that these machines enable the couple to experience a transgression from the bourgeois family norm; yet, John and Mary's voyeuristic sexual game will ultimately lead to their own destruction. The breaking of this relationship that, although striving to be unconventional, cannot help but fall into contrived puppetry, foreshadows the agency of the futurist machines in activating mechanisms that drastically reboot the bourgeois *modus vivendi*. Marinetti further elaborates on the demolition of family ties in *Mafarka il futurista*. To prepare for the birth of Gazurmah – the solipsist futurist overhuman – the novel symbolically dismembers marital bonds, through the atrocious death of Uarabelli-Ciarciar and her caring husband Magmal, Mafarka's brother. This exotic disguise of the "perfect" bourgeois family is mercilessly destroyed. Under the effect of a powerful venom, Magmal attacks his wife and then dies. Once torn to bloody pieces, Uarabelli reveals her true essence: she is nothing more than disgusting pulp staining the couple's bedroom. Turning the bourgeois hearth into a charnel house, futurism does not solely dissolve family ties but also unmasks the nauseating substance hidden under every respectable marriage.

Futurism's rejection of the politics of love that bourgeois society has institutionalized involves an astute dual process of destruction and (re)monopolization of the social space. In the manifesto "L'uomo moltiplicato e il regno della macchina," Marinetti hints at this twofold strategy, when he states that the propaganda in support of free love emancipates people from romantic love and strict family bonds (*TIF* 301, *F* 92). The ruins of this bourgeois institution become a fertile ground for implanting a politics of affect founded on the (seemingly) autarkic brotherhood of futurism. As a relational institution, Marinetti's avant-garde male cohort recalls a type of masculine bond that ancient Greek society had institutionalized through similar types of sociocultural practices. For instance, attending symposia played a key function in creating cohesion among the Greek male ruling elite, while providing the social space for a subaltern definition of womanhood. A literary testimony of this type of socialization that excludes, yet simultaneously defines, women is the satire "On Women" by Semonides of Amorgos. In this work, conceived to be performed during symposia, the poet stigmatizes female characters, associating their awful vices with animal and vegetal elements. The invective against women – "the worst evil which gods have ever inflicted upon man" – ends with the celebration of the only virtuous feminine type, the industrious bee-woman.[28] In a similar way, throughout the social satire that *Mafarka il futurista* "stages," Marinetti defines female stereotypes for his brotherhood, using a number of zoomorphic images. This derogatory use of animal language provides a patriarchal "justification" of women's inferior nature:[29] the caring housewife Uarabelli is a giant, repulsive snail and a night bird; Colubbi, the lover, is a breeder of hyenas; Langurama, the mother, is a mummy with a pig snout. Although *Mafarka il futurista* does not redeem a single woman-type, the novel serves a similar purpose to Semonides's invective, which is to solidify an alternative male-only "family," based on intellectual solidarity rather than on blood and heterosexual relationships.[30]

The futurist fellowship can be strengthened only if competitive forms of relational rituals and institutions, such as courtship and marriage, lose their affective power. As Marinetti clarifies through a comparison with fashion in the manifesto "Distruzione della sintassi – Radio Immaginazione – Parole in libertà," the issue with (heterosexual) love is that it has lost any intriguing potential for innovation. In his words,

> La donna trova tutto l'ignoto dell'amore nella scelta di una toilette straordinaria … L'uomo non ama la donna priva di lusso. L'amante ha perso ogni prestigio, l'Amore ha perso il suo valore assoluto. (*TIF* 67)
>
> [The element of mystery once found in love now resides in the selection of an amazing outfit … Men no longer love a woman who is without *luxus*. The lover has lost all prestige, and Love has lost its absolute value.] (*F* 144).

Compared to the vibrant intellectual solidarity of the futurist male brotherhood, relationships with women can only be exciting for the intense, fleeting time of a quick conquest. In *Come si seducono le donne*, the futurist founder showcases how to enjoy intensified yet "synthetic" forms of pleasure with random female prey. The idea of conquering a woman – a love metaphor for war – offers the "situational" aphrodisiac as well as the background for Marinetti's view of sexual emancipation.[31] For instance, in his manual of seduction, he recounts an occasional love affair with a woman from Bologna, which serendipitously occurred on a train. The fleeting intensity of this event takes the space-time of an incisive futurist formula: "Controllore sagace + treno direttissimo + notte d'agosto + assenza di viaggiatori nello scompartimento X seduttore = bellissima bolognese mangiata e bevuta" ["Shrewd ticket inspector + super express train + August night + absence of travellers in the carriage X seducer = great Bolognese feast and drink"].[32]

Marinetti's emphasis on free love acquires a different meaning after the First World War, when futurism feels the need to further reassert a jeopardized male agency. Once again, we can notice that the strategy of clamour is pivotal for the affirmation of patriarchal schemes. This conservative agenda surfaces from a proposal of radical sexual egalitarianism, which aims to finally break the enslavement fostered by marriage. In the manifesto "Contro il matrimonio" ["Against Marriage"], collected in *Democrazia futurista* [*Futurist Democracy*] (1919), the futurist founder claims the necessity of introducing divorce because, without it, family is a deleterious prison, solely comparable to a Bedouin tent, filled with a lurid blend of impaired old people, women, children, pigs, donkeys, camels, hens, and excrement (*TIF* 368). For futurism, any institutionalized relationship relies on a distorted idea of possession, which negates any sentimental freedom for women. As Marinetti explains, "La donna non appartiene a un uomo, ma bensì all'avvenire e allo sviluppo della razza" ["women do not belong to men but to a collective future that renovates itself through the development of the species"] (*TIF* 370), therefore:

> Dire: *la mia donna* non può essere altro che una cretineria infantile o una espressione da negrieri. La donna è *mia* quanto io sono suo, oggi, in questo momento, per un'ora, un mese, due anni, secondo il volo della sua fantasia e la forza del mio magnetismo animale o ascendente individuale. (*TIF* 369)

> [To say: *my woman* cannot be anything other than an infantile silliness or an expression of slave traders. The woman is as much *mine* as I am hers; now, today, in this moment, for an hour, a month, two years, according to the flights of fancy and the strength of my animal magnetism or individual influence.]

However, in the aftermath of the First World War, futurism aimed to liberate people from the social imprisonment of marriage, not least because futurists believed this form of relationship enslaved women, while institutionalizing adultery and prostitution. The movement acutely perceived women's enfranchisement as creating "dangerous" power dynamics within the family. The postwar society had witnessed a gender role reversal, generating a "tipico grottesco matrimoniale" ["grotesque marriage type"], in which the unemployed husband took the role of unproductive man-housewife, while the working woman-husband provided for the family:

> Rovesciamento completo di una famiglia dove il marito è diventato una donna inutile con prepotenze maschili e la moglie ha raddoppiato il suo valore umano e sociale.
>
> Urto inevitabile fra i due soci, conflitto e sconfitta dell'uomo. (*TIF* 371)

> [Complete overturning of a family wherein the husband has become a useless woman with male presumptions and the wife has doubled her human and social value. Inevitable clash between the two partners, conflict and defeat of man.]

The social changes caused by the war – women played a greater social role, developed a stronger collective identity, and worked outside the home – triggered the need for patriarchal protective measures. Under the guise of an emancipatory message, the dissolution of marriage bonds is instrumental to avoid a "dangerous" gender "imbalance" that jeopardizes male sovereignty by emasculating men's function in the social sphere. Furthermore, destroying the institution of marriage leads to a new regulatory system that, while freeing women from marital life, institutionalizes their procreative function. In the early 1920s, futurism turns its praise of joyful free intercourse into a rigid control over children born outside marriage, though state-owned "Istituti di allevamento e di educazione della prole" ["Institutions for raising and educating children"] (*TIF* 378). Freedom from the prison of marriage evolves into imprisonment in a bigger cage, namely a prescriptive practice of "free" copulation that guarantees the State's biopolitics. The dream of unconstrained love, which informs the "heroic phase" of the avant-garde, degrades into the fascist regime of affect; and this regime, once again, turns to the "rhetoric of noise" – propaganda, emphatic speeches, and worship of the leader's charismatic voice.

Women's Voice of Dissent

In both crepuscular and futurist reinventions, love constitutes an "unconventional" feeling, namely, an agent of change that threatens to impair any understanding of love as "a placeholder relation, a proxy, a stand-in."[33] Nevertheless, through their criticism of the homogenizing script of bourgeois love, both movements ambiguously reinforce gender stereotypes, such as the confinement of women – especially women perceived as too "feminine" – into the marginalized space of the "Other" or the *natural* "Mother." As Karen Warren contends, in Western cultures, "wherever there has been a historical identification of women and other human Others with inferior nature, the domination of women and other human Others has been explained and 'justified' by their connection with nonhuman nature."[34] Thus, the innovative narratives of love that crepuscularism and futurism unfold in parallel ways, by exploring the relational silences created by this feeling or by shouting out loud the faults of romantic love, hide a conservative agenda that is deeply rooted in a marginalization of different *natures*.

However, these transgressive-regressive proposals were also pivotal in fostering a broad discourse about changing the "rules" of love, which constructively involved women. This discourse is quite latent in crepuscularism and mainly documented in the correspondence of Gozzano and poet Amalia Guglielminetti. Futurism, on the other hand, created a heated debate about women's agency in the emotional and socio-political territory of love. Contributions to this discussion span from actress Lyda Borelli's preface to Mario Carli's *Retroscena* [*Backstage*] (1915) to the works published by the Azure Patrol group in the journal *L'Italia futurista*. Overall, this dialogue combined purely aesthetic observations with articulated reflections on socio-political themes such as free love, marriage, and the right to divorce. From this dialogic perspective, we can see how, when a text interacts with a community of readers, it activates an "in-between process" of co-transformation that affects placeholder relations. In the case of avant-garde texts, the hybrid process of circulation, reception, and renegotiation of meanings visibly shaped the women's counter-discourse of love. It generated new "sounds" that are revealed to be more original than the seemingly groundbreaking ideas of non-binary gender that futurist women elaborated on.

As for crepuscularism, women's contribution to the redefinition of love remains a niche discourse, and yet this peripheral narrative develops fundamental questions, which the futurist women would loudly voice. The love letters of Gozzano and Guglielminetti offer a private lens on the complex situation of a woman writer and lover, who experienced a precarious balance between independence, poetic recognition, and the social stigma faced by unmarried women. Through these private documents, she attempts to untangle her troubled relationship with Gozzano – a tense relationship suspended between love and intellectual friendship – while renegotiating her own ambiguous identity. In an early letter, dated 26 October 1907, Guglielminetti meditates on the threat her female allure projects onto her intellectual affirmation. She asks Gozzano if he can disconnect her spiritual charisma from her physical appearance. Yet, soon after, the prescriptive "guilt" for her status as a bourgeois "signorina" ["unmarried woman"] violently arises, and Guglielminetti wonders whether perhaps she does not deserve to be loved for her intellectual capabilities. Restricted by patriarchal standards, she concludes that if her feminine beauty is an obstacle to her intellectual identity, she would rather be a man:

> Voi rimpiangete ch'io non sia un uomo. E lo rimpiango anch'io intensamente. Almeno potrei far valere il meglio di me stessa, dare a ciò che amo la mia forza più buona, dare a voi una fraternità non solo di parole vane. Invece non sono che un essere ibrido male adatta a vivere fra gli schermi anche leggiadri della pura femminilità, sospettata male e male giudicata se tento di varcarne i confini.[35]

> [You regret I am not a man. And I regret it too, intensely. At least I could claim the best of myself, give my best force to what I love, give you a brotherhood made not only of vain words. Whereas I am nothing more than a hybrid being, ill suited to living within the schemes, albeit graceful, of pure femininity, suspected of bad intentions and badly judged if I attempt to escape its confines.]

The unresolved issue with her ill-suited femininity appears again in a letter from 14 November 1907. Commenting on an early version of Gozzano's poem "La signorina Felicita," she praises his decision of not "amoreggiare in versi e in rime con la solita classica antipatica noiosa donna bella che tutti i poeti hanno posseduto o detto di possedere come una cortigiana qualunque" ["flirting in verses and rhymes with the usual, classic, unpleasant, boring, beautiful woman, whom all the poets have possessed or said they have possessed, like a common prostitute"].[36] As Guglielminetti contends, "la bruttezza è tanto più profonda e originale ormai quanto è superficiale e di maniera la bellezza" ["ugliness is much deeper and original nowadays as beauty is superficial and stereotypical"].[37] Yet, these statements can be connected to her own frustration with being a "misfit hybrid," trapped in a beautiful feminine body that interferes with the "male" business of her literary engagement. Guglielminetti's problematic identity further emerges in a literary review of her poetry book *Le seduzioni* [*The Seductions*]. In a letter from 22 July 1909, she tells Gozzano that, according to the literary critic Bertinetti, her book is "un libro di mascolinità" ["a book of masculinity"], a book written by a man "che si foggi un suo tipo di donna perversa e avida: quella che l'uomo perverso e avido sogna" ["who shapes his own type of perverse and avid woman: the woman whom a perverse and avid man dreams of"].[38] Once again, Guglielminetti's status as a woman writer is overpowered by a barely visible yet pervasive patriarchal violence that cannot quite locate her affirmative voice as a feminine lover, except as a misplaced or literally concealed male voice. Her hazy identity recalls Bruno Corra's ironic meditation on the figure of the "signorina borghese" ["unmarried bourgeois woman"], in *Ti amo: il romanzo dell'amore moderno* [*I Love You: The Novel of Modern Love*] (1918). Commenting on the fact that a bourgeois woman acquires a defined identity only through marriage, he writes: "la signorina borghese è un essere *che non esiste ancora completamente*" ["the bourgeois unmarried woman is a being that *does not yet fully exist*"].[39] Corra's ironic statement about the non-existence or silenced presence of a "signorina borghese" may help contextualize why, in a patriarchal society, Guglielminetti – a woman lover undefined by marriage – suffers the condition of someone who "*non è ancora nato del tutto*" ["*hasn't fully been born*"][40] and does not see how to cultivate her own "wholeness."

Transposed into the futurist arena, the issue about love and women lovers' agency takes on the shape of an articulated debate, and involves many female writers in the columns of *L'Italia futurista* and beyond. If, according to Badiou's equation, "love is a re-invention of life. To re-invent love is to re-invent that re-invention,"[41] then the futurist women's discourse on love entails a creative (re)construction of the early twentieth-century socio-political space. As Paola Sica has noted, the women who contributed to *L'Italia futurista* were particularly influenced by the progressive agenda of European and North American feminist groups, which brought forward a wide range of ethical and legal demands including "free love, the gradual devaluation of marriage, the rethinking of motherhood, the right to divorce, the right to vote and the incentive to engage in employment."[42] In addition, the "creative challenge" for futurist women is to begin sketching an identity for female lovers that delineates a separate path from the virile homogenization suggested by Marinetti and Valentine de Saint-Point. Is there a realistic profile for loving women, beyond the masculine imagery of the futurist Amazon of lust? The issue analysed in chapter 3 about gender and masculinization of women returns, and, this time, by focusing on the discourse of love, we can see how women started to voice an actual reinvention of affective relationships.

In her preface to Mario Carli's novel *Retroscena*, actress Lyda Borelli, a progressive woman who was close to futurist circles, makes an observation that foreshadows a possible alternative to the futurist staple model of virile women lovers, a gendered notion strictly based on the bias of the "weak sex."[43] She states she has found a quasi-feminine sensibility in Carli's writing. Yet her understanding of "feminine sensibility" defines an imaginative sensibility that arises from what she dubs creative "morbidezza" ["softness"]. Borelli's notion of "imaginative softness" provides a diverse bodily attitude and mindset, from which a new profile of the woman lover can arise, beyond the futurist rigid norm of metallic "masculine femininity."

Redefining love and social life, the creativity of women writers particularly targets the figure of the "signorina." The unmarried girl is the fictionalized character as well as the physical reader inscribed in many bourgeois novels. She is the political pawn of a system that allows women to have an identity only through the (male) recognition that marriage guarantees. Addressing these issues in her prose "Chopin cade in disgrazia" ["Chopin Falls Disgraced"], published in *L'Italia futurista* on 24 June 1917, Fulvia Giuliani demystifies the social constructions surrounding any respectable "signorina." Every spring – she explains – young women conform to the unnatural flirtations and artificial poses that the script of courtship imposes. Embodying a voice of dissent, Giuliani says farewell to the romantic politics of love that spring enables: "Addio primavera! Addio noiosissima regina delle ammalate di nervi!!!" ["Farewell spring! Farewell very boring queen of hysterical ladies!!!"] (*SF* 138–9). The futurist woman writer welcomes summer as a liberating time. She envisions freedom as a time-space nourished with ideals but also steeped in the spontaneity of everyday objects, practices, and behaviours. Thus, her celebration of summer declares Chopin's languid nocturnes out of season and greets a new life, freed of affectations and social games: it is finally time to "bere la birra perché … è estate e fa caldo" ["drink beer because ... it is summer and is hot"]. Through this statement, Giuliani associates her emancipation from social scripts with an alcoholic beverage, beer, that had become fashionable at the end of the nineteenth century. At the time, beer and breweries were very popular among educated and cosmopolite upper-bourgeois consumers. In Giuliani's discourse, drinking beer comes to symbolize a cultural switch in younger consumers' habits, which simultaneously suggests a change in relational practices.

If the passéist "signorina" urges reinventing, marital life is also called into question. An exemplary, yet also peculiar, case of detachment from the myth of the bourgeois family is Flora Bonheur's *Diario di una giovane donna futurista* [*Journal of a Young Futurist Woman*].[44] The first volume of the *Diario*, ironically entitled *L'amore per il marito* [*Love for the Husband*], narrates the relationship of the protagonist, Albina Folgore, with her inept husband, Ildebrando Martelli. Bonheur's work is idiosyncratic because it indulges in a parodic use of the futurist poetics. Her diary is a "mixed-media project" combining textual narrative, illustration, and artistic typography. Through this "verbo-visual" language, Bonheur ironically mingles images that recall old-fashioned "illustrated novels – chiefly the Victorian and fin de siècle novels" with avant-garde words-in-freedom.[45]

The "dissonant textures" of Bonheur's *Diario* mirror the jarring couple of Albina and Ildebrando. The husband's physical description – long nose, sharp chin, long ears, swollen stomach, giant hands – culminates in the futurist equation "Ildebrando Martelli = coniuge = marito = sfortunato" ["Ildebrando Martelli = spouse = husband = unlucky"].[46] Ildebrando evolves into a repulsive quasi-human, "un ignorantone, una bestia, un cretino, tutto quello che di più imbecille, di più lurido si può immaginare" ["an ignoramus, a beast, an idiot, the most stupid, filthiest one can imagine"].[47] A line of animalistic associations – all regarding horned beasts – suggests that Ildebrando is not only ugly and stupid but also a cuckold. This aspect is explored in the second volume, *L'amore per l'amante* [*The Love for the Lover*], in which Albina decribes her "amore con l'A maiuscola" ["love with a capital A"] for the futurist Enrico, a feeling that pervades her body and soul.[48] In *L'amore per il marito* Albina emphasizes the pettiness of her husband and, playing with Marinetti's motif of the "slap and punch," she describes a fight with Ildebrando, in which she repeatedly hits him – "Cazzotto primo sul grugno. Cazzotto secondo sul grugno. Quarto, quinto, sesto, settimo!" ["First punch on the snout. Second punch on the snout. Fourth, fifth, sixth, seventh!"]. Only in the midst of the physical confrontation does she find her own joyful accomplishment:

> Così così la vita coniugale mia.
> Futurista?
> Passatista?
> A voi il responso.

Finirà?
Quandо?
Esulto: mi divido, diffondo gioia. Trionfo.
Vittoria!
Brrr! Brrr! Ssstt! … Psss! Psss! …
Cirr … cirr … cirr … cirr … Flutt flutt flutt …
Ciac … ciac … ciacc …
Che è?
Che non è?
Sono felice![49]

[So this is my married life.
Futurist?
Passéist?
The response is yours.
Will it end?
When?
I exult: I divide myself, I diffuse joy. Triumph.
Victory!
Brrr! Brrr! Ssstt! … Psss! Psss! …
Cirr … cirr … cirr … cirr … Flutt flutt flutt …
Ciac … ciac … ciacc …
What is it?
What is not?
I am happy!]

In her eccentric narrative of marital "love," Bonheur creates a topsy-turvy world. As if in a Roman Saturnalia, Albina forges a carnival universe in which the woman "dresses up" as a perpetrator of domestic violence and the man becomes the victim of abuse. As Janaya Lasker-Ferretti highlights, *L'amore per il marito* "effectively directs the futurist disdain towards women onto men, and transfers the aggression that occurs in the public sphere during the futurist evenings to the private sphere of the home."[50] Furthermore, as Lasker-Ferretti continues, this parody empowers the woman protagonist, by reinventing the futurist despair of romantic love into "a feminist version of futurism."

The metaphor of love as a fight against bourgeois conformism appears from another perspective in the literary work of Fanny Dini. In the prose "Al futurismo trionfante" ["To Triumphant Futurism"] (1917), the writer expresses her horror of "camere imputridite di felicità" ["rooms rotten with happiness"] and stereotypical settings, such as moonlit and Neapolitan serenades. Dini rewrites the romantic topos of the lover's extreme sacrifice into a ritual murder for intellectual emancipation; as she writes, "– Vorrei uccidere la persona che amo – di più – fare del suo teschio una lampada – e andare a conversare di cose meravigliose con tutte le notti del mondo" ["– I would like to kill the person I love – even more – make a lamp out of his skull – and go talk about wonderful things with all the nights of the world"] (*SF* 264). Similarly, in "Protesta" ["Protest"] (1917), Irma Valeria engages with a rewrite of traditional love topoi, which ideally combines Bonheur's topsy-turvy world with Dini's cathartic murder. She twists the fates of well-known heroines from the tradition; thus the Shakespearian Ophelia turns into a cocotte who carelessly kills Hamlet, and Poe's Berenice has fake teeth.[51] Isabeau, the protagonist of Pietro Mascagni's 1911 eponymous opera, poses as an uninhibited nude model, while in the original medieval legend she is forced to ride naked through the city because she refuses to pick a spouse. Goethe's Margarete has fake braids, and, finally, the murderous Lady Macbeth, who according to Shakespeare's tragedy has her hands stained with blood, dirties her bony finger with mud "per presentarlo coscienziosamente al pubblico" ["to diligently show it to the audience"] (*SF* 219). In this world under protest, in which Lady Macbeth seemingly gives the middle finger to her spectators, the loss of aura of female lovers – its "murder on stage" – is pivotal to forge new social roles for women. As Sica contends, through this radical transformation of female models, women "will be free to show their human flaws, to choose their lovers, and to ignore all the traditional bonds that would restrain their actions and deny them liberation."[52]

Yet, how can women liberate themselves from pre-imposed models of femininity? Valeria's "Protesta" makes a proposal in its sibylline last line, which reads: "Eppure le ranocchie si sgolano a ripetermi che il fango è delizioso" ["And yet frogs loudly croak to tell me over and over that mud is delicious"] (*SF* 219). Muddling the traditional female image, Valeria reveals the receptive porousness and affective potential of a female body that can be alive only when it encounters the messy "deliciousness" of life. Mud turns into a productive element if women engage with it and finally cross the swamp of romantic love. The image of the muddy waters of love tradition also appears in Fulvia Giuliani's prose "Avanzando nella notte" ["Proceeding in the Night"] (1917). In this text, she portrays female social isolation as a "*zona di avvelenamento*" ["*poisoning area*"], concealed as a beautiful, yet clearly delimited, meadow – the idyllic seclusion that romanticized love fuels. Giuliani rejects the tempting promise of that perfect space, declaring:

> Ho vinto, ho riso di tutto questo apparato scenico di cartapesta che voleva piegarmi che voleva farmi agonizzare nel languore più velenoso di un vecchio motivo di poesia romantica. (*SF* 145)

> [I won, I laughed at this scenic apparatus of papier mâché that wanted to bend me and make me agonize in the most poisonous longing of an old motif of romantic poetry.]

She realizes that the field was a cover-up for a swamp harbouring "i miasmi più terribili per uccidere la vita" ["the most terrible miasma, in order to kill life"] (*SF* 145). Only by overcoming that "poisonous area" of perfection – by reinventing love as a space that embraces change and flows – can she eventually reinvent her own life.

The dyad "reinvention of love–reinvention of life" constitutes a central element in the cultural renovation – in the counterpoint, we might say – that futurist women modulate. This redefinition became an important topic of discussion after the publication of Marinetti's *Come si seducono le donne*, when *L'Italia futurista* provided a concrete platform to address the futurist leader's androcentric assumptions. *Come si seducono le donne* was eventually republished in 1918, with an appendix entitled "Polemiche sul presente libro" ["Polemics Regarding This Book"], which included a synopsis of articles published in *L'Italia futurista*. The modified material of the book proves the agency women authors were exercising in the public sphere. By rewriting love, they were literally reshaping their readers' horizon of expectations, while exposing their audience to a more articulated understanding of society.

The first text in the appendix is Enif Robert's open letter to Marinetti. This piece is especially interesting because it rejects the twisted logic of the predator-prey game that the verb "to seduce" fosters. In Robert's view, love is not a matter of seduction, but of intelligent cooperation; as she affirms:

> E che aspettiamo a definire l'amore come una intelligente cooperazione tra due esseri che cercano insieme con eguali diritti, egual volontà la soluzione di un problema psico-fisiologico più o meno urgente?[53]
>
> [What are we waiting for to define love as an intelligent cooperation between two human beings who together find the solution to more or less urgent psychophysical problems with equal rights, and equal will?]

However, her redefinition of love as an egalitarian collaboration of peers implies a subordination of this feeling to a pressing psychophysiological issue. Although Robert asserts women's right to love – a basic notion that in the early twentieth century was far from common – her conception of right is virtually unemotional and not too far from Marinetti's debasement of love to the "mechanics" of copulation. Indeed, her right to love is a recognition of a biological coercion that cannot be escaped, but could be regulated through intelligent commonality. Robert's position reveals its limitations when compared to Rosa Rosà's proposal on female diversity and self-affirmation. In Rosà's piece, "Le donne cambiano finalmente …" ["Women Finally Change …"] (also included in the appendix), she grasps one of women's most stringent issues, an issue that does not emerge so clearly in her other works. She notes women's inability to define themselves beyond male categories – as objects, as illogical, inconsistent, irresponsible, stupid, yet beautiful dolls.[54] Only if women fight these patriarchal stereotypes, Rosà maintains, can they acquire greater spiritual qualities, which will make them independent from men. Women will finally become aware of their free "I," untraceable and inaccessible to the commodified seductions of male "consumers," who enjoy a woman as if she were a glass of Fernet tonic. Unlike Robert's contractual perspective, in this article, Rosà does not seem to find a social compromise between the woman lover, customized and objectivized by man, and the spiritual lover any woman can potentially evolve into. Nevertheless, in another passage of the appendix, her "Risposta a Jean-Jacques …" ["Reply to Jean-Jacques …"], Rosà seems to controvert her previous affirmations of spiritual difference, embracing the eugenic perspective of "orthodox" futurism.[55] Echoing Valentine de Saint-Point, she affirms that it is useless to divide humanity into women and men, when we should rather divide healthy, strong, intelligent, and able individuals from stupid, weak, sick, and disabled ones. Futurist love falls into a Darwinian alliance between the strongest members of the human species, an alliance that leaves any weakness and emotional nuance – the creative intuition of love, its unpredictable incongruences – out of the picture.

In the debate that reshaped Marinetti's manual of seduction, Shara Marini expresses an interesting view on love, which could serve as a bridge between the crepusculars' and the futurists' poetics. In her article "Rivendicazione" ["Demand"], Marini declares that love entails a barely definable experience as, in the words of Emilio Settimelli, "'Si ama quello che non si è toccato e non si toccherà mai'" ["'One loves what one never has touched and never will touch'"]. This image of love as a lost relationship with the untouched recalls Gozzano's images of the unpicked rose and unreached isle. For Marini, the extremely fragile nature of love may explain why men are unable to appreciate it. Men have "sempre goduto e calpestato questo fiore per poterlo amare" ["always enjoyed and stepped on this flower to be able to love it"].[56] Marini, along with Settimelli, is not the only futurist voice that embraces a "crepuscular" approach to love, conceiving this feeling as the delicate potential of the unexperienced, the untouched, the unheard. A similar view appears in a prose by Ardengo Soffici, collected in his work *Arlecchino* [*Harlequin*] (1914). This text shows the personal evolution of this futurist author outside Marinetti's mainstream futurism. Through his first-person narrator, Soffici recalls a crucial moment in which he could have revealed his feelings to a girl, but he did not. As he explains, the highest form of love was letting the partner go and preserving her from a declared love:

> Io sentii allora che potevo amarla, che forse l'amavo … – ma non dissi nulla e non mi mossi. A che pro? Tutti gli amori finiscono così male, che l'atto più profondamente amoroso è forse di nascondere agli esseri amati i palpiti del nostro cuore.[57]
>
> [I then felt that I could love her, that perhaps I loved her – but I did not say anything and I did not move. What for? Every love ends so badly that the most loving act is maybe hiding the palpitations of our heart from the one we love.]

The impasse of love – its slippery nature of embodied potentiality, visible agent of change, and untouchable virtuality – is what nourishes the crepuscular and futurist reinvention of lover-beloved relations. This reinvention, as typical of the avant-garde, did not reach any positive or unanimous definition, yet triggered an intense debate and firmly denied the notion of love as an idyllic resting place. Both movements, including the futurist women of the Azure Patrol, struggled with representing the "substance" of love relationships, which paradoxically remains an unnamable vacuum – a silence.

The Grand Solidarity of Sounds

In the poem "Noia" ["Boredom"], Soffici states that "Fuori delle contingenze / Il prisma dei tempi e dei sentimenti / Muore al dettaglio" ["beyond contingences / The prism of times and feelings / dies in singularity"].[58] These few lines address a fundamental issue with the avant-garde reinvention of love: the prismatic dimension of feelings that crepuscularism and futurism try to grasp cannot be contained within the human borders of lover-beloved relations. Thus, both movements attempt to translate the limited human discourse of love onto an inhuman (or non-humanistic) scale. Carlo Vallini articulates this issue of scale in his poem "L'amore" ["Love"], in which he states that "l'amore è la vanità / maggiore d'ogni altra, poiché / vorrebbe racchiudere in sé / l'idea dell'eternità" ["love is a vanity / bigger than any other, as / it would like to enclose / the idea of eternity"] (*UG* 47). According to Vallini, the question of love precisely resides in the fact that our finitude cannot contain the wholeness this feeling embraces. From this "dimensional perspective," Govoni's open question – "Where, then, will the others be?" – should be reformulated in these terms: what set of relations arise when love is mapped outside human boundaries, outside the lover-beloved traditional space of interaction? What happens, indeed, when we draw a "reverse affective map" that, instead of focusing on the couple, highlights the untraced extra-border territories in which affective relations unfold? How would the "sound of love" change?

Marinetti implicitly answers the issue of "love's scale" in "Lo splendore geometrico e meccanico e la sensibilità numerica" (1914). In this manifesto, he affirms that the futurists have fostered a shift in the general understanding of affective engagement; therefore, if "le grande collettività umane, maree di facce e di braccia urlanti, possono talvolta darci una leggiera emozione" ["vast human collectivities, tides of screaming faces and arms, sometimes give us a slight emotion"], what they aim to access is "la grande solidarietà dei motori preoccupati, zelanti e ordinati" ["the grand solidarity of nervous motors, eager and arrayed"] (*TIF* 99–100, *F* 176). In Marinetti's effervescent universe of feral factories and urban jungles, love must be (re)envisioned as a *material solidarity* that connects dissonant elements into an organic-mechanic manifold. Noise, for its capacity to assimilate disparate voices through its binding dissonance, becomes the medium of the "empathetic materiality" of this human-nonhuman manifold. As Marinetti continues,

> il rumore, essendo il risultato dello strofinamento o dell'urto di solidi, liquidi o gas in velocità, l'onomatopea, che riproduce il rumore, è necessariamente uno degli elementi più dinamici della poesia. (*TIF* 105)
>
> [noise is essentially the result of speeding solids, liquids, or gases that are in friction with or crash into one another. It follows that onomatopoeia, which reproduces noise, is one of the most dynamic elements of poetry.] (*F* 179).

Noise arises as the ultimate poetics of "translatability," offering a hybrid language that transposes love from the narrow space of human relations to the multifarious "grand solidarity" that makes life.

Prior to the futurist exploration of noise, crepuscularism had engaged in a similar attempt to render love beyond human coordinates, through the mediating agency of silence. The movement is deeply fascinated with the emotional potential of silence as a universal medium, as well as with the literary borderline experience of creating the sounds of silence through words. As a form of non-verbal language, silence is bare unshaped matter, from which sounds, words, and ultimately poetry arise. Yet its presence also materializes as a lurking threat to human language, a threat that these poets of the *crepuscolo* – an ambiguous term for the twilight or the dawn – were very much feeling.

Before discussing the crepuscular and futurist sonic environments, it is important to mention that sound, as a physical phenomenon, physiological perception, and element of any auditory communication, is a complex compound object. In its "materiality," sound is the outcome of a chain of interactions. It generates from waves that propagate through a medium, such air or water, and are eventually perceived by animal ears, receptor organs, or mechanical receptive devices. The undulatory motion of the vibrations transforms into the sensation of hearing. Thus, from an ontological perspective, a perceived sound is quintessentially a cluster of matter caught in the process of its transformation – in the manifestation of its interacting potential. Sound waves, as catalysers of air particles, mechanical and electrical events, embody a relational capability embedded within nature and barely mediated by humans. Yet, human or animal intervention can further transform chains of sounds – alternations of silences and noises – into codified communication. Sound then becomes matter charged with a mediating function, allowing for intraspecies and interspecies interactions.

The constitutional hybridity of sound – compound object and medium for further mediations – provides a material platform for crepuscularism and futurism to "reinvent" love. Transposed into an inhuman scale, this feeling is redefined as a diffused yet embedded sense of solidarity that pervades affective soundscapes. A soundscape, according to Italian ecologist Almo Farina, is "the entire sonic energy produced by a landscape and is the result of the overlap of three distinct sonic sources: geophonies, biophonies, and anthrophonies."[59] Very often, a soundscape is the combination of a geophysical entity and a "cultural domain"; namely, the sonic encounter of a landscape and its cultural heritage. Crepuscular and futurist texts create a peculiar sonic environment, which is simultaneously an innovative representational site and a stratified territory of previous literary experiences. In this environment, a heritage of sounds is being radically transformed by new voices. For both movements, experimentation with new sounds – with silences and noises that disturb harmonious tradition – complements their retracing of the traditional anthropocentric landscape. By giving voice to a soundscape no longer dominated by human voices, crepuscularism and futurism situate humans as listeners to the universal noise. Love transmutes into the feeling of belonging to a complex sonic ambience, where humankind tunes into or plays out of tune with nonhuman silences and sounds.

Crepuscular poetry creates a distinct soundscape of barely perceptible noises: whispered prayers, quiet churches and mansions, meowing cats, weaving spiders, and the soft music of hand organs. Govoni turns this muffled melody into the text of his poem "La musica" ["Music"] and affirms that he has always loved "la musica defunta, condensata / come il fondo sintetico d'un fiale" ["the dead music, condensed / like the synthetic bottom of a honeycomb"] (*P* 33). The murmuring white noise of this dead music, which underscores everything, is quintessential to the crepuscular nostalgic reuse of a lost poetic sound that is still perceivable as a blurry echo. "La musica" is collected in Govoni's book *Armonia in grigio et in silenzio* [*Harmony in Grey and in Silence*] (1903), in which the synaesthetic neutrality of grey blends with the acoustic tonality of the pervasive crepuscular whispering. These "images of sound" elicit a hiss – a latent disturbing presence – that the monotonous sing-song cadence of the crepuscular verses intensifies. Yet, while this hissing sound constitutes a unifying score, its meanings range from Corazzini's "plenum," an inhabited mystical silence, to the comforting natural silence of "the school of irony."

In "Desolazione del povero poeta sentimentale," the Roman crepuscular author delineates a path from noise to silence, which traces a parallel passage from poetry, conceived as a form of active communication, to poetry, understood as intimate communion. The text opens with a crying child and unfolds as the child's monologue to an unnamed "You." Corazzini's infantilized persona performs the "tantrum" of a young poet who confronts a personified "adult" tradition and confesses, by breaking the fourth wall, that he does not make conventional verse – "io so che per esser detto: poeta, conviene / viver ben altra vita!" ["I know that to be called a poet, one would have / to live a very different life"], he admits (*SE* 34–5). Yet, what if poetry were rising out of silence rather than out of words? What if being unconventional meant listening to rather than producing noises?

This crying child affirms that he has only tears "da offrire al Silenzio" ["to offer up to the Silence"] (*SE* 30–1), evoking Silence with the capital letter as an intermediary of the divine. Poetry is the transcription of inhuman meanings that silence mediates. As Corazzini's persona states, he "[s]i comunic[a] del silenzio, cotidianamente come di Gesù" ["receive[s] the Holy Communion of silence, daily, like that of Jesus" (*SE* 32–3). In this verse, the poet adopts the Italian verb "mi comunico" ["I receive communion"] and astutely plays on its Latin root, *communio* – "sharing in common." This term connects poetry with the communion between the human, the material, and the divine that the Eucharist enables. During this sacrament, the flesh and blood of Christ coexist in the transubstantiated matter of the bread and wine, and, according to the Catholic dogma, the Eucharist maintains its outward form – bread and wine do not change from bread and wine yet they become divine flesh and blood. Suggesting a metaphoric "transubstantiation" of poetry, Corazzini states that via the medium of silence, his writing retains its human quality, but undergoes a mystical union, fraught with meaning. As he explains, strengthening his religious comparison, "E i sacerdoti del silenzio sono i romori, / poi che senza di essi io non avrei cercato e trovato il Dio" ["the priests of silence are the outcries, / since without them I would not have sought and found God"] (*SE* 33).

In his reflection on the binding agency of silence – the material medium that brings the human closer to the inhuman boundary – Corazzini's meditation can be connected to Maurice Blanchot's reflection on the quiet violence of silence. For the early twentieth-century Roman poet, silence is simultaneously the end of a poetry founded on the centrality of human voice and the promise of a new mystical poetry that accesses a space-time of intense communion. Blanchot similarly highlights this twofold nature of silence, as a locus wherein absence of meaning and potentiality for meaning converge. According to the French author, silence can evoke an "ancient fear" of loss, namely "the fear of time and the absence of time, time which … is not gathered into memory but fragmented in the return."[60] Yet, this returning silence, outside of human linear temporality – this terrifying absence of articulated meaning – is also a joyous opening of unexpected signification.

In his lyric prose *Esortazione al fratello*, which takes the shape of a guide for a novice, Corazzini further explores the interrelated notions of listening to silence and achieving a space of *koinonia*, a sense of joint participation or communion with the universe. In this mystical view, silence is the acoustic perception of a dense swarming presence, a ubiquitous flow of invisible interrelations. When perceived through this participative sonic experience, the conceptualization of otherness acquires a different material status. In such a flowing continuum, the distance from "the other" is reduced – it becomes a "close distance" – as otherness comes to be materially included in the unifying network that silence pervades.[61] In the *Esortazione*, Corazzini creatively reuses Gospel and Nietzschean aphorisms to summon the affective presence of silence, as the jarring status of feeling-together in solitude. Cultivating inner life means to experience *koinonia* through a bodily immersion in the richness of silence. In this way, the soul can become itself a whole, yet a whole opened to the affective connection that silent solitude discloses. Corazzini writes to his novice brother:

> Lo spasimo bianco sarà per tenerti ognuna ora: tutto che di più infantile e di più lontano verrà a battere alla tua porta, dovrai accogliere nel profondo e goderti.
>
> La tua tristizia sarà quella de l'uomo che sempre ritorna: tristizia e letizia maggiore tu non saprai, né mai sapesti. (*O* 234)
>
> [The white spasm will occupy each hour: all the more infantile and remote things will knock at your door, you will have to receive them inside and enjoy yourself in this intimacy.

> Your sadness will be that of the man who always returns: neither will you be able to experience greater sadness and joy, nor were you.]

The Roman poet turns the "white spasm" of silence into an active sensorial fullness that is overwhelmingly dense. One may compare this plentiful whiteness to Dante's inability to render the staggering vision of God in human terms. Corazzini's conception of silence as the material soundscape of an ineffable universal communion – the unfillable shadow of any word – was most certainly influenced by Maurice Maeterlinck's notion of "active silence." According to the symbolist author, silence is the medium of spiritual knowledge and soul-to-soul communication; as he asserts in his essay "Silence," "It is idle to think that, by means of words, any real communication can ever pass from one man to another." For Maeterlinck, silence is active because it allows humans to overcome the communicative limitations that any verbal interaction entails. As he continues, "the true life, the only life that leaves a trace behind, is made up of silence alone."[62] In Corazzini's *Esortazione*, the path of silence and solitude culminates in the final encounter with the voice of Death. This Franciscan "sweet sister" comes singing an incomprehensible lullaby and takes the novice with her, as if he were an exile who, upon his return home, happened to find all his oldest and dearest things (*O* 234). Through this ultimate experience of communion, everything coexists and is intuitively grasped in the binding material solidarity that silence holds together.

In Gozzano's poetry, silence does not carry the same spiritual intensity of Corazzini's mystical poetry, but exercises a healing power that words cannot quite provide. Silence is the refuge that Gozzano's persona finds after undergoing the dialogic path of his second collection, *I colloqui*. This work closes its conversational effort with an invocation to quietness, which hides a transtextual reference to Leopardi's "Ricordanze" ["Memories"]: "Meglio tacere, dileguare in pace / or che fiorito ancora è il mio giardino, / or che non punta ancora invidia tace" ["Better to fade away without a peep, / now while my garden's still in bloom today, / now while the tongue of envy's still asleep"] (*TM* 164–5). To the white noise of the bourgeois "favoleggiare" ["telling fictional stories"], Gozzano's "I" prefers the truthful silence that literature cannot help but counterfeit. If, according to the Turinese author, "Non la vita foggia la letteratura: la letteratura foggia la vita" ["Life does not shape literature: literature shapes life"],[63] the medium of the poetic logos creates a verisimilar "reality," yet life remains somewhat trapped within the silence of the untold. In the poem "I colloqui," which eponymously ends the book, Gozzano's poetic persona declares his plan to recover the silence that literature has polluted. He declares his will to disappear and leave his young self's *imago* in his place:

Col mio silenzio resterò l'amico
che vi fu caro, un poco mentecatto;

il fanciullo sarò tenero e antico
che sospirava al raggio delle stelle,
che meditava Arturo e Federico,

ma lasciava la pagina ribelle
per seppellir le rondini insepolte,
per dare un'erba alle zampine delle

disperate cetonie capovolte …

[And with my silence I will always be
the friend you loved, a trifle scatterbrained.

I'll stay the tender boy eternally
who looked up at the glowing stars and sighed,
who sifted Arthur and Friedrich's philosophy

but left the rebellious page and went outside
to bury the unburied swallows there,
to extend a blade of grass to the terrified

overturned beetles clawing at the air …] (*TM* 166–7)

Gozzano's silence ultimately takes the shape of a return to shelter – *La via del rifugio* is the title of his first poetry collection – which the poet identifies with nature's refuge from human noise. If literature can only speak through a manipulation of life, the only way to heal from this concealment is to step "outside" and embrace silence. And yet, for Gozzano, this return to nature's voice would not represent the end of poetry, but the exploration of a new poetry that directly draws from the vegetal and animal world. Discussing the tension between fiction and authenticity, literature and silence in *I colloqui*, Andrea Rocca has noted that this tension eventually resolves in the poet's late work, *Le farfalle*. In these "epistole entomologiche" ["entomologic letters"], "nate dal silenzio e silenziosamente cresciute, nel 'laboratorio' delle morte fedi" (*TP* 369) ["born from silence and silently grown in the 'laboratory' of dead faiths"], Gozzano engages with nature's "primal forms" and their constituent incommensurability (*TP* 369). However, as Rocca points out, this search for a more authentic wor(l)d coincides with reaching a poetic "altrove" ["elsewhere"]. *Le farfalle* delimits a sacrificial place for literature, wherein words arise from silence, from the capacity of listening to nature (*TP* 370). Yet, through this silent shadowing, Gozzano feels that he has achieved a better understanding of his own humanity. As he explains, the fact that nature silently displays its imperfections is a source of consolation for us; "così ci sentiamo meno soli, meno sbigottiti davanti al mistero, sentiamo che tutta l'intelligenza sparsa nel mondo lotta e soffre come noi contro gli stessi limiti di superarsi" ["so we feel less alone, less astonished before the mystery, we feel that all the intelligence diffused in the world, like us, fights against and suffers from the same limitations to overcome"] (*TP* 469–70).

With the due differences, Gozzano's desire to listen to natural silence, to regain a lost sense of authentic commonality with his human roots, can be compared to the experience of acoustic ecologist Gordon Hempton. An activist for the preservation of soundscapes, he has been recording natural "silences" across the world. Hempton has described his listening to nature as the "wordless process of receiving honest impressions"; for him, the richness of silence relies on the expectation that this sonic ambience inevitably triggers. Silence might then be defined as the "sound of anticipation: the silence of a sound about to be heard, the space between the notes."[64] Hempton's reference to the honesty and anticipation that converge into the acoustic experience of silence can guide us to conceive of Gozzano's seeking shelter in the wordless realm of nature as the possibility of recasting our sense of belonging. The question that his poetry eventually poses is whether our community is not exclusively founded on a civilized speaking *humanitas*, counterpoised to a mute(d) natural world, but also on a joined interspecies alliance. Being receptive to silence, the human can suddenly detect a "stronger sense of embeddedness in a larger field of life" by perceiving (or anticipating) the virtual co-presence of sounds that inhabit silence.[65]

Vallini similarly explores natural silence as a medium of a renewed sense of vital communion. In "I sonetti della casa" ["Sonnets of the House"], a group of six sonnets collected in *La rinunzia*, the poet elaborates on a typical crepuscular topos, the return to the grandfather's house. In this place, "l'odor d'un tempo ora scomparso esala / acutamente nel silenzio inerte" ["the smell of a time now disappeared exhales / sharply in the inert silence"] (*UG* 89). Vallini's poetic "I" cannot establish any connection with this house "senza vita e senza suono" ["lifeless and soundless"] (*UG* 90), suspended in an eternal waiting. All of a sudden, he hears the ticking of a clock that sounds as a memento mori: "Lasciate i morti nelle loro bare" ["You must leave the dead in their coffins"] (*UG* 91). He then leaves the house and goes outside, where vegetal and animal life is fervent: "Cingono ancor le rondini d'un volo / la casa: ancora il verde è nei canneti; / tutto ancor vive" ["With their flight, the swallows still encircle / the house: still the rushes are green; / everything still lives"] (*UG* 92). The encounter with nature transforms Vallini's persona, triggering a will to live: "e tu non gioirai anche una volta / del sapore fuggevole d'un frutto, / dell'ombra della nuvola che passa?" ["Won't you rejoice even only once / at the fleeting flavour of some fruit, / at the shadow of the cloud that goes by?"], he asks himself (*UG* 92).

Vallini's return to the grandfather's house is a story of metamorphosis, from the deadly silence (of tradition) to a (new) wordless potential. Unlike the silent house, immersed in the immobility of past things, nature retains the living capability to be simultaneously grounded and self-transforming. This early twentieth-century story about abandoning a dead cultural heritage to reconnect with the soundscape of life can be linked to a memory Luce Irigaray shared in *Through Vegetal Being* (2016). In this work, co-written with Michael Marder, the feminist thinker describes her experience of being banned from the human community, which led to a renewed closeness with nature. After the publication of *Speculum* (1974), Irigaray was rejected by her academic peers. She then found comfort in the natural world, rediscovering the caring function of mediation that exists between nature and humanity, a mediation Western culture has partially erased. As she writes, our relationship with vegetal life is so basic that it emerges through the act of breathing: "Air put us into living relations even if we did not assume the same role with respect to it. Through air, I participated in a universal exchange from which my tradition cut me off. Thus, I was alone and not alone. I took part in a universal sharing."[66] Yet, throughout the book, Irigaray clarifies that her connection with nature does not imply a nihilistic dissolution of her subjectivity or a "fusional process"; breathing rather reminds her that her communion with the world is founded on difference, "the difference between the outside and the inside … between the other and myself." Irigaray's return to nature is a (re)affirmation of an identity founded on collective breathing, which respects interspecies sharing, as well as natural idiosyncrasies. From this perspective of binding difference, crepuscularism uses silence as a medium for accessing a commonality with the cosmos that human logos cannot grant.

If crepuscularism "pauses" human communication to experience universal communion through silence, futurism finds a very similar connective element in noise. In the manifesto "L'arte dei rumori" ["The Art of Noise"] (1913), musician Luigi Russolo illustrates the key points of the futurist art of noises, an art that enables humans to fully participate in modern techno-life. According to Russolo, while "La vita antica fu tutta silenzio" ["in older times life was completely silent"], the Industrial Revolution has created a new soundscape in which "il Rumore trionfa e domina sovrano sulla sensibilità degli uomini" ["Noise is triumphant and reigns supreme over the sensibility of men"] (*MDF* 83, *F* 133). Tracing a brief history of sound, the futurist musician notices that, among primitive peoples, noises were regarded as marvellous signs, deemed sacred and disconnected from the human. Because of this separation, music created "[un] mondo fantastico sovrapposto al reale, [un] mondo inviolabile e sacro" ["a fantastic world superimposed on the real one, an inviolable and sacred world"] (*MDF* 83, *F* 133). The musical works that this selective paradigm generated were strictly ruled by a prescriptive, yet artificial, notion of harmony; "L'arte musicale ricercò ed ottenne dapprima la purezza, la limpidezza e la dolcezza del suono" ["at first the art of music sought and achieved purity, limpidity, and sweetness of sound"] by caressing the ear (*MDF* 84, *F* 134). Today, as Russolo proclaims, music must mirror a renovated human-nonhuman soundscape, wherein noisy machines "collaborano dovunque coll'uomo" ["everywhere are collaborating with man"] (*MDF* 84, *F* 134). To a passéist notion of inauthentic harmony, the futurists oppose a dissonant intensity that echoes the noise pollution of industrial life and its "più ampie emozioni acustiche" ["greater range of acoustical emotions"] (*MDF* 84, *F* 134). For the futurist musician, listening to the noises **"[de]i rumori di tram, di motori a scoppio, di carrozze e di folle vocianti"** [**"of trams, internal combustion engines, carriages, and noisy crowds"**] is a richer experience than rehearing classics, like the "Eroica" or the "Pastorale"" (*MDF* 85, *F* 135). While the tradition has "intoxicated" listeners with its repetitions and "snobbish ecstas[ies]," futurism aims to reconnect human ears to the noise that interweaves life (*F* 135):

> Attraversiamo una grande capitale moderna, con le orecchie più attente che gli occhi, e godremo nel distinguere i risucchi d'acqua, d'aria o di gas nei tubi metallici, il borbottìo dei motori che fiatano e pulsano con una indiscutibile animalità, il palpitare delle valvole, l'andirivieni degli stantuffi, gli stridori delle seghe meccaniche, i balzi dei tram sulle rotaie, lo schioccar delle fruste, il garrire delle tende e delle bandiere. Ci divertiremo ad orchestrare idealmente insieme il fragore delle saracinesche dei negozi, le porte sbatacchianti, il brusìo e lo scalpiccìo delle folle, i diversi frastuoni delle stazioni, delle ferriere, delle filande, delle tipografie, delle centrali elettriche e delle ferrovie sotterranee. (*MDF* 86)

> [Let us wander through a great modern city with our ears more alert than our eyes and we shall find pleasure in distinguishing the rushing of water, gas, or air in metal pipes, the purring of motors that breathe and pulsate with indisputable animality, the throbbing of valves, the pounding of pistons, the screeching of mechanical saws, the jolting of trams on their tracks, the cracking of whips, the flapping of curtains and flags. We shall amuse ourselves by creating mental orchestrations of the crashing down of metal shop shutters, the slamming of doors, the bustle and

shuffling of crowds, the varied racket of railroad stations, iron foundries, spinning mills, printing plants, subways, and electrical power stations.] (*F* 135)

As "Ogni manifestazione della nostra vita è accompagnata dal rumore" ["Every manifestation of life is accompanied by noise"] (*MDF* 87, *F* 137), rendering noises means rendering the complex irregularity that makes life – a wide gamut of hybrid timbres and "arrhythmias" that harmonious rhythms try to artificially conceal. In its fascination with the dissonances that inform its techno-animal soundscape, futurism engages in a practice of listening that, although seemingly opposite to the crepuscular return to the primal voice of silence, responds to a similar call to authenticity and universal communion. The futurist creation of an "inebbriante orchestra di rumori" ["intoxicating orchestra of noises"] (*MDF* 89, *F* 138) might sound paradoxical to our twenty-first-century ears, rightfully concerned with the threat of sound pollution and endangered ecosystems. Yet, in a quite counter-intuitive fashion and with evident incongruences, for the futurists, acoustic intoxication is an ecological practice: it is a way to preserve the richness of a soundscape oozing with dissonant sonorities and intermeshing timbres. Hence, while in the past arts have muted the diversity produced by clashing noises, futurism strives to render the communion that the rowdy cacophony of life's variety produces.

Chaotic noise is the original – or we might say, cosmological – matter of the futurist explosive intermixing of living sounds. Yet, noise is also a pivotal component in the movement's communication strategy. As Ara Merjian remarks, "the hybridization of media perhaps constitutes Futurism's chief contribution to twentieth-century modernism."[67] This contribution largely happened through a skilful repurposing of noise into an awakening call. The futurist message originated in a confusing anarchist program and evolved into a profession of nationalism and colonial pan-italism.[68] To shape and promote his political agenda, Marinetti used a variety of media and highly affective "platforms," including manifestos, heated *serate* ["futurist theatrical nights"], and public speeches. Through a cross-media approach, the futurist rhetoric particularly played on detecting a general "white noise" of fear and weakness, and feeding it back to the Italian audience in an amplified way, "in a way that somehow change[d] its [disturbing] quality" into a sense of communion, nourished with "pride and patriotism."[69]

The futurist fostering of a pro-war culture pivoted on the construction of new associations between art, politics, and noise. Noise becomes the medium of a rebirth that (re)connects the human with the primal authenticity of blood, violence, and animalistic freedom. In 1911, upon the outbreak of war in Libya, Marinetti released a political manifesto in which he exhorted his futurist peers to make a sacrifice, namely, to temporarily put aside the representational realm of "**I versi, i pennelli, gli scalpelli e le orchestre!**" ["**verses, paint brushes, scalpels, and orchestras!**"] to engage with vital noises. From out-and-out creators, futurist artists must become creative listeners to "**le formidabili sinfonie degli shrapnels e le folli sculture che la nostra ispirata artiglieria foggia nelle masse nemiche**" ["**the formidable symphonies of shrapnel and the crazy sculptures that [the Italian-] inspired artillery creates among the enemy masses**"] (*TIF* 339).[70] In line with this immersive acoustic paradigm, between 1911 and 1912, Marinetti composed *La battaglia di Tripoli* [*The Battle of Tripoli*] and *Zang Tumb Tumb*, while serving as a war correspondent, respectively in Libya and in the First Balkan War. In these works, the futurist founder expresses the universal communion with the living potential that war intensifies. In the accelerated flow of life that war generates, noise is the medium that binds together acoustic, visual, and olfactory inputs. Marinetti's job as a correspondent was in fact to receive this cluster of raw inputs and quickly convert them into information. Thus, as Timothy Campbell contends, "the machinery of war" and "its more accelerated arena" provided Marinetti with the ideal conditions – with an artistic laboratory of noises – to experiment with "the symbolic relation between objects and *parole in libertà* [words in freedom]."[71]

Being the generative matter of futurist communication, noise also plays a central role in the artistic poiesis that Giacomo Balla and Fortunato Depero elaborate in the manifesto "Ricostruzione futurista dell'universo" ["Futurist Reconstruction of the Universe"] (1915). In this seminal text, the two futurist artists affirm that to effectively express the rich complexity of the universe, we must merge the visual materiality of the words-in-freedom and plastic dynamism with the acoustic potential of noise. As they state, only this cross-media merging can render "l'espressione dinamica, simultanea, plastica, rumoristica della vibrazione universale" ["a dynamic, simultaneous, plastic, noise-ist expression of universal vibrations"] (*MDF* 161, *F* 209). Such clustering condenses the synoptic solidarity of disparate elements into a creative synthesis of the world. The artistic process described in this 1915 manifesto is an automorphic artistic action that denies the traditional understanding of aesthetic creation as a necessary separation between genius and the artwork. The futurist notion of "reconstruction" blends human inventiveness with the (re)creation of the inner sound embedded within matter: cinematographic dynamism, the impalpable nature of light, the brightness of colours, olfactory stimuli, and "noise-making" agents, all converge to express the unfolding of life, in its erratic noise-making process (*MDF* 162, *F* 210). Thus, while in the past art could only evoke "un Oggetto perduto (felicità, amore, paesaggio)" ["an Object lost (happiness, love, a landscape)"], futurist art is "Presenza, nuovo Oggetto, nuova realtà creata cogli elementi astratti dell'universo" ["Presence, new Object, new reality created with the abstract elements of the universe"] (*MDF* 162, *F* 210). As Balla and Depero exemplify,

> Nel veder salire velocemente un aeroplano, mentre una banda suonava in piazza, abbiamo intuito il **Concerto plastico-motorumorista nello spazio** e il **Lancio di concerti aerei** al di sopra della città. (*MDF* 163)
>
> [Watching the speedy ascent of an airplane, seen while a band was playing below in the square, we intuited the **Plastic–Motornoise-ist Concert in Space** and the **Launching of Aerial Concerts** above a city.] (*F* 211)

Through their poiesis of interconnections, the futurists redefine artistic creativity as the ability to combine singular sensorial phenomena into a dissonant, viscous continuum – a "noise-ist" soundscape, wherein single objects maintain their sound while creating a symphony of cacophonic relations.

Ballan and Depero's "noise-ist" soundscape finds a precursor in Arnaldo Ginna's experimentation with bare sounds. Ginna composed a series of poems, which he dubbed "poesie fonetiche" ["phonetic poems"]. The idea behind this type of avant-garde poetry was to create experimental texts, wherein phonetics and meaning coincide. One of these poems, entitled "Gioia di vivere" ["Joy of Living"], reads: "Ginnà lamp lampit / Corr fat berit / Ginnà, Ginnà, corr lampit / fat/Lamperit / Vitamot Vivraromit."[72] This text exemplifies the belief behind Ginna's idea: that while we can use many means of expression, the essence of the arts – its true meaning – is univocal. Through his unintelligible soundscape, Ginna conveys an impression of lively intensity in a phonetic form that purposely escapes the decipherability of codified phonemes.

Through its poiesis of uncodified noise, futurism challenges the audience, transforming the spectators into active contributors to its "intoxicating orchestra." During the futurist *serate*, the relation with the public heavily relied on verbal and physical "penetration" of the audience's space, as well on signals that provoked predictable yet unconscious physiological reflexes.[73] These practices maximized the "margin of manoeuvrability" that the audience offered, to experimentally observe what type of unpredictable (re)action people might have when provoked by unexpected vitality. For example, the futurist concerts of *intonarumori* ["noise-intoners"], musical instruments designed to produce unpleasant sounds, were designed to "hit" the spectators with the turmoil of life while simultaneously generating a vital reaction – occasional scuffles and "pathetic cries of 'no more' ... from all the excited quarters of the auditorium."[74] Through this affective strategy, the futurists exercised a powerful physiological control over their spectators, exposing them to an addictive message that constantly instigated a reaction.

However, it would be reductive to assume that the futurist soundscape is an ambience that has banned silence. Silence is an important presence in Ginanni's literary work and provides a possible bridge with crepuscularism. She maintains that the experience of silence allows us to engage in an intimate auscultation of our being, of the "otherness" that resides within us. Cultivating silence is a form of inner care for our relational capability. By fostering a nourishing solitary dialogue, we strengthen our possibility to affect, while potentiating the capability to be affected by, the world's noise. Even Marinetti explored silence as a medium of communion in the mid-1930s, in a collection of radio compositions entitled *Sintesi radiofoniche* [*Radio Synthesis*]. In the third synthesis, "I silenzi parlano tra loro" ["Silences Speak among Themselves"], intermissions of "pure silence" interrupt sequences of sounds – notes of various musical instruments as well as mechanical and human noises. In the fifth piece, "Costruzione di un silenzio" ["Building a Silence"], the futurist founder experiments with the creation of silence out of sounds – a drum roll, trumpeting, gurgling, birdsong. Yet, in these compositions, Marinetti moves away from a distinction between producing and interrupting sounds. Like the crepusculars' active silence and Ginanni's relational practice of self-auscultation, Marinetti's radiophonic silence is not "the empty background filled in by the fullness of media communication."[75] As Federico Luisetti contends, "the apparently triumphal efficacy of interconnected global networks rests on the fragile foundation of virtual silences, of silences that 'speak among themselves,' penetrating and overcoming the barriers of human and technological communication."[76] By retaining the idiosyncratic virtuality of sound, silence enables the power of connectivity that sounds eventually release.

The avant-garde use of noise reshapes the relational process of creation, reception, and interpretation of the artistic event, transposing this network of human-nonhuman interactions into an intersubjective territory wherein the "noise-ist" potential of matter, the noise of artistic creation, and the further noise of its reception meld. Dislodged from lover-beloved relations, love evolves into a diffused connective potential that fills the distance between heterogeneous elements and creates a material sense of belonging. For both crepuscularism and futurism, finding "the others" implies acting as affective listeners – to humans, nature, the mystical inhuman, the noise-ist expressions of machines – who retrace the voice of the human speaker in relation to a wholeness of diverse living sounds.

Chapter Five

Avant-Garde Immersive Onto-Cognition

Limits and Possibilities of Human Knowledge

Before I begin to explore, in this last chapter, how crepuscularism and futurism reformulate the notion of cognition, I will briefly recall the overarching thesis that frames this work: the groundbreaking proposal of the Italian avant-garde – an early twentieth-century proposal that foreshadows the current "nonhuman turn" – is its non-hierarchical and hybrid representations of the relationship between human and nonhuman. As we have seen, this revolutionary perspective on human-nonhuman relations changes the traditional rules of the anthropocentric game. In the avant-garde universe, material objects become agents or even out-and-out animated beings, the human body is portrayed as a "*natureculture* site" of organic and inorganic, physical and social intermeshing, and the romantic motif of love transmutes into a "grand solidarity" that affects all particles of the universe. In essence, crepuscularism and futurism envision fictional worlds wherein agency is not limited to *homo sapiens*. Thus, if agency is not distinctively human, knowledge – as a form of cognitive agency – must also be revised and extended beyond the boundaries of the mind of the *animal rationale*.

The vast inquiry into the limits and possibilities of knowledge is a theme that links the Italian avant-garde to both the origin of the modernist lineage and the later development of avant-gardes such as surrealism and dada. This investigation into the nature of cognition opens a series of pressing questions that are central to these literary and artistic discourses:

> What is there to be known?; Who knows it?; How do they know it, and with what degree of certainty?; How is knowledge transmitted from one knower to another,

and with what degree of reliability?; How does the object of knowledge change as it passes from knower to knower?; What are the limits of the knowable?[1]

Investigating these queries, crepuscularism and futurism exhibit the other face of modernity, namely, the fact that extreme "faith" in progress, in verifiable evidence and universally valid laws, spurs a parallel intellectual attraction for the non-verifiable, for the "unknowable" that reason disregards or demonizes. These two movements delineate parallel epistemologies that are based not on a detachment from the object of inquiry but on our deep participation in the matter that surrounds us. Cognitive engagement then takes the shape of an immersion, an "immersive knowledge." Through merging intuition and bodily experience, the crepuscular and futurist personas *comprehend* their being mired in an articulated yet fragile web of relations that *comprises and informs* them.

The adoption of this immersive cognitive paradigm by crepuscularism and futurism triggers a redefinition of the notion of ignorance and a parallel rethinking of the nature-culture binary. Two texts by Nino Oxilia, "La canzone folle" ["The Foolish Song"] and "L'intestino presidente di repubblica" ["The Intestine President of the Republic"], can guide our preliminary exploration of these interrelated discourses. An author who eclectically blended the crepuscular and futurist poetics, Oxilia puts in verse a shared scepticism of rational knowledge, conceived of as a privileged form of human inquiry and source of wisdom. In "La canzone folle" he writes, "Voglio tendere la rete / sopra tutte le assemblee / e pescare la sapienza / per gettarla ai cani" ["I want to pull my net / on all the assemblies / and fish the wisdom / to throw it to the dogs"] (*PO* 128). Oxilia revises the biblical image of the "fishers of men," expressing his desire to be a fisherman whose intellectual catch will be chewed, dismembered, and destroyed by voracious dogs acting on primal instinct. In these lines, the poet expresses a fundamental point of the crepuscular and futurist approach to knowledge: both movements call for a rediscovery of ignorance, whether it be infantile absence, Socratic virtue, bare creative potential, or liberating irrationality. "Agnotology" – the logos (discourse) about what humans do not know[2] – is the focus of the cognitive perspective of the avant-garde, which metaphorically throws away a static "catch of wisdom" to dive into the rich reservoir of ignorance.

More generally, the fascination of the crepusculars and futurists with the unknown echoes the widespread irrationalism of Italian culture at the turn of the twentieth century, with its medley of fading positivism and rising anti-rational approaches. The avant-garde mistrust of wisdom is symptomatic of an epoch that rejected the supremacy of rigorous scientific methodology over intuitive perception. Within this context of mistrust, the two movements point towards the limitations of rational cognition and expose the circular logic underlying the identification of the human mind with the boundaries of attainable knowledge. Both movements seek to understand the mesmeric experience of being in the world: in Karen Barad's words, the discursive "inseparability of knowing, being, and doing."[3] Immersion in matter comes to constitute the ontological foundation of a revised epistemology of doubt, in which intuition, bodily sensations, and abandonment to the dynamism of life are favoured over reason. As Marinetti, Settimelli, and Corra suggest in the manifesto "Teatro futurista sintetico" ["Futurist Synthetic Theatre"] (1915), perfect knowledge is an illusion. While being merged within the continuum of knowing-being-doing,

> nella vita non ci accade mai di afferrare un avvenimento interamente, con tutte le sue cause e conseguenze, perché la realtà ci vibra attorno assalendoci con *raffiche di frammenti di fatti combinati tra loro, incastrati gli uni negli altri, confusi, aggrovigliati, caotizzati.* (*MDF* 153)

> [one never grasps an event entirely, in all its causes and consequences, because reality throbs around us, assaulting us with *bursts of fragments of interconnected events, interlocking together, confused, jumbled up, chaotic.*] (*F* 206).

In a parallel way, in "Desolazione del povero poeta sentimentale," Corazzini's persona parodies the construction of solid arguments that seemingly support our choices. In the guise of a logical explanation, he illogically affirms: "Io voglio morire, solamente, perché sono stanco; / solamente perché i grandi angioli / su le vetrate delle catedrali / mi fanno tremare d'amore [e] di angoscia" ["I want to die, only because I'm tired; only because the large angels / in the windows of the cathedrals / make me shiver with love and anguish"] (*SE* 30–1).

Yet if immersive knowledge unfolds from our "diving" into the matter that shapes our *humanitas*, how do we humans distinguish and position ourselves in relation to the other-than-human natures that we are attempting to comprehend? In "L'intestino presidente di repubblica," Oxilia pinpoints this question, proposing that we reconsider humans as citizens "della vasta repubblica animale" ["of the vast animal republic"] (*PO* 173) rather than as sovereigns. The poet contends that the issue with intellectualism is precisely that it separates the human mind – Descartes's "macchina che pensa" ["thinking machine"] – from the "animal" body that we share with other animals (*PO* 172). However, Oxilia suggests, if one considers humanity from the physiological perspective of the guts – from their exclusive viewpoint of the "water-closet dell'umanità" ["toilet of humanity"] (*PO* 172) where "totus homo fit excrementum" ["all men become excrement"] (*PO* 175) – would the distinction between *animal rationale* and instinctive animal still make sense? How would the rational animal's waste be different from that of nonhuman animals? Perhaps, through this intestinal point of view, we would rediscover that we belong to an "interspecies republic," bonded by a foundational relationship of coexistence.

However, as we will see, both crepuscularism and futurism struggle with overcoming the separation between culture and nature that informs the modern framework, in which civilization is attained by abandoning the savage natural world. They demonize bourgeois culture to embrace a cognitive approach that often naturalizes irrationalism, viewing irrationalism as an antidote to traditional wisdom. Nevertheless, in doing so, they construct ignorance as a concealed form of "nature." One may think of the futurist manifesto's anti-intellectual regression, which Marinetti expresses through the image of being fed again by his Sudanese nurse (*TIF* 9, *F* 50). And yet, is ignorance the "natural" condition of a feminized nature? What does nature know? And what are we learning when we interact with the animal and plant world? Gozzano's "school of irony" engages with these questions in particular, offering fascinating representations of a wise nature that teaches modern culture a lesson of non-anthropocentric humanism and material spirituality.[4]

In this chapter, I examine the discourse on nature and culture underlying the crepusculars' and futurists' proposals on knowledge through the lens of current theories that have redefined the human cognitive process as "a confusing balance between ontology and epistemology."[5] According to philosopher Maurizio Ferraris, the experience of being in the world coincides with the attitude T.S. Eliot expresses in the lines of "The Love Song of J. Alfred Prufrock": "Oh, do not ask, 'What is it?' / Let us go and make our visit."[6] Diving into matter constitutes the ontological dimension of a precarious cognitive process that cannot be isolated from our entanglement in systems of material and symbolic relations.

Such an embodied approach to knowledge is shared by a number of environmental perspectives that will be adopted in this analysis. These theories generally share a critique of the nature-culture binary that Western epistemology has fostered. For example, ecofeminist Karen Warren has highlighted that the concept of nature is not static, but "socially, historically, and materially constructed"; consequently, what is meant by "nature" depends on factors such as "race/ethnicity, class, age, affectional orientation, geographic location, and religion of humans who name, describe, judge, understand, and interact with 'nature.'"[7] Thus, for Warren, examining the development of nature as a socio-cultural construct is important in order to challenge biases that enable sexist, racist, and colonial views by naturizing "inferior" groups. Yet, recasting "naturization" is not solely an essential tool of critical thinking; it can also lead to an emancipatory path that questions monoculturalism. Feminist philosopher Luce Irigaray has affirmed that returning to nature would lead to a process of liberation based on the recognition of human sexual difference, since "the natural, aside from the diversity of its incarnations or ways of appearing, is at least two: male and female."[8] Irigaray has been criticized for her biological determinism; however, as Christopher Cohoon explains, her redefinition of nature is "fundamentally unteleological"; for Irigaray, nature is a principle that unfolds a potentially infinite number of modalities of becoming for men and women, which are set in opposition to a neuter monoculture of masculinity.[9] Many other feminist perspectives have seen nature as a multifaceted reality that women need to reinterpret and reconnect with. For example, Maria Mies and Vandana Shiva, in their critique of the "eurocentric universalism developed via the Enlightenment and the rise of capitalist patriarchy," emphasize that ecofeminism does not posit human rights into abstract concepts, such as freedom and knowledge, separate from basic needs. Rather, ecofeminist activists affirm that common human needs "can be satisfied only if the life-sustaining networks and processes are kept intact and alive" through a symbiotic relationship with nature.[10] Nature, as Stacy Alaimo has argued, would be better understood as a site of trans-corporeality, in which human and nonhuman bodies, politics, and culture interact.[11] This material and cultural space has affected not only female identity but also queer identities. Queer ecology indeed investigates how dominant cultures have manipulated nature into a heteronormative principle, while identifying homosexual or transgender people as "against nature." However, this heteronormative perspective overlooks the fact that nature includes a rich variety of genders and sexualities.[12]

If feminist and queer studies have analysed the nature-culture connection from the perspective of gender, other types of research – including the studies of Karen Barad, Robin Wall Kimmerer, and Michael Marder – have adopted scientific and philosophical theories to show how nature, rather than being the opposite of culture, expresses more-than-human forms of knowledge and communication. An example of this "natural culture" are trees able to exchange information or nonhuman animals that create sophisticated social structures. While this research aims to erode the modern nature-culture dualism by studying nature, anthropologist Philippe Descola, in his studies of the Amazonian understanding of nature as a social subject, has illustrated how Amerindian cultures provide a non-dualistic view of the relationship between humans and the environment. For instance, the Achuar people have engendered "an ontology that is sometimes labeled 'perspectivism,' which denies a privileged point of view from on high to human beings and holds that multiple experiences of the world can cohabit without contradiction."[13] The open question, though, is how Western culture could mend its centuries-old divide between nature and culture. A provocative solution comes from Timothy Morton's theory of "ecology without nature," which challenges the very idea of nature as a construct. According to this proposal, a respectful coexistence between human and nonhuman agents can become a reality only if we begin deconstructing our Western notion of nature as a separate, organic entity. Coexistence, according to Kate Rigby, might also be attained by embracing forms of "materialist spirituality" and ecotheologies in which salvation does not entail transcending matter but participating in a collective effort of care, as well as in a dialogue between science, politics, religions, and philosophies.[14]

Through their parallel reflections on old-fashioned knowledge and childhood ignorance, immersive knowledge and return to nature, crepusculars and futurists anticipate – yet also problematize – theories that have attacked the paradigm of the "Great Divide," the artificial cognitive divide between mind and body, human and nonhuman, culture and nature.[15] The avant-garde desire to "[u]sci[re] dalla saggezza come da un orribile guscio" ["break out of wisdom, as if out of a horrible shell"] (*TIF* 9, *F* 50) raises a series of environmental perspectives and issues that can enrich the ecocritical debate in unexpected and thought-provoking ways.

Crepuscular Wisdom, or the Return to Nature and Childhood

> Chi troppo studia e poi matto diventa!
> Giova il sapere al corpo che ti langue?
> Vale ben meglio un'oncia di buon sangue
> che tutta la saggezza sonnolenta.
>
> [Study too much and soon you'll fry your brains.
> What's learning when the body starts to fall?
> Better one ounce of good red blood than all
> the drowsy wisdom that the world contains.] (*TM* 178–9)

This quatrain from Gozzano's poem "L'analfabeta" ["The Illiterate"] is part of a long dialogue between an eighty-year-old illiterate and the well-educated poetic narrator, who returns to visit his family's villa in the countryside. In these lines, the old man expresses a folksy version of Marinetti's disgust for a world "fradicio di saggezza" ["rotten with wisdom"], a world filled with knowledge that decays in library catacombs (*TIF* 16, *F* 55). The elderly caretaker of the villa proposes that books be eschewed in favour of learning directly from nature, "nel gran Libro sublime" ["the great Book sublime and vast"], and discerning "la voce delle cose prime" ["the voice of the first things speaking clear"] (*TM* 172–3).

This wise illiterate enjoys the privilege of speaking "la parola non costretta" ["unforced streams"] (*TM* 176–7) because he has actively trained himself to "read" by studying the natural world before him. His idiosyncratic "literacy" typifies a non-Western viewer who is not "*outside* or *separate from* the territory ... he surveys" but, in Leslie Marmon Silko's words, is as "much [a] part of the landscape as the boulders [he] stand[s] on."[16] Through his participative reading of nature, the elderly man comprehends many marvellous phenomena:

Come dal tutto si rinnovi in cellula
tutto; e la vita spenta dei cadaveri
risusciti le selve ed i papaveri
e l'ingegno dell'uomo e la libellula.

Come una legge senza fine domini
le cose nate per se stesse, eterne ...
Tanto discerne quei che non discerne
i segni convenuti dagli uomini.

[How from the All, cells re-create the All,
and how the spent life of cadavers can
reanimate the woods, the mind of man,
the mayfly, and all creatures great and small.

How things born of themselves are subject to
the eternal sway of a law without an end ...
He comprehends this, who can't comprehend
the symbols man has given meaning to.] (*TM* 178–9)

In these two quatrains, the verb "to comprehend" is a key word combining the notions of cognitive retention and corporeal capacity. For Gozzano's illiterate, learning marries the cognitive practices of observation and verification that positivist science prescribes with a vital sense of materiality as realized through a broader ontogenetic process of cellular transformation. Gozzano describes this continuous process as "the eternal sway of a law without an end" – a physical law that exceeds the physicality of our human finitude.

The view of the universe that the poet expresses through this illiterate character shows the influence of Arturo Graf, a writer and professor of Italian Literature at the University of Turin, who was an important figure for young intellectuals in early twentieth-century Turin. His poetry, which blends positivism with, over time, an increasingly religious sentiment, testifies to the collapse of positivist theories and the emergence of cognitive approaches that were fascinated with knowledge beyond human rationality. In particular, Gozzano borrows from Graf the attitude of combining very broad concepts regarding cosmic life into dyads, such as "il Tutto e il Niente" ["the Whole and the Nothing"] or "il Tempo e lo Spazio" ["the Time and the Space"].[17] Compared to these cosmic dimensions, human life comprehends its own fragility, which is to say, citing from Morton, "at Earth magnitude, anthropocentric distinctions don't matter anymore," and the civilized man rediscovers he is an illiterate of the world.[18] He rediscovers his limitations, limitations that are often falsely converted into unlimited possibilities or into the Kantian boundaries of worldly knowledge. In the words of the elderly caretaker, the anthropocentric perspective is drastically scaled down as he, for example, explains the principles of conservation of mass and energy in a modern retelling of the phoenix myth that emphasizes the self-regenerating narrative of life:

> … Ritorna il fiore e la bisavola.
> Tutto ritorna vita e vita in polve:
> ritorneremo, poiché tutto evolve
> nella vicenda d'un'eterna favola.
>
> [The flower and the ancestor are able
> to come back. All come back, all turn to dust.
> We'll come back. Everything, just as it must,
> evolves in the whirling of an eternal fable.] (*TM* 178–9)

The illiterate's participative engagement in the "whirling of an eternal fable" entails a corporeal journey that ties together the decomposition of cadavers with vegetal, animal, and human development. This cognitive perspective, which posits a need for bodily participation in the natural transformations that we observe, can be connected to Barad's use of the neologism "intra-action," as contrasted with the notion of interaction. As Barad explained in an interview with Adam Kleinman:

> The usual notion of interaction assumes that there are individual independently existing entities or agents that preexist their acting upon one another. By contrast, the notion of "intra-action" queers the familiar sense of causality (where one or more causal agents precede and produce an effect), and more generally unsettles the metaphysics of individualism (the belief that there are individually constituted agents or entities, as well as times and places). According to my agential realist ontology, or rather ethico-onto-epistemology (an entanglement of what is usually taken to be the separate considerations of ethics, ontology, and epistemology), "individuals" do not preexist as such but rather materialize in intra-action. That

> is, intra-action goes to the question of the making of differences, of "individuals," rather than assuming their independent or prior existence. "Individuals" do not not exist, but are not individually determinate. Rather, "individuals" only exist within phenomena (particular materialized/materializing relations) in their ongoing iteratively intra-active reconfiguring.[19]

For Gozzano's illiterate, there is no real or ontological separation between the phenomena he participates in and his mind, which he realizes has been nourished with the transforming cells of decomposing bodies. These cells, in turn, will compost the soil and feed "creatures great and small." According to this (proto-)"agential realist," phenomena *are* indeed "the entanglement – the ontological inseparability – of intra-acting agencies."[20] This ontological approach ushers in a parallel epistemological turn; as Barad clarifies, while Cartesian epistemology relies "on the given-ness of a distinction or a Cartesian cut between subject and object, the epistemology of agential realism ... does not start with a set of given or fixed differences, but rather makes inquiries into how differences are made and remade, stabilized and destabilized, as well as their materializing effects and constitutive exclusions."[21]

By abolishing the separation between subject and object, culture and nature, human and nonhuman, Gozzano's "wise illiterate" embodies a virtuous Socratic ignorance that challenges the modern paradigm of intellectual emancipation as a distancing from a mythicized static nature. The metaphor of nature as a *book* implies a reconceptualization of the modern "Great Divide," as the intellectual development of the illiterate wise child – "La tua pupilla è quella d'un fanciullo" ["You look out at the world through a child's eye"] (*TM* 180–1) – is located within a material continuum of intra-actions. This illiterate embraces his belonging to the environment as a form of cultural affirmation, as an ecological and ethical continuing education, set in opposition to the dry knowledge of the intellectual poetic narrator. The sage illiterate represents an alternative path to culture that neither conceptualizes nature as a fixed entity nor sacralizes it as lost Eden on earth. Gozzano's character suggests the unexplored path of human cognition as a daily practice of "becoming with," of being human by coexisting with other animal and vegetal forms of life.[22] The illiterate challenges the notion of ecological preservation based on an aestheticization or metaphysical transposition of nature, of an idealized and benign nature that ultimately does not exist. He does not speak to his literate friend about how to preserve nature as the ultimate cultural endowment; more simply, the old man cannot conceive of a life that exists outside his sense of belonging to the environment.

The cognitive perspective of coexistence embodied by the wise illiterate resonates with Morton's environmental discourse at many levels: first, it similarly abolishes the idea of nature as a separate world or as an intellectual process of world making that posits nature "as a 'thing' that is 'over there,'" distanced from the human; second, the old man's experience of intimacy with the environment implies a radical reshaping of our cognitive approach to nature.[23] As Morton explains, we should rather "think our coexistence not as a world [that we created], but as a disturbing proximity between strangers, for whom I, in the core of my existence, am formally responsible, even when they cause me harm."[24] In Gozzano's poetry, this way of ecological thinking as an onto-cognitive space in which strangers encounter each other and coexist offers an alternative to the creation of "worlds" or to the modern separation between the world of nature and the one of culture.

However, if the caretaker abolishes the nature-culture divide, Gozzano, through this character, still affirms the dualistic perspective that separates blissful ignorance from tormented knowledge. The poet places the caretaker in a peripheral land of childhood memories, a land that the well-read poetic "I" has left for good. Therefore, although Gozzano portrays a rebellious figure of "onto-ecologist" whose being is inseparable from the environmental concept of "being with," he himself cannot help but confirm the modern nature-culture dualism. In his poetic ecosystem, the caretaker's "ecology without nature" or without separate worlds is strictly dependent on a logic of inclusive exclusion that modern culture enables.[25] The elderly man has preserved an uncontaminated view of life – his infantile poiesis – because he is a pariah of modernity who is included in this civilized cultural paradigm as an exceptional anomaly, as an inclusive exclusion. Thus, recalling the ecofeminist perspective of Warren, we can notice that, while Gozzano's dialogue between the young educated master and the old illiterate servant provides a paradigm of coexistence and co-knowledge, the conversation is still framed within a logic of domination that distinguishes "Ups," in this case people equipped with culture, from "Downs," people and nonhuman "others" that seemingly have inferior or infantile cultural skills.[26]

The motif of retraining ourselves to have a more innocent mindset regarding nature is similarly present in Vallini's work. In the poem "Il sogno" ["The Dream"], the poet personifies his soul as a "bimba smarrita / sopra la via della vita" ["lost girl / on the path of life"] (*UG* 58). He then asks a guardian angel to teach the little girl to view nature with wonder: "fa' ch'ella guardi con occhi / stupiti la rosa e l'insetto" ["make her look with astonishment / at the rose and the insect"] (*UG* 58). In this poem, Vallini describes his desire to experience a renewed fascination and respect for the environment, thus devising an alternate route for human cognitive development. As he contends in "La folla" ["The Crowd"], the failure of the modern mindset is that people ask many questions but rarely investigate "il gran perché della vita" ["the great questions of life"] (*UG* 43). They look at things, he explains in "Il teschio fiorito," without wondering about the unfolding relations that exist between them, without wondering about "quali forme viventi / d'insetti o di chicchi di grano, / o d'altro che viva o non viva, / si trasformerà la passiva / carcassa dell'essere umano?" ["what living forms / of insects or grains of wheat / or of other living or not living beings / the passive carcasses / of the human will turn into?"] (*UG* 37).

In "Gli affetti," Vallini comments on the enchanting sense of *intra*-relationality that we lose when we become adults, remembering his childhood as the blissful space-time in which he could love the world simply because the entire world resided within him and he was unable to conceptualize boundaries – "avevo in me tutto il mondo" ["I had the whole world inside me"] (*UG* 40). Similarly, in "Fascino" ["Fascination"], Govoni, a poet who bridged yet also blended crepuscular and futurist poetics, describes a return to the cognitive paradigm of childhood, in which knowledge transforms into a caring attachment to the world. This long and decidedly "crepuscular" poem was published in Govoni's futurist collection *Poesie elettriche* [*Electrical Poems*] (1911), showing once again the connections between these two movements. In "Fascino," the poet, along with a group of peers, imagines engaging in a carousel of memories: love, death, religious sentiment, lust, nature – everything they experienced – continually flows and returns. In the midst of reminiscing, the protagonists of Govoni's poetic narration turn back into children and, like Vallini's soul, are amazed by flowers and insects: "Tornammo bambini coi fiori graziosi / con gli insetti innocenti" ["We became children again, with the pretty flowers / with the innocent insects"] (*P* 142). The unnamed group of friends, a collective and empathetic "we" that Govoni leaves unspecified, comes to the conclusion that in this overwhelming reliving of their past – in this (re-)emerging multiplicity – they indeed found deep meaning, enlightenment, and comfort:

> Ed amammo la vita molteplice e moltanime
> con tutte le sue gioie e i suoi dolori,
> con la sua primavera e il fatale inverno
> con il suo continuo rinnovarsi e morire,
> fascino eterno. (*P* 144)
>
> [And we loved the multifaceted life that has many souls
> with all its joys and pains,
> with its spring and fatal winter
> with its continuous renewal and dying,
> eternal fascination.]

Govoni's text can be read as a provocation against modern *normative* knowledge, which relies on a process of reflexive and analytic subtraction. By contrast, crepuscularism adopts an infantile cognitive approach as, during the developmental stage, the subject-object divide is still blurry, and experiences can be spontaneously lived as processes of sum and diffraction. If, as social theorist Brian Massumi remarks, cognition is indeed the "impossibility of grasping [a] field in all of its cognizable effects," the *diversity* of the crepuscular approach relies on a non-reductionist attempt to engage with the surplus of information that a field of experience unfolds, "as an adventure of integrally renewed self-composition and emergent variation."[27] This cumulative cognition, then, is not portrayed as a moment of self-reflection and achieved clarity, but as a process of diffraction, through which this rich knowledge, passing through an embodied self, spreads out and produces new ripples and modulations.[28]

From a literary perspective, it is important to note that the crepuscular focus on the imaginative power of infancy as the "alternative path" to rational adulthood was not an innovation of early modernism or the avant-garde. As Judith Plotz explains, Romanticism created a fixed and reified figure of the absolute child, identifying this character with a force that was at once creative and destructive, joyful and sorrowful.[29] Yet, unlike traditional poetics, crepuscularism relinquishes the subtle identification of the innocent child with the innate voice of civic values, with the *natural* emergence of modern culture. This provocative discourse becomes evident if one compares Corazzini's figure of the poet-child with Pascoli's seminal work, *Il fanciullino* [*The Little Child*] (first edition, 1897).[30] As mentioned in chapter 1, Pascoli was a central figure of Italian symbolism, and in his declaration of poetics, the child rises as the embodiment of "the beginning of creativity, as the child-like expression of the immediate feelings man experiences in contact with nature and the objects it presents to him."[31] Through his innocent gaze and word, this character animates "objects that were alive and now are frozen, at the edge of life,"[32] and he can act as an animator of a dormant nature because he speaks the awakening voice of culture. By creatively naming things – "Egli adatta il nome della cosa più grande alla più piccola, e al contrario" ["He adapts the name of the bigger thing to the smaller and vice versa"][33] – he welcomes these objects into the dominion of culture, drawing a line between the realm of names and the unnamed dominion of nature.

The disquieting figure of the "child who wants to die," a recurrent character in Corazzini's poetry, parodies Pascoli's tiny civic demiurge who acts as "ispiratore di buoni e civili costumi, d'amor patrio e familiare e umano" ["an inspirer of good and civil customs, of love of country, family and mankind"].[34] The crying poetic "I" of "Desolazione del povero poeta sentimentale" represents the primal innocence that modern society has sacrificed to logic, reason, and custom. Through his illogical crying, Corazzini's young outcast denounces the practice through which modernity attains purified scientific progress by expelling mystery from life. In a 1906 letter to his friend Giuseppe Caruso, the poet suggests that knowledge paradoxically generates "pollution" through its purification practice, namely through its filtering of irrational impurities – its banning of innocence, ignorance, and fantasy. Evoking the myth of the Garden of Eden, the crepuscular author recounts a dreamlike vision in which childhood is transfigured into a cognitive state of innocence, the state that humans lost after being banned from the garden. In this *hortus conclusus*, children are angels, uncontaminated by the sinful fruit of knowledge. As the poet writes, the path to agape – a form of unconditioned natural love – is subordinated to ignorance, to its blissful unawareness:

> Imagina che essi [i fanciulli] siano dei piccoli angeli mortali sulle cui bocche fiorisca il più divino inno, quello dell'ignoranza. Essi non sanno e amano.
>
> [Imagine children were little mortal angels, on whose mouths would blossom the most divine hymn, ignorance. They don't know, and just love.] (*O* 290).

Yet going back to Gozzano's impasse, how is it possible to conjugate "natural" ignorance with the literacy that poetry seemingly implies? For Corazzini, this is not even an issue, as poetry is the expression, or the recovery, of an angelic "riso di gioia e d'inconscienza" ["laughter of joy and unconsciousness"] (*O* 290). As the poet affirms: "Solamente i fanciulli sono degni della nostra anima. L'anima del poeta abita nell'anima del fanciullo" ["Only children are worthy of our soul. The soul of a poet inhabits the soul of a child"] (*O* 290). This infantile poetry queers the familiar certainties of modern culture by delicately engaging with the frightening incoherence of life, which for this young poet is the threat of tuberculosis, and the realization that life is material fleetingness – "Io sento fuggirmi la vita" ["I feel my life escaping"], he writes (*O* 290).

Unlike Pascoli's *fanciullino* – the genuine herald of culture who acts as the agent dividing culture from nature – Corazzini's children, angels, and poets work within a divine realm of unity, in which the human still inhabits the garden of Heaven. His children are closer to an image that French symbolist poet Francis Jammes used in his literary manifesto, *Le Jammisme* (1897). In this work, which delineates a guide to naturalism filtered through mystic contemplation, Jammes compares poets who copy from nature to children who are learning how to write. Just as children diligently copy a model of calligraphy, poets transcribe nature guided by their trusting innocence. It is in disengagement from analytical learning and self-abandonment to an unfiltered imitation of nature that cognitive purity and poetic literacy are found. And yet, for Corazzini, this cognitive purity is achievable only in a world that escapes modern reality, a world where poets are angels who enjoy the unity of nature and culture, good and evil, human and nonhuman. Corazzini's view of unmediated knowledge as a divine unity with an otherworldly nature translates into a mystical escape from everyday life. In the previously mentioned letter to Caruso, the poet explores this escape. He self-identifies with Christ at Gethsemane, a vulnerable Jesus who cries so much that he wets his feet with tears, and then smiles at the "angioli che non si vedono, che ci sono e ci vedono" ["angels who we don't see, who exist and see us"] (*O* 290). This fantastic description proceeds with a Franciscan scene in which nature and culture beautifully merge in a pastoral image: the poet dreams of talking with trees and stars while travelling from village to village, telling fairy tales "piene d'oro e d'ombra" ["filled with gold and shadow"], accompanied by a court of young boys (*O* 290). Corazzini's heavenly vision ultimately coincides with a return to nature. This is his ideal life:

> Il mare infinito, il cielo eterno, soli, fra cielo e mare … raccogliendo le piccole conchiglie sulla povera spiaggia e cantando canzoni di gioia al sole, dormendo fra i fiori selvaggi, vivere così fino alla seconda vita! (*O* 290)
>
> [The infinite sea, the eternal sky, being alone, between sky and sea … collecting little shells on the poor beach and singing joyful songs under the sun, sleeping amid wildflowers, living like this until the second life!]

As for Gozzano and Vallini, Corazzini's cognitive and poetic dream erases the distinction between knowledge and detachment from nature. Ignorance is the cognitive path to wisdom that poets must explore to recover a primal union with the world. Knowing then equates to a constant metamorphic process that combines diffracting from the self and empathetically merging within the entire world contained within our body. Yet for the crepusculars, this "natural" path of coexistence seems attainable only as a fantastic, mystical, or poetic retreat from the normative culture they live in.

Futurist Ignorance, or a Different Return to Nature and Childhood

While crepuscularism equates ignorance with an innocent wisdom, with an exceptional virtue that is rarely found in modern life, futurism charges childhood ignorance with a compelling anti-intellectual message. The 1909 manifesto fosters this message by tying the cognitive rebellion of futurism to a mythical renaissance: after an epic car accident, Marinetti falls into a muddy ditch and feels energized by a powerful rebirth. A baby again, the futurist founder goes back to his childhood memories, when he was sucking milk from his wet nurse's breast:

> Oh! materno fossato, quasi pieno di un'acqua fangosa! Bel fossato d'officina! Io gustai avidamente la tua melma fortificante, che mi ricordò la santa mammella nera della mia nutrice sudanese … (*TIF* 9)
>
> [Oh! Maternal ditch, nearly full of muddy water! Fair factory drain! I gulped down your bracing slime, which reminded me of the sacred black breast of my Sudanese nurse.] (*F* 50).

Overall, the basis for the futurist "reconstruction of the universe" is a return to childhood, imagined as the age of unconstrained learning from contingencies and strikes of intuition. Yet, if we apply Irigaray's feminist view, we can also see that the futurist reconstruction entails a departure from the original relationship with the mother – Marinetti emerges from his "maternal ditch" – and the beginning "of a competitive conquest of the universe by and between those who are (reborn) the same: men."[35] Through the identification of infancy with a polemic counter-culture of masculinity, futurism aims to disconnect civilization from cultural maturity. Summarizing this regressive perspective, Ardengo Soffici affirms in his poem "Mattina" ["Morning"], "Ogni nuova civilizzazione esce dal riso dei bambini" ["Every new civilization comes out from the laugh of children"].[36]

In the futurist elaboration of the motif of regressive education, infancy symbolizes an original space untouched by any form of adult speculation. In line with this return to pre-reason, in "La mia anima è puerile" ["My Soul Is Childish"], one of Marinetti's French poems,[37] he draws on an archetypical essentialism that posits nature as a primal principle, creating what Morton has dubbed "essentialism plus metaphysics of presence."[38] In other words, Marinetti criticizes modernity, embracing a pre-modern metaphysical faith in an essential reality – say, nature – that is constantly present "while humans [or, say] spoons are just epiphenomena."[39] In this text, the futurist founder sings a hymn to the sea that recalls Rimbaud's early poem "Soleil et Chair" ["Sun and Flesh"] (1870). In Rimbaud's reinvention of the classic hymn to the gods, the pre-modern and pre-Christian cultures of "fertility, passion, youth – *antique jeunesse* – and strength" are set in opposition to the enlightened myth of reason.[40] A world of primal corporeality, of primal presence, stands as a warning against the transformations that modern culture has caused:

> Misery! For now [Man] says: I know everything,
> And therefore wanders, eyes closed, ears shut. – And yet,
> No more gods! No more gods! Man is King!
> Man is God! …[41]

The symbolist French author characterizes nature as a source of innate divinity and erotic vitality – Cybele whose breasts spill "the pure stream of eternal life"[42] – a depiction that the futurist avant-garde would later borrow and extend to mechanical matter, the new "electrified" *nature.*[43] Similarly, in "La mia anima è puerile," Marinetti addresses a primal divinity, the sea, yet he frames his prayer as the tantrum of a misbehaving child: "la mia anima è puerile / e strilla e si dibatte per avere un giocattolo! ..." ["my soul is childish / and screams and flounders to get a toy! ..."], he declares (*PF* 333). Marinetti implicitly counteracts the linearity of modern discourse with a synaesthetic orgy of senses, smells, and flavours that inebriates the mind of this capricious child before the sight of a mercantile port:

> Tutti i miei nervi acuìti s'esaltano
> agli effluvî eccitanti del catrame,
> e a quando a quando s'afflosciano
> nella fragranza mista – miele dorato e nera liquirizia –
> dei frutti rancidi o fradici! ...
> Poi, l'odore selvaggio e crepitante del sandalo
> rilancia verso l'odio e la demenza il mio cuore,
> ebbro così da morire, che subito balza nel ballo tondo,
> come un negro piumato che pianga
> in una rossa ubbriachezza forata da bianche risate ... (*PF* 341)

> [All my intensified nerves are exalted
> to the exciting scent of tar,
> and from time to time wilt
> in the mixed fragrance – golden honey and black licorice –
> of rancid or rotten fruit! ...
> Then, the savage and pungent smell of sandalwood
> revamps my heart towards hate and dementia,
> so much inebriated to die, that [it] immediately jumps into a round dance,
> like a plumaged negro who cries
> in a red drunkenness pierced with white laughter ...]

In this passage, Marinetti uses exotic perfumes and the comparison of his heart with a dancing black native to suggest a *natural* cognitive approach that challenges Western *culture* through an exaltation of savage inebriation. While criticizing the paradigm of modern reason, Marinetti remains anchored to a dualistic perspective that divides the artificiality of culture from the savage authenticity of nature. Engaging again with Morton's deconstruction of the idea of nature as a separate ontological and cognitive "world," we can see the impasse: Marinetti's search for an essential reality, freed from the reason that pollutes it, clashes against the fact that, yes, ultimately "there are things, but they don't come with a handy little dotted line that says 'Cut Here' to separate the essence from the appearance."[44] If, as Morton concludes, "a thing [or anything that exists] is strangely physical and semiotic at the same time," Marinetti's alternative to modern reason and to its system of the Great Divide is incoherent because it brings forward a cognitive theory of primal ignorance – of primal vital elements – that, while merging physical substance and semiotics, art and life, human and nonhuman, still attempts to draw a dividing line between nature and culture, or instinct and reason. Marinetti envisions his futurist revolution as the awakening of concealed forces that, although incompatible with traditional anthropocentric rationality, falls into the same logic of separation that it tries to muddle and subvert. Furthermore, the ebullient "will to movement" that animates futurism clashes with the notion of an archetypical irrational violence, a vital living force or brutal nature that paradoxically spurs change by remaining unchanged.

The dualist cognitive approach in which futurism remains incoherently entangled emerges, for instance, in the manifesto "Uccidiamo il chiaro di luna." In this text, Marinetti returns to the idea of an unruly infancy that breaks the order of rational adulthood. He exalts foolishness as the purest form of intellectual energy and as having the power to awaken a sluggish world. Yelling at his futurist friend Paolo Buzzi, Marinetti argues for the crucial role of madness as a key component of this awakening:

> Il nostro cuore è ancora pieno di un ciarpame immondo: code di pavoni, pomposi galli di banderuole, leziosi fazzoletti profumati! ... E non abbiamo ancora scacciate dal nostro cervello le lugubri formiche della saggezza ... Ci vogliono dei pazzi! ... Andiamo a liberarli! (*TIF* 19)

> [Our hearts are still full of filthy rubbish: peacocks' tails, pompous weathercocks, fancy perfumed handkerchiefs! And we still haven't emptied our brains of the lugubrious ants of wisdom ... We need madmen! Let's go and free them!] (*F* 56)

As is typical of futurism, this cognitive enterprise turns into a military battle: the manifesto proceeds with the narration of the siege of Paralysis, a symbolic town ruled by dull conformity. The liberating narrative that futurism delineates connects the unruly energy of mad people with the rejuvenating force of futurism, creating a double dualism, old versus new, rational versus irrational: "Dalle porte spalancate, pazzi e pazze scamiciati, seminudi, eruppero a migliaia, torrenzialmente, così da ringiovanire e ricolorare il volto rugoso della Terra" ["From the wide-open doors, madman and women poured out by the thousands, shirtless madmen and half-naked, a torrent, enough to rejuvenate and give new color to the Earth's wrinkled face"] (*TIF* 19, *F* 57).

In associating madness with a "living thought" – a vitalist, unrestrained thought that overflows the banks of reason – the manifesto creates a further juxtaposition: on the one hand, static norms are opposed to fast-moving action, while on the other hand, the inertia of old-fashioned thinking is opposed to the mad liveliness of young ideas. Enrico Cavacchioli, one of the futurist "brothers" mentioned in this manifesto, experiences this abrupt awakening and suddenly feels himself to be as free as when he was an infant:

> – Io sento ringiovanire il mio corpo ventenne! … Io ritorno, d'un passo sempre più infantile, verso la mia culla … Presto, rientrerò nel ventre di mia madre! … Tutto, dunque, mi è lecito. (*TIF* 18)
>
> [– I feel my twenty-year-old body growing younger! … I'm returning, with ever more infantile steps, to the cradle … Soon, I'll reenter my mother's womb! Everything, then, is permitted!] (*F* 56)

The association between unlimited infantile power and the futurist overcoming the chains of intellect is restated by Cavacchioli himself, in the futurist ballad "Danza della pazzia" ["Dance of Foolishness"]. In this text, inspired by orgiastic Dionysian dances, euphoria triumphs over reason. Foolishness becomes the last dance performed before death. The obsessive movements of this dance will reveal the *vision* that the intellect has always obscured:

> noi danzeremo una danza infinita: prima di morire.
> E sarà l'ultima ebbrezza
> quella che canterà a martello nelle tempie sensibili
> i riti inesprimibili della ragione!
> …
> e l'anima ci fa male, tanto male
> perché la nostra pazzia
> vede più della Ragione che ci abbandona! (*PF* 197, 199)
>
> [we will dance an infinite dance: before dying.
> And it will be the last exaltation
> that one that will sing pounding in the sensitive temples
> the ineffable rites of reason!
> …
> And the soul hurts us so badly
> because our madness
> sees more than the Reason that leaves us.]

The futurist avant-garde envisions a new episteme that fosters regression, infantilism, and praise of folly: ultimately, what humanity needs to learn is to cultivate ignorance, that is, to regain an innate love for that which is rationally unknown. The motif of infantile regression, combined with the liberating ritual of dancing beyond the boundaries of reason, ties Marinetti's futurism with the futurist group of the Azure Patrol.

Maria Ginanni denies the idea that childhood is merely an isolated phase of human development; instead, she imagines childhood as a cross-generational channel where the mind can wander, oblivious to the mental paths that "adult" thinking imposes. In the passage "Come una danza" ["Like a Dance"], Ginanni describes her rebirth as a little girl who thinks outside the confines of her womanhood: "Attraverso i pori delicatissimi dell'aria. Mi sono immersa nel filtro profumatamente titanico con le mie ansie, le mie complicatezze di donna e ne sono uscita bambina." ["Through the extremely delicate pores of the air, I immersed in the filter, fragrantly titanic, with my anxieties, my complications as a woman, and I came out a little girl"] (*MT* 111). Yet, for all its overwhelming aliveness, infancy can also turn into a "crepuscular" space wherein the human acknowledges its inadequacy before the infinite unknown. As Ginanni affirms, recalling Corazzini's crying child:

> Mi sento così bambina, così ingenua stasera in questo punto proiezione del mio filo infinito.
>
> Accanto alla mia sorellina ho sentito, stasera, di essere ancora più bimba di lei: il desiderio di piangere sulle sue mani per l'intenerimento della mia infantilità.[45]
>
> [I feel like such a little girl, so ingenuous tonight in this projection-point of my infinite thread.
>
> Tonight, near my little sister, I felt littler than she: desiring to cry on her hands for the softening of my infantilism.]

Ginanni's reflection on childish ignorance epitomizes two parallel motives within the futurist movement: an electrifying enthusiasm for a constant surplus of creativity, and an uncontainable eagerness to create by absorbing the intensity of this surplus. In these passages from *Montagne trasparenti*, Ginanni voices these coexisting yet conflicting tendencies, expressing the fuel of her writing as an awareness of the mystery of Life, an awareness that turns into inspired creativity:

> Urlo di creazione disperata: dare nuove pazzie all'universo, scompigliare le leggi esistenti, attaccare fulmini di poesia penetranti a zig-zag nell'anima della vita.
>
> …
>
> Sparpagliare la mia anima nei suoi atomi più essenziali per avere la potenza di ricostruire un nuovo universo. (*MT* 70–1)

[Scream of desperate creation: to give new foolishness to the universe, to throw into confusion the existing laws, to attack lightning strikes of poetry, penetrating zigzag into the soul of life,

...

To disperse my soul in her most essential atoms to have the potency to build a new universe.]

Infancy is indeed the realm of unawareness of all those "truths" that weigh heavily on our shoulders. Futurism does not seek balance between the "cervello analitico" ["analytic brain"] and the "spirito entusiasta" ["enthusiast spirit"], as Ginanni defines these two vehicles of cognition.[46] The movement draws a "dotted line" between the two approaches to knowledge, denying that to understand is to achieve a clear outcome through mental processing. As Ginanni declares, in her work *Il poema dello spazio*, the actual cognitive challenge is "vivere della nostra interiorità come di un altro misterioso universo" ["to live our interiority as another mysterious universe"] (*MT* 11). According to her, human knowledge is an illusion, as we can barely control the unknown that surfaces in our own lives. She believes there is an "unseen something" that lives within us, yet "Noi riusciamo a contenerlo tutto questo 'qualcosa' smisurato: i nostri sensi sono la lente che ce lo condensa e ce lo dona cristallizzato" ["We can contain this endless 'something': our senses are the lens that condenses this and gives it to us crystallized"] (*MT* 29).

The pedagogical value of cultivating ignorance through a non-standard education is discursively formalized in the 1916 manifesto "La scienza futurista" ["Futurist Science"], co-signed by Bruno Corra, Arnaldo Ginna, Remo Chiti, Emilio Settimelli, Mario Carli, Oscar Mara, and Neri Nannetti. As the subtitle of the manifesto specifies, futurist science is "anti-tedesca-avventurosa-capricciosa-sicurezzofoba-ebbra d'ignoto" ["anti-German-adventurous-capricious-securityphobic-inebriated with the unknown"].[47] Employing the usual rhetoric of attack and demolition that characterizes other futurist programmatic works, this manifesto bitterly criticizes the traditional association of science with the imposition of rigid methods and prejudices, with deliberative slowness, with the patient practice of research, and with the "dogma" of scientific truth. The pedantic routine of science is, for the futurists, "tradizionalismo eterna rimasticazione e ridigestione di tutto ciò che è stato fatto, disprezzo dei giovani, degli audaci, dei geniali non diplomati, degli irregolari, dei *nuovi*" ["traditionalism eternal rechewing and redigestion of everything that has been done, contempt of youth, of the audacious, of the not-graduated geniuses, of the borderlines, of *people who are new*"] (*MT* 205). By contrast, the futurists affirm an alternative, self-taught model of culture: "*l'unico genere di coltura utile è quella che uno spirito originale sa procurarsi da sé, qua e là, con uno studio a fiuto, caotico, profondamente sregolato*" ["*the only type of useful culture is that which an original spirit can provide for himself, here and there, having a flair for studying, engaging in chaotic and deeply disorganized study*"] (*MT* 206).

Futurist science is a vibrant exploration of the unknown, "*frammentaria, contradditoria, felice di scoprire oggi una verità che distrugga la verità di ieri, tutta inzuppata di ignoto*" ["fragmentary, contradictory, happy to discover today a truth that will destroy the truth of yesterday, all drunk in the unknown"] (*MT* 206). From the rigorous search for universally applicable laws, science devolves into all-out worship of immediate empirical finding. The futurists resort to the most obvious experience, claiming that the reality displayed before our eyes might not need to be studied at all: "*quanto più si è ignoranti tanto più si vede chiara, semplice e sicura la realtà*" ["*the more ignorant one is, the more one sees reality clearly, simply, and with certainty*"] (*MT* 206). Therefore, science must embrace a new mission, namely:

> *La scienza non deve avere più che uno scopo: ingigantire sempre più l'ignoto precisando e frastagliando la zona di realtà che ci è meno sconosciuta ... Il fine supremo della scienza sarebbe, ipoteticamente, non farci capire più niente*: rivolgere la faccia dell'umanità verso il mistero totale. (*MT* 207)
>
> [*Science must have only one aim: to constantly enlarge the unknown, specifying and feathering the area of reality that is less unknown to us ... The supreme goal of science would be, hypothetically, to make us no longer understand anything*: to turn the face of humanity towards the absolute mystery.]

Through a provocative logic that borders on absurdity, this 1916 manifesto recasts science as the exploration of an unverifiable area of ignorance, including the phenomena "del medianismo, dello psichismo, della rabdomanzia, della divinazione, della telepatia" ["of mediumistic and psychic practices, rhabdomancy, divination, telepathy"] (*MT* 208). This hyper-provocative identification of science with a form that the futurists dub "ignotofilia" ["love for the unknown"] (*MT* 209) provides an ideal link between the crepuscular and futurist cult of ignorance. Both movements reconceptualize knowledge as a lack, a void, a frontier that has never been explored. The only way to access this obscure realm is by "regressing" into unconventional forms of cognitive ignorance. The cult of infantilism would indeed lead to a regenerative reaction against the "elephantine slowness" of adult scientific norms.[48]

The iconoclast futurists' proposal of rising ignorance as a new form of regenerative culture is groundbreaking in destabilizing the traditional function of *homo sapiens*, yet it does not erase the modern distinction between culture and nature. Although affirming a non-anthropocentric cognitive perspective, the avant-garde regressive view of knowledge still enforces the divide between the irrational unknown – the escape into an infantile and pre-rational nature – and the enlightened culture that has contaminated this space. Futurist ignorance thus becomes a cognitive-ontological framework that brings (or "regresses") humans closer to the presence of primal elements, wherein a fantasized savage nature – or, in Marinetti's imagery, the naturalized urban forest of the Anthropocene – stands as the essential mystery. Yet, the issue with equating irrationality to a return to nature is that this correspondence denies nature its own nonhuman "thought." Why should humans search for irrationality in nature?

Barad has meditated on nature's intelligence, using the example of the hypertechnological optical system of the brittlestar, a relative of the starfish. In short, this animal without a brain "has a skeleton with crystals that function as a visual system, apparently furnishing the information that lets the animal see its surroundings and escape harm."[49] Barad highlights that the brittlestar is a living optical system, for which "being and knowing, materiality and intelligibility, substance and form entail one another."[50]

Botanist Robin Wall Kimmerer has expressed a similar position by examining vegetal life. She has shown that nature follows patterns of reason and communication that escape our limited human capacity, while challenging our *naturization of nature* as irrational. Using a case study on the masting, or synchronized reproduction, of pecan trees, Wall Kimmerer proves that, although the way trees communicate is still unknown to us, undoubtedly, they do *communicate*. Sophisticated networks of fungi guarantee that each tree in a certain area has the same amount of nutrients, allowing them to bear fruit simultaneously. This "web of reciprocity," created by a chain of chemical reactions (of relational and logical intra-actions), allows for mutual flourishing and survival through unity, so that "soil, fungus, tree, squirrel, boy – all are the beneficiaries of reciprocity."[51] Knowing and communicating is embedded in the *natural* mode of being of both the brittlestar and the pecan tree, and yet, who could argue that "high-tech" brainless animals and "speaking" pecan trees are irrational? Who could argue, indeed, that being close to nature equates to being irrational feral creatures or passive vegetal life, uniquely designed for survival and satisfaction of primal needs?

Investigating these questions, in the last few decades, theoretical and scientific perspectives have extended the understanding of communication and semiotics beyond human and nonhuman animals to include plants. For example, trees are used in seismology as biotic measuring devices, and tomato plants attacked by pathogens have been studied for their ability to "warn" healthy plants of the impending danger. Michael Marder, in his essay "To Hear Plants Speak," reflects on how to listen to the language of plants without translating vegetable life into symbolic or numeric ways to convey human meanings. Rather, his goal is to achieve "an interchange between two languages: the biosemiotics of vegetal life and human signification" that does not deprive plants of their untranslatable specificity – their intrinsic ability to self-express while materially joining different natural elements.[52] Interestingly, Marder's conclusion echoes Morton's view of ecology without a world (or a separate natural world). For Marder, "plants [indeed] *form* a world, by which they, themselves, are shaped. The world is neither an empty container for reality nor the seemingly unlimited stuff it contains; rather, its character is deeply relational, dependent on the interconnections between the beings that populate it."[53] Once again, knowing – or "translating things" into cultural codes – shows itself to be inseparable from our being and doing in the world, from being corporeal natures that speak, affect, and enter into relations with each other.

Although crepuscularism and futurism give voice, in different ways, to the fascinating and "untranslatable" language of nonhuman elements, they are unable to fully conjoin the intelligence of nature with the intellectual inquiry of culture. They cannot quite envision a complex network of human-nonhuman relations that we respectfully access without having to choose between rational and irrational, mindfulness and instinct, reality and fantasy, male and female. However, in the following section we will see that both the crepuscular and futurist redefinitions of knowledge and ignorance move away from the idea of cognition as a process that transcends the encounter with material reality. Immersion and action within matter are explored as new cognitive and relational modalities.

Crepuscular Immersive Knowledge

Through their recasting of ignorance, crepuscularism and futurism further develop the reflection on the three "errors" of scientific knowledge that Nietzsche discussed in *The Gay Science* (1882), namely, thinking that science could promote a human understanding of God; believing that knowledge, morality, and happiness are interdependent; and viewing science as a disinterested, peaceful, and self-sufficient form of knowledge.[54] Yet, what is behind these unveiled "errors"? Put differently, once Tantalus's chains have been cut and the horrible shell of wisdom has been broken, once we are no longer anchored to reason, what is there waiting for us? If being (something in relation to something else) precedes the possibility of rationally knowing something, and yet also exceeds that possibility, then both movements venture into a cognitive abyss – Marinetti's "profondi pozzi dell'Assurdo" ["deep wells of the Absurd"] (*TIF* 9, *F* 50) – wherein the capabilities of the human mind cannot cope with the depths of being. However, if in "Dai 'Soliloquî di un pazzo'" ["From 'A Mad Man's Soliloquies'"] Corazzini can boldly declare that "morte stecchite, [sono] le idee di una volta" ["stone dead, [are] the ideas from the past"] and, echoing Nietzsche, "L'anima è morta ed io ne son sicuro" ["The [human] soul is dead, and I am sure of this"] (*O* 136–7), the problematic aspect remains reconstructing on the rubble of this loss.

In parallel ways, crepuscularism and futurism create an epistemology founded on the material certainty of our immersive presence in matter. In other words, knowing implies a constant repositioning and re-emergence of a self that is strictly dependent on – and even constituted by – its relations (of movement) with other beings. Knowing then means diving into the "well" of an entangled participation. It means being a presence that apprehends its own "*haecceity*," its own contingent "thisness," in a web of relations that is both material and discursive, both bodily and cultural.[55] Consequently, any fixed human certainty is gone; this is the only positive assurance.

At a linguistic level, the crepuscular notion of embodied *comprehension*, which overthrows the traditional cognitive model of the "I-knower" as the subject of intellectual speculation, is especially noticeable in the peculiar use of *sapere* ["to know"] in the mystical poetry of Corazzini. This verb strays from the semantic field of "knowing" or having a certain practical knowhow, and trespasses into the semantics of the verb *conoscere*, which in Italian means to be acquainted with someone and is usually adopted to describe human relationships. In his semiotic blending, the Roman poet also recovers *sapere*'s Latin root, *sapio*, "to taste of," and only figuratively connotes its usual meaning of "to discern." "To know" thus comes to designate a participative assimilation of surrounding matter; matter is tasted, swallowed, and metabolized, while the brain only superficially detects its "flavour." For example, in "Dai 'Soliloquî di un pazzo,'" Corazzini vividly describes Christ's cross: "I chiodi terribili che sanno / le ossa dell'uomo e il legno della croce" ["The terrible nails that know / the bones of the man and the wood of the cross"] (*O* 136). Such hermetic lines engage with the verb *sapere* in all its semantic shadows: the cross never rationally understood Jesus's divinity, yet its wood was physically interpenetrated with Christ's human flesh and soaked with his martyrdom, becoming the tangible synecdoche of the mystery of the passion. By blending mind and bodily knowledge, Corazzini proposes a cognitive model in which human "subjects" *are known* by things and unconsciously infused with their taste, essence, meaning. He envisions a "situated, interactive, and carnal kind of knowing: one that entails a mutual opening of the one to the other, full of unpredictability and risk, in which neither party is ever fully revealed to the other or totally in control of the outcome of their encounter."[56]

The model of incarnated revelation – a form of immersive knowledge in which bodily matter and symbolic meaning coincide – is at the heart of Corazzini's elaboration of intuitive knowledge as messianic epiphany. Crepuscular knowledge is a waiting for the final disclosure of a meaning that is largely unintelligible, and only graspable through instants of inexplicable plenitude. Paradoxically, real knowledge is indeed only glimpsed, never fully understood; as Corazzini declares in a letter to Antonello Caprino:

> La dedizione del mio corpo al *Nulla* o al *Tutto*, secondo l'ora che passa, s'intensifica in un desiderio così folle e così enorme come se nella cessazione della mia esistenza io intravedessi ciò che tiene gli occhi del prigioniero, rimasto per un caso, privo di sorveglianza. (*O* 284)
>
> [The dedication of my body to the *Nothing* or to the *Everything* depends on the time, intensifies in such a foolish and enormous desire, as if at the end of my existence I glimpsed what captures the eyes of the prisoner who happened to remain without surveillance.]

A similar epistemological crisis characterizes Gozzano's poetry. In the poem "Nemesi" ["Nemesis"], his persona overthrows human certitudes like rationality and inner life, even wondering about the entire human species and asking "ma 'chi' sono gli uomini? / Chi sono?" ["'Who' are humans? / Who are they?"] (*TP* 125). Here, Gozzano portrays the disbelief he feels in touching his skull and doubting his own existence; "comincio a dubitare / se sono o se non sono!" ["I begin doubting / if I am or if I am not"], he provocatively affirms, referencing "La via del rifugio," the text that eponymously opens his first poetry collection (*TP* 125). Gozzano's doubt is an evident parody of Descartes's assertion of the necessary correlation between thinking and being. Yet the poet moves beyond his individual humanity. He wonders about the universal sense of life – the existence of *homo sapiens*, the stone, the grass, the sparrow (*TP* 126) – from the perspective of the end of times, when the earth on which "tronfieggia il querulo / sciame dell'Uman Genere" ["lives buffed up the querulous / swarm of the Human Genus"] is an incinerated "povero glomerulo" ["poor glomerulus"] (*TP* 126). Gozzano's ironic verses, which mercilessly represent the Anthropocene as the fleeting space-time of human hubris on earth, disclose an environmental poetic message. In the midst of early twentieth-century Italian industrialization, these lines provocatively downsize human *techne* to "Earth magnitude," showing a *meshed* timeframe.

Technical advancement, solely understood as self-interested human becoming, is neither a realistic nor an attainable path. Vallini's meditation on human life expresses this ecocritical message while embracing the ontological paradigm of "being and becoming with" – which, for Donna Haraway, is a participative paradigm of coexistence and co-evolution.[57] In the poem "Il teschio fiorito," the poet uses the image of the dead cogito, representing his random encounter with a skull, disturbingly repurposed into a grotesque vase with leaves of grass springing out like a lock of hair. The deadly "sorriso … / di scherno eterno" ["laugh … / of eternal mocking"] of the bony vase, in which the poetic "I" virtually glimpses "la vera / parola che mai non sapremo!" ["the true word we will never know"], is evocative of an unbalanced relationship between humanity and the environment (*UG* 36). Yet this unbalanced relationship provocatively reverses the socio-historical paradigm that equates man with the colonizer and a feminized nature with the colonized. In Vallini's text, human characters emerge in their bodily and emotional fragility, as powerless objects of nature; not by chance, the poetic narrator comes to this luxuriant cemetery as "la trista / cosa che chiede perdono" ["the anguished thing / that asks forgiveness"] (*UG* 37–8). In the poem's setting – an "eremo pregno / di succhi e d'odori" ["hermitage full / of juices and smells"] surrounded by a "selva vivente" ["living forest"] (*UG* 37, 36) – the skull is a vestige of humanity. Nature springs from the cranial bones, renewing life through the abandoned skull. Within the context of this inverted relationship between human and nonhuman, the poetic "I" symbolically embraces a new ethical perspective. He humbly asks earth to dispose of his life as earth wishes, constructing a relationship in which man serves the environment rather than owning it.

In the sixth sonnet of the "Sonetti della casa," Vallini pushes his provocation forward to the modern paradigm of emancipatory human reason. He affirms that his generation is enslaved to the "novella maga" ["new sorceress"] of rational investigation and solely "il bene in un'indagine ripone" ["values intellectual inquiry"] (*UG* 92). Yet, for the poet, the inquiry of the mind, "purified" from its bodily entanglement, will not lead humanity to an understanding of the world, for "nature with biological bodies is the material site where we become aware of our embodiment in the earth process."[58] However, in the poem "Alcuni desideri" ["A Few Wishes"], Vallini polemically wonders whether the real cognitive privilege would be to exchange reason for the lethargic, yet deeply *worldly*, existence of a dog that quietly sleeps under the sun:

> Oh come darei le parole
> inutili e l'opere vane

dell'uomo, per essere un cane
che dorma placido al sole!
Per essere la foglia o l'insetto
o l'albero o il gufo o il leone,
per non aver la ragione,
per non aver l'intelletto. (*UG* 62)

[Oh, how I'd give the useless
words and the vain works
of man, to be a dog
that placidly sleeps under the sun!
To be the leaf or the insect
or the tree or the owl or the lion,
not to have reason,
not to have intellect.]

The ultimately intellectual provocation is to deny reason and to find a new form of material and intuitive *comprehension* in animal and vegetal life – in the bodily intelligence of the insect, the tree, and the lion. In Vallini's writing, the perspective of entangled co-dependence, the notion of dependent origination (the belief that things originate with a dependence on other things), and the rejection of the human self were highly influenced by his interest in Buddhist philosophy. Through this non-theistic religion, which poses that "no one thing exists apart from another," the Italian poet blends a precursory spiritual ecology with a vitalist view of matter as vibrant and agentic.[59]

This renewed "eco-cognitive" relation, a cognitive engagement that involves a material *comprehension* of (and in) a living mystery, similarly appears in Gozzano's second collection, *I colloqui*. In the poem "Una risorta" ["A Woman Resurrected"], he portrays a conversation with a woman in which his poetic alter ego explains a supreme mystery to her, namely, that the life that pervades minerals, stones, and crystals is like an all-encompassing breath, physically linking our existence to a surrounding world that is not inert or insentient:

Nel disco della lente
s'apre l'ignoto abisso,
già sotto l'occhio fisso
la pietra vive, sente …
Cadono i dogmi e l'uso
della Materia. In tutto
regna l'Essenza, in tutto
lo Spirito è diffuso …

[Those depths so long unknown
are pierced under the lens.
Intent, the eye can sense
the breathing of the stone …
The customs and the creeds
of Matter fall. In all
The Essence reigns, in all
the living Spirit breathes …] (*TM* 134–5)

Gozzano's breathing stones are the material embodiment of a cognitive approach that recognizes the interrelated uniqueness of any form of existence and overcomes, in Irigaray's words, the "dependence on a truth, a discourse, or a master presumed to know the whole."[60] The feminist philosopher continues by arguing that this rejection of a unique knowing agent fosters respect for the (closely intertwined) diversity that is part of life; therefore, to reject a unique human account of knowledge "is to recognize another life as transcendent to my own and to my world, forever unknowable to myself."[61] It is interesting to note that, just as Vallini's and Gozzano's ecological notion of inter-being was influenced by Eastern philosophies, Irigaray is similarly informed by non-Western approaches. Her reflections were inspired by the practice of mindful breathing that yoga flow and meditation foster.[62]

However, in Gozzano's poetic reflections, the desire for cognitive abandonment is always counterbalanced by the lucid awareness of searching for an answer that neither science nor spirituality can fully provide.[63] In his letters from India, the poet exalts the contemplative Buddhist lifestyle. "Amo la religione buddista" ["I love the Buddhist religion"], he writes to Candida Bolognino in April 1912, meditating about a possible conversion; yet his expression of yearning for asceticism is rife with hypothetical constructions that sound very unlike an actual plan for conversion. Although Gozzano was interested in Eastern religions, in many passages of his travel journal, *Verso la cuna del mondo*, he also reveals an inability to let go of the occidental perspective.[64] In a passage from "Un Natale a Ceylon" ["Christmas in Ceylon"], the poet shares his culture shock and struggle, confessing that "ci si può illudere d'essere un Robinson e un cenobita buddista" ["one can pretend to be Robinson Crusoe or a Buddhist monk"], but it is impossible to deny one's European essence, which is based on "millenni di evoluzione europea e venti secoli di cristianesimo" ["thousands of years of European evolution and twenty centuries of Christianity"].[65]

It is more accurate to say that Gozzano creatively hybridized his fascination with Eastern spirituality with his Western readings. As is typical of the early twentieth-century epoch, the poet elaborated on an eclecticism that combined, though not always harmoniously, a variety of different approaches. Gozzano's private journal, published posthumously with the title *Albo dell'officina* [*Diary of the Laboratory*] (1991), shows this eclectic tendency. The poet meditates on the meaning of knowledge, drawing from the Nietzschean conception of the eternal return. He writes that everyone is like an hourglass, continuously turned over and exposed to repeating conditions. From this cyclical perspective, knowledge translates into a symbiotic encounter with the other – with otherness, generally speaking – that implies finding one's own experience in any suffering, joy, friend, enemy, hope, mistake, blade of grass, or ray of sun.[66] Even Vallini, who in that epoch most likely converted to Buddhism, seems to echo the ironic scepticism about human knowledge that pervades Gozzano's work. Vallini opens his poetry collection *Il giorno* [*One Day*] with the question, "Ma quale / Buddha c'insegnerà come si vive?" ["But which / Buddha will teach us how to live?"] (*UG* 30). At the end of his meditative journey, he has indeed found an answer, albeit a negative one: "Mai nessun Buddha / c'insegnerà come si vive!" ["No Buddha will ever / teach us how to live!"] (*UG* 71–2). However, Vallini's irony might not be irony at all, but rather the admission that teaching and learning are inseparable from the process of living; in other words, teaching and learning occur as beings continually encounter teachers and learners across human and nonhuman natures. In fact, *Il giorno* closes with an insight, with the vision of a truth that the poetic "I" finally *sees*, namely the mindful awareness of being a sentient particle in a cyclical Whole that the human intellect cannot comprehend, despite being comprehended by it:

sentivo di tendere verso
il Tutto, di esser la parte
minima dell'Universo,
la parte che vede e che sente,
che esiste in eterno e che cade
col tutto continuamente
per una china infinita
senza principio, né fondo,
per ove in eterno si fondono
insieme la Morte e la Vita. (*UG* 72)

[I felt myself tending towards
the Whole, to be the minimal
part of the Universe,
the part that sees and feels,
that exists eternally and that falls

with everything continuously
on an infinite incline
without beginning, or end,
through which eternally
Death and Life
fuse themselves together.]

Vallini identifies the only truth worth knowing with the contemplation of a self-generating movement through which Life and Death cyclically interchange their roles.

Overall, the crepuscular participative notion of cognition recalls Morton's image of the "weird twist" or the "loop," wherein knowing takes the shape of a circular string; knowing is "more like letting be known" and also "something like coexisting."[67] Crepuscularism represents cognition as a terrestrial immersion and lingering within a Whole that moves, animated by its own will, a world independent from human reasoning, "in which objects are suffused with and surrounded by mysterious hermeneutical clouds of unknowning," in which fragility, fragile coexistence, and inter-breathing are the names of the (human) cognitive game.[68]

Futurist Action-Thinking

Crepuscular cognition is participative because it arises from instantaneous glimpses of our "intra-connections" with matter. Particularly for the proto-ecologist "school of irony" of Gozzano and Vallini, perceiving and thinking are an integral part of our corporeal mingling with the universe, rather than a privileged distinction that separates the human mind from its surroundings. On a different level, these conceits return in the futurist immersive paradigm of cognition, which pivots on "**la psicologia intuitiva della materia**" ["**the intuitive psychology of matter**"], a notion that in the "Technical Manifesto of Futurist Literature" Marinetti describes as an analogic chain of "Le intuizioni profonde della vita congiunte l'una all'altra, parola per parola, secondo il loro nascere illogico" ["Profound intuitions of life linked together one by one, word by word, according to their illogical surge"] (*TIF* 52, *F* 123). Yet unlike the crepusculars' abandonment to a constantly transforming Whole, the futurists' cognitive involvement in a web of "relations of movement" relies on active engagement. This call for action informs an articulated cognitive paradigm that Marinetti's avant-garde partially elaborated on from other sources, including Henri Bergson's intuitionism, William James's pragmatism, and the artistic experimentalism of Ginna and Corra. Futurism thus assembled these contributions to further its own blending of immediate thinking and active engagement. The movement also used intuition and action to foster a pseudo-religious faith that identified intuitive speed with the divine.

Futurists assume that being part of an intrinsically vibrant matter enables a type of immediate and multifarious action-thinking. As Serge Milan states, the new futurist sensibility is "a constitutive element of perception and cognition; it is intuitive rather than discursive, but emotive and pulsating as well, coming only partly from consciousness and depending above all on conditions of life and the milieu in which the sensing individual is at home."[69] Since the futurist avant-garde views intuitive thinking and immediate action as interdependent, the movement strives to transform the way people process ideas in order to, consequently, change the way people act. As Bruno Corra and Emilio Settimelli declare in the manifesto "Pesi, misure, e prezzi del genio artistico" ["Weights, Measures, and Prices of Artistic Genius"] (1914), the issue with knowledge is not so much understanding how the brain works physiologically – "Non c'è nessuna diversità essenziale tra un cervello umano e una macchina. Maggiore complicazione di meccanismi, nient'altro"[70] ["there is no essential difference between a human brain and a machine. It is mechanically more complicated, that is all"] (*F* 181) – but rather what type of associations the brain-machine is able to process when reacting to a complex system of relations:

> Se il nostro mondo fosse diverso, noi ragioneremmo diversamente. Esempio: se il rovesciarsi delle sedie producesse di solito in tutti i capitani di cavalleria la sordità dell'orecchio sinistro, questo rapporto sarebbe vero per noi. Così, la più gran parte delle nozioni sono poste in ogni cervello in un determinato ordine. Esempî: neve-bianco-freddo-inverno, fuoco-rosso-caldo, danza-ritmo-gioia ... Chiunque è capace di associare azzurro a cielo. Mentre invece vi sono pezzi di conoscenza tra i quali è difficile stabilire un rapporto perché non sono mai stati associati, perché non esistono somiglianze evidenti tra di loro.[71]
>
> [If our world were different, we would reason differently: if chairs falling over typically led to deafness of the left ear in all cavalry officers, that relationship would be true for us. Thus, in every mind most notions are arranged in a definite order. For example, snow-white-cold-winter, fire-red-hot, dance-rhythm-joy. Everyone is capable of associating blue and sky. But there are other pieces of knowledge between which it is difficult to establish a relationship, because they have never been associated together, because there are no obvious similarities between them.] (*F* 181)

Futurism knots together elements that have never been associated, proposing a transformative action that is simultaneously a cognitive effort and a physical rearrangement of the traditional or "natural" order of things. When relations in the world change, the world itself automatically changes; yet seeing or creating less predictable connections between things requires a much higher effort for the brain – an additional intellectual "action," we might say. As Corra and Settimelli affirm, "La quantità di energia che è riuscita a scoprire dei rapporti, a istituire delle relazioni, tra un certo numero di elementi, dev'essere stata tanto più grande quanto più gli elementi combinati erano distanti, estranei gli uni agli altri e quanto più sono complessi e numerosi i rapporti scoperti"[72] ["the quantity of energy necessary to discover kinships and establish relationships between a given number of elements is greater when the elements to be combined are more distant, more unlike each other, and when the relationships discovered are more complex and more numerous," because this distance requires further engagement of cerebral energy"] (*F* 182). Based on this quantitative parameter, they posit that a futurist work of art is indeed more valuable as it leads to increased effort by the brain.

To exemplify the aesthetic value and outcome of the futurist cognitive action, we can think of the introduction to *Mafarka il futurista*, in which Marinetti compares his novel to a weapon, a "grenade" used to destroy a slow-moving and obtuse way of thinking. Through this exploding grenade, the traditional conception of mental processing immediately turns from a reflective meditation into a relational process of detonating "diffraction." This form of active knowledge combines acceleration of action with an acceleration of the cognitive process that rethinks the world while reshaping it.

The intrinsic action-diffraction that informs the futurist cognitive experience also emerges in Boccioni's manifesto "Le fondazioni plastiche della scultura e pittura futuriste" ["The Plastic Foundations of Futurist Sculpture and Painting"] (1913), in which the futurist artist explicitly quotes Bergson's *Matter and Memory*. As Christine Poggi explains, through Bergson's works and intuitionist philosophy, the futurist artist expressed a new empathy that arises from objects in movement:

> Boccioni understood absolute motion to be the result of the inherent volatility of matter with its whirring electrons and propensity to "disaggregate," whereas relative motion was the displacement of one object in relation to another. He theorized that artists could intuit the absolute motion of an apparently still object by empathically identifying with its core in order to sense the dynamic forces inherent to its forms and materiality, and the way these forces would propel the object to fuse with its environment. (*F* 317)

Movement, in Boccioni's view, is an inborn quality of any object, and the artist's role is to intuitively and emotionally grasp this movement. Futurism radically abolishes Descartes's split between the mind – "the thinking thing" – and the non-thinking body. Neurologist Antonio Damasio has provocatively dubbed this divide "Descartes' error," namely, the idea "that mind and brain are related, but only in the sense that the mind is the software program run in a piece of a computer hardware called brain."[73] By recasting knowledge as a multi-textured object in movement, the futurist avant-garde envisions intuitive thinking as an action that involves "a whole organism possessed of integrated body proper and brain and fully interactive with a physical and social environment."[74] The futurist cognitive "revolution" is in fact strictly related to the new techno-media culture of the early twentieth century. In this environment, for the first time in history, people began to embrace the more-than-human dream of telegraphic ubiquity and cinematic motion. Futurist manifestos, such as Marinetti's "Distruzione della sintassi – Immaginazione senza fili – Parole in libertà" (1913), anticipate the twentieth-century conquests of digital communication, foreseeing a world of erased distances and infinite potential for interaction:

> La terra rimpicciolita dalla velocità. Nuovo senso del mondo. Mi spiego: Gli uomini conquistarono successivamente il senso della casa, il senso del quartiere in cui abitavano, il senso della città, il senso della zona geografica, il senso del continente. Oggi posseggono il senso del mondo; hanno mediocremente bisogno di sapere ciò che facevano i loro avi, ma bisogno assiduo di sapere ciò che fanno i loro contemporanei di ogni parte del mondo. Conseguente necessità, per l'individuo, di comunicare con tutti i popoli della terra. Conseguente bisogno di sentirsi centro, giudice e motore dell'infinito esplorato e inesplorato. Ingigantimento del senso umano e urgente necessità di fissare ad ogni istante i nostri rapporti con tutta l'umanità. (*TIF* 68–9)

> [The earth shrunk by speed. New sense of the world. Let me explain: men have successively conquered a sense of the house, the neighborhood in which they live, the city, the region, the continent. Today man possesses a sense of the world; he has only a modest need to know what his forebears have done, but a burning need to know what his contemporaries are doing in every part of the globe. Whence the necessity, for the individual, of communicating with all the peoples of the earth. Whence the need to feel oneself at the center, to be judge and motor of the infinite both explored and unexplored. A gigantic increase in the sense of humanity and an urgent need to coordinate at every moment our relations with all humanity.] (*F* 144–5)

Yet the futurist redefinition of knowledge as intuitive action and as an "urgent need" to escape the material limitations of the human mind was also the result of the creative combination of a number of epistemological perspectives. For instance, as philosopher Norberto Bobbio noted, in Italy, Bergson's theories were mostly filtered through the activity of two prominent intellectuals, Giovanni Papini and Giuseppe Prezzolini, who heavily influenced the early reception of the French philosopher's works. They turned Bergson into a champion of irrationalism and a defender of the primacy of intimate life and mystic individualism over scientific and practical knowledge.[75] This tendency clearly appears in Papini's *Ventiquattro cervelli* [*Twenty-Four Brains*] (1912). In his essay on Bergson, Papini sets the innovative method of the French philosopher in opposition to the narrow-minded perspective of "i carabinieri della Ragione" ["the police of Reason"].[76] According to Papini, Bergson succeeded in explaining that intelligence can only explain a part of reality, since it is limited to the field of basic activities and finalities, as well as geometrical and mathematical rules. Intelligence is limited by its need to account for that which is measurable, calculable, solid; "quello che c'è nella realtà di fluido, di vivente, di mobile, di oscuro, le sfugge" ["that which exists in reality as fluid, living, mobile, obscure, escapes intelligence"]. Consequently, to explore what Papini dubs "il mondo della vita" ["the world of life"], we need to engage with a type of knowledge that derives from intuition. Translating from Bergson, Papini defines intuition as the intellectual sympathy through which we can transform ourselves into the inner part of an object, to coincide with whatever it has of the unique and therefore the ineffable. Papini continues by saying that only intuition – which is not pure instinct, but is more similar to instinct than to rational intelligence – can lead to finding "l'assoluto nella possessione profonda e diretta della realtà più quotidiana" ["the absolute in the profound and direct possession of the most quotidian reality"].[77]

The futurist notion of "intuitive thinking-in-action" also connects with the popularization of the pragmatic theories of American philosopher William James in early twentieth-century Italy. His ideas circulated in Italy mainly through the journal *Leonardo*, and this Italian journal presented James's theories as an application of Bergson's intuitionism on the field of praxis.[78] In the *vulgata* of pragmatism that *Leonardo* contributed to diffusing – especially through Papini's cultural activity – action and intuition are considered equivalent. This perspective emerges, for example, in Papini's article "Gli estremi dell'attività teorica" ["The Extremes of Theoretical Activity"], in which the Italian writer affirms: "poiché vivere è agire, e agire è possedere, e l'intuizione è possessione immediata del reale, il ritorno all'intuizione significa anche ritorno all'azione" ["as living is acting, and acting is possessing, and the intuition is immediate possession of reality, the return to intuition is also a return to action"].[79]

In discussing the sources and components of the futurist intuition, it is important to mention that the avant-garde imaginative power is particularly related to a new understanding of emotional life, which welcomes nonhuman emotions, as "La pittura futurista. Manifesto tecnico" declares:

> Il dolore di un uomo è interessante, per noi, quanto quello di una lampada elettrica, che soffre, e spasima, e grida con le più strazianti espressioni di colore; e la musicalità della linea e delle pieghe di un vestito moderno ha per noi una potenza emotiva e simbolica uguale a quella che il nudo ebbe per gli antichi. (*MDF* 31)
>
> [The suffering of a man is of the same interest to us as the suffering of an electric lamp, which can feel pain, suffer tremors, and shriek with the most heartrending expressions of [colour]. The music discernible in the lines and folds of modern clothing works upon our sensibilities with the same emotional and symbolic power as the nude once possessed for the old masters.] (*F* 65)

This attempt to render emotional intuition beyond the human realm is particularly evident in Boccioni's trilogy of paintings entitled *Gli stati d'animo* [*States of Mind*] (1911) – "Gli addii" ["The Farewells"], "Quelli che restano" ["Those Who Stay"], and "Quelli che vanno" ["Those Who Go"]. In this tryptich, the artist experiments with the "pittura degli stati d'animo" ["painting of the states of mind"], namely a visual language that allows for the expression of complex emotions and feelings through the dynamic plasticity of lines and colours in movement. Once again, intuition is the key to capturing the dynamic force of life – its plastic dynamism – as explained by the co-signatories of the catalogue of the first futurist exhibition:

> Il pubblico deve dunque convincersi che per comprendere delle sensazioni estetiche alle quali non è abituato, deve dimenticare completamente la propria cultura intellettuale, non per *impadronirsi* dell'opera d'arte, ma per *abbandonarsi* a questa ... Noi creiamo così, in qualche modo, un ambiente emotivo, cercando a colpi d'intuizione le simpatie e gli attaccamenti che esistono fra la scena esterna (concreta) e l'emozione interna (astratta). Quelle linee, quelle macchie, quelle zone di colore apparentemente illogiche e inesplicabili sono appunto le chiavi misteriose dei nostri quadri.[80]
>
> [The public must also be convinced that in order to understand aesthetic sensations to which one is not accustomed, it is necessary to forget entirely one's intellectual culture, not in order to assimilate the work of art, but to deliver one's self up to it heart and soul ... We thus create a sort of emotional ambience, seeking by intuition the affinities and the links which exist between the exterior (concrete) scene and the interior (abstract) emotion. Those lines, those spots, those zones of

color, apparently illogical and meaningless, are actually the mysterious keys of our pictures.] (*F* 108)

Boccioni's "emotional ambience," in which cognition springs from the affective space that observer and observed share, had been previously explored by Ginna and Corra. Thus, the hypothesis has been advanced that Boccioni elaborated his own cognitive conception of the "states of mind" after reading the Corradini brothers' essay "Arte dell'avvenire" ["Art of the Future"] (1910), a manifesto deeply influenced by theosophical and anthroposophical theories, as well as occultism and parapsychology.[81] In "Arte dell'avvenire," Ginna and Corra conceived of the material possibility of expressing ideas, feelings, and states of mind through colours *immediately*, as if they were sounds:

> Artista è colui che toglie dalla natura i su detti elementi fondamentali e, conscio delle rispondenze tra essi e i suoi sentimenti, variamente li compone a rappresentare le passioni e i giochi di forze tra esse. Ecco definita l'opera d'arte: passioni in tali reciproci rapporti da formare un sistema – ; un sistema *identico* a quelli che si ruotano in cielo o a quelli tra le molecole nella materia: né più né meno.
>
> Tale è la condizione dell'Artista: Sentimenti dentro; colori, o forme o suoni o linee o parole fuori; relazioni tra quelli e questi. Dato nell'anima dell'Artista un sentimento, egli potrà, per esprimerlo, valersi di uno qualunque degli elementi offerti dalla Natura e in tal scelta sarà guidato dalle tendenze e condizioni individuali …
>
> Riprendo: *è necessario che noi diamo alle cose della natura la nostra passione perché esse ci si facciano sentire intensamente.*[82]
>
> [An artist is he who removes from nature the fundamental elements mentioned above and, aware of the correspondences between them and his feelings, composes them variously to represent the passions and the games of forces between them. Here you have defined the work of art: passion in such reciprocal relations to form a system – a system identical to those that rotate in the sky or to those between the molecules in matter; neither more nor less.
>
> Such is the condition of the Artist: feelings inside; colours, or forms or sounds or lines or words outside; relations between those and these. Given a feeling in the soul of the Artist, [he] be will be able to express it, to use any of the elements offered by Nature, and in such a choice will be guided by his individual tendencies and conditions …
>
> Once again: *it is necessary that we give our passion to the things of nature for them to make themselves intensely felt by us.*]

As art historian Mariastella Margozzi reports, Boccioni, along with Russolo and Carrà, met with the two Corradini brothers in 1911 at Marinetti's Casa

Rossa [Red House] in Milan and, on that occasion, discussed plastic dynamism and the possibility of abandoning geometric shapes to express pure colours and forms. As Ginna recounts in a later document composed in the 1950s, while Carrà and Russolo strongly disagreed with Ginna and Corra's new concept of "chromatic music" freed from geometric forms, Marinetti and Boccioni showed a vivid interest in this proposition. Yet what still seemed to divide the brothers from Marinetti's group was the use of "colori liberamente aleggianti" ["freely waving colours"] as a way to express "stati d'animo supersensibili" ["ultrasensitive states of mind"].[83] Ginna's experimentalism, an artistic path between futurism and a proto-abstractism, was a language able to reconstruct a deep and ungraspable affectivity with colours that flow like sounds – "l'espressività di uno stato d'animo dato dai colori" ["a state of mind given through colours"][84] – something that, for the Corradini brothers, not even Kandisky accomplished.

For Ginna, rendering states of mind through colour ultimately meant overcoming the barrier that divided matter from spirit, expressing an extra-phenomenal dimension through the sensorial language of colours.[85] Exploring forms of occult spirituality, akin to theosophy, Ginna and Corra, as well as the Florentine group of the Azure Patrol in which they later took part, conceived of art as an active way to penetrate other worlds and "*pesca(re) nel lontano substrato universale*" ["*fish in the faraway substratum of the universe*"] by experiencing a state of "*subcoscienza cosciente*" ["*conscious subconsciousness*"].[86] However, Ginna admits the limitation of this cognitive dimension, which is, for him, the impossibility of establishing whether the psyche creates the "forms" of his visions or if these forms come to his mind from the outside when he opens the "finestra della [sua] anima" ["window of [his] soul"].[87] The Florentine venue of futurism assimilates the artistic experience with an esoteric pre-conscious "knowledge" that is attainable only through experiences of trance and temporary exit from the physical space of the physical body-mind. Maria Ginanni describes this experience as an expansion of one's own cognitive horizons and receptive possibilities:

> Essere *capaci* di comprendere sempre di più, vedere sempre di più, sentire sempre di più.
>
> Allargare la propria orbita interna almeno di qualche millimetro ogni giorno, aumentare ogni giorno la porosità della propria anima, non essere mai contenti della propria grandezza.[88]

> [Having the *capacity* to comprehend more, to see more, to feel more.
>
> To widen one's orbit at least some millimetres every day, increase every day the porosity of one's soul, not ever be content with one's greatness.]

Yet the interest in otherworldly knowledge was not a trait of only Florentine futurism. Marinetti used the notion of intuition to create an ethical binary paradigm founded on the dichotomy of velocity-slowness. In the manifesto "La nuova religione – morale della velocità" ["The New Religion – Morality of Speed"] (1916) he states, "*La velocità*, avendo per essenza la sintesi intuitiva di tutte le forze in movimento, è naturalmente *pura*" ["*Velocity*, its essence being an intuitive synthesis of all forces in movement, is naturally *pure*"]; conversely, "La lentezza, avendo per essenza l'analisi razionale di tutte le stanchezze in riposo, è naturalmente *immonda*" ["Slowness, its essence being the rational analysis of forms of exhaustion in repose, is naturally *unclean*"] (*TIF* 132, *F* 225). As anthropologist Mary Douglas maintains, analysing the concept of dirt in primitive religions, the discourse on the impure – on a dirt that is not absolute, but rather "exists in the eye of the beholder" – "involves reflection on the relation of order to disorder, being to non-being, form to formless, life to death," and is therefore a way to demarcate the difference between inside and outside.[89] Thus, while diluting the ontological human-nonhuman demarcation line, futurism imposes a new semblance of cognitive ordering founded on the moral contradiction between fast and slow "things." On the basis of the binary distinction "speed-slowness," Marinetti affirms the purifying role of war, the sole – and devastatingly fast – cleanser of the world, and proposes a cognitive renegotiation of basic morality founded on a new concept of purity: "Dopo la distruzione dell'antico bene e dell'antico male, noi creiamo un nuovo bene: la velocità, e un nuovo male: la lentezza" ["After destroying traditional good and evil, we are creating a new good, speed, and a new evil, slowness"] (*TIF* 132, *F* 225).

Marinetti's dualistic cleansing ritual still offers an alternative to the modern paradigm of the "Great Divide," as, for the futurist founder, "L'Ebbrezza delle grandi velocità in automobile non è che la gioia di sentirsi fusi con l'unica *divinità*" ["The Inebriation of great speeds in cars is simply the joy of feeling oneself merged with the only *divinity*"] (*TIF* 133, *F* 226). In defining gradations of purity, futurism regards "velocità aerea" ["aerial velocity"] as the supreme form of "misticismo perpendicolare" ["perpendicular mysticism"], "ascensione spiralica dell'Io verso il Nulla" ["spiraling ascension of the 'I' towards Nothing"] (*TIF* 137, *F* 228). Yet in Marinetti's manifesto, the word "Nothing-" is hyphenated and followed by the word "Dio" ["God"] in the following line: as in crepuscular poetry, nothingness coincides with its opposite, a fullness saturated with the presence of the divine. Marinetti identifies his futurist god with the totalizing experience of aviation – not with the overwhelming and overhuman act of flying, but with the lubricating action of castor oil, which was commonly used in First World War aircraft: "Dio = Aviazione, agilità purgativa dell'olio di ricino" ["God = Aviation, the cleansing agility of castor oil"] (*TIF* 137, *F* 228).

Castor oil was also used in medicine as a laxative; thus, with its purging agency and its ubiquity in early aviation, this fluid substance combines the holy purity of speed with the techno-simultaneity of time and space.

In futurism's cult of speed, the divine is manifest in a material "Santità della ruota e delle rotaie" ["Holiness of wheels and rails"] (*TIF* 132, *F* 225), a sense of sacredness that turns kinetic and electromagnetic phenomena into divine epiphanies. Describing the saints of the futurist religion, Marinetti writes:

> Nostri santi sono gli innumerevoli corpuscoli che penetrano nella nostra atmosfera a una velocità media di 42.000 metri al secondo. Nostre sante sono la luce e le onde elettromagnetiche 3 x 10^{10} metri al secondo. (*TIF* 132–3)

> [Our male saints are the innumerable small bodies that are penetrating our atmosphere at an average velocity of 42,000 meters a second. Our female saints are light and electromagnetic waves at 3×10^{10} meters a second.] (*F* 226).

The futurist intermixing of life, art, and religion-morality shapes a "living thought" that, drawing from philosopher Roberto Esposito, offers an alternative to the process of rational "immunization" from life that modernity aims to attain through the purity of its intellectual discourse. Marinetti's anti-modern thinking seeks "a channel for transfer and contamination between the languages of reason and sense, deduction and narration, logos and myth – that elsewhere had been hermetically sealed in the interest of furthering the project of the complete mathematization of the world."[90] Yet, once again, it would be misleading to identify this bodily and material contamination of thinking as a full emancipation from the binary order of modernity. "Contaminating" the language of reason with the corporeal language of a warlike action-intuition is not emancipatory when this hybridized language still asserts a phallocentric mindset – male versus female, futurist culture versus nature – as the principle of its liberation from traditional knowledge. In his introduction to *Mafarka il futurista*, Marinetti expressed confidence that by breaking the deadly cadence of the "litanies of wisdom," the art-action of futurism would act as agent to enrich the underused human mind. As he proudly announces, "io vi annuncio che lo spirito dell'uomo è una ovaia inesercitata … E noi lo fecondiamo per la prima volta!" ["*I tell you that the mind of man is an unpracticed ovary … It is we who are the first to impregnate it!*"] (*M* 5, *MF* 3).

The sexual metaphor of fecundation shows how the futurists' cognitive action enables the violent behaviour of war predators, the logic of domination of irrational rapists who carnally *know* by permeating unknown flesh and impregnating it with their own semen. Raping one's enemy's women is a notorious war crime, and, in *Mafarka il futurista*, Marinetti turns this practice into an exemplum of the futurist cognitive process. Through the metaphors of fecundation and, then, through the scene of wartime rape that opens the novel, Marinetti attempts to justify the political dream of a "bourgeois empire" and its mechanisms of exploitation, under the guise of the futurist myth of brave penetration into the wilderness of the Unknown.[91]

The futurist founder's image of colonialist rape, perpetrated on naturalized Indigenous women – complacent bodies who scream with pleasure like animals – presents us with an immersion in nature that is radically different from the crepusculars' blending in a natural mystery of inter-being. As we have examined by discussing gender and love relationships in chapters 3 and 4, Marinetti's ontological alliance of human bodies and animated machines can be achieved only by colonizing a gendered and racially "inferior" *natural* world. Translated into ecofeminist terms, for futurism to achieve the goal of an enhanced mechanical humanity of (male or masculinized) equals, parallel mechanisms of exploitation of women and nature need to be in place. Through Marinetti's subjugation of a feminized "black" nature and his *natural* appropriation of a gendered knowledge – the unpractised ovary of man's mind – we clearly see how, in the words of Karen Warren, "important connections exist between the treatment of women, people of color, and the underclass on one hand and the treatment of nonhuman nature on the other."[92] In the case of Marinetti's Africa, nature evolves from a romanticized "green background" into a political environment of domination. Thus, the approach that sexualizes nature and naturizes women as slaves is revealing of the problematic relationship between nature and culture that underlies futurist art and literature. Ultimately, what futurism cannot envision is a culture of "coexistence in difference," a culture in which a variety of human and nonhuman subjects can simultaneously express their corporeal, sexual, and cultural identities.[93]

However, the futurist cognitive immersion does not exhaust itself in a gendered image of penetration. The group of the Azure Patrol proposes alternatives to Marinetti's "cognitive action." Fulvia Giuliani describes a peculiar process of cognition in her hermetic writing: her soul exercises an energy that magnetically attracts all nearby life forces, creating an "intreccio bislacco" ["odd twist"]. In this weird twisting, the divisions between external phenomena and internal appropriation of meanings are erased. In Giuliani's cognitive network, her cerebral activity expands to incorporate electromagnetic waves, light, heat, senses, and feelings:

> Io vorrò; ed io comanderò che l'enorme condensamento di suoni si illumini di luci proprie, si accenda di spasimi, e irradi di elettricità violette l'intreccio bislacco dei mille motivi, così per tutta una notte invernale la mia anima assorbirà le più

fantastiche, vibranti caloriche ispirazioni, venutemi ipnoticamente dalla fame e dal dolore che spinse mille ignoti suonatori girovaghi a gettare rabbiosamente al cielo tetro le loro melodie strane e malefiche.[94]

[I will want; and I will command that the enormous condensation of sounds will illuminate with its own lights, will light up with spasms, and irradiate with violet electricity, the odd twist of a thousand patterns; in this way, for an entire winter's night, my soul will absorb the most fantastic, vibrant caloric inspirations, which came to me hypnotically due to the hunger and pain that drove one thousand wandering musicians to throw their horrific melodies to the sky with rage.]

After this intense moment of interpenetration, Giuliani devises a further cognitive step, similar to that of Vallini. Her own will regresses until she becomes like a lazy pet: "Io starò accoccolata nella mia tiepida ed armonica cuccia ad attendere il sole" ["I will be nestled in my lukewarm and harmonic dog basket to wait for the sun"].[95] Lying in her nest, like a nonhuman animal, she releases her "weird twist" from her magnetic grip, setting it free to dissipate into atoms and cosmic dust – into "polvere vivificante di concetti musicali ultrapotenti sapenti d'amarezza, di gioia, di sogno" ["vivifying powder of ultra-powerful musical concepts that taste of bitterness, joy, dream"].[96] From a linguistic point of view, this passage recalls the ambiguous nuances of the verb *sapere*, highlighted previously in my discussion of crepuscular mystical poetry. Knowledge acts as an intrusive "powder," a pervasive universal truth, breathed in, savoured, exhaled through the body and yet never entirely processed by the mind. Either as a saturated taste, replete with the richness of life, or as the muscle memory that action engraves within the body, knowledge remains for both crepuscularism and futurism an odd twist, a loop that cannot be unfolded through either pure theorization of knowledge or an experiential actualization. Only in the dimension of the network – the twist, the Whole, the war, the whirling fable – can this "twisted" experience manifest itself as a material compound of interconnected energies and agencies. This is indeed the proposal of "becoming and knowing with" that the avant-garde brings forward, and yet this proposal implies incongruences. Particularly in the case of futurism, Marinetti's "liberating" framework of human-nonhuman co-agency clashes against the rape of nature that enables this ontological meshing. Yet the futurist women's notion of material and spiritual vibration opens fascinating proposals in line with current ecotheological perspectives characterized by "reconceptualization of matter as a lively and communicative participant in more-than-human meaning-making processes."[97]

To summarize, crepuscular immersive knowledge fosters an ethical, ecological, and spiritual relationship of interdependence with nature. Nevertheless, for the crepusculars, this knowledge does not develop into a praxis of care, but "freezes" into a meditative "being known" that can easily fall into disengagement or even nihilism. On the other hand, in Marinetti's futurism, active knowledge escalates into a violent will and "religious" mission to conquer or trespass on a feminized/naturalized territory. Cognitive involvement becomes the paradoxical "rationale" for pro-war culture, colonial mindset, and sexism, which are ultimately incompatible with any inclusive form of relationality and respect for difference.

Conclusion

What to Do with the Avant-Garde "Grammar of Animacy"?

The biggest challenge that the avant-garde undeniably presents to its readers is its deep incoherence. We are dealing with creative movements that neither strived to make sense nor wanted to entertain in a traditional manner. As futurism proves in particular, the avant-garde brought its iconoclastic destruction, pro-war propaganda, and affective politics of violence far beyond the realm of art. The futurists dragged their dynamic cluster of life and art to experience the First World War trench warfare and, later, the populist order of the fascist regime. Marinetti's vitalist hymn to industrialization, to a rising automated "life," was foreshadowing in many ways, perhaps also in its naïve disregard of environmental consequences. The futurist passion for new "stuff" fostered a proto-capitalist logic in which objects quickly became outdated and a constant hunger for cutting-edge consumables was rampant. On the other hand, while crepuscularism anticipated the anti-traditional stance of futurism, it proposed a very different representation of modern bourgeois life. Crepuscular poetry, with its horde of useless "things," engaged in an ecocritical recycling of old objects into new poetic materials. Nevertheless, its delicate yet ironic wondering about the "close alterity" of human and nonhuman life remained circumscribed within a rebellious literary elite that self-indulgently cultivated its difference from the bourgeoisie.

Yet the untarnished beauty of crepuscularism and futurism relies on the fact that their quintessentially asystemic and often incoherent art invites participative readings, unfolding a work in progress that remains open to interpretation. The interpretative challenge that these two interrelated movements leave open is to make sense of their provocative proposals in an epoch in which the coexistence of human and other-than-human forms of life is a pressing concern. Put in other terms, how does the avant-garde still succeed in cognitively engaging its contemporary readers? The analysis conducted in these pages suggests that the *quiet* and rather unexplored message of futurism and crepuscularism is found in their parallel yet equally problematic hybridization of modern dichotomies. In redefining a series of dualisms – life-art, human-nonhuman, mind-body, culture-nature, masculinity-femininity – both movements raise a new awareness "of the interactions between acting/living bodies, the materiality of the physical context, and the discursive-ideological contexts in which they are framed."[1] Through their complementary poetics of things, crepuscularism and futurism defy the taken-for-granted anthropocentric system of modernity, which is founded on the idea that the nonhuman can be reduced to an object of knowledge or to a static possession. By contrast, they create alternative fictional worlds in which organic and inorganic "objects" come to life either as futurist agentic machines, which prefigure the perspective of material vitalism, or as crepuscular silent witnesses that, in line with the thought of object-oriented ontology, are a mysteriously "withdrawn" alterity. In these worlds, human bodies are portrayed as ambiguous spaces where nature and culture co-mingle. This encounter raises questions of the possibility of freezing the multiplicity of nature into fixed genders – including the seemingly emancipatory pansexual virility of futurism – and social behaviours. In the crepuscular and futurist poetics, love itself, as a relation connecting a wide range of bodies, genders, sexualities, and identities, is recast into a broad discourse of change. This new narrative of love, while setting in opposition patriarchal regressive views and feminist responses, also unfolds a new type of material "grand solidarity" that re-envisions love as a feeling, or a deep "sound," of interconnectedness pervading the universe. Finally, in the crepusculars' and futurists' alternative systems, knowledge is rethought beyond the mind-body binary. The cognitive process engenders a complex interaction between the experience of being merged – or comprehended – in the world and the embodied awareness of this continuous and unavoidable immersion.

However, it is important to clarify that neither crepuscularism nor futurism foresaw the ethical and environmental impact of their rebellious anti-models. For example, the two movements discussed, yet did not problematize, the capacity of material life – goods, technology, and even waste products – to affect human life. In addition, their shared vitalism of "things" struggled with redefining the connection between culture and nature outside hierarchical systems. The futurists often endorsed a monoculture of techno-virility dominating over a feminized landscape, and the crepusculars hinted at, but never fully articulated, the link connecting the suffering of the intellectual with the vulnerability of nonhuman matter.

Besides the evident contradictions that these poetics generated, what is still fascinating for contemporary readers is that crepusculars and futurists created an innovative "grammar of animacy," a verbal, visual, sonic, and tactile system that denies "that the only way to be animate, to be worthy of respect and moral concern, is to be human."[2] Both movements experimented with a language in which "nonhuman" ceases to signify "dead stasis" or "separation from the human." In their work, "nonhuman" embraces a variety of more-than-human meanings, all related to a notion of vital materialism. If the world is a space pervaded by interacting (and intra-acting) agencies, humanity comes to signify an embodied relation of hybridity, a "stain" left on objects and vegetal life, yet also the "mark" that they leave on us, in turn.

The avant-garde revolutionary message of hybridization is summarized in a passage of *Arlecchino* (1914) by Ardengo Soffici, an author who, like many writers of that epoch, adhered to futurism yet participated in the movement in an unorthodox way. In this excerpt, he states a core concept of the avant-garde "quiet revolution," namely, that the only way towards relational knowledge, towards "becoming with," is to abandon the epistemological tyranny of the human subject over the nonhuman object:

> Perché volete che mi decida a dire se l'esistenza di tutti questi esseri e queste cose sia subordinata al mio essere che li concepisce; se essi sono in me o fuori di me; se per me il soggetto si identifica con l'oggetto? … Che mi importa a me della verità? Io non voglio che vivere e amare. Amare non vuol dire comprendere?[3]
>
> [Why do you want me to resolve to say whether the existence of all these beings and these things is subjected to my being that conceives them; whether they are within or outside myself; whether for me the subject identifies itself with the object? … What do I care of the truth? I only want to live and love. Doesn't loving mean comprehending?]

"Why do you want me to resolve to say whether the existence of all these beings and these things is subjected to my being that conceives them?" Soffici's question expresses in a nutshell the destructive and creative journey of the avant-garde, from the crepuscular "quiet avant-gardism" to the scream for attention of the futurist manifestos. Crepuscularism reveals its pre-futurist – and as we have seen, proto-avant-gardist – function in undermining a modern mindset that poses the human subject as the sole cognitive agent able to measure the knowable.

The crepuscular movement criticizes the role of *homo sapiens* and *politicus*, endowed with intellect, civic sense, and ruling power over inanimate things. To invalidate this order, crepuscularism adopts a series of weak anti-heroes, who cast doubt on people's ability to distinguish themselves from things and dominate material life. Sick children, old illiterates, bigoted women, forgotten "stuff," and kitsch furniture invade literature – the pure dominion of the human mind – challenging scientific knowledge, teleology, and the philosophy of the limit with ambiguity, disorder, and intermeshing. The cognitive thread linking all these scattered objects is an unsettling question: where does the human begin and the nonhuman end? This query connects crepuscularism with futurism, and is central in, for example, the work of Palazzeschi, an author who was tied to both movements. His man of smoke, the protagonist of the novel *Il codice di Perelà*, embodies the impossibility of finding a clear line of separation; this surreal character made from mist, vapours, and chimney residue lands on earth equipped with only a pair of shoes. For the king's guards, who first meet him, Perelà's boots are the only thing that identifies such a strange creature as a man: "Voi siete poco un uomo, di uomo mi sembra non abbiate che le scarpe" ["You, sir, are very little a man, it seems to me that of a man you have nothing other than your shoes"].[4] This bizarre encounter highlights the apparent absurdity of two men needing a pair of shoes to determine that a man of smoke is a weird "thing" with human shoes. Perelà's boots recall the peasant shoes in a painting by Van Gogh that Heidegger uses in his essay "The Origin of the Work of Art." As the German philosopher argues, those boots go far beyond their utility and the notion of artistic mimesis; they can reveal a web of discursive, yet also material, relations to human existence. One may think of Perelà's "body without organs" as the material representation of a territory without borders, the territory of a cloud of smoke that affects and is affected by other agents, by mingling with them materially and symbolically. Where does Perelà end? – the question returns. In its alien materiality that interferes with the life of his hosting community, the body of the man of smoke exposes "the social and ethical blind spots of social constructs and political practices"; this extra-rational and extra-human body reveals "the irrational practices and the cognitive dissonances of an uneven and discriminating society" that ultimately condemns Perelà only to preserve its foundational lies, divides, and inconsistencies.[5]

Through its army of men of smoke – disturbing queer objects that unhinge a system of dualities and separations – crepuscularism and futurism leave us the complex heritage of an asystemic "material thought" that puts under siege classic anthropocentrism and blends the notions of being and knowing into an experience of metamorphic *sympatheia* with the world. Marinetti states this groundbreaking idea when he affirms that understanding the nonhuman does not mean humanizing it:

> L'immaginazione senza fili, e le parole in libertà c'introducono nell'essenza della materia. Collo scoprire nuove analogie tra cose lontane e apparentemente opposte noi le valuteremo sempre più intimamente. Invece di *umanizzare* animali, vegetali, minerali (sistema sorpassato) noi potremo *animalizzare, vegetalizzare, mineralizzare, elettrizzare o liquefare lo stile*, facendolo vivere della stessa vita della materia. Es., per dare la vita di un filo d'erba, dico: "sarò più verde domani." (*TIF* 73)

> [Wireless imagination and words-in-freedom will transport us into the essence of matter. With the discovery of new analogies between things remote and apparently contradictory, we shall value them ever more intimately. Instead of *humanizing* animals, vegetables, and minerals (a bygone system) we will be able to *animalize, vegetize, mineralize, electrify, or liquefy* our style, making it live the very life of matter. For example, to render the life of a blade of grass, we might say: "I will be greener tomorrow."] (*F* 147)

Yet, what does it mean today for readers to inherit the avant-garde polemic message of hybridity and its "grammar of animacy"? What does it mean to reconceptualize humanism, at the twilight of the anthropocentric gods? In an era in which living things animated by artificial intelligence proliferate, casting doubt on our intellectual superiority, and "the man multiplied by the machine" has come to be, triggering epochal changes in the conception and distribution of labour, crepuscularism and futurism have renewed their provocative spirit. To (re-)encounter the avant-garde rebellion in the twenty-first century undoubtedly implies an ecocritical questioning of the Anthropocene: in a new geological epoch in which humans are simultaneously main agents of change and victims of their own transformative agency, who is in control of what, in dealing with recycling issues, toxic waste, and environmentally unsustainable sources of energy? Confronting the Anthropocene, as both a timeframe of ecological crisis and a platform to develop new socio-political and environmental proposals, the human-nonhuman hybridity that the avant-garde represented more than one hundred years ago acquires new relevance.

To (re)read the works of crepusculars and futurists as a precursory "nonhuman turn" also implies a political and ethical debate, as well as a questioning of human agency as an independent force. Marinetti's wireless – and rather impersonal – imagination and Gozzano's estranging experience of seeing his own life through his double make us meditate on the affective power of our life collectively running on social media. We are indeed all creative contributors, virtual activists, and flattened agents of change. Yet who is in control of what, when clicking on a computer and smartphone keyboard, and generating a myriad of data though that action? In an epoch in which the *homo faber* has evolved into *homo clicker* – we may briefly recall the viral success of the Cow Clicker game on Facebook – we are simultaneously estranged from and controlled by our relations with objects.[6] Clicking gives us the immediacy of buying more "stuff" on Amazon and enjoying same-day delivery, signing up to a Community Supported Agriculture Program, and reading articles about politics, while being tracked and having our consumer profiles constructed and perfected. The *homo clicker* is indeed a hybrid of flesh and data embodied in every click or touch, and the machine is only an interface by which this dialogue runs.

Ushering in a provocative "terminal realism" that denies the assumed fixedness of the real, crepuscularism and futurism deeply provide contemporary readers with an epistemo-ontological framework that suits – and challenges – our epoch of late capitalism and its dynamics of global intermeshing, creations of material and immaterial borders, and proliferations of virtual and actual checkpoints. As things among other things, as agents among other agents, humans are consumers of the global economy, yet also entangled clickers who feed precious human data into the system. Nevertheless, such an entanglement is also a material site from where alternative embodied thoughts emerge and "the dominant image of thought as the expression of a white, masculine, adult, heterosexual, urban-dwelling, property-owning subject" can be challenged.[7] The alternative to the dominant image, an icon primarily constructed on obliviousness – first and foremost on the obliviousness of its ecological and ethical impact – is also the possibility of embracing a humbler interspecies humanism, what Iovino has defined as a "non-anthropocentric humanism."

From this perspective of anthropocentric crisis, the crepuscular "avant-gardism" resides in repositioning the human "in a universe of finitude and fragility"[8] and in a possible revaluation of vulnerability into a positive drive of non-hierarchical coexistence. As Vallini states in a profane prayer to "madre Natura" ["Mother Nature"], the crux of such revised and self-ironic humanism is exactly this: "l'uomo, pur se gli dispiaccia / non essere il solo immortale, / è un essere medio, che vale / né più né meno del resto" ["man, although disappointed / for not being the sole immortal creature, / is an average being, which is worth / neither more nor less than the rest"] ("L'ironia," *UG* 66). However, as average beings living in a shared space that "uomini e cose affratella" ["fraternizes humans and things"], humans must embrace their own resizing and redefine their relationship with the cosmos as an "osmotic individuality," founded on inter-breathing alterity rather than on self-sufficiency. As Vallini remarks in "L'ironia," "L'ignoto non teme la luce / del nostro cervello" ["the unknown doesn't fear / the light of our brain"] (*UG* 72). From this perspective of ironic debasement, crepuscularism lends itself to environmental and new materialist readings, and reveals itself as being far more contingent than the futurists' mechanical dream, a dream that is now frighteningly actualized yet unsustainable for future survival. Crepuscular poetry, with its levity and delicate acerbity, still spurs reflection on our vulnerability and the ethical responsibilities that such vulnerability implies. Furthermore, in an epoch in which it seems difficult, yet is fundamental, to find new alliances between STEM and the humanities in order to envision more sustainable socio-political platforms, reading and reinterpreting the message of the crepusculars shows that literature is particularly meaningful for its creative potential "to actualize in always new forms the fundamental relationship between matter and mind, nature and culture, as a source of its creative processes."[9]

This poetry leaves the reader with many questions and one challenge for future coexistence, which is indeed the challenge of being human:

> Come si muore e si vive
> all'ombra del Tutto e del Nulla?
> Silenzio. Mai nessun Buddha
> c'insegnerà come si vive!
>
> [How to die and live
> in the shadow of Everything and Nothing?
> Silence. No Buddha will
> ever teach us how to live!] (*UG* 71–2)

Notes

Introduction: Poetry at the Twilight

1 *Black Mirror*, "Be Right Back," directed by Owen Harris (Channel Four, 1 February 2013).
2 *Her*, directed by Spike Jonze, Warner Bros, 2013.
3 Francesco Verso, *Nexhuman* (2013), trans. Sally McCorry (Surry Hills: Xoum Publishing, 2014), 112.
4 See *The Multispecies Salon*, ed. Eben Kirksey (Durham, NC: Duke University Press, 2014).
5 Peter Moskowitz, "A Picture Book without Pictures," *New York Times*, 28 May 2012, accessed 28 January 2017, http://lens.blogs.nytimes.com/2012/05/28/a-picture-book-without-pictures/?_r=0. See also *Photographs Not Taken*, ed. Will Steacy (New York: Daylight, 2012).
6 Steacy, "Will Steacy's Photographs Not Taken," accessed 28 January 2017, http://www.thephotographsnottaken.com/.
7 Paolo Bartoloni, *Objects in Italian Life and Culture: Fiction, Migration, and Artificiality* (New York: Palgrave Macmillan, 2016), 81.
8 On the Lampedusa cross, see the online collection of the British Museum: http://www.britishmuseum.org/research/collection_online/collection_object_details.aspx?objectId=3691920&partId=1
9 Felipe Fernández-Armesto, *So You Think You're Human* (Oxford: Oxford University Press, 2005), 27. See, in particular, the chapter "The Animal Frontier," 9–54.
10 See Eben Kirksey, Craig Schuetze, and Stefan Helmreich, "Introduction: Tactics of Multispecies Ethnography," in *The Multispecies Salon*, ed. Kirksey, 2.
11 Federico Luisetti, "Demons of the Anthropocene: Facing Bruno Latour's Gaia," *Philosophy Kitchen* 5.3 (2016): 162.

12 Richard Grusin, Introduction, in *The Nonhuman Turn*, ed. Grusin (Minneapolis: University of Minnesota Press, 2015), xix.

13 Bruno Latour, *Reassembling the Social: An Introduction to Actor-Network Theory* (Oxford, New York: Oxford University Press, 2005), 7.

14 Jane Bennett, *Vibrant Matter: A Political Ecology of Things* (Durham, NC: Duke University Press, 2010), 20.

15 Ibid., 21.

16 Monica Seger, *Landscapes in Between: Environmental Change in Modern Italian Literature and Film* (Toronto: University of Toronto Press, 2015), 7.

17 Besides Seger's book, recent publications engaging with Italian Studies through the perspective of ecocriticism include the volume *Thinking Italian Animals: Human and Posthuman in Modern Italian Literature and Film*, ed. Deborah Amberson and Elena Past (New York: Palgrave Macmillan, 2014); Serenella Iovino, *Ecocriticism and Italy: Ecology, Resistance, and Liberation* (New York: Bloomsbury, 2016); *Ecocritical Approaches to Italian Culture and Literature: The Denatured Wild*, ed. Pasquale Verdicchio (Lanham, MD: Lexington Books, 2016); and the collection of essays edited by Iovino, Enrico Cesaretti, and Past, *Italy and the Environmental Humanities: Landscapes, Natures, Ecologies* (Charlottesville: University of Virginia Press, 2018). In addition, the work of Karen Pinkus, *Fuel: A Speculative Dictionary* (Minneapolis: University of Minnesota Press, 2016), features an intriguing comparative view by proposing an eclectic "dictionary" of fuel.

18 This quote is from the website of the first conference on OOO, hosted at Georgia Tech University on 23 April 2010. See "Object Oriented Ontology: A Symposium at Georgia Teach," *Gatech.edu*, accessed 17 November 2017, http://ooo.gatech.edu/#.

19 Graham Harman, "brief SR/OOO tutorial," Object-Oriented Philosophy (blog), 23 July 2010, https://doctorzamalek2.wordpress.com/2010/07/23/brief-srooo-tutorial/.

20 Levi Bryant, "The Ecological Thought: A Reply to a Critic," Larval Subjects (blog), 26 August 2010 (3:00 am), https://larvalsubjects.wordpress.com/2010/08/26/the-ecological-thought-a-reply-to-a-critic/.

21 Here I have summarized arguments that Morton makes in the following books: *Dark Ecology* (New York: Columbia University Press, 2016); *Ecology without Nature: Rethinking Environmental Aesthetics* (Cambridge, MA: Harvard University Press, 2007); and *Hyperobjects: Philosophy and Ecology after the End of the World* (Minneapolis: University of Minnesota Press, 2013).

22 Bill Brown, "Thing Theory," *Critical Inquiry* 28.1 (2001): 12.

23 I am borrowing the idea that humans and objects share a "processes of co-belonging" from Bartoloni, *Objects in Italian Life and Culture*, 4. For the concept of trans-corporeality, see Stacy Alaimo, *Bodily Natures: Science, Environment, and the Material Self* (Bloomington: Indiana University Press, 2010).

24 Among studies on futurism that appeared in the last few decades are works on gender, like Cinzia Sartini Blum, *The Other Modernism: F.T. Marinetti's Futurist Fiction of Power* (Berkeley: University of California Press, 1996), and Barbara Spackman, *Fascist Virilities: Rhetoric, Ideology, and Social Fantasy in Italy* (Minneapolis: University of Minnesota Press, 1996). In the collection of essays *Modernitalia* (Oxford, New York: Peter Lang, 2012), Jeffrey Schnapp conducted research on the futurist obsession with speed and machines. Other theorists have explored the political evolution of this avant-garde, from its anarchist rebellion to its alignment with fascism; see, for example, Günter Berghaus, *Futurism and Politics: Between Anarchist Rebellion and Fascist Reaction (1909–1944)* (Oxford: Berghahn, 1996). Focusing on visual arts, Christine Poggi has reread the most popular futurist myths as masks of modern traumas in *Inventing Futurism: The Art and Politics of Artificial Optimism* (Princeton: Princeton University Press, 2009). Recently, Paola Sica has published *Futurist Women: Florence, Feminism and the New Sciences* (New York: Palgrave, 2016).

25 See Geert Buelens and Monica Jansen, "Futurism: An Introduction," in *The History of Futurism: The Precursors, Protagonists, and Legacies*, ed. Buelens, Harald Hendrix, and Jansen (Lanham, MD: Lexington Books, 2012), 1–7.

26 Poggi, *Inventing Futurism*, 30.

27 Alberto Asor Rosa, *Storia dell'Italia. Dall'Unità ad oggi*, vol. 4, *La cultura* (Turin: Einaudi, 1975), 1271.

28 Norma Bouchard, "Introduction: Risorgimento as an Unfinished Story," in *Risorgimento in Modern Italian Culture: Revisiting the Nineteenth-Century Past in History, Narrative, and Cinema*, ed. Bouchard (Madison: Fairleigh Dickinson University Press, 2005), 9.

29 See Giuseppe Antonio Borgese, "Poesia crepuscolare," in *La vita e il libro. Seconda serie con un epilogo* (Turin: Fratelli Bocca, 1911), 149–60, in particular 158.

30 On crepuscularism, see Edoardo Sanguineti, *Tra liberty e crepuscolarismo* (Milan: Mursia, 1961); Giuseppe Farinelli, *"Perché tu mi dici poeta?" Storia e poesia del movimento crepuscolare* (Rome: Carocci, 2005); Angela Ida Villa, *Il crepuscolarismo. Ideologia, poetica, bibliografia* (Pesaro: Metauro, 2008); and Marziano Guglielminetti, *La "scuola dell'ironia." Gozzano e i viciniori* (Florence: Olschki, 1984).

31 Luciano Anceschi, Introduction, in *Lirica del Novecento. Antologia di poesia italiana*, ed. Anceschi and Sergio Antonielli (Florence: Vallecchi, 1953), xvii. On Anceshi's choice to open this anthology with the crepusculars, see also Tommaso Lisa, *Le poetiche dell'oggetto da Luciano Anceschi ai novissimi. Linee evolutive di un'istituzione della poesia del Novecento* (Florence: Firenze University Press, 2007), 72 (especially footnote 8).

32 See Raffaele Donnarumma, "Tracciato del modernismo italiano," *Sul modernismo italiano*, ed. Romano Luperini and Massimiliano Tortora (Naples: Liguori, 2012), 13–38, 15–16.

33 Deborah Amberson, *Giraffes in the Garden of Italian Literature: Modernist Embodiment in Italo Svevo, Federigo Tozzi and Carlo Emilio Gadda* (Cambridge: Legenda, 2012), 7.
34 See Farinelli, *"Perché tu mi dici poeta?"* 22.
35 Anceschi, Introduction, xii.
36 Giosuè Carducci, "The Poet," in *Giosuè Carducci: A Selection of His Poems, with Verse Translations, Notes, and Three Introductory Essays*, trans. Geoffrey Langdale Bickersteth (London: Longmans, Green and Co., 1913), 191.
37 See Giovanni Pascoli, *Poems of Giovanni Pascoli*, trans. Arletta M. Abbott (New York: Harold Vinal, 1927), 42; and Natale Tedesco, *La condizione crepuscolare. Saggi sulla poesia italiana del '900* (Florence: La Nuova Italia, 1970), 50.
38 Gabriele D'Annunzio, "The Roots of Song," in D'Annunzio, *Halcyon*, trans. J.G. Nichols (Manchester: Fyfield Books, 2003), 72.
39 Jole Soldateschi, "La questione crepuscolare," in Anna Nozzoli and Jole Soldateschi, *I crepuscolari* (Florence: La Nuova Italia, 1978), 2.
40 Carducci, "The Poet," 187, 189.
41 As Idolina Landolfi noted, Corazzini most likely readapted the motif of the crying child from Pascoli's *Il fanciullino* and from the poetry of Jammes and Samain. See Landolfi, Introduction, in Sergio Corazzini, *Poesie* (Milan: Rizzoli, 1999), 15. François Livi has shown that the genesis of Corazzini's poetic denial is documented in a letter in which the Roman author quoted Jammes: "Penser cela, est-ce être poète? / Je ne sais pas" ["I think so, is this to be a poet? / I don't know"]. See Livi, *Dai simbolisti ai crepuscolari* (Milan: IPL, 1974), 185–6.
42 On the crepuscular metrical experimentation, see Paolo Giovannetti, *Metrica del verso libero italiano* (Milan: Marcos y Marcos, 2007), especially ch. 2.2; 4.2. On Corazzini's free verse, see also the doctoral dissertation of Patrick Cherif: "Le strategie versoliberistiche di Sergio Corazzini. Studio del versoliberismo corazziniano in relazione all'orizzonte d'attesa metrico primo novecentesco" (Università di Cagliari).
43 Corrado Govoni, *Lettere a F.T. Marinetti (1909–1915)*, ed. Matilde Dillon Wanke (Milan: Scheiwiller, 1990), 103.
44 Francesco Flora, *Dal romanticismo al futurismo* (Milan: Mondadori, 1925), 19–20.
45 Carlo Chiaves, "Maldicenza" ["Gossip"], in Chiaves, *Sogno e ironia. Versi 1910*, ed. Aldo Camerino (Venice: Neri Pozza, 1956), 138. On the provincial bourgeois atmosphere of crepuscular poetry, see also Farinelli, *"Perché tu mi dici poeta?"* 22, and Sanguineti, *Tra liberty e crepuscolarismo*, 60.
46 Renato Barilli, *Art Nouveau*, trans. Raymond Rudorff (New York, London: Hamlyn, 1969), 9–10.
47 Stephen Escritt, *Art Nouveau* (London: Phaidon, 2000), 11.
48 Guido Gozzano, "Il misticismo moderno," in *Poesie e prose*, ed. Alberto De Marchi (Milan: Garzanti, 1961), 990.

49 This return to thirteenth-century models is very evident in Palazzeschi's poetry as well. As Adele Dei notes, later in his career, the author stressed his initial choice of going back to "i primi vagiti della poesia" ["the first crying of poetry"] ("Giocare col fuoco," *TTP*, xii).
50 Guglielmo Genua, "La virtù del colore," *Cronache Latine* 1.3 (1906): 9.
51 Raul Dal Molin Ferenzona, *La ghirlanda di stelle* (Rome: Tipografia Concordia, 1912), 44.
52 See Mario Perniola, *The Sex Appeal of the Inorganic: Philosophies of Desire in the Modern World*, trans. Massimo Verdicchio (New York: Bloomsbury, 2004).
53 Manuel DeLanda, *Assemblage Theory* (Edinburgh: Edinburgh University Press, 2016), 148.
54 See Lawrence R. Schehr's note in Michel Serres, *The Parasite*, trans. Schehr (Baltimore, London: Johns Hopkins University Press, 1982), 225. The note refers to the quoted passage.
55 Ibid., 227.
56 Maurizio Ferraris, "Prologue," in *Manifesto of New Realism* (2012), trans. Sarah De Sanctis (New York: SUNY Press, 2014), xiv.
57 Robert Sullivan, "Hello Great North Road Related," *Poetry* 208.4 (2016): 391.

1 A Matter of Things: Modernity, Modernism, Avant-Garde

1 Charles Baudelaire, "The Painter of Modern Life," in *The Painter of Modern Life and Other Essays*, ed. and trans. Jonathan Mayne (London, New York: Phaidon, 2003), 13.
2 Fredric Jameson, *A Singular Modernity: Essay on the Ontology of the Present* (London, New York: Verso, 2002), 41.
3 For a broader understanding of the notion of modernity in the contemporary scholarly debate, see Peter Wagner, *Modernity: Understanding the Present* (Cambridge: Polity, 2012).
4 G.W.F. Hegel, *Aesthetics: Lectures on Fine Art*, vol. 2, trans. T.M. Knox (Oxford: Oxford University Press, 1975), 1092.
5 Massimo Fusillo, "Epic, Novel: The Obsession with Origins," *The Novel*, vol. 2, ed. Franco Moretti (Princeton: Princeton University Press, 2006), 34.
6 Marshall Berman, *All That Is Solid Melts into Air: The Experience of Modernity* (New York: Penguin, 1988), 16.
7 Giorgio Agamben, *What Is an Apparatus? and Other Essays*, trans. David Kishik and Stefan Pedatella (Stanford: Stanford University Press, 2009), 3.
8 Here Berman is engaging a metaphor that Marx used in an 1856 speech in London: "The so-called revolutions of 1848 were ... small fractures and fissures in the dry crust of European society. But they denounced the abyss. Beneath the apparent solid surface, they betrayed oceans of liquid matter" (*All That Is Solid*, 19).

9 Edmundo O'Gorman, *The Invention of America: An Inquiry into the Historical Nature of the New World and the Meaning of Its History* (Bloomington: Indiana University Press, 1961), 122. As O'Gorman clarifies, in the *Lettera* dated Lisbon, 4 September 1504, Vespucci provided "the earliest written evidence of the conception of the new-found lands as a single geographic entity"; however, the *Lettera* also shows Vespucci's indecision regarding "the being of that new entity." The explorer "must have been fully aware that he had resorted to an inadmissible concept, that of plural worlds, but either he could think of no alternative or he hesitated to assume responsibility for proposing a new concept to express the new geographical picture of the world which he evidently had in mind" (122).

10 See Carolyn Merchant, *The Death of Nature: Women, Ecology and the Scientific Revolution* (San Francisco: Harper and Row, 1980).

11 Val Plumwood, *Feminism and the Mastery of Nature* (London, New York: Routledge, 1993), 3.

12 Michel Foucault, "What Is Enlightenment?" in *The Foucault Reader*, ed. Paul Rabinow (New York: Pantheon Books, 1984), 39.

13 Dante Alighieri, *Inferno* 26.119–20, trans. Mark Musa in *Dante's Inferno. The Indiana Critical Edition*, ed. Musa (Bloomington: Indiana University Press, 1995), 192.

14 See Bruno Latour, *On the Modern Cult of the Factish Gods*, trans. Catherine Porter and Heather MacLean (Durham, NC: Duke University Press, 2010).

15 Jameson, *A Singular Modernity*, 52. Here Jameson is drawing from Heidegger's theories of modernity; see, in particular, 46–57.

16 Alfred Tennyson, "Ulysses," in *Poems of Alfred Lord Tennyson*, ed. Ruth Greiner Rausen (New York: Crowell, 1964), 90.

17 Steven Shaviro, *The Universe of Things: On Speculative Realism* (Minneapolis: University of Minnesota Press, 2014), 135.

18 Wagner, *Modernity*, 20.

19 For the identification of modernity as a crisis, and the reference to *Labor of Dionysus* by Michael Hardt and Antonio Negri, see Cesare Casarino, *Modernity at Sea: Melville, Marx, Conrad in Crisis* (Minneapolis: University of Minnesota Press, 2002), 1–3.

20 In providing a brief overview of critiques to modernity, I am referring to Wagner's chapter "Changing Views of Modernity," in *Modernity*, 11–27, especially 18–19.

21 Max Horkheimer and Theodor W. Adorno, *Dialectic of Enlightenment: Philosophical Fragments*, ed. Gunzelin Schmid Noerr, trans. Edmund Jephcott (Stanford: Stanford University Press, 2002), 1; 28–9.

22 Horkheimer and Adorno, "Preface (1944 and 1947)," in ibid., xvii.

23 Ibid., xvi–xvii.

24 Slavoj Žižek, *Violence: Six Sideways Reflections* (New York: Picador, 2008), 81–2.

25 I am using Maurizia Boscagli's translation in *Stuff Theory: Everyday Objects, Radical Materialism* (New York: Bloomsbury, 2014), 1.

26 Giovanni Verga, "La roba," in *Tutte le novelle*, ed. Giuseppe Zaccaria (Turin: Einaudi, 2011), 261

27 Boscagli, *Stuff Theory*, 1.

28 See Verga, "Fantasticheria," in *Tutte le novelle*, 123–4.

29 Boscagli, *Stuff Theory*, 1.

30 Purification and translation are terms that Bruno Latour adopts in *We Have Never Been Modern*, trans. Catherine Porter (Cambridge, MA: Harvard University Press, 1993); see in particular figure 1.1, 11.

31 Cary Wolfe, *What Is Posthumanism?* (Minneapolis: University of Minnesota Press, 2009), xv.

32 Ibid., xxv.

33 Ibid.

34 Giosuè Carducci, "Hymn to Satan," in *Poems of Giosuè Carducci Translated with Two Introductory Essays*, ed. Frank Sewall (New York: Dodd, Mead and Co., 1892), 65.

35 Ibid., 64.

36 Jeffrey Schnapp, "Why Speed Is a Religion-Morality," in *Modernitalia*, ed. Francesca Sansovetti (Oxford, New York: Peter Lang, 2012), 12.

37 See Giampaolo Pignatari, Introduction, in Paolo Buzzi, *Aeroplani. Canti Alati* (1909) (Milan: Lampi di Stampa, 2009), xv–xvi.

38 Timothy Campbell, "D'Annunzio and the 'Marconigram': Crowd Control at Fiume," in *Wireless Writing in the Age of Marconi* (Minneapolis: University of Minnesota Press, 2005), 64.

39 Giovanna Rosa, *Il patto narrativo. La fondazione della civiltà romanzesca in Italia* (Milan: Il Saggiatore, 2008), 9–11.

40 For a thorough discussion of this topic, see Lucy Riall, *The Italian Risorgimento: State, Society and National Unification* (London: Routledge, 1994).

41 Silvio Ramat adopts the term "object" to refer to the metamorphic evolution of Italy in an essay on the Florentine futurist author Ardengo Soffici, "Oggetto e genio nei taccuini di Ardengo Soffici," in *Protonovecento* (Milan: Il Saggiatore, 1978), 378.

42 "Io nacqui Veneziano ai 18 Ottobre del 1775, giorno dell'Evangelista San Luca; e morrò per la grazia di Dio Italiano quando lo vorrà quella Provvidenza che governa misteriosamente il mondo" ["I was born Venetian on 18 October 1775, the day of the Evangelist Luke; and I will die by God's grace Italian when the Providence that mysteriously rules the world wants it"]. Ippolito Nievo, *Confessioni d'un Italiano*, ed. Sergio Romagnoli (Venice: Marsilio, 2000), 3.

43 Cesare De Michelis, "Introduction," in ibid., xv.

44 Stephanie Hom, "'Patria'-otic Incarnations and Italian Character: Discourses of Nationalism in Ippolito Nievo's *Confessioni d'un Italiano*," *Italica* 84.2/3 (2007): 228.

45 In the first chapter, Carlino explains: "Ecco la morale della mia vita … questa morale non fui io ma i tempi che l'hanno fatta" ["Here is the moral of my life … I didn't create this moral, but time did"]. Nievo, *Le Confessioni d'un Italiano*, 3.
46 Ibid., 916.
47 The Kingdom of the Two Sicilies included the Kingdom of Naples and the Kingdom of Sicily. At the time of the Expedition of the Thousand (1860), through which the south of the peninsula and Sicily were annexed to Italy, both kingdoms were under the domination of the Bourbon family.
48 Verga, "Libertà," in *Tutte le novelle*, 318.
49 Giolitti's first government lasted only a year, from 1892 to 1893, because of the economic scandal of the Banca Romana and the opposition of powerful Italian industrialists and landlords. After his first experience as prime minister, Giolitti had another four terms, from 1903 to 1921.
50 See Alexander J. De Grand, *The Hunchback's Tailor: Giovanni Giolitti and Liberal Italy from the Challenge of Mass Politics to the Rise of Fascism, 1882–1922* (Westport: Praeger, 2001), 161–2.
51 Martin Clark, *Modern Italy: 1871 to the Present* (Harlow: Pearson Longman, 2008), 145.
52 Ibid., 198–9.
53 On the notion of futurist war, see Günter Berghaus, "Violence, War, Revolution: Marinetti's Concept of a Futurist Cleanser for the World," *Annali d'Italianistica* 27 (2009): 33.
54 Michael Levenson, *Modernism* (New Haven: Yale University Press, 2011), 5.
55 I am adopting Guido Waldman's translation of canto 34, in Ludovico Ariosto, *Orlando Furioso* (Oxford: Oxford University Press, 1983), 419–20. References to the translated stanzas will be provided within the text.
56 Astradur Eysteinsson, "'What's the Difference?' Revisiting the Concepts of Modernism and the Avant-Garde," in *Europa! Europa? The Avant-Garde, Modernism and the Fate of a Continent*, ed. Sasha Bru, Jan Baetens, Benedikt Hjartarson, Peter Nicholls, and Tania Orum (Berlin: De Gruyter, 2009), 33.
57 Bill Brown, *A Sense of Things: The Object Matter of American Literature* (Chicago: University of Chicago Press, 2003), 12.
58 Virginia Woolf, *Mrs. Dalloway*, with a foreword by Maureen Howard (San Diego: Harcourt Brace and Company, 1990), 3–4.
59 T.S. Eliot, *The Waste Land*, in *The Annotated Waste Land with Eliot's Contemporary Prose*, ed. Lawrence Rainey (New Haven: Yale University Press, 2006), 58.
60 Introduction, in *Oggetti della letteratura italiana*, ed. Gian Mario Anselmi and Gino Ruozzi (Rome: Carocci, 2010), 10.
61 Eugenio Montale, "Non chiederci la parola che squadri da ogni lato," in *Tutte le poesie* (Milan: Mondadori, 1977), 47.

62 Charles Baudelaire, "Correspondences," in *French Symbolist Poetry*, trans. F. Macintyre (Berkeley: University of California Press, 2007), 13. I am adopting this translation, as it is more literal than other renderings of the French text.
63 Baudelaire, "Elevation," in *Les Fleurs du Mal*, trans. Richard Howard (Boston: Godine, 1982), 14.
64 Peter Nicholls, *Modernisms: A Literary Guide* (London, New York: Palgrave Macmillan, 2009), 30.
65 Charles Russell, *Poets, Prophets, and Revolutionaries: The Literary Avant-Garde from Rimbaud through Postmodernism* (New York: Oxford University Press, 1985), 53.
66 Ibid., 52.
67 Stéphane Mallarmé, "Preface to *Traité du verbe*," qtd and trans. Anthony Hartley in his Introduction, in *Mallarmé* (Baltimore: Penguin, 1965), xxviii.
68 Mallarmé, Preface to "Un Coup de Dés Jamais n'Abolira Le Hazard. Poëme," in ibid., 209–10.
69 Giuseppe Gazzola discusses the issues with the periodization of modernism, referencing Michael Levenson, Denis Donaghue, and Susan Stanford Freedman, in *Montale the Modernist* (Florence: Olschki, 2016), 7–8.
70 See Valentino Baldi, "A cosa serve il modernismo italiano?" *Allegoria* 63.81 (2011): 66–82.
71 Peter Bürger, *Theory of the Avant-Garde*, trans. Michael Shaw (Minneapolis: University of Minnesota Press, 1984), 22.
72 See Walter Adamson, *Avant-Garde Florence: From Modernism to Fascism* (Cambridge, MA: Harvard University Press, 1993), 51.
73 Gabriele D'Annunzio, *Pleasure*, trans. Lara Gochin Raffaelli (New York: Penguin, 2013), 35.
74 Ibid., 36.
75 See Nicoletta Pireddu, *Antropologi alla corte della bellezza. Decadenza ed economia simbolica nell'Europa fin de siècle* (Verona: Fiorini, 2002), in particular 376.
76 D'Annunzio, *Pleasure*, 7.
77 Ibid., 9.
78 D'Annunzio, *Versi d'amore e di gloria*, vol. 1, ed. Annamaria Andreoli and Niva Lorenzini (Milan: Mondadori, 1982), 234.
79 I am adopting the translation by James McGowan, in Baudelaire, *The Flowers of Evil* (Oxford, New York: Oxford University Press, 2008), 63.
80 I am slightly adapting Nicolas J. Perella's translation, in "Arrigo Boito's Short Stories," *California Italian Studies* 1.2 (2010): 2.
81 According to Anglo-American chess nomenclature, the black ensign is the black bishop.

82 Perella, "Arrigo Boito's Short Stories," 4.
83 Arrigo Boito, "L'Alfier nero" in *I racconti neri della Scapigliatura*, ed. Gilberto Finzi (Milan: Mondadori, 1980).
84 Giovanni Pascoli, "La tovaglia," in *Poesie e prose scelte*, vol. 1, ed. Cesare Garboli (Milan: Mondadori, 2002), 768.
85 Gianfranco Contini, "Il linguaggio di Pascoli," in *Pascoli. Poesie*, vol. 1, ed. Augusto Vicinelli (Milan: Mondadori 1981), xxiii–lviii.
86 Ibid., xli.
87 Pascoli, *Poems of Giovanni Pascoli*, trans. Arletta M. Abbott (New York: Harold Vinal, 1927), 42.
88 Cinzia Sartini Blum, *The Other Modernism: F.T. Marinetti's Futurist Fiction of Power* (Berkeley: University of California Press, 1996), 7.
89 F.T. Marinetti, "The Old Sailors," in *Selected Poems and Related Prose*, ed. Paolo Valesio, trans. Elizabeth R. Napier and Barbara R. Studholme (New Haven: Yale University Press, 2013), 3.
90 Aldo Palazzeschi, Introduction, in Filippo Donini, *Vita e poesia di Sergio Corazzini* (Turin: De Silva, 1949), xii.
91 Emilio Cecchi, "La via del rifugio," in *Studi critici di Emilio Cecchi* (Puccini: Ancona, 1912), 113.
92 Ibid., 112.
93 For a detailed account of the Roman crepuscular circle, see Angela Ida Villa, *Il crepuscolarismo. Ideologia, poetica, bibliografia* (Pesaro: Metauro, 2008).
94 Villa, "Sergio Corazzini 'poeta sentimentale': un poeta del neomisticismo simbolista nella Roma Neolatina d'inizio secolo" (*O* 29).
95 Corazzini only attended the first two years of *liceo classico* (a type of high school centred on classical education).
96 Fausto Maria Martini, *Si sbarca a New York*, ed. Guido Baldassarri (Rome: Salerno editrice, 2008), 54.
97 Giovanni Papini, *Passato remoto (1885–1914)* (Florence: L'Arco, 1948), 206–7.
98 Raul Dal Molin Ferenzona, *La ghirlanda di stelle* (Rome: Tipografia Concordia, 1912), 195.
99 The 1909 edition did not contain all the poems by Corazzini, but only a selection that his friends chose.
100 See Roberto Carnero, *Guido Gozzano esotico* (Anzio: De Rubeis, 1996).
101 Marino Moretti, *Tutti i ricordi* (Milan: Mondadori, 1952), 1015.
102 See Giuseppe De Robertis, *Scrittori del novecento* (Florence: Le Monnier, 1940).
103 See, in particular, Pietro Pancrazi, "Gozzano senza i crepuscolari," in *Scrittori italiani del Novecento* (Bari: Laterza, 1934).
104 François Livi, *Dai simbolisti ai crepuscolari* (Milan: IPL, 1974), 236–7.

105 See Mimmo Cangiano, "Gozzano (o del Modernismo apparente)," *Critica letteraria* 173 (2016): 684–705.

106 See Eugenio Montale, "Gozzano, dopo trent'anni," in *Sulla poesia*, ed. Giorgio Zampa (Milan: Mondadori, 1976), 54–62.

107 While Vallini, Ragazzoni, and Oxilia geographically shared the same cultural entourage as Gozzano, Moretti had only a correspondence with him, as well as with Corazzini. Marziano Guglielminetti traces the literary evolution of Moretti towards an ironic poetry and includes the poet in the "school of irony." See *La "scuola dell'ironia." Gozzano e i viciniori* (Florence: Olschki, 1984).

108 Scipio Slataper, "Perplessità crepuscolare (a proposito) di G. Gozzano," in *I crepuscolari*, ed. Aldo Vallone (Palermo: Palumbo, 1960), 66, 68.

109 This document is quoted in Villa, *Il crepuscolarismo*, 88.

110 Walter Binni, *La poetica del decadentismo* (Florence: Sansoni, 1977), 152.

111 Ibid., 165.

112 Corrado Govoni, *Lettere a F.T. Marinetti (1909–1915)*, ed. Matilde Dillon Wanke (Milan: Scheiwiller, 1990), 54.

113 See Gino Severini, *La vita di un pittore* (Milan: Edizioni di Comunità, 1965), 27–8.

114 Gerald Graff, "Babbitt at the Abyss: The Social Context of Postmodern American Fiction," *TriQuarterly* 33 (1975): 321.

115 Bill Brown, "Thing Theory," *Critical Inquiry* 28.1 (2001): 12.

116 Jane Bennett uses and explains her adoption of the term "vital materialities" in the preface to *Vibrant Matter: A Political Ecology of Things* (Durham, NC: Duke University Press, 2010), x–xi.

117 Ian Bogost, *Alien Phenomenology, or What It's Like to Be a Thing* (Minneapolis: University of Minnesota Press, 2012), 123.

118 On the topic of death and the motif of the corpse as a subversion of social order in Western society, see Michel Vovelle, *La Mort et l'Occident de 1300 à nos jours* (Paris: Gallimard, 1983).

119 Luciano De Maria, Introduction (*TIF* xliii).

120 Laurence Rainey, "Introduction to Part One" (*F* 5).

121 "L'ossessione lirica della materia" has commonly been translated as "the lyric obsession with matter" (see *F* 121); yet to render the nonhuman perspective that futurism embraces, by singing the lyrical obsession embedded within matter, I literally translated the Italian "della" with "of."

122 Mario Carli, "Vulcanizziamo le grandi città," *L'Italia futurista*, 25 August 1916, 2.

123 Timothy Campbell, "Vital Matters: Sovereignty, Milieu, and the Animal in Futurism's Founding Manifesto," *Annali d'Italianistica* 27 (2009): 158.

124 Bruno Corra and Arnaldo Ginna, *Manifesti futuristi e scritti teorici di Arnaldo Ginna e Bruno Corra*, ed. Mario Verdone (Ravenna: Longo, 1984), 100.

125 Quentin Meillassoux defines correlationism in these terms: "Correlationism consists in disqualifying the claim that it is possible to consider the realms of subjectivity and objectivity independently of one other. Not only does it become necessary to insist that we never grasp an object 'in itself,' in isolation from its relation to the subject, but it also becomes necessary to maintain that we can never grasp a subject that would not always-already be related to an object. If one calls 'the correlationist circle' the argument according to which one cannot think the in-itself without entering into a vicious circle, thereby immediately contradicting oneself, one could call 'the correlationist two-step' this other type of reasoning to which philosophers have become so well accustomed – the kind of reasoning which one encounters so frequently in contemporary works and which insists that 'it would be naïve to think of the subject and the object as two separately subsisting entities whose relation is only subsequently added to them.'" Meillassoux, *After Finitude: An Essay on the Necessity of Contingency*, trans. Ray Brassier (New York: Continuum, 2008), 5–6.

2 The Avant-Garde Is Made of Useless Objects

1 Massimo Fusillo, *Feticci. Letteratura, cinema, arti visive* (Bologna: Il Mulino, 2012), 160.
2 Bill Brown, "Thing Theory," *Critical Inquiry* 28.1 (2001): 4.
3 Ibid., 4.
4 Raymond Malewitz, *The Practice of Misuse: Rugged Consumerism in Contemporary American Culture* (Stanford: Stanford University Press, 2014), 10.
5 See Graham Harman, *Tool-Being: Heidegger and the Metaphysics of Objects* (Chicago: Open Court, 2002), 20.
6 See Remo Bodei, *La vita delle cose* (Bari: Laterza, 2009), 49.
7 Diana Coole and Samantha Frost, "Introducing the New Materialisms," in *New Materialisms: Ontology, Agency, and Politics*, ed. Diana Coole and Samantha Frost (Durham, NC: Duke University Press, 2010), 11.
8 Danila Cannamela, "What Is a Little Thing? Crepuscular Still Lifes and the Italian Avant-garde," *Modernism/Modernity* 24.4 (2017): 844.
9 Serenella Iovino, "'Un po' troppo incorruttibile.' Ecologia, responsabilità e un'idea di trascendenza," in *Ecocritica ed ecodiscorso. Nuove reciprocità tra umanità e pianeta*, ed. Elisa Bolchi and Davide Vago, special issue of *L'analisi linguistica e letteraria* 24.2 (2016): 25.
10 Here Benjamin is quoting Baudelaire's "Pierre Dupont"; see footnote 41, in Walter Benjamin, "Paris, the Capital of the Nineteenth Century," in *The Writer of Modern Life: Essays on Charles Baudelaire*, ed. Michael W. Jennings, trans. Howard Eiland, Edmund Jephcott, Rodney Livingstone, and Harry Zohn (Cambridge, MA: Harvard University Press, 2006), 42.

11 Ibid.
12 Edoardo Sanguineti, "Sopra l'avanguardia," in *Ideologia e linguaggio* (1965) (Milan: Feltrinelli, 2001), 55.
13 Ibid.
14 Giorgio De Rienzo, editor's Introduction, in Guido Gozzano, *Lettere a Carlo Vallini con altri inediti*, ed. De Rienzo (Turin: Centro Studi Piemontesi, 1972), 11.
15 Gozzano, *Lettere a Carlo Vallini*, 51–2
16 Ibid., 50.
17 Ibid., 60.
18 Benjamin, "Paris, the Capital of the Nineteenth Century," 41.
19 Commenting on the function of the avant-garde, Peter Bürger noticed that "Only after art has in fact wholly detached itself from everything that is the praxis of life can two things be seen to make up the principle of development of art in bourgeois society: the progressive detachment of art from real life contexts, and the correlative crystallization of a distinctive sphere of experience, i.e., the aesthetic." See Bürger, *Theory of the Avant-Garde*, trans. Michael Shaw (Minneapolis: University of Minnesota Press, 1984), 23.
20 This is a central concept that Vittorio Spinazzola illustrates in many of his critical works, including *Critica della lettura* (Milan: Editori Riuniti, 1992) and the essay "La teoria della lettura," in *La modernità letteraria* (Milan: Fondazione Arnoldo e Alberto Mondadori, 2001).
21 Carlo Chiaves, "Nel secolo duemila trecento," in *Sogno e ironia. Versi 1910*, ed. Aldo Camerino (Venice: Neri Pozza, 1956), 13.
22 Ibid., 14.
23 Ardengo Soffici, "Atelier," in *BÏF & ZF + 18. Simultaneità e chimismi lirici* (Florence: Vallecchi, 1919), 45.
24 Paolo Buzzi, *Aeroplani. Canti Alati* (1909) (Milan: Lampi di Stampa, 2009), 156.
25 Renato Poggioli, *The Theory of the Avant-Garde* (Cambridge, MA: Harvard University Press, 1968), 26.
26 See Francesco Orlando, *Gli oggetti desueti nelle immagini della letteratura. Rovine, reliquie, rarità, robaccia, luoghi inabitati e tesori nascosti* (Turin: Einaudi, 1993).
27 Malewitz, *The Practice of Misuse*, 8.
28 Matei Calinescu, *Five Faces of Modernity: Modernism, Avant-Garde, Decadence, Kitsch, Postmodernism* (Durham, NC: Duke University Press, 1987), 226.
29 Poggioli, *The Theory of the Avant-Garde*, 120.
30 Jochen Shulte-Sasse, "Theory of Modernism versus Theory of the Avant-Garde," in Bürger, *Theory of the Avant-Garde*, ix.
31 See Sanguineti, *Tra liberty e crepuscolarismo* (Milan: Mursia, 1961).
32 See Bürger, *Theory of the Avant-Garde*, 22.
33 Walter Benjamin, "The Paris of the Second Empire in Baudelaire," in *The Writer of Modern Life*, ed. Jennings, 118–19.

34 Timothy Campbell, "Vital Matters: Sovereignty, Milieu, and the Animal in Futurism's Founding Manifesto," *Annali di Italianistica* 27 (2009): 171.

35 See Roberto Tessari, "Crepuscolo di 'giovinezza' e 'bontà' nella poesia di Nino Oxilia," in *PO* 5–24, 17–20.

36 Guido Oldani, "Terminal Realism," *Annali di Italianistica* 29 (2011): 301.

37 On Duchamp's ready-mades as forms of "in between," see Federico Luisetti, "Reflections on Duchamp: Bergson Readymade," trans. David Sharp, *Diacritics* 38.4 (2008): 79.

38 Ian Bogost, *Alien Phenomenology, or What It's Like to Be a Thing* (Minneapolis: University of Minnesota Press, 2012), 38.

39 Ibid., 40.

40 Bogost, "Seeing Things," Vimeo, accessed 10 December 2017, https://vimeo.com/29092112.

41 Harman, *Tool-Being*, 24.

42 Harman discusses the notion of "carpentry of things" – how things are made – in *Guerrilla Metaphysics: Phenomenology and the Carpentry of Things* (Chicago: Open Court, 2005).

43 "Carnival of things" is another expression that Harman adopts in his *Guerrilla Metaphysics*.

44 Matt Miller compares Whitman's poetic listing to Duchamp's ready-mades in *Collage of Myself: Walt Whitman and the Making of Leaves of Grass* (Lincoln: University of Nebraska Press, 2010), 233.

45 In his review of *Le canzoni rosse* by Federico De Maria, Corazzini opens a brief digression on Whitman, praising his "maravigliose epiche che ci fanno sempre fremere di entusiasmo" ["marvellous epic poems that make us always shudder with enthusiasm"] (*O* 254).

46 Miller, *Collage of Myself*, 231.

47 Walt Whitman, "There Was a Child Went Forth," in *Poetry and Prose*, ed. Justine Kaplan (New York: Library of America, 1996), 492–3.

48 Charles Baudelaire, "The Painter of Modern Life," in *The Painter of Modern Life and Other Essays*, ed. and trans. Jonathan Mayne (London, New York: Phaidon, 2003), 8.

49 This is an expression that Ernst Bloch adopts in *Spuren* [*Traces*] (1930), quoted in Bodei, *La vita delle cose*, 91.

50 Maurice Merleau-Ponty, "Eye and Mind," in *The Primacy of Perception and Other Essays on Phenomenological Psychology, the Philosophy of Art, History and Politics*, ed. James E. Edie, trans. Carleton Dallery, annotation by Leila Wilson (Evanston, IL: Northwestern University Press, 1964), 163.

51 Ibid.

52 As is typical of Corazzini, the female figure is purposely ambiguous and never mentioned by name, according to the medieval poetic practice of the *senal*. Some critics have argued that "Elegia" is the poet's soliloquy with his soul (the Italian

"anima" is a feminine noun). I would suggest, though, that here Corazzini is addressing an unnamed woman.

53 Merleau-Ponty, "Eye and Mind," 163.

54 Ibid., 164.

55 "Materiality: An Introduction," in *Materiality*, ed. Daniel Miller (Durham, NC: Duke University Press, 2005), 5.

56 Pierre Bourdieu, *Distinction: A Social Critique of the Judgement of Taste*, trans. Richard Nice (Cambridge, MA: Harvard University Press, 1984), 249. See also the chapter "From Duty to Fun Ethics," 365–71.

57 See also the letter to Giuseppe Caruso, dated 20 August 1906 (*O* 291).

58 Bodei, *La vita delle cose*, 35.

59 Harman, *Tool-Being*, 22.

60 Ibid., 152.

61 Steven Shaviro, *The Universe of Things: On Speculative Realism* (Minneapolis: University of Minnesota Press, 2014), 42.

62 Ibid.

63 "Enchanted materialism" is a definition by Jane Bennett that Diana Coole and Samantha Frost recall in their Introduction, in *New Materialisms: Ontology, Agency, and Politics* (Durham, NC: Duke University Press, 2010), 9.

64 Bogost, *Alien Phenomenology*, 65.

65 Lawrence Buell, *Emerson* (Cambridge, MA: Harvard University Press, 2004), 162.

66 The passage, collected in Maeterlinck's work *The Treasure of the Humble*, is quoted by Paul Revere Frothingham in an early twentieth-century article that highlights the mystic role of the Belgian author: "The Mysticism of Maeterlinck," *Harvard Theological Review* 5.2 (1912): 259.

67 Guido Gozzano, *Verso la cuna del mondo. Lettere dall'India (1912–1913)* (Milan: Treves, 1917), 263; *Journey toward the Cradle of Mankind*, trans. David Marinelli (Evanston, IL: Marlboro Press Northwestern, 1996), 99.

68 Giuseppe Vannicola, "Vagamente," *Cronache Latine* 1.2 (1906): 5.

69 Giordano Bruno (1548–1600) was a Dominican friar, philosopher, and cosmologist, who was condemned by the Catholic Church as a heretic for postulating the infinity of the universe and the possibility of cosmic pluralism.

70 Friedrich Nietzsche, *The Gay Science with a Prelude in German Rhymes and an Appendix of Songs*, ed. Bernard Williams, trans. Josefine Nauckhoff and Adrian De Caro (Cambridge: Cambridge University Press, 2001), 168. I am appropriating here a quotation that may seem far from the crepuscular mystic position. Yet, it is important to highlight that Corazzini, especially, read Nietzsche as an ascetic writer and, in the prose "Esortazione al fratello" [Exhortation to the brother], quoted Nietzsche along with Saint Francis. Therefore, Nietzsche's declaration about the chaos that informs the world can be connected to the irrational crepuscular adhesion to a world that, albeit

pervaded by the divine, is ultimately intelligible. Commenting on this Nietzschean passage, Christopher Cox explains that "what Nietzsche has been urging all along is that we withdraw from the world all those things that we have imagined God to have put there and orchestrated: purpose, order, aim, form, beauty, wisdom, eternal novelty, law, hierarchy, and so forth. What we are left with, Nietzsche tells us, is a world that is 'in all eternity chaos'"; see Cox, *Nietzsche: Naturalism and Interpretation* (Berkeley: University of California Press, 1999), 102–3.

71 Serpil Oppermann, "Rethinking Ecocriticism in an Ecological Postmodern Framework," in *Literature, Ecology, Ethics: Recent Trends in European Ecocriticism*, ed. Timo Müller and Michael Sauter (Heidelberg: Universitätsverlag Winter Verlag, 2012), 43.

72 Coole and Frost, Introduction, in *New Materialisms*, 10.

73 The translation in *F* reads "you-have-to-left-yourself-3-centimeters" (129); assuming that "left" is a typo, I am translating the original Italian "bisogna-arrampicarsi-3-centimetri" as "you-have-to-lift-yourself-3-centimetres."

74 I am referring to Eduardo Viveiros De Castro's reflections on animism and Guattari, reported in an article by Angela Melitopoulos and Maurizio Lazzarato, "Assemblages: Félix Guattari and Machinic Animism," *e-flux* 36 (2012): https://www.e-flux.com/journal/36/61259/assemblages-flix-guattari-and-machinic-animism/.

75 Fortunato Depero, "Quest'è la mia esistenza," in *Pestavo anch'io sul palcoscenico dei ribelli. Antologia degli scritti letterari*, ed. Michele Ruele (Langhirano, Trento: Cucùlibri, 1992), 22.

76 See Melitopoulos and Lazzarato, "Assemblages."

77 Gilles Deleuze and Félix Guattari, *A Thousand Plateaus: Capitalism and Schizophrenia*, trans. Brian Massumi (Minneapolis: University of Minnesota Press, 1987), 21.

78 Umberto Boccioni, "Perché non siamo impressionisti," in *Pittura scultura futuriste: Dinamismo plastico*, ed. Zeno Birolli (Florence: Vallecchi, 1977), 49.

79 Ibid., 51.

80 Boccioni et al., "Prefazione al catalogo della 1ª Esposizione di Pittura futurista," in *Gli scritti editi e inediti*, ed. Zeno Birolli (Milan: Feltrinelli, 1971), 15–17.

81 F.T. Marinetti, "Vengono," in *Teatro Futurista sintetico*, ed. Guido Davico Bonino (Genoa: Il Melangolo, 1993) 165–7.

82 Here and in the following quotations, see Melitopoulos and Lazzarato, "Assemblages."

83 Amazonian animistic ontology generally extends the condition of humanity to animal and natural elements. As for objects-artefacts, Viveiros De Castro explains that "artifacts have [an] interestingly ambiguous ontology. They are objects that necessarily point to a subject; as congealed actions, they are material embodiments

of nonmaterial intentionality. What is nature to us may well be culture to another species." For example, "what is blood to us is manioc beer to jaguars, a muddy waterhole is seen by tapirs as a great ceremonial house." Viveiros De Castro, "Exchanging Perspectives: The Transformation of Objects into Subjects in Amerindian Ontologies," *Common Knowledge* 10.3 (2004): 471.

84 Ibid., 466–7.

85 On the reference to Neoplatonism and the difference between various types of animisms, see Melitopoulos and Lazzarato, "Machinic Animism," *Deleuze Studies* 6.2 (2012): 243.

86 Arnaldo Ginna, "Pittura dell'avvenire," in Bruno Corra and Ginna, *Manifesti futuristi e scritti teorici di Arnaldo Ginna e Bruno Corra*, ed. Mario Verdone (Ravenna: Longo, 1984), 202.

87 Jeffrey Schnapp, "Why Speed Is a Religion-Morality," in *Modernitalia*, ed. Francesca Sansovetti (Oxford, New York: Peter Lang, 2012), 12.

88 Maria Ginanni, *Il poema dello spazio* (Milan: Facchi, 1919), 24.

89 Anselm Franke, Introduction, in *e-flux* 36 (2012): https://www.e-flux.com/journal/36/61244/introduction-animism/.

90 Michael W. Jennings, Introduction, in Benjamin, *The Writer of Modern Life*, 17.

91 Serenella Iovino, "Death(s) in Venice: Bodies and the Discourse of Pollution from Thomas Mann to Porto Marghera," 10. Paper presented at the James K. Binder lecture, University of California, San Diego, 15 May 2014; the paper was then collected in *The James K. Binder Lectureship in Literature* 8 (2014): 1–33.

92 Quoted by Iovino, ibid.,10.

93 Maurizia Boscagli, *Stuff Theory: Everyday Objects, Radical Materialism* (New York: Bloomsbury, 2014), 12.

94 Onto-cartography is a term that Levi Bryant coined in *Onto-Cartography: An Ontology of Machines and Media* (Edinburgh: Edinburgh University Press, 2014). The reflection of things as co-agents in the process of forging relations came from a conversation I had with Bryant.

95 Harman, *Tool-Being*, 39.

96 Coole and Frost, Introduction, in *New Materialisms*, 10.

97 Harman, *Tool-Being*, 4.

98 Ibid., 4–5.

99 Ibid., 5.

100 Graham Harman, "Objects, Matter, Sleep, and Death," in *Towards Speculative Realism: Essays and Lectures* (Winchester: Zero Books, 2009), 205.

101 Ibid.

102 Levi Bryant, *The Democracy of Objects* (Ann Arbor: Open Humanities Press, 2011), 71.

103 Peter Gratton, *Speculative Realism: Problems and Prospects* (London, New York: Bloomsbury, 2014), 96.

104 See Shaviro's reflection on Whitehead's "immanent place for transcendence," in *The Universe of Things*, 23.
105 The animistic prospective of crepuscularism and the futurist avant-garde comes close to Alfred North Whitehead's view of universal interconnections; see Shaviro, *The Universe of Things*, 30.
106 The two references are respectively dated 10 and 12 April 1956. In a journal entry dated 6 November 1956, Paci writes a similar consideration: "Sperimento che le cose sono dure, impenetrabili" ["I experience that things are hard, impenetrable"]. See Paci, *Diario fenomenologico* (Milan: Il Saggiatore, 1961), 13, 21.
107 This is an expression that Corazzini uses in his review of Aldo Palazzeschi's *I cavalli bianchi*; see *O* 259.
108 Maurizio Ferraris, *Positive Realism* (Winchester: Zero Books, 2015), x.
109 Friedrich Nietzsche, aphorism no. 638, in *Human, All Too Human: A Book for Free Spirits*, ed. Arthur C. Danto, trans. Marion Faber and Stephen Lehmann (Lincoln: University of Nebraska Press, 1996), 266–7.
110 See Eugene Gendlin, "An Analysis of What Is a Thing?" in Martin Heidegger, *What Is a Thing?*, trans. W.B. Barton, Jr, and V. Deutsch (Chicago: H. Regnery, 1968), 256.
111 Shaviro, *The Universe of Things*, 55.
112 Harman, *Guerrilla Metaphysics*, 251.
113 Ibid., 251.
114 See Val Plumwood, *Feminism and the Mastery of Nature* (London, New York: Routledge, 1993), 33.
115 See Elizabeth Grosz, "Feminism, Materialism, and Freedom," in *New Materialisms*, ed. Coole and Frost, 139–57.
116 I am paraphrasing Merleau-Ponty's definition of a painting, see: "Eye and Mind," in *The Primacy of Perception*, 169.
117 On the text as a distributive network of bodies, see Jane Bennett, "Systems and Things: On Vital Materialism and Object-Oriented Philosophy," in *The Nonhuman Turn*, ed. Richard Grusin (Minneapolis: University of Minnesota Press, 2015), 234.
118 Rosi Braidotti, *Nomadic Theory: The Portable Rosi Braidotti* (New York: Columbia University Press, 2011), 35.
119 See Serpil Oppermann, "From Ecological Postmodernism to Material Ecocriticism: Creative Materiality and Narrative Agency," in *Material Ecocriticism*, ed. Serenella Iovino and Oppermann (Bloomington: Indiana University Press, 2014), 21.
120 Arjun Appadurai, "Mediants, Materiality, Normativity," *Public Culture* 27.2 (2015): 235.

3 Being a Living Thing: Towards a New Notion of Body

1 Serenella Iovino and Serpil Oppermann, "Introduction: Stories Come to Matter," in *Material Ecocriticism*, ed. Iovino and Oppermann (Bloomington: Indiana University Press, 2014), 6.

2 This view of war is not widely accepted; while Lucia Re contends that the war provided an important context for female emancipation, Silvia Contarini provides a quite different account, based on the study by historian Françoise Thébaud, *Storia delle donne in occidente. Il Novecento*, ed. Françoise Thébaud (Rome: Laterza, 1996).
3 Lucia Re, "Maria Ginanni vs. F.T. Marinetti: Women, Speed, and War in Futurist Italy," *Annali d'Italianistica* 27 (2009): 104–5.
4 See *Le futuriste. Donne e letteratura d'avanguardia in Italia (1909–1944)*, ed. Claudia Salaris (Milan: Edizioni delle donne, 1982), 56, note 2.
5 See Val Plumwood, *Feminism and the Mastery of Nature* (London, New York: Routledge, 1993), 27.
6 See Stacy Alaimo, *Undomesticated Ground: Recasting Nature as Feminist Space* (Ithaca: Cornell University Press, 2000).
7 See in particular the section "The Flâneur" of "The Paris of the Second Empire in Baudelaire," in Walter Benjamin, *The Writer of Modern Life: Essays on Charles Baudelaire*, ed. Michael W. Jennings, trans. Howard Eiland et al. (Cambridge, MA: Harvard University Press, 2006), 66–96.
8 Félix Guattari, *Chaosmosis: An Ethico-Aesthetic Paradigm*, trans. Paul Bains and Julian Pefanis (Bloomington: Indiana University Press, 1995), 9.
9 Maria Ginanni, *Il poema dello spazio* (Milan: Facchi, 1919), 15, 31.
10 Guattari, *Chaosmosis*, 65.
11 Ginanni, *Il poema dello spazio*, 69.
12 Guido Gozzano, *Poesie e prose*, ed. Alberto De Marchi (Milan: Garzanti, 1961), 1255.
13 Palazzeschi published a revised version of this novel in 1958.
14 Aldo Palazzeschi, *Il codice di Perelà*, in *Tutti i romanzi*, ed. Gino Tellini (Milan: Mondadori, 2004), 264–5. My translation is based on the 1911 version of this novel.
15 On this topic, see Jack Wilson, *Biological Individuality: The Identity and Persistence of Living Entities* (Cambridge: Cambridge University Press, 1999), 112.
16 Georges Bataille, *Inner Experience*, trans. Leslie Anne Boldt (New York: SUNY Press, 1988), 35.
17 Irma Valeria, *Morbidezze in agguato* (Florence: Edizioni dell'Italia Futurista, 1917), 61.
18 Ginanni, *Il poema dello spazio*, 24.
19 Palazzeschi, *Il codice di Perelà*, 148.
20 Jeffrey Schnapp, "The Statistical Sublime," in *The History of Futurism: The Precursors, Protagonists, and Legacies*, ed. Geert Buelens, Harald Hendrix, and Monica Jansen (Lanham, MD: Lexington Books, 2012), 107.
21 Michel de Certeau and Marsanne Brammer, "Mysticism," *Diacritics* 22.2 (1992): 22.
22 The first version of the novel appeared in 1909 in French; the novel was translated by Marinetti's secretary, Decio Centi, and published in Italian in 1910.
23 Hal Foster, *Prosthetic Gods* (Cambridge, MA: MIT Press, 2004), 121.
24 Friedrich Nietzsche, *Thus Spoke Zarathustra: A Book for All and None*, ed. Adrian Del Caro and Robert B. Pippin (Cambridge: Cambridge University Press, 2006), 7

25 Fortunato Depero, *Pestavo anch'io sul palcoscenico dei ribelli. Antologia degli scritti letterari*, ed. Michele Ruele (Langhirano, Trento: Cucùlibri, 1992), 58.

26 For a thorough study of the rhetoric of sickness and health in nineteenth-century French and Italian culture, see Barbara Spackman, *Decadent Genealogies: The Rhetoric of Sickness from Baudelaire to D'Annunzio* (Ithaca: Cornell University Press, 1989).

27 Marino Moretti, *Via Laura. Il libro dei sorprendenti vent'anni* (Milan: Treves, 1931), viii.

28 Palazzeschi, *Il codice di Perelà*, 179–80.

29 Mirella Bentivoglio, "Futuriste italiane tra linguaggio e immagine," in *L'arte delle donne nell'Italia del novecento*, ed. Laura Iamurri and Sabrina Spinazzè (Rome: Meltemi, 2001), 42.

30 On *Ventre di donna*, see also Re, "Enif Robert, F.T. Marinetti e il romanzo *Un ventre di donna*: bisessualità, trauma e mito dell'isteria," *California Italian Studies* 5.2 (2014): 43–82, https://escholarship.org/uc/item/2dt2z4wx.

31 Cecilia Bello Minciacchi uses the definition "sperimentalismo terapeutico" ["therapeutic experimentalism"] for Robert's writing, in *Scrittrici della prima avanguardia. Concezioni, caratteri e testimonianze del femminile nel futurismo* (Florence: Le Lettere, 2012); see in particular 362–95.

32 Julia Kristeva, *Powers of Horror: An Essay on Abjection* (New York: Columbia University Press, 1982), 14.

33 See Robert C. Fuller, *Spirituality in the Flesh: Bodily Sources of Religious Experiences* (New York: Oxford University Press, 2008).

34 Ibid., 160.

35 Caroline Walker Bynum, *Christian Materiality: An Essay on Religion in Late Medieval Europe* (New York: Zone Books, 2011), 257.

36 Ibid.

37 Gozzano composed "L'ipotesi" in 1907, and this text is considered an early stage of the writing process that led to the final version of "La signorina Felicita."

38 Bruno Corra, *Sam Dunn è morto* (Milan: Studio Editoriale Lombardo, 1917), 68. I am using John Walker's translation in *Sam Dunn Is Dead* (London: Atlas Press, 2015), 69–70.

39 Corra, *Sam Dunn è morto*, 68; *Sam Dunn Is Dead*, 70.

40 Corra, *Sam Dunn è morto*, 68; *Sam Dunn Is Dead*, 70.

41 Corra, *Sam Dunn è morto*, 77; *Sam Dunn Is Dead*, 77.

42 Kristeva, *Powers of Horror*, 10.

43 Ibid., 12.

44 Carolyn Merchant, *The Death of Nature: Women, Ecology and the Scientific Revolution* (San Francisco: Harper and Row, 1980), 155.

45 On this topic, see Willy Jansen and Grietje Dresen, "Fluid Matters: Gendering Holy Blood and Holy Milk," in *Things: Religion and the Question of Materiality*, ed. Dick Houtman and Birgit Meyer (New York: Fordham University Press, 2012), 218.

46 See Elaine Scarry, *The Body in Pain: The Making and Unmaking of the World* (New York: Oxford University Press, 1985), 36.
47 Like the Homeric heroes, Mafarka, although committing cruel acts and massacres, is always presented as the righteous hero, who fights for a personal and universal cause.
48 See Silvia Contarini, "Guerre maschili/guerre femminili: corpi e 'corpus' futuristi in azione/trasformazione," *Annali d'Italianistica* 27 (2009): 125–36. See also Contarini, *La Femme futuriste. Mythes, modèles et représentations de la femme dans la théorie et la littérature futuristes (1900–1919)* (Nanterre: Presses Universitaires de Paris 10, 2006).
49 Lucia Re, "Women, Sexuality, Politics, and the Body in the Futurist Avant-Garde during the Great War," in *Modernism and the Avant-Garde Body in Spain and Italy*, ed. Maria Truglio and Nicolás Fernández-Medina (New York: Routledge, 2016), 184–5.
50 Paola Sica, "Maria Ginanni: Futurist Woman and Visual Writer," *Italica* 79.3 (2002): 340.
51 In *Fascist Virilities: Rhetoric, Ideology, and Social Fantasy in Italy* (Minneapolis: University of Minnesota Press, 1996), Barbara Spackman borrows this notion from Christine Buci-Glucksmann to develop her argument on the virile homosexualization of values attained by Marinetti (23).
52 Kent L. Brintnall, *Ecce Homo: The Male-Body-in-Pain as a Redemptive Figure* (Chicago: University of Chicago Press, 2012), 30.
53 Ibid.
54 F.T. Marinetti, *Come si seducono le donne*, 2nd ed. with preface by Bruno Corra and Emilio Settimelli (Milan: Edizioni Excelsior, 1918), 146.
55 Ibid., 148.
56 On this topic, see Stacy Alaimo, *Bodily Natures: Science, Environment, and the Material Self* (Bloomington: Indiana University Press, 2010), 5.
57 Rosa Rosà, "Le donne del posdomani," *L'Italia futurista*, 17 June 1917.
58 Contarini, "Guerre maschili/guerre femminili," 131.
59 Greta Gaard, "Living Interconnections with Animals and Nature," in *Ecofeminism: Women, Animals, Nature*, ed. Gaard (Philadelphia: Temple University Press, 1993), 5.
60 Greta Gaard, "New Directions for Ecofeminism: Toward a More Feminist Ecocriticism," *ISLE: Interdisciplinary Studies in Literature and Environment* 17.4 (2010): 656.
61 Michael Worton, "Behold the (Sick) Man," in *National Healths: Gender, Sexuality and Health in a Cross-Cultural Context*, ed. Worton and Nana Wilson-Tagoe (London: UCL Press, 2004), 152.
62 Ibid., 153.

63 Mario Perniola, *The Sex Appeal of the Inorganic: Philosophies of Desire in the Modern World*, trans. Massimo Verdicchio (New York: Bloomsbury, 2004), 10.

64 Guido Gozzano and Amalia Guglielminetti, *Lettere d'amore di Guido Gozzano e Amalia Guglielminetti*, ed. Spartaco Asciamprener (Milan: Garzanti, 1951), 30.

65 Cinzia Sartini Blum, *The Other Modernism: F.T. Marinetti's Futurist Fiction of Power* (Berkeley: University of California Press, 1996), 32.

66 *Le futuriste*, ed. Salaris, 24.

67 The letter, quoted in Véronique Richard de la Fuente, *Valentine de Saint Point (1875–1953): une poétesse dans l'avant-garde futuriste et méditerranéiste* (Céret: Editions des Albères, 2003), 125, belongs to the *Correspondances Marinetti–Saint Point* (private collection).

68 Perry Willson, *Women in Twentieth-Century Italy* (New York: Palgrave Macmillan, 2010), 8.

69 See Eve Sedgwick, *Epistemology of the Closet* (Berkeley: University of California Press, 1990), 27.

70 Spackman, *Fascist Virilities*, 53.

71 Ibid., 76.

72 Lucia Re, "Mater Materia: Maternal Power and the Futurist Avant-Garde," in *The Great Mother: Women, Maternity, and Power in Art and Visual Culture, 1900–2015*, ed. Massimiliano Gioni (Milan: Skira, 2015), 48–9. On midwifery, see also Merchant, "Production, Reproduction, and the Female," in *The Death of Nature*, 149–63.

73 Donna Haraway, "A Cyborg Manifesto: Science, Technology, and Socialist-Feminism in the Late Twentieth Century," in *Simians, Cyborgs, and Women: The Reinvention of Nature* (New York: Routledge, 1991), 150.

74 Marino Moretti, *Poesie scritte col lapis* (Naples: Ricciardi, 1910), 113–14.

75 For a further exploration of the metaphor of the abortion in Govoni, see Francesco Capello, *Città specchio. Soggettività e spazio urbano in Palazzeschi, Govoni e Boine* (Milan: Franco Angeli, 2013).

76 Fausto Martini, *Tutte le poesie*, ed. Giuseppe Farinelli (Milan: Istituto di Propaganda Libraria, 1969), 136.

77 Ibid., 137.

78 Corra, *Sam Dunn è morto*, 87; *Sam Dunn Is Dead*, 81.

79 See Angela Ida Villa, *Il crepuscolarismo. Ideologia, poetica, bibliografia* (Pesaro: Metauro, 2008), 58. The *puer aeternus* is a figure of classical mythology representing the divine status of eternal youth, often connected with the god Dionysus. In addition, in *Thus Spoke Zaratustra*, the man who wants to die represents a stage of nihilism that humans have to experience as a consequence of the death of God (the episode of the tightrope walker is exemplary of this stage).

80 Here Hollywood is commenting on Bataille's *Theory of Religion*; see Amy Hollywood, *Sensible Ecstasy: Mysticism, Sexual Difference, and the Demands of History* (Chicago: University of Chicago Press, 2001), 58.
81 Paolo Buzzi, *Aeroplani. Canti Alati* (1909) (Milan: Lampi di Stampa, 2009), 163.
82 Aldo Palazzeschi, *The Arsonist*, trans. Nicholas Benson (Los Angeles: Otis Books 2013), 19.
83 Corra, *Sam Dunn è morto*, 52; *Sam Dunn Is Dead*, 59.
84 Corra, *Sam Dunn è morto*, 77; *Sam Dunn Is Dead*, 74.
85 On the topic of "ineffable positivity" see Vladimir Jankélévitch, *Le je-ne-sais-quoi et le presque-rien* (Paris: Seuil, 1980).
86 Haraway, "A Cyborg Manifesto," 154.

4 Love and the Grand Solidarity of Sound

1 For a more exhaustive explanation of the difference between affect and emotion, see Brian Massumi, "The Autonomy of Affect," *Cultural Critique* 31 (1995): 96, and *Politics of Affect* (New York: Polity, 2015).
2 Jeanne Heuving, *The Transmutation of Love and Avant-Garde Poetics* (Tuscaloosa: University of Alabama Press, 2016), 33.
3 Aaron Jaffe, "Who's Afraid of the Inhuman Woolf?," *Modernism/Modernity* 23.4 (2016): 495.
4 Ibid.
5 Lauren Berlant, "Love, a Queer Feeling," in *Psychoanalysis and Homosexuality*, ed. Tim Dean and Christopher Lane (Chicago: University of Chicago Press, 2001), 433–4.
6 Alain Badiou, with Nicolas Truong, *In Praise of Love*, trans. Peter Bush (New York: New Press, 2012), 61.
7 Berlant, "Cruel Optimism," *Differences: A Journal of Feminist Cultural Studies* 17.5 (2006): 20.
8 The philosophical concept of entelechy was originally formulated by Aristotle and later used by Leibniz, as the core principle of his monad.
9 Dino Cervigni, "The Petrarchan Lover's Non-Dialogic and Dialogic Discourse: An Augustinian Semiotic Approach to Petrarch's 'Rerum Vulgarium Fragmenta,'" *Annali d'Italianistica* 22 (2004): 124.
10 Berlant, "Love, a Queer Feeling," 448.
11 Martha C. Nussbaum, "Love's Knowledge," in *Love's Knowledge: Essays on Philosophy and Literature* (Oxford, New York: Oxford University Press, 1990), 267.
12 Melissa Gregg and Gregory Seigworth, "An Inventory of Shimmers," in *The Affect Theory Reader*, ed. Gregg and Seigworth (Durham, NC: Duke University Press, 2010), 2.

13 Allan Pero, "A Fugue on Camp," *Modernism/Modernity* 23.1 (2016): 31.
14 Sianne Ngai, *Ugly Feelings* (Cambridge, MA: Harvard University Press, 2007), 10.
15 See Roy Campbell's translation in *Poems of Baudelaire* (New York: Pantheon Books, 1952).
16 Michael Hardt, "Foreword: What Affects Are Good For," in *The Affective Turn: Theorizing the Social*, ed. Patricia Ticineto Clough and Jean Halley (Durham, NC, London: Duke University Press, 2007), x.
17 Nussbaum, "Love's Knowledge," 268.
18 See Alberto Toscano, "The Promethean Gap: Modernism, Machines, and the Obsolescence of Man," *Modernism/Modernity* 23.3 (2016): 595.
19 Clare Hemmings, "Invoking Affect: Cultural Theory and the Ontological Turn," *Cultural Studies* 19.5 (2005): 551.
20 Gregg and Seigworth, "An Inventory of Shimmers," 9–10.
21 Massumi, *Politics of Affect*, 25.
22 On this topic, see also Lucia Re, "Women, Sexuality, Politics, and the Body in the Futurist Avant-Garde during the Great War," in *Modernism and the Avant-Garde Body in Spain and Italy*, ed. Maria Truglio and Nicolás Fernández-Medina (New York: Routledge, 2016).
23 See Luciano Caruso, "Post-fazione," in Paolo Buzzi, *L'ellisse e la spirale. Film più parole in libertà* (Florence: SPES, 1990), i–xi.
24 See Ara H. Merjian, "Manifestations of the Novel: Genealogy and the Sculptural Imperative in F.T. Marinetti's *Mafarka le futuriste*," *Modernism/Modernity* 23.2 (2016): 382.
25 Laurence Rainey, Introduction (*F* 4).
26 Minsoo Kang, *Sublime Dreams of Living Machines: The Automaton in the European Imagination* (Cambridge, MA: Harvard University Press, 2011), 255.
27 Ibid., 254.
28 Semonides of Amorgos, "On Women," in *Semonides: Testimonia et fragmenta*, ed. Ezio Pellizer and Gennaro Tedeschi (Rome: Edizioni dell'Ateneo, 1990), 18–29.
29 On the feminization of animals, see in particular Carol Adams, *The Sexual Politics of Meat: A Feminist-Vegetarian Critical Theory* (New York: Continuum, 1990).
30 This is a concept Marinetti emphasizes on many occasions, initially in terms of brotherhood, then as an "intellectual solidarity." See, for instance, the "Manifesto and Foundation of Futurism" and "Multiplied Man and the Reign of the Machine."
31 Lucia Re, "Maria Ginanni vs. F.T. Marinetti: Women, Speed, and War in Futurist Italy," *Annali d'Italianistica* 27 (2009): 103–24.
32 Marinetti, *Come si seducono le donne*, 2nd ed. with preface by Bruno Corra and Emilio Settimelli (Milan: Edizioni Excelsior, 1918), 76.
33 Berlant, "Love, a Queer Feeling," 448.

34 Karen Warren, *Ecofeminist Philosophy: A Western Perspective on What It Is and Why It Matters* (New York: Rowman and Littlefield, 2000), 24.

35 Guido Gozzano and Amalia Guglielminetti, *Lettere d'amore di Guido Gozzano e Amalia Guglielminetti*, ed. Spartaco Asciamprener (Milan: Garzanti, 1951), 58–9.

36 Ibid., 64.

37 Ibid.

38 Ibid., 149.

39 Bruno Corra, *Io ti amo: il romanzo dell'amore moderno* (Milan: Studio Editoriale Lombardo, 1918), 17–18.

40 Ibid., 20.

41 Badiou, with Truong, *In Praise of Love*, 33.

42 Paola Sica, *Futurist Women: Florence, Feminism and the New Sciences* (London, New York: Palgrave Macmillan, 2016), 26. See this work for a detailed historical overview of the futurist women's discourse on female identity and social rights.

43 Lyda Borelli, Preface to Mario Carli's *Retroscena*, in *Le futuriste*, ed. Salaris, 49.

44 Flora Bonheur's *Diario d'una giovane donna futurista* was published in Bologna by Stabilimento Poligrafico Emiliano. The *Diario* does not have a publication date, yet most likely it appeared between 1914 and 1917. Bonheur's work is still at the margin of futurist scholarship, for her parodic take on futurism. Bonheur is anthologized in Salaris's collection *Le futuriste* (1982). For a detailed analysis of the *Diario*, see Janaya Sandra Lasker-Ferretti, "Between Word and Image: Women Futurists and Parole in Libertà 1914–1924" (PhD diss., University of California, Berkeley, 2012).

45 See ibid., 38.

46 Flora Bonheur, *Diario d'una giovane donna futurista, L'amore per il marito*, vol. 1, in *Le futuriste*, ed. Salaris, 46.

47 Ibid., 46.

48 See Lasker-Ferretti, "Between Word and Image," 26.

49 Bonheur, *Diario d'una giovane donna futurista, L'amore per il marito*, 48.

50 Lasker-Ferretti, "Between Word and Image," 26–7.

51 As Sica highlights, in Edgar Allan Poe's eponymous short story, Berenice is "affected by a mysterious disease, attacking all her body, apart from her teeth"; see Sica, *Futurist Women*, 55.

52 Ibid., 55.

53 Enif Robert, "Come si seducono le donne (Lettera aperta a Marinetti)," in Marinetti, *Come si seducono le donne*, iv.

54 Rosa Rosà, "Le donne cambiano finalmente …" in ibid., vi–vii.

55 Rosà, "Risposta a Jean-Jacques …" in ibid., x–xi.

56 Shara Marini, "Rivendicazione," in ibid., xiv, xiv.

57 Ardengo Soffici, *Arlecchino* (Florence: Vallecchi, 1921), 81.

58 Ardengo Soffici, *BÏF & ZF + 18. Simultaneità e chimisi lirici* (Florence: Vallecchi, 1919), 30.

59 As Farina explains, geophonies are the result of sonic energy produced by nonbiological natural agents such as winds, biophonies are the results of animal vocalizations, and anthrophonies are the result of all the sounds produced by technical devices. For a more detailed explanation, see Almo Farina, *Soundscape Ecology: Principles, Patterns, Methods and Applications* (London: Springer, 2014), 7–11.

60 Karmen MacKendrick, *Immemorial Silence* (Albany: SUNY Press, 2001), 19.

61 See Remo Bodei, *La vita delle cose* (Bari: Laterza, 2009), 87.

62 Maurice Maeterlinck, "The Silence," in *The Inner Beauty* (London: Arthur L. Humphreys, 1910), 32, 33.

63 Guido Gozzano, "Intossicazione," in *Prose e poesie*, ed. Alberto De Marchi (Milan: Garzanti, 1966), 1078.

64 Gordon Hempton, with John Grossman, *One Square Inch of Silence: One Man's Quest to Preserve Quiet* (New York: Free Press, 2009), 6.

65 Massumi, *Politics of Affect*, 5–6.

66 Luce Irigaray and Michael Marder, *Through Vegetal Being: Two Philosophical Perspectives* (New York: Columbia University Press, 2016), 22.

67 Merjian, "Manifestations of the Novel," 367.

68 See Ernest Ialongo, "Futurism from Foundation to World War: The Art and Politics of an Avant-Garde Movement," *Journal of Modern Italian Studies* 21.2 (2016): 306–23.

69 I am borrowing from Massumi's reflection on the media strategy of creating a discourse on terrorism after 9/11; see *Politics of Affect*, 32.

70 I am adopting Ialongo's translation, in "Futurism from Foundation to World War," 314.

71 Timothy Campbell, *Wireless Writing in the Age of Marconi* (Minneapolis: University of Minnesota Press, 2005), 89.

72 Arnaldo Ginna, "Gioia di vivere," in Bruno Corra and Ginna, *Manifesti futuristi e scritti teorici di Arnaldo Ginna e Bruno Corra*, ed. Mario Verdone (Ravenna: Longo, 1984), 258. "Gioia di Vivere" is included in Ginna's essay "A proposito di 'Arte dell'avvenire' (e altre pagine di taccuini) (1913–1967)."

73 On futurist media practices, see Michael Kirby, *Futurist Performance*, trans. Victoria Nes Kirby (New York: E.P. Dutton, 1971), 31; and Arndt Niebisch, "Cruel Media: On F.T. Marinetti's Media Aesthetics," *Annali d'Italianistica* 27 (2009): 344.

74 Kirby reports a review by *The Times* on the concert of noise-intoners at the Coliseum in London on 15 June 1914.

75 Federico Luisetti, "A Vitalist Art: Filippo Tommaso Marinetti's sintesi radiofoniche," in *The History of Futurism: The Precursors, Protagonists, and Legacies*, ed. Geert

Buelens, Harald Hendrix, and Monica Jansen (Lanham, MD: Lexington Books, 2012), 289–90.

76 Ibid., 289.

5 Avant-Garde Immersive Onto-Cognition

1 Here Brian McHale is referencing questions posed by Dick Higgins in *A Dialectic of Centuries: Notes toward a Theory of the New Arts*; see McHale, *Postmodernist Fiction* (New York, London: Methuen, 1987), 9.

2 I am borrowing the term "agnotology," coined by linguist Iain Boal, from *Agnolotology: The Making and Unmaking of Ignorance*, ed. Robert N. Proctor and Londa Schiebinger (Stanford: Stanford University Press, 2008).

3 Karen Barad, "Invertebrate Visions: Diffractions of the Brittlestar," in *The Multispecies Salon*, ed. Eben Kirksey (Durham, NC: Duke University Press, 2014), 233.

4 I am referring to the notion of non-anthropocentric humanism that Serenella Iovino has elaborated; see, in particular, Iovino, "Ecocriticism and a Non-Anthropocentric Humanism: Reflections on Local Natures and Global Responsibilities," in *Local Natures, Global Responsibilities: Ecocritical Perspectives on the New English Literatures*, ed. Laurenz Volkmann, Nancy Grimm, Ines Demers, and Katrin Thomson (Amsterdam: Rodopi, 2010), 29–54.

5 Maurizio Ferraris, *Positive Realism* (Winchester: Zero Books, 2015), 36.

6 Ibid., 36–7.

7 Karen Warren, *Ecofeminist Philosophy: A Western Perspective on What It Is and Why It Matters* (New York: Rowman and Littlefield, 2000), 58.

8 Christopher Cohoon, "The Ecological Irigaray?" in *Ecocritical Theory: New European Approaches*, ed. Axel Goodbody and Kate Rigby (Charlottesville: University of Virginia Press, 2011), 210.

9 Ibid., 211.

10 Maria Mies and Vandana Shiva, *Ecofeminism* (New York: Zed Books, 1993), 13.

11 See Stacy Alaimo, *Bodily Natures: Science, Environment, and the Material Self* (Bloomington: Indiana University Press, 2010).

12 On queer ecology, see in particular the works of Catriona Sandilands, Simon Estok, and Joan Roughgarden, as well as the inclusive feminism of Stacy Alaimo, Greta Gaard, and Noël Sturgeon.

13 Philippe Descola, *Beyond Nature and Culture*, trans. Janet Lloyd (Chicago: University of Chicago Press, 2013), 11.

14 See Kate Rigby, "Spirits That Matter: Pathways toward a Rematerialization of Religion and Spirituality," in *Material Ecocriticism*, ed. Serenella Iovino and Serpil Oppermann (Bloomington: Indiana University Press, 2014), 283–90.

15 Donna Haraway, *When Species Meet* (Minneapolis: University of Minnesota Press, 2007), 11.

16 Here I am quoting from Marmon Silko's discussion of the term "landscape," in the culture of her Native American tribe, the Pueblo people; see Marmon Silko, *Yellow Woman and a Beauty of the Spirit* (New York: Simon and Schuster, 1997), 27.

17 Marziano Guglielminetti, Introduction, in *La "scuola dell'ironia." Gozzano e i viciniori* (Florence: Olschki, 1984), xv.

18 See Timothy Morton, *Dark Ecology* (New York: Columbia University Press, 2016), 32.

19 Karen Barad, "Intra-actions," interview by Adam Kleinman, *Mousse* 34 (2012): 77.

20 Ibid.

21 Ibid.

22 For the notion of "becoming with," see Donna Haraway's introductory chapter and chapter 4 ("Examined Lives: Practices of Love and Knowledge in Purebred Dogland"), in *When Species Meet*.

23 The deconstruction of the construct of nature as a separate "whole" and the redefinition of cognition as proximity or as a "loop" are essential topics in Morton's theory; a summary of these views can be found in his essay "Coexistence and Coexistents: Ecology without a World," in *Ecocritical Theory*, ed. Goodbody and Rigby, 169.

24 Ibid.

25 See Timothy Morton, *Ecology without Nature: Rethinking Environmental Aesthetics* (Cambridge, MA: Harvard University Press, 2007).

26 See Warren, *Ecofeminist Philosophy*, 47.

27 Erin Manning and Brian Massumi, *Thought in the Act: Passages in the Ecology of Experience* (Minneapolis: University of Minnesota Press, 2014), 15, 19.

28 For the notion of diffraction versus reflection, as adopted by Haraway and Barad, see in particular, Donna Haraway's *Modest_Witness@Second_Millennium. FemaleMan©Meets_OncoMouse™: Feminism and Technoscience* (New York, London: Routledge, 1997), and Barad's "Nature's Queer Performativity."

29 Judith Plotz, "Preface: The Romantic Fixation," in *Romanticism and the Vocation of Childhood* (New York: Palgrave Macmillan, 2001), xii–xvi.

30 The first version of *Il fanciullino*, which featured only a few chapters, was published for the first time in 1897. Yet, Pascoli worked on this text for ten years.

31 See Rosamaria LaValva, "Preface" in *The Eternal Child: The Poetry and Poetics of Giovanni Pascoli* (Chapel Hill, NC: Annali d'italianistica, 1999), viii–ix. In the quoted passage, LaValva makes a comparison with Giambattista Vico, in *The New Science* (1725).

32 LaValva, "Preface," in *The Eternal Child*, ix.

33 LaValva, *The Eternal Child*, 14–15.

34 Ibid., 38–9. For an analysis of the figure of the "child who wants to die," see chapter 3 of this book.

35 Irigaray, "There Can Be No Democracy without a Culture of Difference," in *Ecocritical Theory*, ed. Goodbody and Rigby, 195.
36 Ardengo Soffici, *BÏF & ZF + 18. Simultaneità e chimismi lirici* (Florence: Vallecchi, 1919), 56.
37 The poem was later translated into Italian by Delio Cinti and included in the anthology *Poeti futuristi*.
38 Morton, "Weird Embodiment," in *Sentient Performativities of Embodiment: Thinking alongside the Human*, ed. Lynette Hunter, Elisabeth Krimmer, and Peter Lichtenfels (London: Lexington Books, 2016), 20.
39 Ibid., 20–1.
40 Arthur Rimbaud, "Sun and Flesh," in *Rimbaud Complete*, trans. Wyatt Mason (New York: Modern Library, 2002), 13.
41 Ibid.
42 Ibid.
43 On the representation of nature in futurism, see in particular Enrico Cesaretti, "Eco Futurism? Some Thoughts on Nature, Matter, and Body in F.T. Marinetti," in *Modernism and the Avant-Garde Body in Spain and Italy*, ed. Maria Rosa Truglio and Nicolás Fernandez-Medina (New York: Routledge, 2016), 232–47.
44 Morton, "Weird Embodiment," 24.
45 Maria Ginanni, *Il poema dello spazio* (Milan: Facchi, 1919), 33.
46 Ginanni uses this terminology in ibid., 41.
47 Bruno Corra, Ginna, et al., "La scienza futurista," in Corra and Ginna, *Manifesti futuristi e scritti teorici di Arnaldo Ginna e Bruno Corra*, ed. Mario Verdone (Ravenna: Longo, 1984), 205. Henceforth referenced within the text.
48 In the conclusion of the 1916 manifesto of futurist science, the "passatista" [old-fashioned] science is described as "pachidermica" ["enormous and slow like an elephant"], see "La scienza futurista," 209.
49 Barad, "Invertebrate Visions," 222.
50 Ibid., 227.
51 Robin Wall Kimmerer, *Braiding Sweetgrass: Indigenous Wisdom, Scientific Knowledge, and the Teaching of Plants* (Minneapolis: Milkweed Editions, 2013), 20.
52 Michael Marder, "To Hear Plants Speak," in *The Language of Plants: Science, Philosophy, Literature*, ed. Monica Gagliano, John C. Ryan, and Patrícia Vieira (Minneapolis: University of Minnesota Press, 2017), 109.
53 Ibid., 122.
54 Friedrich Nietzsche, *The Gay Science with a Prelude in German Rhymes and an Appendix of Songs*, ed. Bernard Williams, trans. Josefine Nauckhoff and Adrian De Caro (Cambridge: Cambridge University Press, 2001), 88.
55 See Manuel DeLanda, *Assemblage Theory* (Edinburgh: Edinburgh University Press, 2016), 141.

56 Kate Rigby, "Spirits That Matter," in *Material Ecocriticism*, ed. Iovino and Oppermann, 286.
57 For an articulated discussion of the concept of "becoming with," see Donna Haraway, *When Species Meet* (Minneapolis: University of Minnesota Press, 2007).
58 Serpil Oppermann, "Feminist Ecocriticism: A Posthumanist Direction in Ecocritical Trajectory," in *International Perspectives in Feminist Ecocriticism*, ed. Greta Gaard, Simon C. Estok, and Oppermann (New York: Routledge, 2013), 31
59 On the relation between Buddhism and material vitalism, see Greta Gaard, "Mindful New Materialisms: Buddhist Roots for Material Ecocriticism's Flourishing," in *Material Ecocriticism*, ed. Iovino and Oppermann, 292.
60 Luce Irigaray and Michael Marder, *Through Vegetal Being: Two Philosophical Perspectives* (New York: Columbia University Press, 2016), 50.
61 Ibid.
62 See the chapter "Sharing Universal Breathing," in ibid., 21–6.
63 These excerpts from the letter to Mrs Bolognino are quoted by Vincenzo Faraci in the article "Sensibilità umana e religiosa in Guido Gozzano," *Torino. Rivista mensile municipale* 27.11 (1951): 25–8.
64 On this topic, see Roberto Carnero, *Guido Gozzano esotico* (Anzio: De Rubeis, 1996).
65 Gozzano, *Verso la cuna del mondo. Lettere dall'India (1912–1913)* (Milan: Treves, 1917), 70; *Journey toward the Cradle of Mankind*, trans. David Marinelli (Evanston, IL: Marlboro Press Northwestern, 1996), 16.
66 Guido Gozzano, *Albo dell'officina*, ed. Nicoletta Fabio and Patrizia Menichi (Florence: Le lettere, 1991), 102.
67 Morton, *Dark Ecology*, 5.
68 Ibid., 6.
69 Serge Milan, "The 'Futurist Sensibility': An Anti-Philosophy for the Age of Technology," in *Futurism and the Technological Imagination*, ed. Günter Berghaus (Amsterdam, New York: Rodopi, 2009), 68.
70 Bruno Corra and Emilio Settimelli, "Pesi, misure e prezzi del genio artistico," in *Prosa e critica futurista: Antologia*, ed. Mario Verdone (Milan: Feltrinelli, 1973), 276.
71 Ibid., 277.
72 Ibid., 278.
73 Antonio Damasio, *Descartes' Error: Emotions, Reason, and the Human Brain* (New York: Putnam, 1994), 247–8.
74 Ibid., 252.
75 Norberto Bobbio, *Profilo filosofico del Novecento* (Milan: Garzanti, 1990), 43.
76 Giovanni Papini, "Enrico Bergson," in *Ventiquattro cervelli. Saggi non critici*, 3rd ed. (Milan: Studio editoriale Lombardo, 1917), 318.
77 Ibid., 324, 326, 328, 327.
78 See Laura Schram-Pighi, *Bergson e il bergsonismo nella prima rivista di Papini e Prezzolini: Il "Leonardo" 1903–1907* (Sala Bolognese: A. Forni, 1982), 74.

79 Giovanni Papini, "Gli estremi dell'attività teorica," *Leonardo* 2 (1904): 34.
80 Umberto Boccioni et al., "Prefazione al catalogo della 1ª Esposizione di Pittura futurista," in *Gli scritti editi e inediti*, ed. Zeno Birolli (Milan: Feltrinelli, 1971), 20.
81 See Mariastella Margozzi, "Dalla pittura animica all' 'antipittura.' Itinerario di Ginna pittore," in *Armonie e disarmonie degli stati d'animo. Ginna futurista*, ed. Micol Forti, Lucia Collarile, and Mariastella Margozzi (Rome: Gangemi, 2009), 33.
82 Arnaldo Ginnanni and Bruno Corradini (Ginna and Corra), "Arte dell'avvenire (1910)," in Corra and Ginna, *Manifesti futuristi e scritti teorici di Arnaldo Ginna e Bruno Corra*, ed. Mario Verdone (Ravenna: Longo, 1984), 106–7.
83 Margozzi, "Dalla pittura animica all' 'antipittura,'" 34.
84 Arnaldo Ginna, "Note sul futurismo," in Corra and Ginna, *Manifesti futuristi e scritti teorici di Arnaldo Ginna e Bruno Corra*, 262; see also Margozzi, "Dalla pittura animica all' 'antipittura,'" 41.
85 See Arnaldo Ginna, "Note sul futurismo," *Manifesti futuristi e scritti teorici di Arnaldo Ginna e Bruno Corra*, 262.
86 See Ginna, "Pittura dell'avvenire" (1915), in ibid., 200–1.
87 Ibid., 201.
88 Ginanni, *Il poema dello spazio*, 73.
89 Mary Douglas, Introduction, in *Purity and Danger: An Analysis of the Concepts of Pollution and Taboo* (New York: Praeger, 1966), 2, 5.
90 I am recontextualizing Esposito's considerations regarding Bruno's philosophy, in *Living Thought: The Origins and Actuality of Italian Philosophy*, trans. Zakiya Hanafi (Stanford: Stanford University Press, 2012), 63.
91 See Barbara Spackman, *Fascist Virilities: Rhetoric, Ideology, and Social Fantasy in Italy* (Minneapolis: University of Minnesota Press, 1996), 76.
92 Karen Warren, "Taking Empirical Data Seriously: An Ecofeminist Philosophical Perspective," in *Ecofeminism: Women, Culture, Nature*, ed. Warren (Bloomington: Indiana University Press, 1997), 3.
93 I am borrowing and readapting the expression "coexistence in difference" from Irigaray, "There Can Be No Democracy without a Culture of Difference," 205.
94 Fulvia Giuliani, "Intreccio bislacco" (*SF* 139–40). This text was originally published in *L'Italia futurista*, on 1 July 1917.
95 Ibid., 140.
96 Ibid.
97 Rigby, "Spirits That Matter," in *Material Ecocriticism*, ed. Iovino and Oppermann, 288.

Conclusion

1 Serenella Iovino, "Toxic Epiphanies: Dioxin, Power, and Gendered Bodies in Laura Conti's Narratives on Seveso," in *International Perspectives in Feminist Ecocriticism*,

ed. Greta Gaard, Simon C. Estok, and Serpil Oppermann (New York: Routledge, 2013), 51.

2 Robin Wall Kimmerer, *Braiding Sweetgrass: Indigenous Wisdom, Scientific Knowledge, and the Teaching of Plants* (Minneapolis: Milkweed Editions, 2013), 55, 57.

3 Ardengo Soffici, *Arlecchino* (Florence: Vallecchi, 1921), 15–16.

4 Aldo Palazzeschi, *Il codice di Perelà*, in *Tutti i romanzi*, ed. Gino Tellini (Milan: Mondadori, 2004), 139.

5 Here I am readapting Iovino's reflections on dioxin in the 1976 environmental crisis of Seveso; see "Toxic Epiphanies," 42.

6 On "Cow Clicker," see also Ian Bogost, *Alien Phenomenology, or What It's Like to Be a Thing* (Minneapolis: University of Minnesota Press, 2012).

7 Rosi Braidotti, *Nomadic Theory: The Portable Rosi Braidotti* (New York: Columbia University Press, 2012), 6.

8 Timothy Morton, *Dark Ecology* (New York: Columbia University Press, 2016), 6.

9 Hubert Zapf, "Creative Matter and Creative Mind: Cultural Ecology and Literary Creativity," in *Material Ecocriticism*, ed. Serenella Iovino and Serpil Oppermann (Bloomington: Indiana University Press, 2014), 51. On literature and cultural ecology, see also Zapf, *Literature as Cultural Ecology: Sustainable Texts* (New York: Bloomsbury, 2016).

Bibliography

Adams, Carol J. *The Sexual Politics of Meat: A Feminist-Vegetarian Critical Theory*. New York: Continuum, 1990.

Adamson, Walter. *Avant-Garde Florence: From Modernism to Fascism*. Cambridge, MA: Harvard University Press, 1993.

Agamben, Giorgio. *Homo Sacer: Sovereign Power and Bare Life*. Translated by Daniel Heller-Roazen. Stanford: Stanford University Press, 1998.

– *Nudities*. Translated by David Kishik and Stefan Pedatella. Stanford: Stanford University Press, 2010.

– *What Is an Apparatus? and Other Essays*. Translated by David Kishik and Stefan Pedatella. Stanford: Stanford University Press, 2009.

Alaimo, Stacy. *Bodily Natures: Science, Environment, and the Material Self*. Bloomington: Indiana University Press, 2010.

– *Undomesticated Ground: Recasting Nature as Feminist Space*. Ithaca: Cornell University Press, 2000.

Alighieri, Dante. *Inferno*. Edited and translated by Mark Musa in *Dante's Inferno. The Indiana Critical Edition*. Bloomington: Indiana University Press, 1995.

– *Vita Nuova: Italian Text with Facing English Translation*. Edited and translated by Dino S. Cervigni and Edward Vasta. Notre Dame, London: University of Notre Dame Press, 1995.

Altomare, Libero, et al. *I poeti futuristi*. Milan: Edizioni futuriste di Poesia, 1912.

Amberson, Deborah. *Giraffes in the Garden of Italian Literature: Modernist Embodiment in Italo Svevo, Federigo Tozzi and Carlo Emilio Gadda*. Cambridge: Legenda, 2012.

Amberson, Deborah, and Elena Past, eds. *Thinking Italian Animals: Human and Posthuman in Modern Italian Literature and Film*. New York: Palgrave Macmillan, 2014.

Anceschi, Luciano. "Dai Crepuscolari ai Vociani." In *Le poetiche del Novecento in Italia*. Milan: Marzorati, 1963.

– Introduction. In *Lirica del Novecento. Antologia di poesia italiana*, edited by Luciano Anceschi and Sergio Antonielli, vii–civ. Florence: Vallecchi, 1953.

Anselmi, Gian Mario, and Gino Ruozzi, eds. *Oggetti della letteratura italiana*. Rome: Carocci, 2010.

Appadurai, Arjun. "Mediants, Materiality, Normativity." *Public Culture* 27.2 (2015): 221–37.

– *The Social Life of Things: Commodities in Cultural Perspective*. Cambridge: Cambridge University Press, 1988.

Ariosto, Ludovico. *Orlando Furioso*. Translated by Guido Waldman. Oxford: Oxford University Press, 1983.

Armstrong, Nancy. "The Fiction of Bourgeois Morality and the Paradox of Individualism." In *The Novel*, vol. 2, *Forms and Themes*, edited by Franco Moretti, 349–88. Princeton: Princeton University Press, 2006.

Asor Rosa, Alberto. *Storia dell'Italia. Dall'Unità ad oggi*, vol. 4, *La cultura*. Turin: Einaudi, 1975.

Badiou, Alain, with Nicolas Truong. *In Praise of Love*. Translated by Peter Bush. New York: New Press, 2012.

Baldi, Valentino. "A cosa serve il modernismo italiano?" *Allegoria* 63 (2011): 66–82.

Barad, Karen. "Intra-actions." Interview by Adam Kleinman. *Mousse* 34 (2012): 76–81.

– "Invertebrate Visions: Diffractions of the Brittlestar." In *The Multispecies Salon*, edited by Eben Kirksey, 221–41. Durham, NC: Duke University Press, 2014.

– "Nature's Queer Performativity." *Qui Parle: Critical Humanities and Social Sciences* 19.2 (2011): 121–58.

Barberi Squarotti, Giorgio. "Chi è il poeta: Carducci, D'Annunzio, Pascoli e tanti altri." *La modernità letteraria* 3 (2010): 87–105.

– Introduction to *Poesie*, by Gozzano, 7–21.

Bardazzi, Emanuele. "Sacro e profano nel simbolismo multiforme di un dandy di casa nostra." In *Raoul Dal Molin Ferenzona. "Secretum meum,"* 11–23. Florence: Saletta Gonnelli, 2002.

Barilli, Renato. *Art Nouveau*. Translated by Raymond Rudorff. New York, London: Hamlyn, 1969.

Bartoloni, Paolo. *Objects in Italian Life and Culture: Fiction, Migration, and Artificiality*. New York: Palgrave Macmillan, 2016.

Basilici, Carlo. "Due critici di Giulio Orsini." *Rivista di Roma*, 19 June 1904, 3.

Bataille, Georges. *Inner Experience*. Translated by Leslie Anne Boldt. New York: SUNY Press, 1988.

Baudelaire, Charles. *Les Fleurs du Mal*. Translated by Richard Howard. Boston: Godine, 1982.

– *The Flowers of Evil*. Translated by James McGowan. Oxford, New York: Oxford University Press, 2008.

– *The Painter of Modern Life and Other Essays*. Edited and translated by Jonathan Mayne. London, New York: Phaidon, 2003.

– *Poems of Baudelaire*. Translated by Roy Campbell. New York: Pantheon Books, 1952.

Bello Minciacchi, Cecilia. *Scrittrici della prima avanguardia. Concezioni, caratteri e testimonianze del femminile nel futurismo*. Florence: Le Lettere, 2012.

Bello Minciacchi, Cecilia, ed. *Spirale di dolcezza + serpe di fascino. Scrittrici futuriste. Antologia*. Naples: Bibliopolis, 2007.

Benjamin, Walter. *The Writer of Modern Life: Essays on Charles Baudelaire*. Edited by Michael W. Jennings. Translated by Howard Eiland, Edmund Jephcott, Rodney Livingstone, and Harry Zohn. Cambridge, MA: Harvard University Press, 2006.

Bennett, Jane. *Vibrant Matter: A Political Ecology of Things*. Durham, NC: Duke University Press, 2010.

Berghaus, Günter. *Futurism and Politics: Between Anarchist Rebellion and Fascist Reaction (1909–1944)*. Oxford: Berghahn, 1996.

– "Violence, War, Revolution: Marinetti's Concept of a Futurist Cleanser for the World." *Annali d'Italianistica* 27 (2009): 23–43.

Bergson, Henri. *Laughter: An Essay on the Meaning of the Comic*. Translated by Cloudesley Brereton and Fred Rothwell. London: Macmillan, 1913.

– "On Some Motifs on Baudelaire." In *Illuminations: Essays and Reflections*, edited by Hannah Arendt, translated by Harry Zohn, 155–200. New York: Schocken Books, 1969.

Berlant, Lauren. "Cruel Optimism." *Differences: A Journal of Feminist Cultural Studies* 17.5 (2006): 20–36.

– "Love, a Queer Feeling." In *Psychoanalysis and Homosexuality*, edited by Tim Dean and Christopher Lane, 432–51. Chicago: University of Chicago Press, 2001.

Berman, Marshall. *All That Is Solid Melts into Air: The Experience of Modernity*. New York: Penguin, 1988.

Bertini, Simona. *Marinetti e le "Eroiche serate."* Novara: Interlinea, 2002.

Binni, Walter, *La poetica del decadentismo*. Florence: Sansoni, 1977.

Birolli, Viviana, ed. *Manifesti del futurismo*. Milan: Abscondita, 2008.

Bobbio, Norberto. *Profilo filosofico del Novecento*. Milan: Garzanti, 1990.

Boccioni, Umberto. *Gli scritti editi e inediti*. Edited by Zeno Birolli. Milan: Feltrinelli, 1971.

– "Perché non siamo impressionisti." In *Pittura scultura futuriste: Dinamismo plastico*, edited by Zeno Birolli, 37–51. Florence: Vallecchi, 1977.

Bodei, Remo. *La vita delle cose*. Bari: Laterza, 2009.

Bogost, Ian. *Alien Phenomenology, or What It's Like to Be a Thing*. Minneapolis: University of Minnesota Press, 2012.

Boito, Arrigo. "L'Alfier nero." In *I racconti neri della Scapigliatura*, edited by Gilberto Finzi, 125–41. Milan: Mondadori, 1980.

Borgese, Giuseppe Antonio. "Poesia crepuscolare." In *La vita e il libro. Seconda serie con un epilogo*, 149–60. Turin: Fratelli Bocca, 1911.

Boscagli, Maurizia. *Stuff Theory: Everyday Objects, Radical Materialism*. New York: Bloomsbury, 2014.

Bouchard, Norma. "Introduction: Risorgimento as an Unfinished Story." In *Risorgimento in Modern Italian Culture: Revisiting the Nineteenth-Century Past in History, Narrative, and Cinema*, edited by Norma Bouchard, 9–22. Madison: Fairleigh Dickinson University Press, 2005.

Bourdieu, Pierre. *Distinction: A Social Critique of the Judgement of Taste*. Translated by Richard Nice. Cambridge, MA: Harvard University Press, 1984.

Braidotti, Rosi. *Nomadic Theory: The Portable Rosi Braidotti*. New York: Columbia University Press, 2012.

– *The Posthuman*. Malden, MA: Polity, 2013.

Branca, Vittore, ed. *I mistici. Fioretti di San Francesco. Lettere di Santa Caterina*. Milan, Rome, Naples, Città di Castello: Società editrice Dante Alighieri, 1964.

Brewer, Marilynn, and Miles Hewstone, eds. *Self and Social Identity*. Malden: Wiley-Blackwell, 2004.

Brintnall, Kent L. *Ecce Homo: The Male-Body-in-Pain as Redemptive Figure*. Chicago: University of Chicago Press, 2012.

Brown, Bill. *A Sense of Things: The Object Matter of American Literature*. Chicago: University of Chicago Press, 2003.

– "Thing Theory." *Critical Inquiry* 28.1 (2001): 1–22.

Bryant, Levi. *The Democracy of Objects*. Ann Arbor: Open Humanities Press, 2011.

– *Onto-Cartography: An Ontology of Machines and Media*. Edinburgh: Edinburgh University Press, 2014.

Buelens, Geert, Harald Hendrix, and Monica Jansen, eds. *The History of Futurism: The Precursors, Protagonists, and Legacies*. Lanham, MD: Lexington Books, 2012.

Buell, Lawrence. *Emerson*. Cambridge, MA: Harvard University Press, 2004.

Bürger, Peter. *The Decline of Modernism*. University Park: Pennsylvania State University Press, 1992.

– *Theory of the Avant-Garde*. Translated by Michael Shaw. Minneapolis: University of Minnesota Press, 1984.

Buzzi, Paolo. *Aeroplani. Canti Alati*. 1909. Milan: Lampi di Stampa, 2009.

– *L'ellisse e la spirale. Film più parole in libertà*. Edited by Luciano Caruso. Florence: SPES, 1990.

Calcaterra, Carlo. *Con Gozzano e altri poeti*. Bologna: Zanichelli, 1944.

Calinescu, Matei. *Five Faces of Modernity: Modernism, Avant-Garde, Decadence, Kitsch, Postmodernism*. Durham, NC: Duke University Press, 1987.

Campbell, Timothy. "Vital Matters: Sovereignty, Milieu, and the Animal in Futurism's Founding Manifesto." *Annali d'Italianistica* 27 (2009): 157–73.

– *Wireless Writing in the Age of Marconi*. Minneapolis: University of Minnesota Press, 2005.

Cannamela, Danila. "What Is a Little Thing? Crepuscular Still Lifes and the Italian Avant-garde." *Modernism/Modernity* 24.4 (2017): 841–66.

Cangiano, Mimmo. "Gozzano (o del Modernismo apparente)." *Critica letteraria* 173 (2016): 684–705.

Capello, Francesco. *Città specchio. Soggettività e spazio urbano in Palazzeschi, Govoni e Boine*. Milan: Franco Angeli, 2013.

Carducci, Giosuè. *Giosuè Carducci: A Selection of His Poems, with Verse Translations, Notes, and Three Introductory Essays*. Translated by Geoffrey Langdale Bickersteth. London: Longmans, Green and Co., 1913.

– *Poems of Giosuè Carducci Translated with Two Introductory Essays*. Edited by Frank Sewall. New York: Dodd, Mead and Co., 1892.

Carli, Mario. "Vulcanizziamo le grandi città." *L'Italia Futurista*, 25 August 1916, 2.

Carnero, Roberto. *Felicità e malinconia. Gozzano e i crepuscolari*. Milan: Baldini Castoldi Dalai, 2006.

– *Guido Gozzano esotico*. Anzio: De Rubeis, 1996.

Caruso, Luciano. Afterword to *L'ellisse e la spirale. Film più parole in libertà*, by Paolo Buzzi, i–xi. Florence: SPES, 1990.

Casarino, Cesare. *Modernity at Sea: Melville, Marx, Conrad in Crisis*. Minneapolis: University of Minnesota Press, 2002.

Cavalcanti, Guido. *Complete Poems*. Translated by Anthony Mortimer. Richmond: Oneworld Classics, 2010.

Cecchi, Emilio. "La via del rifugio." In *Studi critici di Emilio Cecchi*, 109–18. Puccini: Ancona, 1912.

Cervigni, Dino. "The Petrarchan Lover's Non-Dialogic and Dialogic Discourse: An Augustinian Semiotic Approach to Petrarch's 'Rerum Vulgarium Fragmenta.'" *Annali d'Italianistica* 22 (2004): 105–34.

Cesaretti, Enrico. "Eco Futurism? Some Thoughts on Nature, Matter, and Body in F.T. Marinetti." In *Modernism and the Avant-Garde Body in Spain and Italy*. Edited by Maria Rosa Truglio and Nicolás Fernandez-Medina, 232–47. New York: Routledge, 2016.

Chiaves, Carlo. *Sogno e ironia*. 1918. Venice: Neri Pozza, 1956.

Childs, Peter. *Modernism*. London, New York: Routledge, 2008.

Cigliana, Simona. *Futurismo esoterico*. Milan: Feltrinelli, 2002.

Clark, Martin. *Modern Italy: 1871 to the Present*. Harlow: Pearson Longman, 2008.

Cohoon, Christopher. "The Ecological Irigaray?" In *Ecocritical Theory: New European Approaches*, edited by Axel Goodbody and Kate Rigby, 206–14. Charlottesville: University of Virginia Press, 2011.

Comberiati, Daniele. *Nessuna città d'Italia è più crepuscolare di Roma: Le relazioni fra il cenacolo romano di Sergio Corazzini e i simbolisti belgi*. Brussels: Peter Lang, 2014.

Contarini, Silvia. *La Femme futuriste. Mythes, modèles et représentations de la femme dans la théorie et la littérature futuristes (1900–1919)*. Nanterre: Presses Universitaires de Paris 10, 2006.

– "Guerre maschili/guerre femminili: corpi e 'corpus' futuristi in azione/trasformazione." *Annali d'Italianistica* 27 (2009): 125–36.

Contini, Gianfranco. "Il linguaggio di Pascoli." In *Poesie*, vol. 1, by Giovanni Pascoli, xxiii–lviii. Edited by Augusto Vicinelli. Milan: Mondadori 1981.

Contorbia, Franco. *Il sofista subalpino: tra le carte di Gozzano*. Cuneo: L'arciere, 1980.

Coole, Diana, and Samantha Frost, eds. *New Materialisms: Ontology, Agency, and Politics*. Durham, NC: Duke University Press, 2010.

Corazzini, Sergio. *Opere. Poesie e prose*. Edited by Angela Ida Villa. Pisa, Rome: Istituti editoriali e poligrafici internazionali, 1999.

– *Poesie*. Edited with an introduction by Idolina Landolfi. Milan: Rizzoli, 1999.

– *Sunday Evening: Selected Poems of Sergio Corazzini*. Edited and translated by Michael Palma. Stony Brook, New York: Gradiva Publications, 1997.

Corra, Bruno. *Io ti amo: il romanzo dell'amore moderno*. Milan: Studio Editoriale Lombardo, 1918.

– *Sam Dunn è morto*. Milan: Studio Editoriale Lombardo, 1917.

– *Sam Dunn Is Dead*. Translated by John Walker. London: Atlas Press, 2015.

Corra, Bruno, and Arnaldo Ginna. *Manifesti futuristi e scritti teorici di Arnaldo Ginna e Bruno Corra*. Edited by Mario Verdone. Ravenna: Longo, 1984.

Corra, Bruno, and Emilio Settimelli. "Pesi, misure e prezzi del genio artistico." In *Prosa e critica futurista: Antologia*, edited by Mario Verdone, 276–82. Milan: Feltrinelli, 1973.

Corradini, Enrico. *L'ora di Tripoli*. Milan: Treves, 1911.

Cox, Christopher. *Nietzsche: Naturalism and Interpretation*. Berkeley: University of California Press, 1999.

Croce, Benedetto. *Breviario di estetica – Aesthetica in nuce*. Edited by Giuseppe Galasso. Milan: Adelphi, 1990.

– "Rigoglio di cultura e irrequietezza spirituale (1901–1914)." In *Storia d'Italia dal 1871 al 1915*, edited by Giuseppe Galasso, 309–31. Milan: Adelphi, 1991.

Curi, Fausto. *La poesia italiana d'avanguardia. Modi e tecniche. Con un'appendice di documenti e testi editi e inediti*. Florence: Liguori, 2001.

Dalle Vacche, Angela. "Lyda Borelli's Satanic Rhapsody: The Cinema and the Occult." *Cinémas* 16.1 (2005): 91–115.

Dal Molin Ferenzona, Raul. *La ghirlanda di stelle*. Rome: Tipografia Concordia, 1912.

Daly, Selena. *Italian Futurism and the First World War*. Toronto: University of Toronto Press, 2016.

Damasio, Antonio. *Descartes' Error: Emotions, Reason, and the Human Brain*. New York: Putnam, 1994.

D'Annunzio, Gabriele. *Halcyon*. Translated by J.G. Nichols. Manchester: Fyfield Books, 2003.

– *Pleasure*. Translated by Lara Gochin Raffaelli. New York: Penguin, 2013.
– *Versi d'amore e di gloria*, vol. 1. Edited by Annamaria Andreoli and Niva Lorenzini. Milan: Mondadori, 1982.
De Certeau, Michel. *Heterologies: Discourse on the Other*. Translated by Brian Massumi. Minneapolis: University of Minnesota Press, 1986.
De Certeau, Michel, and Marsanne Brammer. "Mysticism." *Diacritics* 22.2 (1992): 11–25.
De Grand, Alexander J. *The Hunchback's Tailor: Giovanni Giolitti and Liberal Italy from the Challenge of Mass Politics to the Rise of Fascism, 1882–1922*. Westport: Praeger, 2001.
DeLanda, Manuel. *Assemblage Theory*. Edinburgh: Edinburgh University Press, 2016.
Deleuze, Gilles, and Félix Guattari. *A Thousand Plateaus: Capitalism and Schizophrenia*. Translated by Brian Massumi. Minneapolis: University of Minnesota Press, 1987.
Depero, Fortunato. *Pestavo anch'io sul palcoscenico dei ribelli. Antologia degli scritti letterari*. Edited by Michele Ruele. Langhirano, Trento: Cucùlibri, 1992.
De Robertis, Giuseppe. *Scrittori del Novecento*. Florence: Le Monnier, 1940.
Descola, Philippe. *Beyond Nature and Culture*. Translated by Janet Lloyd. Chicago: University of Chicago Press, 2013.
Donini, Filippo. *Vita e poesia di Sergio Corazzini*. Turin: De Silva, 1949.
Donnarumma, Raffaele. "Tracciato del modernismo italiano." In *Sul modernismo italiano*, edited by Romano Luperini and Massimiliano Tortora, 13–38. Naples: Liguori, 2012.
Douglas, Mary. *Purity and Danger: An Analysis of the Concepts of Pollution and Taboo*. New York: Praeger, 1966.
Eliot, T.S. *The Annotated Waste Land with Eliot's Contemporary Prose*. Edited by Lawrence Rainey. New Haven: Yale University Press, 2006.
Emerson, Ralph Waldo. "The Over-Soul." In *Essays: First and Second Series*, 153–214. New York: Library of America, 2010.
Escritt, Stephen. *Art Nouveau*. London: Phaidon, 2000.
Esposito, Roberto. *Living Thought: The Origins and Actuality of Italian Philosophy*. Translated by Zakiya Hanafi. Stanford: Stanford University Press, 2012.
– *Le persone e le cose*. Turin: Einaudi, 2014.
Eysteinsson, Astradur. *The Concept of Modernism*. Ithaca, London: Cornell University Press, 1990.
– "'What's the Difference?' Revisiting the Concepts of Modernism and the Avant-Garde." In *Europa! Europa? The Avant-Garde, Modernism and the Fate of a Continent*, edited by Sascha Bru, Jan Baetens, Benedikt Hjartarson, Peter Nicholls, and Tania Orum, 21–35. Berlin: De Gruyter, 2009.
Faraci, Vincenzo. "Sensibilità umana e religiosa in Guido Gozzano." *Torino. Rivista mensile municipale* 27.11 (1951), 25–8.
Farina, Almo. *Soundscape Ecology: Principles, Patterns, Methods and Applications*. London: Springer, 2014.

Farinelli, Giuseppe. *"Perchè tu mi dici poeta?" Storia e poesia del movimento crepuscolare*. Rome: Carocci, 2005.

Fernández-Armesto, Felipe. *So You Think You're Human*. Oxford: Oxford University Press, 2005.

Ferraris, Maurizio. *Manifesto of New Realism*. 2012. Translated by Sarah De Sanctis. New York: SUNY Press, 2014.

– *Positive Realism*. Winchester: Zero Books, 2015.

Fielding, Henry. *The History of Tom Jones, A Foundling*. Edited by Thomas Keymer and Alice Wakely. London, New York: Penguin, 2005.

Flora, Francesco. *Dal romanticismo al futurismo*. Milan: Mondadori, 1925.

Forti, Micol, Lucia Collarile, and Mariastella Margozzi, eds. *Armonie e disarmonie degli stati d'animo. Ginna futurista*. Rome: Gangemi, 2009.

Fortini, Arnaldo. *D'Annunzio e il francescanesimo*. Assisi: Edizioni di Assisi, 1963.

Foster, Hal. *Prosthetic Gods*. Cambridge, MA: MIT Press, 2004.

Foucault, Michel. *The History of Sexuality, Vol. 1: An Introduction*. Translated by Robert Hurley. New York: Pantheon Books, 1978.

Franke, Anselm. Introduction to *e-flux* 36 (2012): https://www.e-flux.com/journal/36/61244/introduction-animism/.

French Symbolist Poetry. Translated by F. MacIntyre. Berkeley: University of California Press, 2007.

Frothingham, Paul Revere. "The Mysticism of Maeterlinck." *Harvard Theological Review* 5.2 (1912): 251–68.

Fuller, Robert C. *Spirituality in the Flesh: Bodily Sources of Religious Experiences*. New York: Oxford University Press, 2008.

Fusillo, Massimo. *Il dio ibrido. Dioniso e le "Baccanti" nel Novecento*. Bologna: Il Mulino, 2006.

– "Epic, Novel: The Obsession with Origins." In *The Novel*, vol. 2, *Forms and Themes*, edited by Franco Moretti, 32–63. Princeton: Princeton University Press, 2006.

– *Feticci. Letteratura, cinema, arti visive*. Bologna: Il Mulino, 2012.

Gaard, Greta. "Living Interconnections with Animals and Nature." In *Ecofeminism: Women, Animals, Nature*, edited by Greta Gaard, 1–12. Philadelphia: Temple University Press, 1993.

– "Mindful New Materialisms: Buddhist Roots for Material Ecocriticism's Flourishing." In *Material Ecocriticism*, edited by Serenella Iovino and Serpil Oppermann, 291–300. Bloomington: Indiana University Press, 2014.

– "New Directions for Ecofeminism: Toward a More Feminist Ecocriticism." *ISLE: Interdisciplinary Studies in Literature and Environment* 17.4 (2010): 643–65.

Garin, Eugenio. *Storia della filosofia italiana*, vol. 3. Turin: Einaudi, 1966.

Gazzola, Giuseppe. *Montale the Modernist*. Florence: Olschki, 2016.

Gendlin, Eugene. "An Analysis of What Is a Thing?" In Heidegger, *What Is a Thing?*, 247–96.

Genua, Guglielmo. "La virtù del colore." *Cronache Latine* 1.3 (1906): 6–9.
Ginanni, Maria. *Montagne trasparenti*. Florence: Edizioni dell'Italia Futurista, 1917.
– *Il poema dello spazio*. Milan: Facchi, 1919.
Giovannetti, Paolo. *Metrica del verso libero italiano*. Milan: Marcos y Marcos, 2007.
Govoni, Corrado. *Confessione davanti allo specchio*. Brescia: Morcelliana, 1943.
– *Lettere a F.T. Marinetti (1909–1915)*. Edited by Matilde Dillon Wanke. Milan: Scheiwiller, 1990.
– *Poesie (1903–1958)*. Edited by Gino Tellini. Milan: Mondadori, 2000.
Gozzano, Guido. *Albo dell'officina*. Edited by Nicoletta Fabio and Patrizia Menichi. Florence: Le Lettere, 1991.
– *Journey toward the Cradle of Mankind*. Translated by David Marinelli. Evanston, IL: Marlboro Press Northwestern, 1996.
– *Lettere a Carlo Vallini con altri inediti*. Edited by Giorgio De Rienzo. Turin: Centro Studi Piemontesi, 1972.
– *Lettere d'amore di Guido Gozzano e Amalia Guglielminetti*. Edited by Spartaco Asciamprener. Milan: Garzanti, 1951.
– *Lettere dell'adolescenza a Ettore Colla*. Edited by Mariarosa Masoero. Alessandria: Edizioni dell'Orso, 1993.
– *The Man I Pretend to Be: The Colloquies and Selected Poems of Guido Gozzano*. Translated by Michael Palma. Princeton: Princeton University Press, 1981.
– *Il paese fuori del mondo: prose per l'esposizione di Torino del 1911*. Edited by Eliana Pollone. Savigliano: Aragno, 2011.
– *Poesie*. Edited by Giorgio Barberi Squarotti. Milan: Rizzoli, 1977.
– *Poesie e prose*. Edited by Alberto De Marchi. Milan: Garzanti, 1961.
– *I tre talismani, La principessa si sposa e altre fiabe*. Edited by Matilde Dillon Wanke. Alessandria: Edizioni dell'Orso, 2004.
– *Tutte le poesie*. Edited by Andrea Rocca. Milan: Mondadori, 1980.
– *Vierso la cuna del mondo. Lettere dall'India (1912–1913)*. Milan: Treves, 1917.
Graf, Arturo. *Rime della selva; canzoniere minimo, semi-tragico e quasi postumo*. Milan: Treves, 1906.
Graff, Gerald. "Babbitt at the Abyss: The Social Context of Postmodern American Fiction." *TriQuarterly* 33 (1975): 305–37.
Gratton, Peter. *Speculative Realism: Problems and Prospects*. London, New York: Bloomsbury, 2014.
Gregg, Melissa, and Gregory Seigworth, eds. *The Affect Theory Reader*. Durham, NC: Duke University Press, 2010.
Grosz, Elizabeth. "Feminism, Materialism, and Freedom." In *New Materialisms: Ontology, Agency, and Politics*, edited by Diana Coole and Samantha Frost, 139–57. Durham, NC: Duke University Press, 2010.
Grusin, Richard, ed. *The Nonhuman Turn*. Minneapolis: University of Minnesota Press, 2015.

Guattari, Félix. *Chaosmosis: An Ethico-Aesthetic Paradigm*. Translated by Paul Bains and Julian Pefanis. Bloomington: Indiana University Press, 1995.

Guglielminetti, Marziano. *La "scuola dell'ironia." Gozzano e i viciniori*. Florence: Olschki, 1984.

Haraway, Donna. "A Cyborg Manifesto: Science, Technology, and Socialist-Feminism in the Late Twentieth Century." In *Simians, Cyborgs, and Women: The Reinvention of Nature*, 149–81. New York: Routledge, 1991.

– *Modest_Witness@Second_Millennium.FemaleMan©Meets_OncoMouse™: Feminism and Technoscience*. New York, London: Routledge, 1997.

– *When Species Meet*. Minneapolis: University of Minnesota Press, 2007.

Harman, Graham. *Guerrilla Metaphysics: Phenomenology and the Carpentry of Things*. Chicago: Open Court, 2005.

– *Tool-Being: Heidegger and the Metaphysics of Objects*. Chicago: Open Court, 2002.

– *Towards Speculative Realism: Essays and Lectures*. Winchester: Zero Books, 2009.

Hegel, G.W.F. *Aesthetics: Lectures on Fine Art*, vol. 2. Translated by T.M. Knox. Oxford: Oxford University Press, 1975.

Heidegger, Martin. "Letter on Humanism." In *Basic Writings: From Being and Time (1927) to The Task of Thinking (1964)*, edited by David Farrell Krell, 141–82. London: Routledge, 2010.

– *What Is a Thing?* Translated by W.B. Barton, Jr, and Vera Deutsch. Chicago: H. Regnery, 1968.

Hemmings, Clare. "Invoking Affect: Cultural Theory and the Ontological Turn." *Cultural Studies* 19.5 (2005): 548–67.

Hempton, Gordon, with John Grossman. *One Square Inch of Silence: One Man's Quest to Preserve Quiet*. New York: Free Press, 2009.

Heuving, Jeanne. *The Transmutation of Love and Avant-Garde Poetics*. Tuscaloosa: University of Alabama Press, 2016.

Hollywood, Amy. *Sensible Ecstasy: Mysticism, Sexual Difference, and the Demands of History*. Chicago: University of Chicago Press, 2001.

Hom, Stephanie. "'Patria'-otic Incarnations and Italian Character: Discourses of Nationalism in Ippolito Nievo's *Confessioni d'un Italiano*." *Italica* 84.2/3 (2007): 214–32.

Horkheimer, Max, and Theodor W. Adorno. *Dialectic of Enlightenment: Philosophical Fragments*. Edited by Gunzelin Schmid Noerr. Translated by Edmund Jephcott. Stanford: Stanford University Press, 2002.

Houtman, Dick, and Birgit Meyer, eds. *Things: Religion and the Question of Materiality*. New York: Fordham University Press, 2012.

Ialongo, Ernest. "Futurism from Foundation to World War: The Art and Politics of an Avant-Garde Movement." *Journal of Modern Italian Studies* 21.2 (2016): 306–23.

Iamurri, Laura, and Sabrina Spinazzè, eds. *L'arte delle donne nell'Italia del Novecento*. Rome: Meltemi, 2001.

Iovino, Serenella. "Death(s) in Venice: Bodies and the Discourse of Pollution from Thomas Mann to Porto Marghera." In *The James K. Binder Lectureship in Literature* 8 (2014): 1–33.

– "Ecocriticism and a Non-Anthropocentric Humanism: Reflections on Local Natures and Global Responsibilities." In *Local Natures, Global Responsibilities: Ecocritical Perspectives on the New English Literatures*, edited by Laurenz Volkmann, Nancy Grimm, Ines Detmers, and Katrin Thomson, 29–54. Amsterdam: Rodopi, 2010.

– *Ecocriticism and Italy: Ecology, Resistance, and Liberation*. New York: Bloomsbury, 2016.

– "'Un po' troppo incorruttibile.' Ecologia, responsabilità e un'idea di trascendenza." In *Ecocritica ed ecodiscorso. Nuove reciprocità tra umanità e pianeta*, edited by Elisa Bolchi and Davide Vago. Special issue of *L'analisi linguistica e letteraria* 24.2 (2016): 21–34.

– "Toxic Epiphanies: Dioxin, Power, and Gendered Bodies in Laura Conti's Narratives on Seveso." In *International Perspectives in Feminist Ecocriticism*, edited by Greta Gaard, Simon C. Estok, and Serpil Oppermann, 37–55. New York: Routledge, 2013.

Iovino, Serenella, Enrico Cesaretti, and Elena Past, eds. *Italy and the Environmental Humanities: Landscapes, Natures, Ecologies*. Charlottesville: University of Virginia Press, 2018.

Iovino, Serenella, and Serpil Oppermann, eds. *Material Ecocriticism*. Bloomington: Indiana University Press, 2014.

Irigaray, Luce. "There Can Be No Democracy without a Culture of Difference." In *Ecocritical Theory: New European Approaches*, edited by Axel Goodbody and Kate Rigby, 194–205. Charlottesville: University of Virginia Press, 2011.

Irigaray, Luce, and Michael Marder. *Through Vegetal Being: Two Philosophical Perspectives*. New York: Columbia University Press, 2016.

Jaffe, Aaron. "Who's Afraid of the Inhuman Woolf?" *Modernism/Modernity* 23.4 (2016): 491–513.

Jameson, Fredric. *A Singular Modernity: Essay on the Ontology of the Present*. London, New York: Verso, 2002.

Jankélévitch, Vladimir. *Le je-ne-sais-quoi et le presque-rien*. Paris: Seuil, 1980.

Kang, Minsoo. *Sublime Dreams of Living Machines: The Automaton in the European Imagination*. Cambridge, MA: Harvard University Press, 2011.

Kay Nelson, Judith. *Seeing through Tears: Crying and Attachment*. New York: Routledge, 2005.

Kierkegaard, Søren. *Fear and Trembling: Repetition*. Vol. 6. Edited and translated by Howard V. Hong and Edna H. Hong. Princeton: Princeton University Press, 1983.

Kirby, Michael. *Futurist Performance*. Translated by Victoria Nes Kirby. New York: E.P. Dutton, 1971.

Kirksey, Eben, ed. *The Multispecies Salon*. Durham, NC: Duke University Press, 2014.

Kristeva, Julia. *Powers of Horror: An Essay on Abjection*. New York: Columbia University Press, 1982.

Landolfi, Idolina. Introduction, in *Poesie*, by Sergio Corazzini, 13–44. Milan: Rizzoli, 1999.

Lasker-Ferretti, Janaya Sandra. "Between Word and Image: Women Futurists and Parole in Libertà 1914–1924." PhD dissertation, University of California, Berkeley, 2012.

Latour, Bruno. *On the Modern Cult of the Factish Gods*. Translated by Catherine Porter and Heather MacLean. Durham, NC: Duke University Press, 2010.

– *Reassembling the Social: An Introduction to Actor-Network Theory*. Oxford, New York: Oxford University Press, 2005.

– *We Have Never Been Modern*. Translated by Catherine Porter. Cambridge, MA: Harvard University Press, 1993.

LaValva, Rosamaria. *The Eternal Child: The Poetry and Poetics of Giovanni Pascoli*. Chapel Hill, NC: Annali d'Italianistica, 1999.

Lease, Gary. "Modernism and 'Modernism': Christianity as Product of Its Culture." *Journal for the Study of Religion* 1.2 (1988): 3–23.

Levenson, Michael H. *Modernism*. New Haven: Yale University Press, 2011.

Lisa, Tommaso. *Le poetiche dell'oggetto da Luciano Anceschi ai novissimi. Linee evolutive di un'istituzione della poesia del Novecento*. Florence: Firenze University Press, 2007.

Livi, François. *Dai simbolisti ai crepuscolari*. Milan: IPL, 1974.

Lucini, Gian Pietro. *Il verso libero. Proposta*. Edited by Pier Luigi Ferro. Novara: Interlinea, 2008.

Luisetti, Federico. "Demons of the Anthropocene: Facing Bruno Latour's Gaia." *Philosophy Kitchen* 5.3 (2016): 157–69.

– "Reflections on Duchamp: Bergson Readymade." Translated by David Sharp. *Diacritics* 38.4 (2008): 77–93.

– "A Vitalist Art: Filippo Tommaso Marinetti's sintesi radiofoniche." In *The History of Futurism: The Precursors, Protagonists, and Legacies*, edited by Geert Buelens, Harald Hendrix, and Monica Jansen, 283–98. Lanham, MD: Lexington Books, 2012.

Luisetti, Federico, and Luca Somigli, eds. *A Century of Futurism: 1909–2009. Annali d'Italianistica* 27 (2009).

Luperini, Romano, and Massimiliano Tortora, eds. *Sul modernismo italiano*. Naples: Liguori, 2012.

Luti, Giorgio, ed. *Critici, movimenti, riviste del '900 letterario.* Rome: Nuova Italia, 1986.

MacKendrick, Karmen. *Immemorial Silence*. Albany: SUNY Press, 2001.

Maeterlinck, Maurice. *On Emerson and Other Essays*. Translated by Montrose J. Moses. New York: Dodd, Mead, 1912.

– "The Silence." In *The Inner Beauty*, 30–49. London: Arthur L. Humphreys, 1910.

Malewitz, Raymond. *The Practice of Misuse: Rugged Consumerism in Contemporary American Culture*. Stanford: Stanford University Press, 2014.

Mallarmé, Stéphane. *Mallarmé.* Translated by Anthony Hartley. Baltimore: Penguin, 1965.

Manning, Erin, and Brian Massumi. *Thought in the Act: Passages in the Ecology of Experience*. Minneapolis: University of Minnesota Press, 2014.

Marder, Michael. "To Hear Plants Speak." In *The Language of Plants: Science, Philosophy, Literature*, edited by Monica Gagliano, John C. Ryan, and Patrícia Vieira, 103–25. Minneapolis: University of Minnesota Press, 2017.

Marinetti, Filippo Tommaso. *Come si seducono le donne*. 2nd ed. with preface by Bruno Corra and Emilio Settimelli. Milan: Edizioni Excelsior, 1918.

– *Mafarka il futurista*. Edited by Luigi Ballerini. Milan: Mondadori, 2003.

– *Mafarka the Futurist: An African Novel*. Translated by Carol Diethe and Steve Cox. London: Middlesex University Press, 1998.

– "Radio Synthesis." Translated by Jeffrey Schnapp. *Modernism/Modernity* 16.2 (2010): 415–20.

– *Selected Poems and Related Prose*. Edited by Paolo Valesio. Translated by Elizabeth R. Napier and Barbara R. Studholme. New Haven: Yale University Press, 2013.

– "Vengono." In *Teatro Futurista sintetico*. Edited by Guido Davico Bonino, 165–7. Genoa: Il Melangolo, 1993.

– *Teoria e invenzione futurista*. Edited by Luciano De Maria. Milan: Mondadori, 2010.

Marmon Silko, Leslie. *Yellow Woman and a Beauty of the Spirit*. New York: Simon and Schuster, 1997.

Martini, Fausto Maria. *Si sbarca a New York*. Edited by Guido Baldassarri. Rome: Salerno editrice, 2008.

– *Tutte le poesie*. Edited by Giuseppe Farinelli. Milan: Istituto di Propaganda Libraria, 1969.

Masoero, Mariarosa. *Gozzano. Libri e lettere*. Florence: Olschki, 2005.

Massumi, Brian. "The Autonomy of Affect." *Cultural Critique* 31 (1995): 83–109.

– *Politics of Affect*. New York: Polity, 2015.

McHale, Brian. *Postmodernist Fiction*. New York, London: Methuen, 1987.

Meillassoux, Quentin. *After Finitude: An Essay on the Necessity of Contingency*. Translated by Ray Brassier. New York: Continuum, 2008.

Melitopoulos, Angela, and Maurizio Lazzarato. "Assemblages: Félix Guattari and Machinic Animism." *e-flux* 36 (2012). https://www.e-flux.com/journal/36/61259/assemblages-flix-guattari-and-machinic-animism/.

– "Machinic Animism." *Deleuze Studies* 6.2 (2012): 240–9.

Menci, Francesca. "L'identità nazionale e la poesia nei 'giovani' del primo Novecento." In *Letteratura e identità nazionale nel Novecento*, edited by Romano Luperini and Daniela Brogi, 55–84. San Cesario di Lecce: Manni, 2004.

Merchant, Carolyn. *The Death of Nature: Women, Ecology and the Scientific Revolution*. San Francisco: Harper and Row, 1980.

Merjian, Ara H. "Manifestations of the Novel: Genealogy and the Sculptural Imperative in F.T. Marinetti's *Mafarka le futuriste*." *Modernism/Modernity* 23.2 (2016): 365–401.

Merleau-Ponty, Maurice. *The Primacy of Perception*. Edited by James E. Edie. Translated by Carleton Dallery. Annotation by Leila Wilson. Evanston, IL: Northwestern University Press, 1964.

Mies, Maria, and Vandana Shiva. *Ecofeminism*. New York: Zed Books, 1993.

Milan, Serge. "The 'Futurist Sensibility': An Anti-Philosophy for the Age of Technology." In *Futurism and the Technological Imagination*, edited by Günter Berghaus, 63–76. Amsterdam, New York: Rodopi, 2009.

Miller, Daniel, ed. *Materiality*. Durham, NC: Duke University Press, 2005.

Miller, Matt. *Collage of Myself: Walt Whitman and the Making of Leaves of Grass*. Lincoln: University of Nebraska Press, 2010.

Miretti, Lorenza. *Mafarka il Futurista. Epos e Avanguardia*. Bologna: Gedit, 2005.

Montale, Eugenio. "Gozzano, dopo trent'anni." In *Sulla poesia*, edited by Giorgio Zampa, 54–62. Milan: Mondadori, 1976.

– *Tutte le poesie*. Milan: Mondadori, 1977.

Moretti, Marino. *Poesie scritte col lapis*. Naples: Ricciardi, 1910.

– *Tutte le poesie*. Milan: Mondadori, 1966.

– *Tutti i ricordi*. Milan: Mondadori, 1952.

Morton, Timothy. *Dark Ecology*. New York: Columbia University Press, 2016.

– *Ecology without Nature: Rethinking Environmental Aesthetics*. Cambridge, MA: Harvard University Press, 2007.

– *Hyperobjects: Philosophy and Ecology after the End of the World*. Minneapolis: University of Minnesota Press, 2013.

– "Weird Embodiment." In *Sentient Performativities of Embodiment: Thinking alongside the Human*, edited by Lynette Hunter, Elisabeth Krimmer, and Peter Lichtenfels, 19–33. London: Lexington Books, 2016.

Możejko, Edward. "Tracing the Modernist Paradigm." In *Modernism*, edited by Astradur Eysteinsson and Vivian Liska, 11–33. Amsterdam, Philadelphia: John Benjamins, 2007.

Ngai, Sianne. *Ugly Feelings*. Cambridge, MA: Harvard University Press, 2007.

Nicholls, Peter. *Modernisms: A Literary Guide*. London, New York: Palgrave Macmillan, 2009.

Niebisch, Arndt. "Cruel Media: On F.T. Marinetti's Media Aesthetics." *Annali d'Italianistica* 27 (2009): 333–43.

Nietzsche, Friedrich Wilhelm. *The Gay Science with a Prelude in German Rhymes and an Appendix of Songs*. Edited by Bernard Williams. Translated by Josefine Nauckhoff and Adrian Del Caro. Cambridge: Cambridge University Press, 2001.

– *Human, All Too Human: A Book for Free Spirits*. Introduction by Marion Faber and Arthur C. Danto. Translated by Marion Faber and Stephen Lehmann. Lincoln: University of Nebraska Press, 1996.

– *Thus Spoke Zarathustra: A Book for All and None*. Edited by Adrian Del Caro and Robert B. Pippin. Cambridge: Cambridge University Press, 2006.
Nievo, Ippolito. *Confessioni d'un Italiano*. Edited by Sergio Romagnoli. Venice: Marsilio, 2000.
Nordau, Max Simon. *Degeneration*. 1892. New York: D. Appleton, 1985.
Nozzoli, Anna, and Jole Soldateschi. *I crepuscolari*. Florence: La Nuova Italia, 1978.
Nussbaum, Martha C. *Love's Knowledge: Essays on Philosophy and Literature*. Oxford, New York: Oxford University Press, 1990.
O'Gorman, Edmundo. *The Invention of America: An Inquiry into the Historical Nature of the New World and the Meaning of Its History*. Bloomington: Indiana University Press, 1961.
Oldani, Guido. "Terminal Realism." *Annali d'Italianistica* 29 (2011): 301–14.
Oppermann, Serpil. "Feminist Ecocriticism: A Posthumanist Direction in Ecocritical Trajectory." In *International Perspectives in Feminist Ecocriticism*, edited by Greta Gaard, Simon C. Estok, and Serpil Oppermann, 19–36. New York: Routledge, 2013.
– "Rethinking Ecocriticism in an Ecological Postmodern Framework." In *Literature, Ecology, Ethics: Recent Trends in European Ecocriticism*, edited by Timo Müller and Michael Sauter, 35–50. Heidelberg: Universitätsverlag Winter Verlag, 2012.
Orlando, Francesco. *Gli oggetti desueti nelle immagini della letteratura. Rovine, reliquie, rarità, robaccia, luoghi inabitati e tesori nascosti*. Turin: Einaudi, 1993.
Oxilia, Nino. *Poesie*. Edited by Roberto Tessari. Naples: Guida, 1973.
Paci, Enzo. *Diario Fenomenologico*. Milan: Il Saggiatore, 1961.
Palazzeschi, Aldo. *The Arsonist*. Translated by Nicholas Benson. Los Angeles: Otis Books, 2013.
– *Il codice di Perelà*. 1911. In *Tutti i romanzi*, edited by Gino Tellini, 133–352. Milan: Mondadori, 2004.
– Introduction to *Vita e poesia di Sergio Corazzini*, by Donini, xii–xv.
– *Tutte le poesie*. Edited by Adele Dei. Milan: Mondadori, 2002.
Pancrazi, Pietro. *Scrittori italiani del Novecento*. Bari: Laterza, 1934.
Papini, Giovanni. "Gli estremi dell'attività teorica." *Leonardo* 2 (1904): 34.
– *Passato remoto (1885–1914)*. Florence: L'Arco, 1948.
– *Pragmatismo (1903–1911)*. Florence: Vallecchi, 1920.
– *Ventiquattro cervelli. Saggi non critici*. Milan: Studio editoriale lombardo, 1917.
Parati, Graziella, and Rebecca West, eds. *Italian Feminist Theory and Practice: Equality and Sexual Difference*. Madison, Teaneck: Fairleigh Dickinson University Press, 2002.
Pascoli, Giovanni. *Poems of Giovanni Pascoli*. Translated by Arletta M. Abbott. New York: Harold Vinal, 1927.
– *Poesie e prose scelte*, vol. 1. Edited by Cesare Garboli. Milan: Mondadori, 2002.
Perella, Nicolas J. "Arrigo Boito's Short Stories." *California Italian Studies* 1.2 (2010): 1–69. https://escholarship.org/uc/item/7541s7r6

Perniola, Mario. *The Sex Appeal of the Inorganic: Philosophies of Desire in the Modern World.* Translated by Massimo Verdicchio. New York: Bloomsbury, 2004.

Pero, Allan. "A Fugue on Camp." *Modernism/Modernity* 23.1 (2016): 28–36.

Pignatari, Giampaolo. Introduction to *Aeroplani. Canti Alati* (1909), by Paolo Buzzi, vii–xlvii. Milan: Lampi di Stampa, 2010.

Pinkus, Karen. "Dematerialization: From Arte Povera to Cybermoney through Italian Thought." *Diacritics* 39.3 (2009): 65–77.

– *Fuel: A Speculative Dictionary.* Minneapolis: University of Minnesota Press, 2016.

Pireddu, Nicoletta. *Antropologi alla corte della bellezza. Decadenza ed economia simbolica nell'Europa fin de siècle.* Verona: Fiorini, 2002.

Plotz, Judith. *Romanticism and the Vocation of Childhood.* New York: Palgrave Macmillan, 2001.

Plumwood, Val. *Feminism and the Mastery of Nature.* London, New York: Routledge, 1993.

Poggi, Christine. *Inventing Futurism: The Art and Politics of Artificial Optimism.* Princeton: Princeton University Press, 2009.

Poggioli, Renato. *The Theory of the Avant-Garde.* Cambridge, MA: Harvard University Press, 1968.

Proctor, Robert N., and Londa Schiebinger, eds. *Agnolotology: The Making and Unmaking of Ignorance.* Stanford: Stanford University Press, 2008.

Propp, Vladimir. *Morphology of the Folktale.* 1928. Translated by Laurence Scott. Austin: University of Texas Press, 1968.

Puncher, Martin. *Poetry of the Revolution: Marx, Manifestos, and the Avant-Gardes.* Princeton: Princeton University Press, 2005.

Quesada, Mario, ed. *Raoul dal Molin Ferenzona: oli, acquarelli, pastelli, tempere, disegni, punte d'oro, punte d'argento, collages, puntesecche, acqueforti, acquetinte, bulini, punte di diamante, xilografie, berceaux, gipsografie, litografie e volumi illustrati.* Rome: Emporio Floreale, 1979.

Rabinow, Paul, ed. *The Foucault Reader.* New York: Pantheon Books, 1984.

Rainey, Lawrence, Christine Poggi, and Laura Wittman, eds. *Futurism: An Anthology.* New Haven, London: Yale University Press, 2009.

Rainey, Lawrence, and Robert von Hallberg, eds. *Marinetti and the Italian Futurists.* Special issue of *Modernism/Modernity* 1.3 (1994).

Ramat, Silvio. *Protonovecento.* Milan: Il Saggiatore, 1978.

Re, Lucia. "Enif Robert, F.T. Marinetti e il romanzo *Un ventre di donna*: bisessualità, trauma e mito dell'isteria." *California Italian Studies* 5.2 (2014): 43–82. https://escholarship.org/uc/item/2dt2z4wx.

– "Maria Ginanni vs. F.T. Marinetti: Women, Speed, and War in Futurist Italy." *Annali d'Italianistica* 27 (2009): 103–24.

– "Mater Materia: Maternal Power and the Futurist Avant-Garde." In *The Great Mother: Women, Maternity, and Power in Art and Visual Culture, 1900–2015*, edited by Massimiliano Gioni, 48–73. Milan: Skira, 2015.

– "Women, Sexuality, Politics, and the Body in the Futurist Avant-Garde during the Great War." In *Modernism and the Avant-Garde Body in Spain and Italy*, edited by Maria Truglio and Nicolás Fernández-Medina, 174–209. New York: Routledge, 2016.

Riall, Lucy. *The Italian Risorgimento: State, Society and National Unification*. London: Routledge, 1994.

Richard de la Fuente, Véronique. *Valentine de Saint Point (1875–1953): une poétesse dans l'avant-garde futuriste et méditerranéiste*. Céret: Editions des Albères, 2003.

Rigby, Kate. "Spirits That Matter: Pathways toward a Rematerialization of Religion and Spirituality." In Iovino and Oppermann, eds., *Material Ecocriticism*, 283–90.

Rimbaud, Arthur. *Rimbaud Complete*. Translated by Wyatt Mason. New York: Modern Library, 2002.

Robert, Enif, and Filippo Tommaso Marinetti. *Un ventre di donna. Romanzo chirurgico*. Milan: Facchi, 1919.

Rosa, Giovanna. *Il patto narrativo. La fondazione della civiltà romanzesca in Italia*. Milan: Il Saggiatore, 2008.

Rosà, Rosa. *Una donna con tre anime. Romanzo futurista*. Edited by Claudia Salaris. Milan: Edizioni delle donne, 1982.

Russell, Charles. *Poets, Prophets, and Revolutionaries: The Literary Avant-Garde from Rimbaud through Postmodernism*. New York: Oxford University Press, 1985.

Saint-Point, Valentine de. *Manifeste de la Femme futuriste*. Edited by Jean-Paul Morel. Paris: Éditions Mille et une nuits, 2005.

Salaris, Claudia, ed. *Le futuriste. Donne e letteratura d'avanguardia in Italia (1909–1944)*. Milan: Edizioni delle donne, 1982.

Salvemini, Gaetano. *Il ministro della malavita e altri scritti sull'Italia giolittiana*. Milan: Feltrinelli, 1966.

Sanguineti, Edoardo. *Guido Gozzano: Indagini e letture*. Turin: Einaudi, 1966.

– *Ideologia e linguaggio*. 1965. Milan: Feltrinelli, 2001.

– *Tra liberty e crepuscolarismo*. Milan: Mursia, 1961.

Sartini Blum, Cinzia. *The Other Modernism: F.T. Marinetti's Futurist Fiction of Power*. Berkeley: University of California Press, 1996.

Scarry, Elaine. *The Body in Pain: The Making and Unmaking of the World*. New York: Oxford University Press, 1985.

Schnapp, Jeffrey. "The Statistical Sublime." In *The History of Futurism: The Precursors, Protagonists, and Legacies*, edited by Geert Buelens, Harald Hendrix, and Monica Jansen, 107–28. Lanham, MD: Lexington Books, 2012.

– "Why Speed Is a Religion-Morality." In *Modernitalia*, edited by Francesca Santovetti. Oxford, New York: Peter Lang, 1–21.

Schram-Pighi, Laura. *Bergson e il bergsonismo nella prima rivista di Papini e Prezzolini: Il "Leonardo" 1903–1907*. Sala Bolognese: A. Forni, 1982.

Schulte-Sasse, Jochen. Foreword to *Theory of the Avant-Garde*, by Bürger, vii–xlvii.

Schulz-Buschhaus, Ulrich. *Il sistema letterario nella civiltà borghese*. Milan: Unicopli, 1999.

Sedgwick, Eve. *Epistemology of the Closet*. Berkeley: University of California Press, 1990.

Seger, Monica. *Landscapes in Between: Environmental Change in Modern Italian Literature and Film*. Toronto: University of Toronto Press, 2015.

Seillière, Ernest. *Le Romantisme et la morale. Essai sur le mysticisme esthétique et le mysticisme passionnel*. Paris: La Nouvelle Revue Critique, 1932.

Semonides of Amorgos. "On Women." In *Semonides: Testimonia et fragmenta*, edited by Ezio Pellizer and Gennaro Tedeschi, 18–29. Rome: Edizioni dell'Ateneo, 1990.

Serres, Michel. *The Parasite*. Translated by Lawrence R. Schehr. Baltimore, London: Johns Hopkins University Press, 1982.

Severini, Gino. *La vita di un pittore*. Milan: Edizioni di Comunità, 1965.

Shaviro, Steven. *The Universe of Things: On Speculative Realism*. Minneapolis: University of Minnesota Press, 2014.

Sica, Paola. *Futurist Women: Florence, Feminism and the New Sciences*. London, New York: Palgrave Macmillan, 2016.

– "Maria Ginanni: Futurist Woman and Visual Writer," *Italica* 79.3 (2002): 339–52.

Slataper, Scipio. "Perplessità crepuscolare (a proposito) di G. Gozzano." In *I crepuscolari*, edited by Aldo Vallone, 66–70. Palermo: Palumbo, 1960.

Soffici, Ardengo. *Arlecchino*. Florence: Vallecchi, 1921.

– *BÏF & ZF + 18. Simultaneità e chimismi lirici*. Florence: Vallecchi, 1919.

– *La giostra dei sensi*. Florence: Vallecchi, 1920.

Somigli, Luca. *Legitimazing the Artist: Manifesto Writing and European Modernism, 1885–1915*. Toronto: University of Toronto Press, 2003.

– "The Mirror of Modernity: Marinetti's Early Criticism between Decadence and 'Renaissance Latine.'" *Romanic Review* 97.3–4 (2006): 331–52.

Somigli, Luca, and Mario Moroni, eds. *Italian Modernism: Italian Culture between Decadentism and Avant-Garde*. Toronto: University of Toronto Press, 2004.

Sontag, Susan. *Notes on "Camp."* New York: Vintage Books, 1982.

Spackman, Barbara. *Decadent Genealogies: The Rhetoric of Sickness from Baudelaire to D'Annunzio*. Ithaca: Cornell University Press, 1989.

– *Fascist Virilities: Rhetoric, Ideology, and Social Fantasy in Italy*. Minneapolis: University of Minnesota Press, 1996.

Spinazzola, Vittorio. *Letteratura e popolo borghese*. Milan: Unicopli, 2000.

Steacy, Will, ed. *Photographs Not Taken*. New York: Daylight, 2012.

Stewart, Susan. *Poetry and the Fate of the Senses*. Chicago: University of Chicago Press, 2002.

Sullivan, Robert. "Hello Great North Road." *Poetry* 208.4 (2016): 391.

Tedesco, Natale. *La condizione crepuscolare. Saggi sulla poesia italiana del '900*. Florence: La Nuova Italia, 1970.

Tennyson, Alfred. *Poems of Alfred Lord Tennyson*. Edited by Ruth Greiner Rausen. New York: Crowell, 1964.

Tessari, Roberto. "Crepuscolo di 'giovinezza' e 'bontà' nella poesia di Nino Oxilia." In Oxilia, *Poesie*, 5–24.

Ticineto Clough, Patricia, and Jean Halley, eds. *The Affective Turn: Theorizing the Social*. Durham, NC, London: Duke University Press, 2007.

Toscano, Alberto. "The Promethean Gap: Modernism, Machines, and the Obsolescence of Man." *Modernism/Modernity* 23.3 (2016): 593–609.

Valeria, Irma. *Morbidezze in agguato*. Florence: Edizioni dell'Italia Futurista, 1917.

Vallini, Carlo. *Un giorno e La rinunzia*. Genoa: San Marco dei Giustiniani, 2010.

Vallone, Aldo, ed. *I crepuscolari*. Palermo: Palumbo, 1960.

Vannicola, Giuseppe. "Modern Style." *La settimana artistica letteraria* 1 (1907).

– "Vagamente." *Cronache Latine* 1.2 (1906): 5.

Verdicchio, Pasquale, ed. *Ecocritical Approaches to Italian Culture and Literature: The Denatured Wild*. Lanham, MD: Lexington Books, 2016.

Verdone, Mario. *Cinema e letteratura del futurismo*. Rome: Bianco e Nero, 1968.

Verga, Giovanni. *Tutte le novelle*. Edited by Giuseppe Zaccaria. Turin: Einaudi, 2011.

Verso, Francesco. *Nexhuman*. 2013. Translated by Sally McCorry. Surry Hills: Xoum Publishing, 2014.

Villa, Angela Ida. *Il crepuscolarismo. Ideologia, poetica, bibliografia*. Pesaro: Metauro, 2008.

– Introduction to *Opere: poesie e prose*, by Corazzini, 13–66.

– "'La morte di Tantalo' nell''Ultima Thule.'" *Otto/Novecento* 1 (2012): 117–39.

– *Neoidealismo e rinascenza latina tra Otto e Novecento. La cerchia di Sergio Corazzini: poeti dimenticati e riviste del crepuscolarismo romano (1903–1907)*. Milan: Led, 1999.

Virgilio, Publio Marone. *Georgiche*. Edited by Alessandro Barchiesi. Milan: Mondadori, 1980.

Viveiros De Castro, Eduardo. "Exchanging Perspectives: The Transformation of Objects into Subjects in Amerindian Ontologies." *Common Knowledge* 10.3 (2004): 463–84.

Vlastos, Gregory. *Socrates, Ironist and Moral Philosopher*. Ithaca: Cornell University Press, 1991.

Von Hochheim, Eckhart. *Sermons*. Edited and translated by Jeanne Ancelet-Hustache. Paris: Édition du Seuil, 1974.

Vovelle, Michel. *La Mort et l'Occident. De 1300 à nos jours*. Paris: Gallimard, 1983.

Wagner, Peter. *Modernity: Understanding the Present*. Cambridge: Polity, 2012.

Walker Bynum, Caroline. *Christian Materiality: An Essay on Religion in Late Medieval Europe*. New York: Zone Books, 2011.

Wall Kimmerer, Robin. *Braiding Sweetgrass: Indigenous Wisdom, Scientific Knowledge, and the Teaching of Plants*. Minneapolis: Milkweed Editions, 2013.

Warren, Karen. *Ecofeminist Philosophy: A Western Perspective on What It Is and Why It Matters*. New York: Rowman and Littlefield, 2000.

Warren, Karen, ed. *Ecofeminism: Women, Culture, Nature*. Bloomington: Indiana University Press, 1997.

Whitman, Walt. *Poetry and Prose*. Edited by Justine Kaplan. New York: Library of America, 1996.

Wilson, Jack. *Biological Individuality: The Identity and Persistence of Living Entities*. Cambridge: Cambridge University Press, 1999.

Willson, Perry. *Women in Twentieth-Century Italy*. New York: Palgrave Macmillan, 2010.

Wolfe, Cary. *What Is Posthumanism?* Minneapolis: University of Minnesota Press, 2009.

Worton, Michael. "Behold the (Sick) Man." In *National Healths: Gender, Sexuality and Health in a Cross-Cultural Context*, edited by Michael Worton and Nana Wilson-Tagoe, 151–65. London: UCL Press, 2004.

Woolf, Virginia. *Mrs. Dalloway*. San Diego: Harcourt Brace and Company, 1990.

Young, Edward. *Pre-Raffaellitism; or, A Popular Enquiry into Some Newly Asserted Principles Connected with the Philosophy, Poetry, Religion, and Revolution of Art*. London: Longman, 1857.

Zaccaria, Giuseppe. *"Reduce dall'amore e dalla morte." Un Gozzano alle soglie del postmoderno*. Novara: Interlinea, 2009.

Zapf, Hubert. "Creative Matter and Creative Mind: Cultural Ecology and Literary Creativity." In *Material Ecocriticism*, edited by Serenella Iovino and Serpil Oppermann, 51–66. Bloomington: Indiana University Press, 2014.

– *Literature as Cultural Ecology: Sustainable Texts*. New York: Bloomsbury, 2016.

Žižek, Slavoj. *Violence: Six Sideways Reflections*. New York: Picador, 2008

Index

www.ingramcontent.com/pod-product-compliance
Lightning Source LLC
LaVergne TN
LVHW090149080826
844660LV00013B/726/J

* 9 7 8 1 4 8 7 5 0 5 0 6 6 *